Encyclopedia of North American
Eating & Drinking
Traditions
Customs
& Rituals

Encyclopedia of North American

Eating&Drinking

Traditions
Customs
Rituals

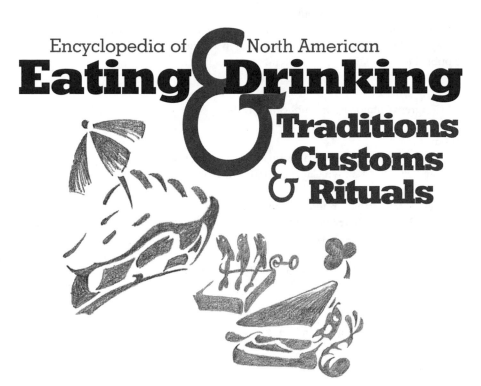

Kathlyn Gay
Martin K. Gay

ABC-CLIO

Copyright © 1996 by Kathlyn Gay and Martin K. Gay

Library of Congress Cataloging-in-Publication Data

Gay, Kathlyn.
    Encyclopedia of North American eating and drinking traditions, customs, and rituals / Kathlyn Gay and Martin K. Gay.
        p. cm.
    Includes bibliographical references and index.
    1. Food habits—United States—Encyclopedias. 2. Drinking customs—United States—Encyclopedias. 3. United States—Social life and customs—Encyclopedias. I. Title.
    GT2853.U5G39 1995   394.1′2′097—dc20   95-15219

ISBN 0-87436-756-5

02 01 00 99 98 96   10 9 8 7 6 5 4 3 2 1

ABC-CLIO, Inc.
130 Cremona Drive, P.O. Box 1911
Santa Barbara, California 93116-1911

This book is printed on acid-free paper ∞.
Manufactured in the United States of America

CONTENTS

ACKNOWLEDGMENTS

We would like to thank Karen and Dean Hamilton for the research they have provided for this book. Their firsthand knowledge about various eating and drinking customs was especially helpful—they presented valuable ideas for entries and pointed out regional and ethnic traditions surrounding foods and beverages, which sparked further investigation.

INTRODUCTION

Eat, drink, and be merry: Take part in a wedding feast. Blow out the candles on a birthday cake before slicing and eating it. Gather around a picnic table to share a potluck during a family reunion. Lift a glass of champagne for a toast to the new year. Attend a food festival and sample the offerings at numerous food booths. These are just a few examples of ways that North Americans participate in rituals or follow customs or traditions that include eating and drinking.

A great many daily rituals, from rising in the morning at the sound of the alarm to reading a newspaper at a particular time in the evening, do not focus on foods and beverages, but other daily activities, such as eating a fastfood lunch or having a bedtime snack, are certainly routine and often ritualistic in nature. Many informal rituals are simple family events—enjoying popcorn and soft drinks while watching television in the evening, for example. Or they are rituals maintained with friends—having coffee together every morning or stopping after work for a beer at a neighborhood tavern.

Throughout life, most people observe rites of passage that include important eating and drinking components. Weddings, christenings, bar and bat mitzvahs, birthdays, anniversaries, and funerals are examples. Some formal rituals that include food and beverages are based on religious observances, such as the Christian Eucharist with symbolic bread and wine, or the light supper that breaks each day's fasting during the month of Ramadan observed by Muslims, or the seder during Jewish Passover.

Certainly eating and drinking are integral factors in holiday celebrations and in harvest festivals, which stem from age-old rituals. Some types of harvest festivals take place in just one state or province where a celebrated crop is grown, such as the Date Festival in California and the Sunflower Festival in Manitoba, Canada. Festivals that focus on seafood—crabs, oysters, salmon, and shrimp—obviously are observed in coastal regions; and apples, blueberries, corn, and similar foods are honored at festivals in many different areas where these crops are produced.

A large number of customs surrounding food and drink stem from practices that Native Americans have long observed. One such custom is the salmon bake held in the Pacific Northwest; another is the Green Corn Festival held in New York State.

Some people of Asian, African, or European descent in North America have maintained eating traditions that have been passed down for generations. For example, a family from Pakistan following national customs may use a piece of flatbread as an eating utensil; and their meals probably would begin with rice or a curry dish. The specifics of any eating or drinking ritual may vary, though, depending on where it occurs and the customs of the group or groups taking part.

Whatever the ethnic cuisine, it is now often modified by the use of commercially prepared food and beverage items so readily available throughout most of North America. In *An American Folklife Cookbook,* Joan Nathan provides examples, such as the cook who makes kale soup in customary fashion, simmering bones for stock and cooking the soup for hours, then "at the last minute, she adds a package of Lipton's Onion Soup Mix." Another elderly woman is proud of her traditional pie crust but "sprinkles Tang on top of her apple pie." In short, "Mushroom soup [from a can], onion-soup mix, Cool Whip, canned tomato sauce, and ketchup have all become the nearly universal concessions to modern life." (Nathan 1984, xiii)

Industrial and commercial changes have also affected the manner in which people eat and drink. Consider the family dinner ritual among mainstream Americans, which Margaret Visser (*Much Depends on Dinner* and *The Ritual of Dinner*) of York University in Toronto, Canada, has so eloquently described. This communal eating ritual has never been associated with any particular country or cuisine, but it is virtually synonymous with a piece of furniture: the dining-room table has been a potent symbol of Western attitudes toward living together since the eighteenth century. (Before that, most people drew up benches to the hearth and sat down in relays to eat. The rich used rough planks to set up temporary trestle tables.)

The dining-room table stands, solid and immobile, in a room of its own. Its size is the size of the family group; when anyone leaves home or is away, the table provides a mute but constant reminder of the absentee, of the space no longer filled. . . . In our culture the dining-room table also represents a distinctive view of the family as a close-knit, independent and extremely disciplined entity. . . . Children learn at the table "how to behave," to express themselves, to listen, to catch conversational nuances. The table also provides a controlled setting where family relations, in all their ambiguity, can safely be played out. . . . By contrast, nothing could more perfectly symbolize the aims as well as the stresses of modernity than the vast proliferation of fast foods: their "anti-hierarchical" uniformity, not only of foods but of venues to eat them in; their sweet and bland flavors (nothing strong enough to displease anyone); the obsessive concern with wrapping and packaging (suggesting technological control and the atmosphere of a children's party with presents); the relaxed and egalitarian

way in which they are eaten (while walking along, using plastic cutlery or one's hands). (Visser 1990)

Because of the hectic (sometimes frantic) life-style in much of North America due in part to divorce, long-distance separations of extended families, and overwhelming job demands, some families have tried to give meaning to their lives by restoring or establishing rituals. Some of the most important appear to be food-oriented—eating dinner together on a daily basis or going for a drive on the weekend to a favorite ice cream shop. Such rituals strengthen family ties, parenting experts claim.

Communicating and Socializing with Food and Drink

Apart from the nuclear family, North Americans participate in numerous eating and drinking rituals that not only provide opportunities to communicate and to broaden social and business contacts but also instill a sense of community. People throughout the continent (and around the world for that matter) transmit a variety of well-understood messages with the food and beverages they offer—or withhold—from others. A gift of homemade bread or homebrewed beer, for example, is a traditional way to say that you care enough to share the product of your labor with someone who will appreciate the effort. A potluck is a customary way for a group of friends, members of clubs and civic organizations, and others to indicate they are willing to cooperate with one another in meal preparation and service. A company banquet—a ritual that usually occurs annually at the end of a year—is a way for executives to show their appreciation for employees.

In North America, people often socialize with friends, relatives, or business acquaintances by attending a dinner at someone's home. If the dinner is formal, guests usually follow a set of defined table manners in order to be considered acceptable members of the group. One example of "proper" behavior is maintaining good table posture, with hands in the lap when not eating rather than propping elbows on the table. When it comes to saying a blessing before a meal, etiquette books advise guests to follow the host's lead. It is not considered polite to use a napkin for a bib or to take more than modest portions of food when dishes are passed. Adding sauces, spices, or salt or putting ketchup on everything before tasting is one other taboo. So is chewing with the mouth open.

It is also customary to follow a set of rules when eating out at a fine restaurant. After ordering a bottle of wine, for example, a diner may adhere to a special protocol that includes tasting a small amount poured in a glass, checking the cork to determine that it is moist, and granting permission to the server to pour the wine for the others at the table.

Eating certain foods in a specific way—gracefully—is another aspect of formal dining rituals. A diner is not supposed to drink soup from a soup bowl, for example, and slurping soup from a spoon is not acceptable in North America, although it is customary among many people of Japanese ancestry to slurp in appreciation for the tasty soup. We are told by etiquette experts how to handle such difficult foods as artichokes, corn-on-the cob, and spaghetti. The latter should be twirled on a fork (sometimes against a large serving spoon) so that it can be transported safely to the mouth. These and many other dining rituals fill the pages of dozens if not hundreds of etiquette books and manuals.

Less formal grazing at food festivals, cocktail parties, buffets, or restaurant lounges during happy hour is also a way that foods and beverages become part of a social event. Backyard barbecues, picnics, luaus, lobster boils, keg parties, and fish fries are other common informal social events that focus on eating and drinking.

The Scope of This Book

Most of the rituals and customs just described are included in the entries for this book, which is by no means all-encompassing. Rather, it includes a sampling of the numerous types of eating and drinking patterns in North America, many of which are a blend of traditions from other continents.

Entries describe foods and beverages that are consumed in ritualistic or customary ways, eating or drinking establishments that are an integral part of a ritual or custom, and eating or drinking events. The events fit a rather loose set of criteria: the activity is one in which foods or beverages are a central focus (most national holidays, for example, include eating and drinking, but a few, such as President's Day, are not necessarily associated with ritual eating); the occurrence is fairly predictable; and the observance is deliberately planned by a broad-based group of people—it is not just an entrenched eating or drinking habit (or addiction) of one individual.

Some entries, especially those for particular foods or dishes, are not easily classified, but the foods included definitely are consumed in ritualistic or customary ways. Frequently, the entries include cross-references for related information. Also, numerous entries end with notations for sources that are listed in the bibliography. Some of the sources contain historical material about foods, others are cookbooks with background information about some dishes, and others describe customs—including foodways—of specific regional, religious, or ethnic groups.

Although traditional ethnic foods associated with particular events are part of some entries in this book, not all ethnic groups are represented, nor are all religious groups. Overall the entries clearly indicate that most people in Canada, the United States, and Mexico believe that eating and drinking rituals and customs—whether they have been practiced for centuries or have been recently established—are important to maintain. Why? Primarily because such rituals provide order in life, fulfill expectations, and allow social interaction. As numerous anthropologists, food historians, sociologists, psychologists, and other experts on human behavior have long pointed out, *what* and *how* we eat and drink help define who we are and our roles or status in society. "Food is one of the most, if not the single most, visible badges of identity, pushed to the fore by people who believe their culture to be on the wane," wrote folklorist Charles Camp in his book *American Foodways* (1989). Camp pointed out that "ordinary people participate in an ongoing—in fact, daily—discourse" on what food means and how it affects their culture simply by choosing certain foods and beverages to consume and determining how these are prepared.

No one set of rituals or customs can define North American foodways, however. Many eating and drinking patterns are likely to be in flux, influenced by the great diversity of rituals, customs, and traditions practiced throughout the continent.

AFTER-DINNER DRINKS

Serving drinks after dinner is a North American custom that has its roots in Europe. Brandy, which is distilled from fermented fruit and served undiluted in a snifter glass, has long been an after-dinner drink, providing a leisurely way to end a meal in Europe. The practice carried over to North America, particularly in the mid-1800s when brandy making began in California. Although that state remains the top producer of American varieties, brandies are imported from a number of other countries. One of the finest and smoothest is cognac, named for the Cognac region in France where it is produced.

Liqueurs—brandy-based beverages flavored with fruit, seeds, barks, spices, or flowers—and cordials made from fruit pulp or juices are also widely used as after-dinner drinks. All liqueurs are quite sweet, and frequently they are used in dessert dishes.

Some liqueurs are made from secret recipes and processes that have been guarded for centuries. Benedictine, for one, is made from an herb formula that Benedictine monks have held in secrecy for over 400 years. A few other liqueurs known throughout the world by their brand names include Amaretto, which is made from apricot pits and almond flavoring; Cointreau, made from brandy and orange peel; Creme de Cacao, flavored with cacao and vanilla beans; mint-flavored Creme de Menthe (both green and white varieties); Galliano, flavored with herbs, roots, and spices; and Sloe Gin, made from the berries (called sloe berries) of the blackthorn bush.

Reference: Suffes. *Mr. Boston Official Bartender's and Party Guide.* 1994.

AFTER-DINNER MINTS

Serving mint-flavored candies after dinner is a custom practiced throughout North America. Although its origin is uncertain, the practice became more widespread with the proliferation of commercially prepared hard candies and mint-flavored chocolates in specialty shops, grocery stores, and supermarkets. In many restaurants, mints are presented with the check for a dinner meal, symbolizing a "thank-you" and the hope that customers will "leave with a sweet taste in their mouth," as the old saying goes.

See also: CHOCOLATE CANDY.

AFTERNOON TEA

In some restaurants and homes in North America, especially in parts of Canada and in the South, serving tea with light fare is a common afternoon ritual. No one is sure when this custom began; however, some historians believe it originated in France during the mid-1700s, although others credit the British Duchess of Bedford with establishing the practice in the mid-1800s when she requested that light refreshments be served with her afternoon tea. Whatever the origin, British colonists continued the ritual in their new country, where it was a way for women to entertain friends in high style. Afternoon tea (or simply "a tea") became a common event among upper-class Victorians. Borrowing from British practice, the perfect tea included triangular- and circular-shaped sandwiches—many open-faced with no crust—and trays of cookies, fruit, cakes, and ice cream. Tea was served from a silver pot and poured into the finest porcelain cups. Those who attended wore formal attire.

At today's afternoon tea, which traditionally occurs between 3:30 and 5:30 P.M., a tea table (buffet) may be set up with a white lace or damask tablecloth and dainty tea napkins trimmed in lace. A silver tea service may be on the table, and all the food items are likely to be finger foods, such as cucumber sandwiches, other bite-size sandwiches, and small biscuits called scones. Usually desserts and fruit are on the table as well.

Although not a widespread practice, the afternoon tea is being revived in some areas of North America, sometimes as a birthday party event, a civic fund-raiser, or a promotional feature at a hotel. One example of a modern tea is that served at the Brown Palace Hotel in Denver, Colorado, where tea is served daily in the sumptuous lobby. Patrons (men and women alike) can select from a variety of teas and from a menu that includes finger sandwiches and scones, sweets such as rich chocolate rum balls, bar cookies, and miniature cream puffs. Although servers are dressed in formal uniforms, tea guests usually are less formal, and those who attend afternoon tea on a regular basis do so to escape the "hustle and bustle" of everyday life.

See also: BUFFET; SANDWICHES.
References: Baldridge. *The New Manners for the '90s.* 1990; Holt. *A Cup of Tea.* 1991.

AFTER-THEATER DINING

Theater-goers in New York City have long maintained the tradition of going to a favorite restaurant for dinner or a light supper after enjoying an evening at the theater. The custom is also followed in major cities such as Boston, Philadelphia, Chicago, and Los Angeles, as well as in smaller cities that support theater leagues bringing in traveling companies for performances.

See also: DINNER THEATER.

AGED MEAT

Aged meats, especially aged steaks, are a staple on the menus of numerous high-quality restaurants in North America, and those who routinely order aged meat when dining out or who prepare it at home usually believe they are getting top quality for the price they pay. (Since the process of aging meat adds to its cost, it is usually an expensive food item.)

In order to improve the flavor and texture of meat, it is aged under controlled conditions—that is, stored for three to four weeks at 34 to 38 degrees Fahrenheit in low humidity. The meat undergoes enzymatic change, which intensifies the flavor, deepens the color, and tenderizes the flesh by softening some of the connective tissue.

Reference: Herbst. *Food Lover's Companion.* 1990.

AGUTUK

A traditional dessert among Native Americans in Alaska, agutuk is a type of ice cream originally made from seal oil, snow, and salmon berries. Today, the basic ice

cream ingredients are more likely to be commercial shortening, sugar, and mashed potatoes with salmon berries for flavoring. This dessert is routinely served at tribal meetings and festivals.
See also: ICE CREAM.

AIRLINE MEALS

Eating and drinking "on the fly" are familiar to anyone who frequently uses airline transportation to travel long distances. These services have been fairly routine on most airlines since the late 1950s, the same time that the majority of flights also began to serve alcoholic beverages along with snacks, lunch, or dinner.

The first airline meals, served during the 1930s, were cold boxed lunches handed out by copilots. Later, when flight attendants became part of the crew, steam chests were brought aboard to house hot meals consisting of fried chicken, rolls, fruit cocktail, and coffee—the same meal no matter what time of day. On some early airlines, passengers were served these hot meals as if they were at a restaurant, seated at tables with cloths, flower vases, wine, and tableware. When planes were designed with row after row of seats in order to carry more passengers, restaurant-style dining was no longer possible.

Today, passengers eat their meals at individual fold-down tables provided at each seat. The meals arrive in plastic containers that can be heated in microwave ovens. Usually a passenger can arrange ahead of time to have a special diet—diabetic, kosher, low-fat, or vegetarian—accommodated. Depending on the flight destination and the carrier, meals may be designed to reflect traditions of a particular nation: traditional Italian, Danish, Dutch, or Mexican, for example.

Once in the air, passengers may purchase alcoholic beverages or order complimentary soft drinks, coffee, or tea, which are routinely served with individually packaged peanuts or a similar snack food. Then attendants push food carts down the aisles, handing out snack boxes or dinner trays, depending on which service is offered with the flight. Each day, millions of airline meals are consumed. (Just one U.S. airline, Delta, reports serving a total of 200,000 meals and snacks and 800,000 beverages on its daily scheduled flights.) After meals are served, it is common practice on some airlines for attendants, using tongs, to pass out damp, heated cloths to passengers who want to wipe their hands after a meal.
See also: SNACK FOODS.

AIRPORT DINING/DRINKING

Although food kiosks, booths, vending machines, restaurants, cafes, and bars have been part of most major airports in North America for decades, the trend in recent years has been to provide passengers and passersthrough some of the same eating establishments that they might find in their favorite shopping area or metropolitan center. For example, travelers going from or through the Dulles International Airport in Washington, D.C., who choose to have a drink before or after a flight may routinely select a locally brewed beer or a regional wine at one of the airport's bars or lounges. At many airports, coffee houses, espresso bars, and food courts (featuring such franchise establishments as TGIFriday's, Burger King, McDonald's, Taco Bell, Pizza Hut, Subway, TCBY, Dunkin' Donuts, Starbucks, Mrs. Field's Cookies, Cinnabon, and Pretzel Time) are common. According to some studies, airport passengers seek comfort in food and beverages; they want to relieve the stress of travel and like ordering food and beverages from fastfood chains because they are known to be safe. Food courts—large areas in airports and malls designated for food stands and vendors—make eating and drinking quick and convenient, which also helps ease anxiety.
See also: COFFEE HOUSES; ESPRESSO BARS; FASTFOOD; FOOD COURTS; VENDING MACHINES.
Reference: Fehr. "The Mall in the Airport." 1994.

ALL KINGS DAY

In Mexico and among people of Mexican heritage in the United States, All Kings Day is celebrated on the sixth of January each year. The day commemorates the journey of the Three Magi to the site of Jesus' birth, where they presented gifts of gold, frankincense, and myrrh. Families gather on the night of the fifth to place their shoes in hay around the Christmas tree, and parents give their children small gifts and food, representing the offerings of the kings.

The next day, almost every Mexican home hosts a gathering of family and friends to take part in the ritual of the Rosca de Reyes, or the "eating of the kings' cake." This tradition is as old as the first Catholic missionaries who brought Christian rituals to the indigenous population of North America. At that time, a cake was served in the evening with hot chocolate. Now, a cake is baked in the shape of a ring and decorated with powdered sugar and candied fruits to symbolize the crowns of the kings, and it is served with coffee, chocolates, pine nuts, and tamales.

The ritual includes baking a small figurine of an infant, symbolizing the Christ child, inside the cake. Each person is allowed to cut his or her own piece of cake, and the person who takes a piece containing the figurine is "crowned" king or queen of the fiesta. The new royalty picks a partner, and the couple has the responsibility of offering the traditional dinner of Candlemas Day, which occurs on 2 February.

See also: CHOCOLATE BEVERAGES; EPIPHANY FEAST; TAMALES.

Reference: Quintana and Haralson. *Mexico's Feasts of Life*. 1989.

ALL SOULS DAY

Paying tribute to the dead is a worldwide custom. The traditional feasting, along with other activities, associated with this ritual among North Americans of Mexican ancestry is an outgrowth of the ancient religious traditions of the Mexican native population and the Spanish Catholic colonizers who came to the Americas. Both societies had strong beliefs in the connections between those souls who were living in earthly flesh and those who had departed for the afterlife.

In Mexico, this belief became the basis for *el Día de los Muertos,* or "the Day of the Dead," wherein all souls who have passed on are celebrated and welcomed into the home for a feast. The ceremonies and traditions surrounding The Day of the Dead have been brought to the United States, particularly to the southwestern United States.

On 31 October, people welcome the spirits of young children by building altars decorated with toys, flowers, and specially made confections or any sweets that were the children's favorites when they were alive. By noon of the next day, 1 November, celebrants have eaten the candies and sweets and *los angelitos* (the young innocents) return to the other world. Other foods are then prepared for the altar as the older souls arrive to feast with their living brethren.

Local variations may call for different foods and beverages, but the following dishes are common. Flan (caramelized egg custard) is always found on the altar along with the most important dish, *tamales oaxaqueos* (pork and chicken tamales wrapped in banana leaves instead of the usual corn husks). Moles (chile sauces), such as the *verde* and *coloradito* (green and little red) varieties, are placed alongside the tamales and roasted pork loin.

Pan de los muertos (bread of the dead) is prepared in Mexican-American communities, particularly in the Southwest. The breads include ornately decorated loaves, such as *estillo valle de bravo* (candied fruit bread) and *pan de yema* (egg bread), and they are often shaped into the form of a person or baked in rounds or loaves with ceramic heads stuck into the surfaces. They may be embellished with braided dough, painted with food coloring, or sprinkled with colored sugar to achieve a festive effect. Throughout the afternoon and evening, relatives and friends visit, celebrate, and eat the special foods. Families may also visit the cemetery, washing the grave markers, decorating them with flowers, playing music, and sharing drinks, offering toasts to those who have gone before.

See also: DRINKING TOASTS; HALLOWEEN.
References: Quintana and Haralson. *Mexico's Feasts of Life.* 1989; West. *Mexican-American Folklore.* 1988.

AMERICAN FOLKLIFE FESTIVAL

At the end of June or in early July each year, the Smithsonian Institution and the U.S. National Park Service stage the Festival of American Folklife on the National Mall in Washington, D.C. Featuring foods, music, and crafts of various states and cultures, the event includes demonstrations showing how traditional meals and baked goods are prepared, arts and crafts exhibits, and music and dance performances.

See also: AMISH FOOD FESTIVALS; ATLANTIC ANTIC; FIESTA FILIPINIANA; GREEK FOOD FESTIVALS; KWANZAA; MEXICAN FIESTAS; NATIVE AMERICAN FEASTS; OKTOBERFEST; SMORGASBORD; UKRAINIAN FESTIVALS.

AMISH FOOD FESTIVALS

In February 1993, the first annual Amish or Pennsylvania Dutch Food Festival was held in Lancaster County, Pennsylvania—the home of many Amish families who are often referred to as Plain People because of their plain dress and simple life-style, which are dictated by religious beliefs. Festival visitors toured Amish farms and markets that sold Amish foods, and they ate at restaurants that prepared such traditional items as chicken pot pies, whoopie pies, grape mush, banana pickles, and soft pretzels. Amish food has also been celebrated each summer at an Amish Acres festival held in Nappanee, Indiana, since the 1980s. Though this festival focuses on arts and crafts, the thousands who attend the festival each year also come to taste Amish food from the booths, shops, and restaurants on the premises.

See also: APPLE PIE; PICKLES; POT PIES; SHOOFLY PIE.

ANIMAL CRACKERS OR COOKIES

Anyone who has ever nibbled on animal-shaped crackers or cookies probably has a special way of eating them. The very personal ritual of eating animal crackers usually begins during childhood. Some kids like to behead the animals immediately. Others save the head until last. The most common ritual, however, is for youngsters to begin chomping on the legs (back ones first) and then moving on to the head and body, according to Nabisco, which has been marketing animal crackers since the early 1900s when the company was known as the National Biscuit Company.

At first, the biscuitlike cookies were sold in boxes designed to look like animal cages in Barnum's Circus, which was very popular at that time. The product was called Barnum's Animals but later became known as Barnum's Animal Crackers. Carolyn Wyman, in *I'm a SPAM Fan: America's Best-Loved Foods* (1993), a book about some of America's most popular brand-name food items, notes that there are 17 different animal shapes produced for the animal cracker menagerie: "bear (sitting and walking), bison, camel, cougar, elephant, giraffe, gorilla, hippopotamus, hyena, kangaroo, lion, monkey, rhinoceros, seal, sheep, tiger and zebra." All 17 varieties, however, do not necessarily end up in each box, since the containers are filled in a random fashion.

So popular are the animal shapes that several other companies have "jumped on the circus wagon," producing a similar product. Frookies, for example, packages a chocolate variety made with fruit juice sweeteners.

See also: CHOCOLATE CHIP COOKIES; COOKIES.
Reference: Wyman. *I'm a SPAM Fan.* 1993.

Boxes containing animal-shaped crackers roll along a Nabisco assembly line. The crackers were first called Barnum's Animals for the nineteenth-century American impresario Phineas T. Barnum who created a traveling circus. The boxes recall the brightly decorated wagons used to transport and display circus animals.

ANNIVERSARY DINNER

A wedding anniversary is one of the most common occasions for celebrating by dining out. The celebration may include only the married couple, or it may be an elaborate affair with many people attending, particularly for a milestone anniversary such as a thirtieth or fiftieth. Other types of anniversaries also prompt festive dinners. Numerous civic, charity, and religious organizations hold anniversary dinners marking their length of service, whether it has been 10, 25, 50, or 100 years. Community dinners may also be held to commemorate significant historic events. Usually such dinners are formal or semiformal and consist of several courses. The meal may be served in a large dining hall, ballroom, conference center, school gymnasium, or a similar setting.

See also: BANQUET; DRINKING TOASTS.

ANTIPASTO

As the word itself suggests (*anti* means before and *pasto* means meal), antipasto is a before-the-meal course of Italian origin. It usually consists of a variety of cold meats and seafoods, cheeses, vegetables, and even fruits presented on a tray, with the selection depending on the cook. Antipasto is served in many Italian restaurants and households in North America. If prepared in the northern Italian style, it is likely to include thinly sliced salami and prosciutto (dry-cured Italian spiced ham), pickled artichokes and mushrooms, anchovies, olives, capers, tuna chunks, sardines, and hardboiled eggs. Northern Italian antipasto is somewhat more elaborate than antipasto served in the southern Italian style, which includes many vegetables, often pickled, and cheeses such as mozzarella and provolone on a tray lined with lettuce.

See also: APPETIZERS.

APERITIF

While North Americans may gather before dinner to enjoy cocktails, the French usually meet for an *aperitif*, which means "opener." The rituals are similar, and many North Americans use the French term, particularly at a formal dinner or lunch, to indicate that guests will be served some form of alcoholic beverage before the meal. These are served to whet the appetite or to allow time for all the guests to arrive and for the cook to finish preparing dinner.
See also: APPETIZERS; COCKTAIL PARTY; COCKTAILS.

APPETIZERS

Appetizers, or hors d'oeuvres, like aperitifs or cocktails, are intended to whet the appetite. They come in hundreds of different shapes and forms and are made out of almost any food imaginable. Some people routinely make a meal out of them, but appetizers are usually served with drinks before a meal. At a cocktail party, they may be served buffet-style or passed around on trays, and they include small open-faced sandwiches with toppings ranging from simple cheese spreads to layers of meat, poultry, fish, cheese, and vegetables or fruit. Other common appetizers include crackers and cheese; salsa and chips; hot items such as small pizzas, tiny meatballs in a sauce, small spring rolls or egg rolls, and small barbecued ribs; crudités—fresh vegetables, mostly raw or lightly steamed, with a dip; pâté, a meat or fish paste eaten with crackers or small bread slices; pastries filled with bits of meat or fish; pickled herring; and smoked fish.

Numerous restaurants offer appetizers such as the popular shrimp cocktail, deep-fried onion rings, and elaborate Italian antipasto. The pupu platter is common in Chinese- and Polynesian-style restaurants (*pupu* is a Hawaiian term for appetizers that include meats, egg rolls, and other items that can be heated on a lighted burner). Hors d'oeuvres of all kinds are also

routinely served in cocktail lounges and bars throughout North America.
See also: ANTIPASTO; COCKTAIL PARTY; COCKTAILS; CRACKERS AND CHEESE; GRAZING; PRETZELS; SALSA; SMORGASBORD; SPRING ROLLS; ZAKUSKI.

APPLE

See APPLE BUTTER; APPLE FESTIVALS; APPLE PIE; CIDER.

APPLE BUTTER

Making, serving, and eating apple butter are end-of-summer and early fall rituals that began centuries ago in Europe and have continued in North America. The ritual of making apple butter is part of some apple festivals across the United States, and individual families also keep the tradition alive.

One northern Indiana family has made apple butter every year since their German ancestors came to the United States in the late 1800s. In fact, a huge kettle brought from Germany when the family immigrated is used in the butter-making process. The kettle holds about 30 gallons and is filled with apple cider, which is boiled for about four or five hours over an open fire. Once the cider has boiled down to about half its original volume, "snitches"—peeled and sliced apples—are added and cooked for another four or five hours. During the final stages of cooking, a member of the family constantly stirs the mixture with a long stick to prevent burning. About 9 gallons of fresh apple butter become the end product that is shared with friends and neighbors.

The ritual is not complete, however, until the kettle has been cleaned, a process that is done the old-fashioned way, too. Scouring pads are never used because they can scratch the surface of the kettle. Instead, tomatoes are rubbed inside the kettle; the acid in the tomatoes does the cleaning job. The kettle is then wiped with

a soft cloth, and, cleaned and polished, it is ready for the next season.
See also: APPLE FESTIVALS; CIDER.

APPLE FESTIVALS

Many apple festivals are held in states such as Washington and California where most of the apples in North America are grown, but the apple and all the many foods that are created with the fruit are also celebrated in the Midwest. One of the most popular of these celebrations is in Fort Wayne, Indiana, the burial site of the legendary John Chapman, better known as Johnny Appleseed, who traveled from New England to the Midwest during the early 1800s carrying apple seeds that he planted along the way or distributed to any pioneer who would plant them. Some of the trees he and others planted in New England and the Midwest still bear fruit.

At almost any apple festival it is common to find signs or plaques with the old saying "eat an apple a day, keep the doctor away." Apples have long been a favorite "health food" (a good source of dietary fiber and some vitamin C), a fact that is emphasized at festivals. But apples—red, yellow, and green ones—are also served as snack foods, in dried forms or in baked or fried goods such as apple cakes, cookies, doughnuts, fritters, and pies. Apples coated with a candied syrup such as caramel or taffy are common, too.

Most apple festivals include traditional apple pie–eating contests: contestants compete with their hands behind their backs and bury their faces in pies, devouring as fast as they can.
See also: APPLE PIE; DOUGHNUTS; FRITTERS; SNACK FOODS.

APPLE PANDOWDY

Typically a late summer or fall dessert, apple pandowdy was very common in the East and in the Midwest until just a few generations ago. Although its popularity has declined, rural folks still make a version

of the dessert, lining a baking dish with sections of pastry dough and then filling it with sliced apples, sugar and molasses, spices, melted butter, and a little water. The combination is covered with rolled-out pastry dough, sealed, then baked. After about ten minutes in the oven, the cook must "dowdy" the dessert—use a sharp knife to cut the crust into the apples. Usually it is topped with ice cream, cream, or milk.
See also: APPLE FESTIVALS.
Reference: *American Heritage* editors. *The American Heritage Cookbook and Illustrated History of American Eating and Drinking.* 1964.

APPLE PIE

Many New Englanders claim that the fruit pie—particularly apple pie—is a New England invention. Certainly, apple pie is a staple among the Amish and other religious groups known as Plain People living in the New England states (as well as in the Midwest). Amish mothers, in fact, bake special half-moon apple pies for their children to eat on Sunday. Known as "preaching pies" (and as "perfect pacifiers"), they are made with dried apples so they will not be juicy and drip as children eat them during Sunday services.

For 100 years it was a custom at Yale University in New Haven, Connecticut, to serve apple pie after every evening meal, and some New Englanders still follow the custom of eating apple pie and drinking a glass of milk after many of their suppers. While on duty in remote places many American military personnel have expressed yearnings for what they call "Mom's apple pie" (that is, a pie baked "from scratch" at home). Although home-baked apple pie has long been considered a traditional American dessert and has been labeled by some as *the* most American food, fewer and fewer cooks prepare this favorite from fresh apples, peeled and baked inside homemade crusts. Most apple pies are now prepared in commercial bakeries or in food processing plants where they can be frozen for future consumption.

When served, apple pie is frequently accompanied with ice cream on the side or à la mode. Apple pie with Cheddar or American cheese is also a popular combination, particularly in the East and Midwest. **See also:** APPLE FESTIVALS; APPLE PANDOWDY. **References:** Hutchison. *Pennsylvania Dutch Cook Book.* 1948; Sokolov. "Insects, Worms, and Other Tidbits." 1989; Trager. *Foodbook.* 1970.

ART SHOW OPENING

Across North America, most openings of art shows, whether in a museum, gallery, studio, or other setting, are accompanied by a long-standing ritual—a reception for the artist, art patrons, and guests where food and beverages are served. Typically, wine or champagne, cheese and crackers, fruits, and various sweets are served, although some receptions may be formal affairs including a more lavish buffet with a great variety of foods and drinks. Guests usually carry their glasses and sip their drinks while viewing the show and conversing with the artists and other guests. **See also:** BUFFET; CRACKERS AND CHEESE.

ARTICHOKE FESTIVAL

In California where some type of food festival is held almost every week, even the artichoke, a thistlelike vegetable, is honored. In fact, folks there are likely to repeat the old tongue twister:

Theophilus Thistle,
    the successful thistle sifter,
In sifting a sieve
    of unsifted thistles,
Thrust 10,000 thistles
    through the thick of his thumb.

Theophilus, after all, represents the many workers who sort the thorny buds of Globe artichoke plants and are likely to have to pick thistles from their thumbs.

On a September weekend each year, the small coastal farm town of Castroville, 70 miles south of San Francisco, attracts

thousands to its Artichoke Festival, dubbed one of America's biggest crop parties. The town has been holding its annual "choke fest" since the 1950s, and, as would be expected, the festival features artichoke-cooking and artichoke-eating contests.

Every year farms in the area produce about 4 million cartons of spherical and oval-shaped Globe artichokes and Baby artichokes, each carton containing 23 to 25 pounds of the vegetable. The Globe artichoke is not native to California, though; it came to North America with the French who settled in Louisiana and the Spaniards who migrated to California. Since most of the artichoke crop in the United States now comes from the Castroville area, the town calls itself the "Arthichoke Center of the World," and emphasizes its title with the Artichoke Inn and the Giant Artichoke Restaurant.

Overabundance has led many of the town's restaurants to include artichokes as appetizers as well as main entrees on their menus. Boiling artichokes and serving them with butter or mayonnaise is one of the most traditional ways to prepare artichokes. First, the stalk is rubbed with lemon (to prevent darkening), then the whole head is boiled in water with a little salt, and finally the petals are pulled off one by one and the fleshy and tender base of each is dipped in butter or mayonnaise (the tip of the petal is tough and usually is thrown away). Artichoke hearts—the center part of small artichokes—are commonly canned and sold as gourmet foods and are frequently used in salads and in appetizers. **See also:** FOOD EVENTS; FOOD FAIRS; GOURMET FOODS.

ASPARAGUS HARVEST

During the damp and cool springs of the Midwest, it is an annual ritual in Olympia Fields, Illinois, to search for wild asparagus. The stalks do not grow wild as many mushrooms do; instead, new growth depends on seeds scattered from older plants during the previous year. The location of the "hunting grounds" for this delicate vegetable is

Artichokes, relatives of thistles, flourish near Castroville, California. Europeans from the Mediterranean Basin introduced the plant to California in 1806. The plant's bud, harvested by hand, can be steamed or boiled and eaten petal by petal. Small buds, once cooked, are so tender that they can be eaten whole. Castroville, self-proclaimed "Artichoke Center of the World," celebrates Monterey County's multimillion dollar crop with a September festival.

known only to the Italian families who have passed down the secret through the generations. Tools needed to find the elusive stalk include a plastic bag or other container for capture, very sharp eyes and concentration, a paring knife, and a long stick to push away the tall grasses under which the asparagus stalks hide. An important rule to remember during the hunt is older or "seeded" plants should not be cut. They are generally considered woody and not good to eat, but more importantly their seeds are needed to secure the next year's crop.

Asparagus is also grown commercially across the United States. It is a major spring crop in western Michigan, where the National Asparagus Festival is held each June in counties near Shelby. An even larger asparagus festival takes place earlier in the year—on the fourth weekend each April—in Stockton, California, where surrounding farms produce about 70 percent of the commercial U.S. asparagus crop. At both festivals the main attractions are the asparagus dishes, of course. In Michigan they are served smorgasbord-style, and in California the asparagus foods are sold from booths. The featured items range from grilled asparagus and asparagus soups to salads and casserole dishes and even desserts made with asparagus.

See also: CASSEROLE DISHES/MEALS; SMORGASBORD.

References: Chalmers. *Great American Food Almanac.* 1986; Hill. *Festivals U.S.A.* 1988; Mariani. *The Dictionary of American Food and Drink.* 1993, 1994; Schulz. *Celebrating America.* 1994.

ATLANTIC ANTIC

Brooklyn, New York, hosts numerous street fairs and festivals; one of the oldest and most popular is Atlantic Antic, an international food festival, which takes place at the end of September along a mile-and-one-half stretch of Atlantic Avenue. Sponsored by the Atlantic Avenue Association Development Corporation, the street fair draws nearly 1 million visitors each year and begins with a parade along Atlantic Avenue. Music, dancing, drama, and other entertainment are part of the fair. The many food booths feature Middle Eastern, Lebanese, Italian, Chinese, Polynesian, Mexican, Spanish, Swedish, and Cuban foods, as well as a variety of other ethnic foods.

See also: NINTH AVENUE FOOD FESTIVAL; TASTE OF . . . FESTIVALS.

BABY FOOD

In the vast majority of North American households, some of the first foods besides mother's milk or a milk formula offered to babies during their first year are hot cereals and pureed fruits, vegetables, poultry, and meats. Since 1928, when Gerber first produced pureed baby food for the mass market, parents have been routinely buying baby food from one of the three major producers in the United States—Gerber, Beech-Nut, and Heinz. These three companies process and sell well over 2 billion jars of baby food each year. Not all of the pureed food, however, is consumed by infants. A recent survey of college students found that baby food—pureed fruit in particular—is high on the list of favorite snack foods among the dormitory crowd, primarily because it is ready to eat and is sweet.

Frozen pureed foods for babies is a new type of baby food that has hit some big city markets (such as Chicago and Denver) in the 1990s. It is especially popular among parents who say they want to feed their children food that has not been in a jar for months or years, has no preservatives, and tastes almost like fresh food. Called Growing Healthy, the product is flash frozen in recyclable trays and comes in more than 30 varieties from pureed bananas to vegeta-bles and chicken (chicken, potatoes, corn, peas, and carrots).

See also: SNACK FOODS.
Reference: Mahany. *"Pablum Rebellion."* 1994.

BACHELOR PARTY

The bachelor party stems from ancient practices, and it has been a long-standing custom in North America. It went out of fashion during the 1960s and 1970s primarily because of its sexist nature; however, the custom has been revived in the 1990s, as more traditional weddings and prewedding events have become popular again.

Bachelor parties have a reputation for being raucous affairs where the prospective groom and male friends and relatives gather to eat, drink, tell off-color stories, and watch exotic dancers or stripteasers. Although excess food and alcohol, drugs, sex, and drunken, destructive brawls are still what some bachelor parties are all about, many others are sedate get-togethers. The tone of the bachelor party is usually determined by the prospective groom, who may not necessarily enjoy carousing and drinking with buddies. He may want to have dinner out with a few male friends or enjoy a golf outing or a weekend at a country retreat that includes a barbecue. Regardless of the nature of the party, the event is generally considered a send-off for the prospective groom, who, in the view of some, is leaving a carefree life for the "shackles" of marriage. Others see it simply as a rite of passage—a transition from one period of life (or life-style) to another. **See also:** BARBECUE.

BAGELS

The bagel is a doughnut-shaped yeast bread that gets its name from a German word meaning twisted or curved bracelet or ring, and it came to America with quite a background of history and lore. One legend says that the stirrup-shaped bagel was invented in the early seventeenth century by a Jewish baker in Vienna to honor horse-loving King John III of Poland, who protected the country from hordes of Turks crossing the Austrian border. Seventeenth-century folklore indicates that the superstitious considered the bagel a chaser of evil spirits. Another piece of ancient history includes the official sanction of bagels as an appropriate gift for women in childbirth in the Polish Community Regulations of 1610.

Authentic bagels are boiled for about 60 seconds and then baked for about 15 minutes. The boiling process, called "kettling," gives bagels their chewiness. Like many American food fads, the more popular something becomes the more outrageous the flavors. Bagel aficionados can now go to a number of bagel chain outlets to choose from anything from fresh blueberry- to spinach-flavored bagels. The original process of preparing the bagels is not always adhered to, and the result is often very different from store to store. Even the round shape is no longer sacred—with merchants also peddling them in seasonal shapes like Christmas trees and Valentine hearts.

The booming $800 million bagel business has also moved beyond the breakfast

Jewish immigrants from Europe brought the recipe for bagels to the United States. Actor Art Metrano played to West Coast patrons with a taste for bagels and cream cheese when he opened the Posh Bagel in Hollywood, California, in 1975.

table to include the sandwich lunch. Essentially, anything that can be served between two slices of bread is now served on bagels. Thus, the average American can now have anything from cream cheese and lox to turkey and bean sprouts on the 3.6 pounds of bagels they consume each year.

See also: BED AND BREAKFAST; BREAD; BREAKFAST; COFFEE HOUSES; CONTINENTAL BREAKFAST; LOX.

References: Chalmers. *The Great Food Almanac.* 1994; Evans. "The Bagel Boom!" 1996; Shosteck. *A Lexicon of Jewish Cooking.* 1979.

BAKE SALE

One of the most popular fund-raising events in many U.S. communities is the bake sale, often organized by a religious group, social club, school, or civic organization. Volunteers bake the breads, cookies, brownies, cakes, pies, and other goods offered for sale. Those who attend can also buy individual desserts to eat on the premises. Bake sales not only raise money for a particular cause or project, but they also provide an opportunity for socializing.

See also: BREAD; CHRISTMAS BAZAAR; COOKIES.

BAKED ALASKA

Originally, Baked Alaska consisted of ice cream encased in whipped cream and pastry. It was known simply as "Alaska" at Delmonico's, a famous restaurant in New York City, where it was a popular dessert in the 1800s and where some historians say that it was invented by the restaurant's chef to mark the United States' purchase of Alaska in 1869. Since that time, there have been numerous variations of the dessert. One was made with layers of white cake spread with preserves and ice cream, rolled and frozen, then topped with meringue just before serving. It was once prepared for festive occasions and formal dinners in many North American homes, but with today's time constraints and demand for convenience foods, Baked Alaska is now

primarily a specialty of fine restaurants and is ordered by diners who want a distinctive and delicate dessert.

See also: ICE CREAM.

Reference: Mariani. *The Dictionary of American Food and Drink.* 1993, 1994.

BAKED BEANS AND BROWN BREAD

The two foods baked beans and brown bread have been combined since the 1700s in North America. Colonial women learned to bake beans by following the example of Native American women, who soaked beans overnight, then combined them with onion and fat in a clay pot, and cooked them in a pit of hot stones. Because many colonial women adhered to religious customs that forbade cooking on Sunday, they prepared baked beans on Saturday evening to serve for Sunday dinner or supper.

Eventually, the Sunday cooking laws faded away, and New England people—specifically those in Boston—began to serve baked beans on Saturday nights. According to food historian James Trager, "the beans were baked by [commercial] bakers, who called each Saturday morning, took the family's bean pot to a community oven, usually in the cellar of a neighboring tavern, and returned the baked beans with a bit of brown bread for Saturday supper or Sunday breakfast." Ever since, "baked beans and brown bread" has been traditional fare in Boston, and it became popular across the United States. Today, however, the combination is seldom served outside New England, although many Americans consume "Boston baked beans," which are distributed across the continent in cans and jars.

Reference: Trager. *Foodbook.* 1970.

BANQUET

Extravagant banquets or feasts were common among ancient people of nobility and those who had great wealth and stature. Many paintings of generations past portray banquet tables laden with enormous

Wives of members of the Philadelphia Eagles host a bake sale in September 1987 to fund tickets home for nonunion, replacement players after the end of a strike.

amounts of food and beverages and people indulging in orgy fashion. Some banquets today can be extremely lavish with entrees including exotic meats such as lion, kangaroo, rattlesnake, and ostrich; but most banquets feature fairly routine food such as chicken dishes and roast beef.

Usually a banquet is a formal dinner served in a large hall, hotel ballroom, motel conference room, school gym or cafeteria, or recreational center in a church or temple. An annual banquet is a typical American way to celebrate major achievements or anniversaries. Professional associations, school sports teams, civic organizations, and many other groups mark a year of activities with such an event. A banquet is also a traditional grand finale for a conference and a typical way for small groups or major organizations to raise funds.

See also: ANNIVERSARY DINNER.

BAR MITZVAH/BAT MITZVAH

This sacred Jewish rite of passage also includes a celebration afterward with food and drink. In accordance with Jewish tradition, a bar mitzvah for a boy and bat mitzvah for a girl mark the time when a child is ready to assume adult responsibilities. The ceremony usually occurs at age 13, although in recent years a number of Americans well into their adult years who have never had a bar or bat mitzvah have gone through the ceremony. Girls were barred from such ceremonies until 1922; and even after a bat mitzvah was allowed, it did not become commonplace until about the 1980s. Thus, some women of advanced age are now going through the ceremony—an 85-year-old Florida woman was bat mitzvahed in 1993, for example.

After studying for months under the guidance of a rabbi, a person who is to be bar or bat mitzvahed stands before a congregation to chant from the Torah—the Five Books of Moses—and the Haftorah—selections from the Prophets. Usually the ceremony is followed by festivities and giftgiving. To symbolize the sweetness of the occasion, members of the congregation

may toss spice drops wrapped in a netting and tied with a ribbon at the bar mitzvah or bat mitzvah, and usually guests are invited to attend a lunch or dinner given for the honoree in a reception room at the temple, or in a hotel, restaurant, or banquet hall. The event may be an elegant sit-down meal and include elaborate decorations and entertainment, or it may be a simple reception with a buffet. A fairly recent custom and an American innovation is inviting selected guests to light candles on a cake shaped like a Torah, which symbolizes God's presence and the light of tradition that has been preserved for centuries.

See also: BANQUET; BUFFET.

BARBECUE

The barbecue (also spelled barbeque or bar b q) is a popular outdoor activity throughout the United States, especially during the summer months. *Barbeque* is the term most often used in the Southeast; it comes from the French *barbe a queue,* meaning "from beard to tail," and referring to a whole hog that is roasted slowly over a pit of coals. By the late 1700s and early 1800s, pit barbeques in North America were weekend events that included butchering a hog, digging a pit, and then cooking the meat. Such a style of cooking is still prevalent in the Carolinas, Georgia, and some other southern states.

Barbecue is the term most widely used in the United States. It usually refers to various methods of outdoor cooking that are combined with a social event. For some reason—no one knows why—most of the technicalities of the barbecue have been designated "man's work," although certainly many women are excellent barbecuers. The cook usually creates the design of the briquette/wood placement, starts the fire, adjusts the grill, and turns and bastes the meat, poultry, fish, and/or vegetables.

The Caribbean islands may have been the site for some of the first barbecues. In the 1700s, the Caribe Indians passed on the custom to settlers, runaway slaves, and others who went to the islands from the new outposts being established in the

Americas. Because there was an abundance of livestock, which had been introduced by the Spanish in previous years, the natives had been able to experiment with meat preparation over a good deal of time. They called the cooking procedure *boucan*, and it required building a fire on animal bones and hides, placing a green wood lattice (*barbacoa*) over the fire, and cooking the meat atop the frame, where it was cooked (usually charred) to perfection.

Today, a commercial barbecue pit is often a round or rectangular appliance that sits outdoors. Hot coals (created by using ready-made briquettes or pieces of burned wood like oak or mesquite) or gas jets provide heat sufficient for cooking appropriate food items on a grill. Hamburgers, hot dogs, steaks, chicken, and fish, such as swordfish or salmon, are the most popular foods cooked in this fashion. Some side dishes also go on the grill or into the coals wrapped in aluminum foil: potatoes, corn-on-the-cob, and the occasional pot of beans. Depending on the event and the time of year, the meal is served outdoors to a group of invited guests or family members at dinnertime. Usually cold side dishes such as coleslaw, jello salads, and vegetable trays accompany the barbecued items.

Barbecue contests have become a traditional summer event in many parts of the continent. Chefs, caterers, and amateurs with monikers like the Baron of Barbecue or the Honorable Sir Lion compete to win monetary prizes and publicity for their barbecued ribs, sausages, chicken breasts, or legs of lamb. The Kansas City Barbeque Society (KCBS), which was founded in the mid-1980s and now has more than 1,100 members, sponsors regional contests as well as national cook-offs in Kansas City, Kansas, and Lynchburg, Tennessee. KCBS requires contestants to abide by KCBS rules, such as the requirement to use only charcoal or hardwood for cooking. Contestants may barbecue pork ribs or shoulder, sausage, beef brisket, lamb, or poultry. Two more prestigious contests are the annual American Royal National Invitational Barbecue Cookoff and the World Invitational Rib Championship.

See also: BARBECUE RIBS; BARBECUE SAUCE; COLESLAW.
References: Clayton. *Cooking across America*. 1993; Funk. *2,107 Curious World Origins, Sayings and Expressions*. 1993; Stern and Stern. *Real American Food*. 1986.

BARBECUE RIBS

Ribs are a favorite menu item with many backyard barbecuers. They are also a mainstay at barbecue cooking contests throughout the United States and Canada. Typically, the ribs are cooked slowly, at a low temperature, by smoking or heating them over hot coals. There are three major variables when barbecuing ribs: (1) the meat, (2) the flavoring (spices, sauces, and marinades), and (3) the wood. Every barbecue "expert" has his or her own special ritual for cooking barbecue ribs, and, in general, people in regions west of the Mississippi tend to focus more on beef ribs, while those in the East use more pork ribs. Sauces can vary from the tomato-based to the vinegar-based varieties. Sometimes no sauce at all is used; in a process known as "dry rub" the spices are rubbed directly on the meat. The type of wood used to smoke and/or cook the meat also imparts a distinct flavor to the finished product. While mesquite is favored in the West, hardwoods such as oak, beech, cherry, and walnut are more traditional in the South.
See also: BARBECUE; BARBECUE SAUCE.
References: Dosier. "BBQ Deep in the Heart of Texas." 1993; Jamison and Jamison. *Smoke and Spice*. 1994.

BARBECUE SAUCE

The sauce used to baste meat while it is barbecuing can vary drastically from region to region in the United States. Adherents to one type of sauce can be fanatical in their devotion to their chosen recipe. For instance, there is a rivalry between the traditional barbecue sauces of eastern and western North Carolina. While both sauces contain coleslaw as an ingredient, the eastern sauce is vinegar- and turmeric-based, and the western sauce is tomato-based.

Most sauces contain some sort of acidic base, such as vinegar, tomato sauce, or Worcestershire sauce. The acid provides not only flavor but also a tenderizing effect. The acidity may be complemented by a sweetening agent such as honey, sugar, or fruit juice. Finally, extra flavor is added to the sauce with chili, horseradish, onion, mustard, paprika, or garlic.

How the sauce is applied to the meat is also a matter of debate among avid bar-becuers. Some add the sauce at the beginning, basting the meat several times throughout the barbecue. Some add the sauce only toward the end of the cooking process. Others cook the meat without sauce and serve the sauce at the end, occasionally on the side.

See also: BARBECUE; CHILI AND CHILI SUPPERS; COLESLAW; MUSTARD.

References: Coyle. *The World Encyclopedia of Food.* 1982; Jamison and Jamison. *Smoke and Spice.* 1994.

A cook bastes meat as it cooks over coals at a barbecue. Considered an art form by some, the Kansas City Barbeque Society of Kansas City, Missouri, holds contests for the best-tasting recipes for cooking beef, pork, chicken, sausage, lamb, or poultry.

BARN-RAISING

In the early days of the United States, it was a custom among farmers to help their neighbors build a barn, but that tradition has faded in most rural areas of North America—except for those where Amish societies prevail. In such states as Pennsylvania, Ohio, Indiana, and Iowa, and in the Canadian province of Ontario, the Amish (often called Plain People because of their plain dress and life-style) gather when an Amish family needs a new barn or has to rebuild a barn lost to fire, a tornado, or another disaster. Dozens of farmers and some members of their families may offer their services for a barn-raising, which is a major social event that includes plenty of food and drink.

The construction work usually begins early in the morning with each Amish farmer engaged in a specific task. Using precut lumber, the men raise the barn structure from the prepoured cement foundation to the roof in a single day. By midmorning, the men pause for a break, and the women and some of the older children serve gallons of lemonade or another type of fruit drink to the workers. When the men go back to their construction tasks, the women and children begin preparing tables for the noon meal, which is likely to include plenty of home-baked bread and butter, fried chicken, ham, vegetable casseroles, baked beans, potato salad, macaroni salad, coleslaw, fresh seasonal garden vegetables, pickles of various sorts, and homemade desserts—fresh pies, cakes, cookies, and puddings—and coffee.

See also: BAKED BEANS AND BROWN BREAD; CASSEROLE DISHES/MEALS; COLESLAW; COOKIES; HAM; PICKLES; PUDDINGS.

BARTENDER SPECIALS

Innovative bartenders often create unique drink concoctions for their restaurants, saloons, taverns, or clubs. Customers who like the concoctions may then routinely order these "bartender specials" when they frequent the establishments. If the specials are exceptional, they make their way into the conventional mixed drink or cocktail repertoire.

Perhaps some of the earliest specials were created when American settlers fermented almost anything they could find—squash, berries, roots—in order to make alcoholic beverages. In commercial drinking establishments, however, two of the earliest specialties to appear were the manhattan and the martini. Some historians suggest that the same mixologist, Jerry Thomas, invented both the manhattan and a forerunner of the martini in the 1870s, while others place the origin of the martini well before the manhattan. Other early specials include the mint julep and the Ramos Gin Fizz. Later concoctions that remain popular include the Bloody Mary, a combination of tomato juice, vodka, and seasonings; the Mai Tai, a mixture of lime, curaçao, and rum that was created in 1944 by Victor "Trader Vic" Bergeron; and the Screwdriver, a vodka and orange juice mixture first invented in the 1950s. The most frequently told story about the origin of the Screwdriver involves American oil rig workers in the Middle East mixing vodka with canned orange juice and stirring the drink with the most readily available implement—a screwdriver.

Factors in the success of these bartender specials include taste, imagination, and a catchy name.

See also: COCKTAIL PARTY; COCKTAILS; IRISH COFFEE; MARTINI; MINT JULEP.

References: Grimes. *Straight Up or on the Rocks.* 1993; Mariani. *The Dictionary of American Food and Drink.* 1993, 1994; Poister. *The New American Bartender's Guide.* 1989; Trager. *The Food Chronology.* 1995.

BASEBALL PARK EATING AND DRINKING

When one thinks of baseball and going to a major or minor league game, certain foods and beverages often come to mind: hot dogs and cold drinks, peanuts, popcorn, caramel corn, and ice cream bars. Some

A vendor at Chicago's Wrigley Field hawks salted peanuts to fans during a 1981 Chicago Cubs and Philadelphia Phillies game.

baseball fans swear that red hots—also hot dogs or frankfurters—and a cold beer taste the best when consumed at a baseball game. According to a recent estimate, 9 percent of the hot dogs consumed in the United States are eaten in baseball parks. The beer flows profusely. In just one stadium—Arlington in Texas—at least 10,000 kegs of beer are poured during an average six-day period.

The vendors who move up and down the stands selling food and beverages throughout the park develop special chants and calls (like the street vendors of days past) to hawk their wares: "Get your red hots, here!" and "Beer! Hey! Cold beer here!" and "PEEEEEEE.......NUTS! Roasted Peanuts! Two bags a buck!" Some vendors have made an art of their job, prompting some fans to routinely look for seats in their favorite vendor's section. The dramatic style of at least one vendor, the "Peanut Man" at Dodger Stadium in Los Angeles, caught the attention of the *Tonight Show,* where the vendor appeared to demonstrate his uncanny accuracy and

range. He has been known to throw bags of peanuts over dozens of rows of people without hitting a hair on anyone's head.

Another tradition has developed in relation to this practice. When the food cannot be delivered air express, as with peanuts or bags of popcorn, fans between the vendor and the buyer readily pass along soda, frozen malts, hot dogs, and the like down the aisle. Money as payment and the return change is handled the same way. The only thing that confounds this system is a great play on the field.

Still another eating ritual has developed at baseball parks. Fans who attend Milwaukee Brewers games (like fans of other teams) often begin their festivities with food; they tailgate, eating prepared food from picnic baskets, cooking on small grills, or buying foods that can be eaten from the back of a car, truck, van, or recreational vehicle parked in the stadium lot. Inside the Milwaukee County Stadium, great foods are served as well, and the most famous is bratwurst covered with a "secret sauce."

Some baseball parks cater to special food preferences. At Pittsburgh's Three Rivers Stadium, a Kidcessions stand offers special children's meals featuring child-sized hot dogs, chips, sodas, lemonades, and slushes. Coloring books and crayons are also offered. In Miami, the Marlins' fans may hale from not only Florida but also from Canada, Puerto Rico, and Latin America. Foods at the concession stands reflect this multiethnic diversity. In Boston, outside Fenway Park and also within the stadium, Italian sausage sandwiches and other Italian foods are among the specialties. At Candlestick Park in San Francisco, the food and beverages reflect not only some of the city's ethnic diversity but also health consciousness, with some stands selling vegetarian, or "veggie," burgers, turkey franks, and mineral water.

See also: CARAMEL CORN; HOT DOGS; ICE CREAM; PICNIC BASKET; POPCORN; SANDWICHES; TAILGATE PARTY.

References: Mariani. *The Dictionary of American Food and Drink*. 1993, 1994; Rand McNally. *The Official Baseball Atlas*. 1994.

BASQUE BOARDING-HOUSE DINING

Numerous ethnic food cookbooks published in recent years contain recipes based on meals served in Basque boarding houses, which are located primarily in the cattle-raising areas of Nevada and Idaho, and in the California hills. There is no longer a Basque nation in Europe, but it was once a small country in the Pyrenees, a mountainous region between France and Spain, where the Basque, who spoke a language known as Euskera, lived since around 200 B.C. Many of these people immigrated to early America, where they survived as sheepherders and spent days, if not weeks, in the hills with their sheep. When they went to a town or village, they stayed at Basque boarding houses, most of which were built along railroad lines so that they could be easily found by any new Basque immigrants arriving in western territory.

A few such boarding houses still exist in the West; some are refurbished bed-and-breakfast accommodations, and others are hotels that serve traditional, family-style boarding-house meals. These meals usually consist of many courses—first soup, then salad and relishes, followed by a bean dish such as garbanzos and sausage or garlic-roasted green beans, all accompanied by bread and wine. Next comes a rice dish, a stew or side-dish course made with tongue or tripe, and finally a main entree of beef steak, roast lamb or beef, or pork chops is served. Dessert is likely to be fruit or cheese. The entire meal comes to a close with an after-dinner drink, usually a liqueur or Winnemucca coffee made with freshly brewed, strong coffee, brandy, anisette, and a twist of lemon.

See also: AFTER-DINNER DRINKS; BED AND BREAKFAST; BREAD; RICE DISHES.

References: Betz. *Tastes of Liberty*. 1985; Smith. *The Frugal Gourmet on Our Immigrant Ancestors*. 1990; Stern and Stern. *Real American Food*. 1986.

BASTILLE DAY

Although primarily a French holiday celebrated on 15 July to mark the storming of the Bastille prison during the French Revolution in 1789, Bastille Day is celebrated the evening before (14 July) among people of French ancestry in the United States and Canada. It is the French version of Independence Day.

A Bastille Day festival is held annually in Kaplan, Louisiana, where numerous families of French heritage and descendants of Acadians (Cajuns) settled. The festival became a town ritual in the early 1900s when a young Frenchman, Eugene Eleazar, moved to the area and encouraged farmers to celebrate a Bastille celebration on 14 July.

One of the most colorful celebrations has been held in Boston since the mid-1970s. Along with parades, singing, and dancing there is plenty of French-style food, including caviar, salmon mousse, and pâtés. In Philadelphia an annual Bastille

Day Waiters' Race is held. Participants must race holding a tray with a split of champagne and a glass in one hand and a French flag in the other hand. When racers arrive at the finish line, they must put down the tray, uncork the champagne bottle, and pour it without spilling a drop.

Some Bastille Day celebrations are fund-raising events. In a Detroit, Michigan, suburb one such event was a benefit for St. Agatha Catholic Church. The $100-a-plate, French-style dinner began with champagne, followed by onion and green peppercorn soup in a pastry dome, then poached halibut with leeks and oysters. After that, a dollop of raspberry sorbet was served—a European custom to refresh the taste buds, or "cleanse the palate," before the main course arrives. The dinner's centerpiece consisted of roasted beef tenderloin in a veal and basil mousse with red wine sauce, and—again in European fashion—a Caesar salad followed. Frozen vanilla soufflé with almond cookies, lemon tartlets, and coffee eclairs topped off the elegant Bastille Day dinner.

See also: CAESAR SALAD; CAVIAR; SORBETS AND GRANITAS.

References: Cohen and Coffin. *America Celebrates!* 1991; Hill. *Festivals U.S.A.* 1988.

BEAN DISHES

A variety of legumes (which include split peas, lentils, and pod beans) are used to make bean dishes that are served on a regular basis across North America. Chili, a widely consumed tomato-based dish, is made with pinto, kidney, or red beans. A two-, three-, or four-bean salad (made of kidney beans, green beans, and/or wax beans, and sometimes garbanzo beans) with a seasoned vinegar or mayonnaise dressing is often served at picnics and potlucks. Bean sprouts are a common garnish for green salads. Minestrone (Italian for "big soup") made with beef or chicken stock and pinto or Great Northern beans and other vegetables, split pea soup, black bean soup, and white bean soup are routinely served in many areas of the conti-

nent. Dips and spreads made from black, white, or pinto beans or lentils are common appetizers or accompaniments to a meal.

While people who are not accustomed to beans often suffer from digestive problems because the bean starches cannot be fully digested, those whose diets regularly include beans often have the digestive enzymes needed to prevent discomfort. In some cases, seasonings help in the digestive process in addition to adding flavor. Hearty seasonings are combined with various types of beans for traditional ethnic dishes. Chiles are mixed with red beans for a typical Mexican dish, and people from the Middle East use cumin to flavor fava beans. Ginger is a common flavoring for legumes used in Chinese dishes, and lentils, split peas, and mung beans may be spiced with curry in dishes originally prepared in India.

Bean dishes are especially popular with vegetarians, who combine them with rice, bread, tortillas, or other grain foods to provide a complete protein for the diet (beans alone are not a complete protein; that is, they do not contain all the essential amino acids the body cells need for proper functioning). Beans are used to make vegetarian dishes ranging from appetizers and salads to casseroles and substitute "meat" loaves.

See also: BAKED BEANS AND BROWN BREAD; BEANS AND FRANKS; BLACK-EYED PEA CELEBRATIONS; CASSEROLE DISHES/MEALS; CHILI AND CHILI SUPPERS; CHILI DOGS; CHINESE NEW YEAR; CURRY; DANISH DAYS; DIWALI; NEW YEAR'S DAY; PERSIAN NEW YEAR; RAMADAN; SUCCOTASH; VEGETARIAN EATING.

Reference: Solomon. *Lean Bean Cuisine.* 1995.

BEANS AND FRANKS

Open up a can of baked beans, slice open a package of frankfurters, combine the ingredients with catsup, mustard, or some other types of condiments or spices, and heat on top of the stove or in the oven and you have a weekend supper, a quick lunch, a picnic dish, or a carry-in specialty. This inexpensive combination dish is a regular part of many North Americans' diets and is popular with youngsters who are just learning how to cook or who routinely prepare their own meals.

See also: HOT DOGS.

BED AND BREAKFAST

So popular are bed-and-breakfast accommodations in North America that numerous guides have been published to help travelers find their way to these places, which total more than 9,000 across the United States. They range from rooms in farmhouses and ranches to bedrooms in restored Victorian mansions in small towns and spare rooms in luxury apartments and townhouses in big cities. Ambiance and a change from the standard motel or hotel room and restaurant are what travelers seem to want. They also want to take part in the breakfast ritual: guests can chat with each other and with their host or hostess while eating, making breakfast more of a social event than what most travelers would find in large hotel and motel chains. While foods vary and often are specialties of the particular host or hostess, muffins and sweet breads are some of the most common items, along with fresh fruits, hot or cold cereals, and various types of egg dishes.

See also: BREAD; BREAKFAST; CEREAL, COLD; CONTINENTAL BREAKFAST; MUFFINS.

BEDTIME SNACK

No particular food or beverage can be labeled the all-time favorite snack at bedtime, but this light meal is habitual for countless Americans, and some popular bedtime snacks include cookies or crackers and milk, tea and toast, popcorn, pretzels and beer, a peanut butter sandwich, fresh or canned fruit, a piece of pie or cake, or even dinner leftovers, such as a slice of pizza or a dish of cold pasta.

See also: COOKIES; PASTA; PEANUT BUTTER; POPCORN; PRETZELS; SANDWICHES; SNACK FOODS.

BEER DRINKING

"Beer is the beverage of celebration, of the shared harvest and communal prosperity. It is what we drink at town festivals and picnics in the park, beach parties and block parties, family reunions and friendly get-togethers . . . the ritual substance that unites us all." That is how Bruce Aidells and Denis Kelly, authors of *Real Beer and Good Eats* (1992), describe the significance of beer drinking in the United States, an activity they say "is always tied to food." Beer, in fact, is a form of food. Its basic ingredient is dried grain—barley, millet, oats, rye, wheat, or other grain—rice, or corn fermented with a sugary liquid solution and yeast, which often forms naturally.

Beer making has been practiced in most parts of the world for thousands of years, and in the past beer brewing usually accompanied bread making with bread sometimes crumbled and allowed to ferment to make more beer. It was common for Europeans to brew beer (called *ale,* a term from the Germanic languages) in their homes as part of the bread-baking process. When Europeans immigrated to North America, they brought their beer-making traditions with them and served beer at nearly every meal. Long before the colonists arrived, however, Native Americans routinely made beer of corn—a sacred event honoring the corn goddess. Colonists sometimes favored corn beer, or "Indian corn," over their own brew made the European way. Corn beer has also long been the basis for corn whiskey made by so-called moonshiners in Kentucky, Tennessee, Arkansas, Georgia, and other parts of the South.

Today, large commercial brewers market a great variety of beers, such as ales, stouts, lagers, bocks, and even nonalcoholic beers, under numerous brand names. Some well-known brands took their names from German brewers like Frederick Pabst and Joseph Schlitz, who in the 1800s began brewing beer in Milwaukee, Wisconsin, known as the beer capital of North America.

Beer drinkers may consume their beverage of choice at an athletic or a recreational or social event, or after a day's work, relaxing in a beer garden, tavern, saloon, cafe, restaurant, or brew pub, where beer is brewed and served on the same premises. Most beer drinkers develop a routine for drinking their beverage— from a cold can or bottle, from a paper cup (especially at ball games or picnics), or from an icy frosted glass or mug (as it is often served in a beer garden or brew pub). It is also a custom for many people who frequent taverns or pubs to eat certain foods while drinking beer. Hot roasted peanuts in the shell, potato chips, pretzels, pizza slices, salsa and chips, crackers and cheese, onion rings, bar chicken (deep-fried), and deep-fried seafoods are popular items. A past custom in some taverns and pubs was to serve hardboiled eggs or a soup (bean soup was popular) as an accompaniment to a "brew," and in a few drinking establishments that custom is still observed.

See also: BASEBALL PARK EATING AND DRINK-ING; BOILERMAKER; BREW PUBS; DRINKING TOASTS; KEG PARTY; OKTOBERFEST; PICNIC; PRETZELS.

References: Aidells and Kelly. *Real Beer and Good Eats.* 1992; Digby and Digby. *Inspired by Drink: An Anthology.* 1988; Fussell. *The story of Corn.* 1992; Morris. *The Great Beer Trek.* 1990.

BELTANE CAKES

Some North Americans of Scotch, Irish, and British ancestry celebrate the first day of May (May Day), or Beltane as it was called when the Celts flourished, by preparing and eating oat cakes or oatmeal cookies and dairy foods such as cheese, custard, and ice cream. Commemorating Beltane began several thousand years ago and stems from Celtic rituals to usher in spring. Festivities usually began on the eve of May Day with Beltane fires—bonfires— to ward off evil spirits and included dances around a Maypole. Green boughs and bowls of milk set beside a door supposedly brought good fairies to help guard against sinister powers—thus the use of dairy products today. Not too long ago in North

America, May Day was commonly cele-brated by children who left "May baskets" of spring flowers on the doorsteps of neighbors' and friends' homes. That prac-tice, however, has faded.

See also: COOKIES; ICE CREAM.

BIKER "HANGOUTS"

For many years, movies, videotapes, and television programs have depicted male motorcyclists as macho, mean, low-down, outlaw types and their female companions as tough "broads"—images that are deserved in some, but not all, cases. Places where bikers gather to "hang out"—road-side cafes, saloons, pool halls—also have been regarded as unsavory, because it has been a common occurrence for bikers to drink to excess and get involved in drunk-en brawls. The hangouts are considered off-limits to most "respectable folks."

The "boozing" ritual, however, is not common for a growing number of bikers. Just outside the metropolitan Chicago area a restaurant on U.S. Highway 41 is a "bikers' scene" on summer weekends. Dozens (if not hundreds) of motorcyclists, including a well-known Chicago radio personality who often discusses his biking adventures on the air, come from miles around to meet for a Saturday or Sunday morning ritual of eating breakfast or brunch and taking part in "biker talk." Many of the bikers are in the middle-age category, and biker couples are frequent customers at this particular biker hang-out, which enjoys a reputation as a peace-ful place to gather. Similar biker hangouts are common in many parts of North America, and it is not unusual for groups of conservative motorcyclists to travel cross-country together, meeting at speci-fied locations for conventions, festivals, or other events.

Some motorcyclists gather for a differ-ent type of ritual and purpose. They are "X-Winos," as some announce with logos on their leather jackets, or ex-addicts of various sorts who hang out in "dry bars" or coffee shops. The Dry Gulch Sober Cantina in St. Paul, Minnesota, is one such biker hangout. In fact, numerous eating and drinking establishments in the twin cities of St. Paul and Minneapolis cater to recovering alcoholics and other addicts who have come to the area for treatment at detoxification centers such as the well-known Hazelden. Some of the recovering addicts stay to make their homes in the area, and, whether they are motorcycle enthusiasts or have other interests, they meet with a sober group in dry cafes, restaurants, dance halls, or clubs where only nonalcoholic beverages are served.

See also: CAFES.

BIRTHDAY CAKE

The birthday cake is the most common special-occasion food in history, though its origin is uncertain. More than likely, a cake was, and is, presented to ensure the honored person's good fortune throughout the coming year.

Although a home-baked birthday cake is traditional in many American homes, the "store-bought" variety has probably taken precedence. Since it is also common for people to celebrate a birthday by eating out, a small birthday cake with lighted candles or sparklers may be presented to the honored guest by restaurant servers. In informal restaurants, the servers also make it a practice to wish a birthday celebrant a happy day in song accompanied by rhythmic clapping.

Wherever a birthday cake with lighted candles is presented, the honoree is encouraged to blow out each flame, no matter how many are on the cake, to ensure that a wish will come true. Adults who fail to make the grade are usually subject to much good-natured teasing. In his book, *The Magic in Food* (1990), Scott Cunningham suggests that originally the candles may have been arranged to represent the person's astrological sign, thereby honoring the sun. He also notes that blowing out the candles and making a wish are steeped in an ancient spiritual magic and that writing in frosting on top of the cake also has its basis in magic; he believes that consuming the written good wishes causes them to be internalized by the recipient.

Reference: Cunningham. *The Magic in Food*. 1990.

Special cakes with messages mark birthdays. Triplets celebrate their second birthday, each with a cake and candles.

BISCUITS AND GRAVY

The simple dish of biscuits and gravy is essentially bread covered with a gravy or sauce sometimes containing meat. Originally it was a poverty meal—considered a poor folks food—and it is now often considered a comfort food and is served in diners or at home for breakfast. The biscuits routinely used are small, raised breads, occasionally yeast-based but more likely leavened with baking soda and/or baking powder, which are especially favored in the South. The gravy is made from fat rendered by pan-fried meat, usually pork. A small amount of flour is cooked in the fat (longer than for a white sauce but not browned as for a roux). This mixture is extended with milk, diluted milk, or plain water in the most dire circumstances. Sometimes the gravy is called "sop" when made with water, or "sawmill gravy," ostensibly because mill crews in the backwoods ate little more than biscuits, gravy, and coffee. If the pan-fried meat is ham, flour is omitted and the drippings are extended with water or (traditionally) black coffee; this variant is called "red-eye gravy," because the reddish ham drippings coalesce to form an eye.

See also: BREAD; BREAKFAST; COFFEE; HAM.
References: Egerton. *Southern Food.* 1993; Jamison and Jamison. *Texas Home Cooking.* 1993.

BISTRO DINING

The ritual of eating at a bistro cafe is certainly common in France, where the term *bistro* probably originated. A French bistro "is a small neighborhood restaurant serving home-style, substantial fare . . . [where] people don't whisper, they shout, and diners are on a first-name basis with the harried waitress," as well as the owner, according to Patricia Wells, author of *Bistro Cooking.* Although a North American bistro may not be as informal as its counterpart in France, it is usually a friendly, intimate place, one where friends enjoy meeting and sharing a meal or just coffee and dessert or a glass of wine. Those who regularly eat at a bistro are likely to order French-style foods, such as bouillabaisse or another type of entree with an ethnic flair, or perhaps a fresh green salad or homemade pastry with an espresso.

See also: CAFES; ESPRESSO BARS.

BLACK-EYED PEA CELEBRATIONS

Sometimes called a "cowpea" or "black-eyed bean," the black-eyed pea is actually a legume. It is celebrated in Athens, Texas, with a Black-Eyed Pea Jamboree every July and eaten for good luck at the beginning of a new year in other southern states.

Known for the single black dot at one end, the kidney-shaped legumes have been cultivated in the United States since the 1700s, when President Thomas Jefferson had them planted at Monticello. Black-eyed peas, however, originated in Africa and were carried to this continent with slaves who were brought to American shores by way of the West Indies and then the territory of Louisiana, where today many Creole dishes make use of the nutritious food.

Black-eyed peas are also a staple in many soul food dishes and are one of the main ingredients in the traditional Hoppin' John dish served on New Year's Day. During the Jamboree in Athens, which claims to be the Black-Eyed Pea Capital of the Planet, foods made with black-eyed peas are naturally part of the festivities, and it is common to find even martinis made with black-eyed peas soaked in crushed chiles.

See also: CHILES; MARTINI; NEW YEAR'S DAY; SOUL FOOD.
References: Pyles. *The New Texas Cuisine.* 1993; Root and de Rochemont. *Eating in America.* 1981; Schulz. *Celebrating America.* 1994.

BLESSINGS

The act of intoning a prayer before eating a meal is one of the most common modern practices hearkening back to a time when

The Kiddush, an age-old Jewish prayer, begins Seder, the festive ceremonial meal of the first night of the eight-day Passover celebration that recalls the Hebrew liberation from Egyptian slavery.

the food source was not taken for granted. The origins of the prayer ritual were undoubtedly pagan. In ancient times, people burned or destroyed a symbolic portion of the meal as a sacrifice—a "thank-you"—to a power responsible for providing sustenance and life itself. Today, many families begin each meal with the practice of linking their food to a deity. The prayer ritual might be as elaborate as a sermon or as simple as the well-known chant, "God is good, God is great. Now we thank Him for this food. Amen. Let's eat!"

BLINTZES

A traditional Jewish dairy dish, blintzes are made from a thin egg batter (like crepes) and filled with sweetened farmer cheese and sometimes seasonal fruits, such as strawberries and apples. The basic cheese blintz as well as other varieties are common menu items in Jewish delis and are served on many Jewish holidays.
See also: DELI FOODS; SHAVOUT.

BLOODY MARY

A popular drink served before brunch and also as a cocktail before dinner, a Bloody Mary is made from vodka, tomato juice, lemon juice, Worcestershire sauce, and a dash of Tabasco sauce. It is usually served with a slice of lime or with a large stalk of celery as a decorative touch. One variation of the drink is the Bloody Maria made with tequila instead of vodka. Another is a vodka-based Bloody Bull made with beef bouillon and tomato juice.
See also: COCKTAILS; SUNDAY BRUNCH.

BLUEBERRY FESTIVALS

Along with attending a community blueberry festival at harvest time, many blueberry lovers also take part in the summer ritual of picking their own fruit at a blueberry farm. A favorite dessert at festival time is fresh-baked blueberry pie topped with a scoop of vanilla ice cream. Other popular foods served during blueberry festivals include blueberry pancakes, blueberry muffins, and blueberry jams and jellies.

Some blueberry festivals commemorate colonial times when blueberries grew wild and colonists picked and served the fruit with sherry or sweetened milk. Blueberries also were covered with a biscuit dough and baked, creating what today would be called a cobbler. Every summer, the National Blueberry Festival is held in South Haven, Michigan, which calls itself the Blueberry Capital of the World. One of the main events is a blueberry pie–eating contest.

See also: MUFFINS; PIES.

BLUE-PLATE SPECIAL

During the 1930s and 1940s, the blue-plate special served in a U.S. diner or cafe was an inexpensive meal—a plate of leftovers— served at the counter where customers lined up on a row of swivel stools. Today, however, in refurbished diners or small restaurants that have revived the Art Deco decor including the neon lights and shiny chrome, the term *blue-plate special* often refers to a specialty of the house or a dish that is being promoted for the day. These eating establishments also serve such traditional items as old-fashioned meat loaf, hot turkey sandwiches, macaroni and cheese, sodas, and homemade pies.

See also: CAFES; MEAT LOAF; SANDWICHES.

BOILERMAKER

For many working people, Friday afternoon or evening is the end of the workweek and a time to relax at a favorite "watering hole" for a beer or other type of drink. One Friday favorite is the boilermaker. The term *boilermaker* dates back to the 1920s when it was considered a drink for the rough and tough, particularly men who made and repaired heavy metal items. It consists of a glass of beer served with a shot of some other alcoholic beverage. That other beverage depends on location. In Milwaukee, Wisconsin, which is famous

for its beer making and drinking, a boilermaker is without question beer with a shot of brandy. Farther north in Wisconsin, a boilermaker is beer and a glass of wine or liqueur. In the East, beer and schnapps or beer and a shot of scotch or Irish whiskey are popular boilermakers.

The ritual of drinking a boilermaker is fairly standard nationwide: you drink the shot in one gulp and chase it with the beer, or sip the shot between swallows of beer. Some drinkers insist on a "depth charge," dropping the shot glass and its contents in the beer glass and guzzling the combination.

See also: BEER DRINKING.

References: Mariani. *The Dictionary of American Food and Drink.* 1993, 1994; Morris. *The Great Beer Trek.* 1990.

BOOKSTORE CAFE OR DELI

Coffee and books (or other published works) have been a twosome for as long as printed material has been distributed in North America, and the tradition of reading poetry, political essays, or short stories while sipping coffee (or other beverage) has not disappeared. Bookstore cafes are popular among literary coffeehouse crowds in numerous upscale city neighborhoods from coast to coast.

Some older independent bookstores are adding cafes to their businesses as a way to lure customers while maintaining literary traditions. Poetry and drama collections may be offered for sale in cafes that also feature storytelling, poetry readings, and dramatic performances. In fact, poetry readings, which have faded in popularity since the 1960s, began making a comeback in the 1990s. Customers seated in a cozy cafe sipping an espresso or cappuccino are once again listening to creative individuals share their thoughts and feelings through their poetry, which ranges in style from haiku and free verse to limericks and song. Quaint coffee houses sometimes have bookstores within, or in the back of, their premises. Chain (mass-market) bookstores often hold autograph parties featuring authors of cookbooks and samples of their favorite creations. Museums of all sorts also often include a bookstore cafe within their walls.

A cafe or deli featuring books for sale or a bookstore that includes a cafe or deli is sometimes a major tourist attraction in a city or town, and such a business can almost always be found in a university community. That is the case in Santa Barbara, California, where the Earthling Bookstore is not only a literary landmark with its whimsical mural depicting dozens of the world's greatest authors, but also a favorite place for residents and tourists alike to meet for a deli lunch or coffee.
See also: CAFES; COFFEE; COFFEE HOUSES; DELI FOODS.

BOX LUNCHES

For children who take their lunch to school, the box lunch means food packed at home, transported in a lunch box, and eaten in the school cafeteria. Those box lunches usually include a sandwich, chips, perhaps some fresh vegetables such as carrot sticks, fresh or canned fruit or a pudding, or some other sweet dessert, and a carton of fruit juice. A thermos of hot soup might also be included in some box lunches.

Lunch boxes are sold in most discount and variety stores, and for most children it is important to choose one that has a pretty design or a popular icon.

For adults, the box lunch is not usually a do-it-yourself meal; rather, it is commercially prepared and served at business meetings, seminars, and conferences and sometimes at concerts or outdoor events. One of the most popular box lunches includes fried chicken, coleslaw, a roll and butter, and usually a dessert such as a brownie or chocolate chip cookie. Some box lunches may be more elaborate, consisting of a croissant filled with a sandwich spread and sliced beef or chicken, a green salad, and a gourmet dessert.
See also: COLESLAW; CROISSANTS; PUDDINGS; SANDWICHES.

BOXED MEALS AND HELPERS

Since the end of World War II, as busy consumers have looked for ways to prepare meals quickly, the demand for convenience foods has grown steadily. In many households quick meals have become common and are a "must" at least once or twice per week. While frozen meals are one type of convenience food routinely consumed, another kind of quick meal is made with packaged pasta and precooked rice and seasonings or sauces that have to be reconstituted with water or other liquid. Macaroni and cheese is one of the most popular meals-in-a-box, with Kraft's brand selling more than 300 million boxes annually. Another traditional quick meal is made with packaged pasta or rice and sauce and seasonings, to which the consumer adds fresh hamburger, chicken, or canned tuna fish. The Helper products (Hamburger, Chicken, and Tuna) are registered trademarks of General Mills, Inc., which introduced its first helper—Hamburger Helper—as an inexpensive way to create a ground-meat dish. The helpers proved to be convenient, too, and along with quick-fix rice, rice and pasta (Rice-A-Roni), and various types of packaged noodle dishes, they are now part of the quick-meal tradition in the United States.
See also: FROZEN MEALS; PASTA; RICE DISHES.

BREAD

Most North Americans consume some type of bread with almost every meal, with the average person eating over 50 pounds of bread per year. Bread and butter or other spread is sometimes a meal in itself. Most breads are made from grains—wheat, rye, barley, oats, and other cereals—ground into flour. Corn, beans (such as lentils and soybeans), and nuts ground into meal have long been used for bread making as well. Although bread has been made for thousands of years, perhaps since the Stone Age, some of the first records of bread making go back to ancient Egypt where both leavened and unleavened breads were baked in public ovens.

One of the first North American breads was a flatbread that Native Americans produced from cornmeal. Colonists adapted this type of bread making and also made bread from cereal grains they planted and harvested. Immigrants brought with them recipes for many varieties of bread that have been passed on and are still baked and served with traditional meals. Examples include Scandinavian dark breads and crispbreads that appear at every smorgasbord, baton-shaped French breads served at many meals, Irish soda bread traditionally served on St. Patrick's Day, and caraway and poppy seed breads that stem from many nations.

Today, numerous types of traditional sweetened and decorated breads, rolls, and buns are associated with holidays, such as hot cross buns served on Easter and St. Lucia Day buns. Some breads have long been allied with particular regions of the continent. Cornbread and spoon bread are southern favorites; brown bread is a New England specialty; English scones (which are more like cake than bread) are popular in many areas of Canada as well as the northeastern United States; and sourdough bread is a northwestern specialty. Certain breads, from toasted garlic bread to pita bread, are also traditionally served at ethnic restaurants.

See also: BAGELS; BUTTER AND OTHER SPREADS; CROISSANTS; CROUTONS; EASTER; FRYING PAN BREAD; GARLIC BREAD; HOT CROSS BUNS; PITA BREAD; SAINT LUCIA DAY; SAINT PATRICK'S DAY; SANDWICHES; SMORGASBORD; SOURDOUGH BREAD; SPOON BREAD; ZUCCHINI BREAD.

References: Simon and Howe. *Dictionary of Gastronomy.* 1970; Trager. *Foodbook.* 1970.

BREAKFAST

Although breakfast is one of the least organized of all meals in North America, there are many individual rituals and family customs associated with foods and beverages consumed in the morning. For some folks,

Sunday breakfast consists primarily of juice and coffee and perhaps a bagel or sweet roll consumed while reading the Sunday newspaper. For others, having a weekend breakfast means going to a pancake house or waffle house to enjoy the house specialties.

Serving hot oatmeal, cornmeal mush, or cold cereal has been a typical breakfast custom since the time of the Civil War. Bacon, steak, sausage, or other meat and eggs, along with hash browns, are also traditional breakfast foods. Another common breakfast item, especially in the southern part of the United States, is biscuits and gravy.

For years nutritionists have labeled breakfast the "most important meal of the day," but a recent Rutgers University survey found that in today's busy U.S. households, 12 percent of the adults do not eat any breakfast and 17 percent simply drink coffee, tea, hot chocolate, milk, or other beverage for breakfast. The survey found that the most common breakfast included cold cereal with a beverage, or it consisted of toast, a muffin, sweet pastry, or bagel and some type of drink. Perhaps orange juice (or another fruit juice) or a piece of fruit is added. More than one in ten persons in the United States eats a breakfast of cold leftovers such as a slice of pizza, a portion of lasagna, or a salad.

The breakfast routine for countless individuals on their way to work or school includes a stop at a fastfood establishment for favorite breakfast items "to go." Some people may stop at a diner for breakfast, while others may eat the morning meal at a school cafeteria. Still others may routinely share breakfast with friends, work colleagues, or schoolmates at a predetermined cafe, coffee shop, or restaurant.

See also: BAGELS; BISCUITS AND GRAVY; BREAKFAST SANDWICHES; CAFES; CEREAL, COLD; COFFEE; COFFEE HOUSES; CORNMEAL MUSH; DOUGHNUTS; MUFFINS; ORANGE JUICE; PANCAKE BREAKFAST; SUNDAY BRUNCH.

BREAKFAST SANDWICHES

Making a sandwich out of bread, fried eggs, and ham or bacon is popular with some Americans who routinely start the day with a sit-down breakfast at home. Today, though, millions of American workers and students have their breakfast "on the run," choosing morning sandwich meals from the nearest fastfood establishment, eating a breakfast sandwich such as the Egg McMuffin or Breakfast Burrito from MacDonald's, a Croissan'wich from Burger King, or a bagel sandwich from a deli. If fastfood is not an option, a frozen muffin or biscuit sandwich heated in the microwave, a Waffle 'Wich made from sliced turkey and cream cheese between frozen waffles, or even pizza toast made with tomato sauce and mozzarella cheese are other types of breakfast sandwiches that have become popular in recent years. **See also:** BAGELS; BREAD; BREAKFAST; FAST-FOOD; MUFFINS; SANDWICHES; SUNDAY BRUNCH.

BREW PUBS

Since the 1980s, several hundred microbreweries and brew pubs have sprung up across the United States, many of them initiated by men and women who have brewed beer at home as a hobby. A microbrewery makes beer in small quantities for local distribution to stores and restaurants, while a brew pub is a restaurant with beer-making facilities on the premises. Some microbreweries are adjacent to restaurants that serve the local brew as well as nationally known brands. The brew pub trend has caught on because apparently people enjoy going to neighborhood bars, and beer lovers like to drink and eat at places where they can watch the brewing process. Brew pubs are also popular tourist attractions in cities where they are located. **See also:** BEER DRINKING.

BROWN BAG LUNCHES

Brown bagging it is the term many people use to describe the practice of taking a lunch in a paper bag to work or school, or sometimes to picnics and other recreational activities. The bag may be recycled from a grocery store, or it may be from a package of purchased "lunch bags."

During the late 1800s and early 1900s, newspaper-wrapped foods and small tin pails were the forerunners to the brown bag. Workers at factories, mines, mills, and constructions sites carried lunch pails that held pieces of meat, cheese, and/or fruit. The same pails were used to boil water to make hot drinks or to heat the food. Manufacturers later produced the lunch bucket—a light metal case—to transport food and the insulated thermos jar to carry hot soup or cold beverages. Eventually, the lunch bucket was made with a place for the thermos to be secured inside. Today, lightweight containers for adults or children are readily available on the market. Children's containers may be lunch boxes with pictures of favorite television or movie characters such as *Sesame Street* notables or Barney, music celebrities, or emblems of a sports team. Other common containers include backpacks, insulated nylon packets or bags, and plastic "coolers." Some are sold as designer products, although the majority are generic goods sold in variety stores, supermarkets, drugstores, and discount stores.

In spite of all the different lunch containers that are now on the market, the paper bag or sack is still widely used to carry a lunch from home. Because the practice of carrying a lunch to work is so common, refrigerators, microwaves, and toaster ovens are available in most workplaces.

Packing a lunch can be a ritual in and of itself. Usually it begins with sandwich making or preparing the sandwich ingredients to be packed separately from the bread. Some people wrap their sandwich with plastic wrap or foil, carefully and meticulously folding the corners. Others place their sandwiches in plastic "sandwich bags" or food storage bags with zipperlike closures or in rigid plastic storage containers especially made for holding sandwiches. Still others save bread wrappers and plastic vegetable bags to use as sandwich wrappers or to carry raw carrots, celery, and other vegetables or perhaps leftover food such as a pizza slice from the previous night's meal.

Some "brown baggers" regularly purchase convenience foods to pack in their lunch bag or box. These foods may be snacks such as potato or corn chips or pretzels; packages of dried fruit; small containers of yogurt, cottage cheese, or pudding; crackers with cheese spread; small cans of tuna or chicken; prepackaged vegetables; packaged salads; candy bars or cookies; and a bottled or canned soft drink, fruit juice, or tea. The contents of a brown bag lunch are determined by individual preference, but the concept is the same: a small meal prepared at home (usually) to eat at a later time while at work, school, or play.
See also: BOX LUNCHES; CONVENIENCE STORE FOODS; FASTFOOD; MICROWAVE COOKING; PICNIC.
Reference: Miller and Schafer. *Lunches To Go!* 1991.

BRUNCH

See SUNDAY BRUNCH.

BUBBLE GUM

Blowing bubbles with bubble gum may be more a habit than a ritual, but whatever it is called, the practice is pervasive among many North Americans—children and adults. Bubble gum came on the scene in 1906 when the Frank H. Fleer Corporation (originator of candy-coated gum) developed Blibber-Blubber. Although no bubble gum by that name exists today, the bubble gum industry has expanded tremendously—around the world. It has been sold with picture cards that are now collectors' items and comics and in a variety of shapes. According to author Robert Hendrickson who wrote *The Great American Chewing Gum Book,* Americans have consumed enough bubble gum over the years to "make a stick nearly 113 million miles long, without even stretching it or blowing a bubble; long enough . . . to reach more than 200 times to the moon and back."

Bubble gum is produced in hundreds of flavors and a great variety of colors from the traditional pink (America's favorite) to a ghastly green. Many who routinely consume the gum feel their day is not complete without a relaxing chew, satisfying snap, and special effort to create a bubble of magnificent proportions.
See also: CHEWING GUM.
Reference: Hendrickson. "Since 1928 It's Been Boom and Bust with Bubble Gum." 1990.

BUFFALO WINGS

Although small ethnic restaurants have served deep-fried chicken wings as an inexpensive dish since about the 1950s, Buffalo wings, as they are known, originated in 1964 with Teresa Bellissimo, owner of the Anchor Bar in Buffalo, New York. Bellissimo needed to use up an oversupply of chicken wings, so when her son asked for a quick snack for himself and his friends, she improvised, cutting off the tips of the chicken wings and disjointing them before frying the meaty parts and preparing a special hot sauce along with blue cheese house dressing for dipping. After Bellissimo served the chicken wings to her customers, the snack became an immediate success, and the prices of other parts of the chicken dropped. Variations of Buffalo wings are now served at bars and restaurants across the United States, and in 1994 such fastfood restaurants as Domino's Pizza and Pizza Hut added Buffalo wings to their menus.
See also: APPETIZERS; FASTFOOD; FOOD SAMPLING; SPORTS BARS.

BUFFET

The word *buffet* once referred primarily to a sideboard or piece of furniture from which food was served, but the term is now used to describe a form of food service that is a popular way to entertain in many American homes: cold and hot food dishes are placed on a table and guests

The Frank H. Fleer Corporation introduced Blibber-Blubber, a chewing gum intended for blowing bubbles in 1906. Little League catcher Clarence Brumm of Colton, California, concentrates on a throw to second base during the 1954 championship game at Williamsport, Pennsylvania, while blowing a bubble gum bubble.

Passengers aboard a Princess Cruise ship hand select lunch items from a buffet. Cruise companies often utilize buffets to serve an array of foods, and they often feature cuisines of ports visited.

help themselves to the various offerings. Serving buffet-style is one way to accommodate a large number of guests for a luncheon or dinner in small quarters. Buffet service is also common at a Sunday brunch or at company parties in restaurants. **See also:** BANQUET; CHINESE BUFFET; COCKTAIL PARTY; SUNDAY BRUNCH.

BURRITO

See TASTE OF . . . FESTIVALS.

BUTTER AND OTHER SPREADS

Bread and butter, or a butter substitute, has been a traditional combination ever since biblical times when ancient herdsmen accidentally discovered the butter-making process, much as they learned yogurt making. According to legend, wandering herdsmen carried goatskin bags of milk on their camels, and, as they traveled, the milk in the bags was agitated, forming but-ter or sometimes yogurt. Herdsmen learned to make butter by beating milk in a bowl and later putting milk in a skin container and pushing it back and forth. Finally, a churn was invented for butter making. Until about the early 1900s, butter was made on family farms and small dairies in Europe and North America. Now large dairy companies produce butter for nationwide distribution and for export.

Although butter has been the favorite spread for bread in the past, alternative spreads (such as olive oil, apple butter, peanut butter, honey, and various marmalades and jams) have also been popular, and with increasing concerns about the high fat and high cholesterol content of some dairy products, butter has fallen into disfavor in North America. Substitutes for butter have become the spreads of choice.

The first butter substitute was made in France in the 1870s by the chemist Hypolite Mège-Mouries. He developed the product by clarifying animal fat and mixing it with milk to form a pearly white spread, which he called margarine after the Greek word for pearly, *margarites*. The product was later refined by blending in peanut, palm, soybean, or coconut oil. The use of margarine increased in the United States during World War II when butter was rationed, but the margarine was sold as a solid white block in a vinyl wrap with a capsule of yellow vegetable coloring that had to be blended in, either by softening and squeezing the margarine inside the wrap or by blending it in a food mixer. Today's factory-mixed product now looks and tastes like butter; one brand even carries the name "I Can't Believe It's Not Butter," although people who prefer the real dairy product would say otherwise.

See also: APPLE BUTTER; BREAD; GHEE; OLIVES AND OLIVE OIL; PEANUT BUTTER.

References: Simon and Howe. *Dictionary of Gastronomy.* 1970; Trager. *Foodbook.* 1970.

BYOB PARTY

A bring-your-own-booze or bring-your-own-bottle party (abbreviated as simply BYO or BYOB) has been common in the United States since at least the 1950s. Asking guests to provide their own beverages is rather like a potluck and helps the person or persons hosting the party to defray costs. The BYOB has been a popular way for many young couples and singles groups to entertain, although people of any age may opt for this type of informal arrangement for a party.

See also: POTLUCK.

CABBAGE SLAW

See COLESLAW.

CAESAR SALAD

In finer eating establishments, the preparation of the Caesar salad is an elaborate tableside presentation, from rolling in a food cart with all the ingredients and utensils to seasoning the wooden mixing bowl to grinding the pepper mill over the finished product. An authentic Caesar salad is made with romaine lettuce, garlic, olive oil, croutons, Parmesan cheese, Worcestershire sauce, egg yolks, lemon, and anchovies (although some people have an aversion to the salty fish and ask that the anchovies be eliminated).

The salad was first created in the 1920s by Caesar Cardini, an Italian immigrant with a chain of restaurants in Tijuana, Mexico, just across the border from San Diego, where he introduced his salad as a main course. It became very popular with the Hollywood movie people, who often traveled to Tijuana. As a result of their patronage, the Caesar salad was next seen in the popular restaurants of Los Angeles and later it was added to menus in New York City and the rest of the country.

Caesars are served as an appetizer or as a main meal. As an appetizer, the Caesar salad can be eaten instead of the traditional green salad seen in most restaurants. As a main meal, it may be served by itself and may be prepared with grilled chicken pieces or shrimp. For the real nontraditionalist, tomato slices can be added.

See also: APPETIZERS; CROUTONS; OLIVES AND OLIVE OIL.

CAFES

The cafe is usually associated with time out from work or a place to take a coffee break while on a long drive. Many U.S. cafes are located in industrial areas, along busy highways, or in the center of small-town business areas. Although cafes serve many food items and beverages other than coffee, the cafe originated as a coffee house; *cafe* is the French and Spanish term for coffee. The first cafes, or coffee houses, were established in the Arabian cities of Mecca and Cairo during the fifteenth century. Since its inception, the cafe has been a place where people can not only drink coffee but also read or socialize or just watch the world go by.

See also: BOOKSTORE CAFE OR DELI; COFFEE; COFFEE BREAK; COFFEE HOUSES; KAFFEEKLATSCH.

CAFETERIA DINING

Just mention the word *cafeteria* and some folks immediately have visions of bland food served in unappetizing fashion. In fact, it is routine for most schoolchildren from the elementary grades on up to complain about cafeteria food with such comments as "it stinks bad" or "nobody eats prunes" or "meat loaf is gross!" Yet some schools, particularly colleges, have changed their traditional fare and are contracting with franchises such as Pizza Hut and Taco Bell to operate inside school cafeterias, offering popular fast-food items to students.

Outside the school setting—in malls, at airports and amusement parks, and in hospitals, corporate buildings, and business centers—cafeteria eating is part of daily life. Convenience and fast service are two factors that motivate many people to choose cafeteria dining. These eating establishments are also popular meeting places for workers and shoppers.

See also: CAMPUS DINING; MEAT LOAF.

CAKEWALK

Once a traditional form of entertainment in the U.S. South, the cakewalk originated with blacks who competed in contests to see who could carry a bucket of water on their head without spilling a drop. The feat required walking as erect as possible and sometimes using grotesque body movements to keep from sloshing the water out of the bucket. Whoever succeeded received a cake as a prize, which 200 years ago was a common way to award people for special accomplishments. In fact, "to take the cake" is an old saying meaning "to be rewarded in some way," and the term for the special walking contest derived from that saying. Eventually, a dance known as the cakewalk became popular among blacks. With arms folded across the chest, a dancer would hold his head high and all but prance to a musical beat. Occasionally, the cakewalk is performed today at black family reunions or Juneteenth celebrations.

See also: JUNETEENTH.

Reference: Funk. *2,107 Curious World Origins, Sayings and Expressions.* 1993.

Cafeteria patrons select foods served from steam-heated counters at Dubrow's in New York City. Rather than choosing items from a menu and ordering through a waiter or waitress, patrons select what they want, pay, and seat themselves.

CAMP/TRAIL FOOD

"Enough to eat but nothing to throw away, minimum weight and bulk, no spoilage, meals that are easy to prepare and tasty and leave one satisfied until the next meal . . ." That is part of the opening sentence in *Food for Knapsackers,* published in 1971 by the Sierra Club. Today, numerous articles and books explain the types of convenience foods that people can carry on camping or hiking trips. These include dried fruits; dehydrated vegetables, soups, and sauces; canned meats and fish; jerky; instant milk powder and other powdered drinks; peanut butter; and various condiments.

See also: INSTANT FOODS AND BEVERAGES; JERKY; MARSHMALLOW ROAST; PEANUT BUTTER.

CAMPUS DINING

Although college students in North America have access to a great deal of information about nutrition and healthful eating, they generally follow eating habits and rituals that may not be conducive to good health. Like Americans across the land, college students seem "addicted" to fastfood, vending machine foods, or convenience items like bagels or doughnuts for breakfast, and frequently campus "dining" refers to a take-out meal or a pizza delivery. Many dormitories are equipped with microwaves, which are used primarily to make popcorn, to heat up soup, or to prepare a packaged meal, such as a noodle dish or a leftover pasta dish (which is the top dinner choice among college students). Surveys and electronic forums on food have shown that college students are also great fans of such processed foods as Spam and baby food (fruit) in jars and that many are avid cola drinkers.

Although take-out and delivery meals are popular, the vast majority of students on a meal-ticket plan go to the campus cafeteria for most of their meals. Companies providing food service on college campuses have taken great strides in recent years to improve the quality of the foods they serve, offering items such as Belgian waffles for breakfast, fajitas for lunch, and grilled salmon for dinner.

Some students choose to truly "dine"—buying fresh meats and poultry, vegetables, and fruit and preparing dinner for themselves most days of the week. Popular meals among these students consist of spaghetti and salad and chicken entrees (which include frozen items). Stir-fry meals are common among the vegetarians.

See also: BABY FOOD; BAGELS; CAFETERIA DINING; CATERING-TRUCK FOODS; CHICKEN ENTREES; DINING ON DELIVERY; FASTFOOD; PASTA; POPCORN; STIR-FRY COOKING; VEGETARIAN EATING.

Reference: Rice. "What's Cooking on Campus?" 1994.

CANDIED SWEET POTATOES (OR YAMS)

In many North American homes, Thanksgiving dinner would not be complete without candied sweet potatoes, or yams as one variety is called. This traditional dish is made with fresh sweet potatoes that have been boiled with their skins on, peeled and placed in a casserole dish, and dotted with butter, brown sugar, or honey and maple syrup. Sometimes orange peel, lemon juice, or crushed pineapple is added for flavor, and marshmallows may be sprinkled over the entire mixture. The casserole is baked until the potatoes or yams are glazed and then served with the turkey and other traditional Thanksgiving foods.

See also: CASSEROLE DISHES/MEALS; SOUL FOOD; THANKSGIVING DAY DINNER.

CANDLELIGHT DINNER

A candlelight dinner is the beginning to the ultimate romantic fantasy evening. Couples who are serious about kindling (or rekindling) the romantic aspects of their relationship will sit down to a dinner whose only illumination comes from the glow of candles placed in the center of the table. (There is something magical about the soft light of flickering flames that makes everyone appear like a magazine model.) The happy duo usually consumes such delectable items as a good wine or champagne, a gourmet entree, preferably served by a waiter in a tuxedo, and a flaming dessert accompanied by a fine cognac. **See also:** GOURMET FOODS.

CANDY AND CARAMEL APPLES

These sweet treats are common sights in supermarkets during apple harvest season and are traditional fare at Oktoberfests, Halloween parties, and similar fall events. For both treats, wooden skewers are inserted into fresh whole apples, which are dipped in a cooked corn syrup mixture dyed red for candied apples or a heated caramel mixture for caramel apples. Sometimes youth groups, religious organizations, or civic groups make these candy-coated apples for fund-raising events such as bazaars.
See also: BAKE SALE; HALLOWEEN; OKTOBERFEST.

CANDY CANES

See CHRISTMAS CANDY.

CANNIBALISM

Considered an abhorrent ritual by most societies today, the "ceremonial eating of man by man" has been practiced in all parts of the world from Australia to Europe to the New World of the Americas. Around the fifth century, humans were sometimes sacrificed to appease angry gods or goddesses, although animals were more often used for such rituals. Cannibalism has also been practiced for greed. In ninth- and tenth-century Europe, for example, professional killers attacked and murdered travelers and cut up the bodies to sell the parts for meat.

Most often cannibalism was associated with religious ceremonies or with acts of revenge (eating the enemy, for example).

The most common reports of cannibalism focus on fifth-century Aztec life; Spanish conquistadors reported finding tens of thousands of skulls, in what is now central Mexico, displayed on racks at temple sites. The Aztecs believed that offering a human heart was the ultimate gift or sacrifice to the gods, and, if the gods gained strength from the sacrificed man or woman, certainly the members of the population could gain strength and magical powers from the consumption of parts of the bodies.

It was believed that the gods needed live, beating hearts, so the priests ripped open the chest cavity of a living victim, reached in to remove the still-beating heart, and placed it on the altar. The body was then butchered, with a thigh going to the ruling elite and other prime cuts to powerful members of the community. The remaining parts were given to the man who had captured the victim, and these were turned into a corn and man stew called *tlacatlaolli*. All the members of his family would then partake of the dish in solemn ceremonial fashion.

Although human sacrifices to the gods are now rare, some religious rituals, such as the Christian communion in which participants partake of symbolic bread and wine (eating of the flesh and drinking of the blood), are linked to pagan rites.
See also: EUCHARIST.
References: Farb and Armelagos. *Consuming Passions.* 1980; Fussell. *The Story of Corn.* 1992; Tannahill. *Food in History.* 1973.

CANOLA OIL

Made from oil found in a type of rapeseed—the seed of a yellow-flowering plant—canola oil has become a popular food product in North America. Since the 1960s, the plants have been grown extensively in Canada, where canola oil (a name that is a shortened version of Canadian oil) is widely used. An increasing number of farmers in the Plains regions of the United States have also been growing the crop since the early 1990s. This trend reflects the demand for vegetable oils low in saturated fat—canola oil is only 6 percent saturated fat—for cooking, baking, and making salad dressings. Since about the mid-1990s, canola oil has replaced vegetable oils high in saturated fat that were once staples used in a variety of U.S. baked goods, canned foods, and other processed foods.

See also: DIETS; EATING TRENDS; OLIVES AND OLIVE OIL.

CARAMEL CORN

Although not as popular as buttered or butter-flavored popcorn today, caramel corn with its sugary coating was once the leading snack food consumed at the movies, and it is still a traditional "fun food" at carnivals, circuses, ballparks, movie theaters, and food fests. Cracker Jack, created in 1872, is the most famous brand of caramel corn, and since 1912 when prizes were added to the boxes to motivate sales, kids and grownups alike have purchased the brand in order to discover what besides caramel corn (and peanuts) might be inside the box.

See also: BASEBALL PARK EATING AND DRINKING; POPCORN; SNACK FOODS.

Reference: Chalmers. *Great American Food Almanac.* 1986.

CARNIVAL AND FAIR FOOD

Watermelon and pie-eating contests; bake-offs; barbecues; food booths that sell hot buttered corn on the cob, corn dogs, cotton candy, elephant ears (large, flat, sugared pastries), and various ices and ice creams are common at carnivals and county or state fairs. These typical summer events take place in most parts of North America, and many who attend are as interested in being part of the eating and drinking rituals as they are in being entertained by carnival rides, animal shows, or celebrity performances.

See also: BARBECUE; BASEBALL PARK EATING AND DRINKING; CORN DOGS; COTTON CANDY; FOOD FAIRS; ICE CREAM; TASTE OF . . . FESTIVALS.

CARRY-OUT FOODS

During any given day, millions of American consumers buy take-out foods, prepared meals, salads, sandwiches, or other food items that can be eaten at home, in the car, at the workplace, in the park, or at the beach or other recreational site. Carry-out service has always been part of fastfood businesses, delis, and various ethnic restaurants, but an increasing number of bistros, family restaurants, supermarkets, and gourmet grocery stores also offer this service, a convenience that many consumers have been willing to pay for since the late 1980s.

See also: DELI FOODS; DINING ON DELIVERY; FASTFOOD; GOURMET FOODS.

CASSEROLE DISHES/MEALS

Although a casserole dish is a type of cooking container, it is also a traditional one-dish meal or food taken to a potluck, church supper, or family gathering. One-dish meals have been common for centuries in most parts of the world, but the casserole dish became increasingly popular in North America after cookware designed especially for casseroles was introduced and marketed during the 1950s. Today, casserole meals are not touted as extensively as are frozen meals that can be microwaved, but a variety of packaged "helper" products—pasta or rice—and dried potato products are designed so that they can be used in casserole dishes, including scalloped potatoes, tuna-and-noodle casseroles, and chicken-and-rice casseroles.

See also: BOXED MEALS AND HELPERS; CHURCH DINNERS/SUPPERS; PASTA; POTATOES; POTLUCK; RICE DISHES.

CATERED EVENTS

Early in the 1900s, catered events were a luxury available only to the very wealthy, but today catered parties are arranged for a broader cross section of society. Where the typical catering used to be associated with a wedding or a grand holiday party, today

While there are many varieties of caramel corn, a mix of caramel-covered popcorn and peanuts, Cracker Jack has almost become a ritual food at baseball games. Originated in Chicago in the 1870s, the snack is forever part of the American pastime with the lyrics "Take me out to the ball game . . . buy me some peanuts and Cracker Jack, I don't care if I never come back. . . ."

Actors in a scene from the 1985 comedy Desperately Seeking Susan *eat carry-out Chinese food with chopsticks from paper cartons. Carry-out foods are a convenience for consumers who buy meals from delicatessens, fast-food chains, restaurants, or grocery stores and take them home, back to the office, or to parks to eat.*

office parties, anniversary parties, birthday parties, and many other events are catered affairs. The trend toward hiring professionals for food preparation and service has helped to create a demand for caterers. Sometimes a party-giver will contract with a caterer to deliver hors d'oeuvres, a special cake, or a few select items that will be used to enhance the homemade meal or the buffet. Another service that caterers provide on a fairly regular basis is consultation. Charges for access to the expert's experience and "vision" are usually by the hour, and can be expensive but invaluable for the accomplished cook who has never put together all of the elements necessary for a successful affair.

On the upper end of the scale, it is not unusual to spend tens of thousands of dollars for a caterer whose reputation and experience can guarantee a perfect event. Attention to detail is the most important factor in evaluating a potential caterer who will be in charge of all of the possible elements of, for example, a wedding. Where will the food be served and what time will the meal be expected? Is the music arranged? Will there be a picture-taking session? Has a photographer been hired? When will the best man be giving the toast? At what point will the cake be cut? Valet parking? When can the rental company deliver? These are just a few examples of the questions that are likely to be asked and answered if the caterer is to serve well.

Food is, of course, the principal responsibility of any caterer. It is in this area that the client usually defers to a professional's expertise and ability to perform. Catering is, in fact, a live performance, where any mistake will be noticed, and where responsive, immediate actions and decisions have to be made throughout the event. The performance is not over until the cleanup is complete.

See also: APPETIZERS; BUFFET; CATERING-TRUCK FOODS.

CATERING-TRUCK FOODS

While many caterers use a truck or van to transport their food, beverages, and equipment for a catered event, the quilted-steel catering truck routinely travels to industrial parks and business centers carrying primarily snack and lunch items for workers. A catering company may be comprised of just one or two trucks selling coffee and sweet rolls or ethnic food items such as tacos along the roadside, or it may be a huge company such as Cater-Craft Foods in southern California with over 50 trucks and sales totaling more than $6 million annually.

Industrial catering trucks, often called lunch wagons or meat wagons or even "mobile food preparation units," usually go to a factory at a specified time, and employees come out of the workplace to make their selections. Some trucks carry only cold foods and beverages and cigarettes, while others are "hot trucks," preparing foods right on the vehicle. One catering company in an industrial Indiana town prepares hot breakfast and lunch specials, such as biscuits and sausage gravy and eggs Benedict, hot chicken and dumplings, and chili, and dinner specials such as beef and noodles and lasagna. Some caterers also contract with various fastfood chains to deliver doughnuts, pizza, burritos, and barbecue chicken. Catering trucks also carry foods to some college campuses where there is no cafeteria, or they may regularly go to flea markets, fairs, ball games, or other outdoor events where large crowds gather.
See also: CAMPUS DINING; CATERED EVENTS.

CATFISH FRY

Fried catfish, coleslaw, and hush puppies go together in the South and are considered traditional southern food. Many people from Arkansas to Louisiana to Texas catch channel catfish in bayous, muddy streams and ponds, and lakes and "fry up a mess of catfish" as a part of their weekly meal routine. Most catfish sold commercially today, however, are raised in clear-water farm ponds and fed with special feed. Catfish usually are dipped in cornmeal and deep fried. In restaurants and cafes known for their catfish meals, patrons may appear on a regular basis—at least once a week—to enjoy a ritual catfish fry.

Catfish is the fifth most popular seafood in America and is a $500 million industry. Willard Scott, famous for his eccentric reports on the *Today Show,* said that he "wants to go down in history as the person who convinced the American people that catfish is one of the finest eating fishes in the world."
See also: HUSH PUPPIES.
Reference: Chalmers. *The Great Food Almanac.* 1994.

CATSUP

See KETCHUP.

CAVIAR

For those who host or attend elegant parties, caviar—the washed and salted eggs, or roe, of fish—is a "must" as an appetizer. Various types of caviar are available, such as salmon caviar from the northern Pacific, lumpfish caviar from Iceland, and golden whitefish caviar from the Canadian Great Lakes. Caviar has long signaled affluence because of its relatively high cost, but it is now called an "affordable luxury," with some types priced at less than half-a-dollar per serving. Traditionally, caviar is served in a bowl of cracked ice surrounded by various side dishes, such as chopped egg, chopped onion, lemon wedges, and unsalted crackers.
See also: APPETIZERS.

CEREAL, COLD

A mainstay of the American breakfast, cereal has many versions. Shredded Wheat was the first ready-to-eat breakfast cereal to hit the store shelves. It was introduced in 1893 in Denver by Henry D. Perky and is still

Catfish, dredged in seasoned cornmeal and fried, is served with hush puppies and coleslaw. Considered by many to be a traditional southern meal, the freshwater fish is raised commercially in ponds.

considered one of the healthiest cereal choices today. John Harvey Kellogg followed suit soon afterward by inventing the first ready-cooked flaked cereal in 1894. A physician, Kellogg was inspired by a patient, who demanded payment of $10 to replace her false teeth, which she broke on the zwieback that the doctor had prescribed. The idea for developing a gentler, ready-cooked food came to him in a dream and started a new breakfast tradition. He boiled wheat and ran it through a machine his wife had for rolling dough. He then spread it on a pan, baked it, and broke it into flakes. Kellogg later invented 60 other cereals. These well-intended foods were the forebearers of today's sugar-filled Cocoa Puffs, Fruit Loops, and Lucky Charms.

Most grocery stores now dedicate a full aisle to about 200 brands of cereal. It is such a popular convenience food that consumers spend nearly $8 billion on it and consume nearly 3 billion pounds every year.

In many U.S. households, cold cereals are more than a common breakfast food. A favorite brand may be purchased and eaten on a regular basis because it has long been associated with a slogan promoting athletic prowess ("Breakfast of Champions"), fun ("Snap, Crackle, and Pop!"), or good health ("Contains oat bran"). Kids may demand a particular breakfast cereal because a cartoon character, a well-known sports figure, or another famous personality endorses the product. Part of the ritual of buying and consuming cold breakfast cereal may be to retrieve a special prize inside—or to save box tops, bar code symbols, or coupons to redeem some commemorative item or money.

While a variety of factory-produced cold cereals have been on the market since Perky and Kellogg's inventions, one of the first cold cereals originated with Native Americans such as the Hopi, who have made thin corn wafers known as piki for hundreds of years. Although the methods may have changed, piki is still prepared from white, yellow, blue, red, or other color corn that has been cracked, ground, roasted, and ground again into a meal. To make piki the traditional way, women, who have practiced the art since childhood, dip their fingers into a bowl of cornmeal batter and quickly spread it across a hot cooking stone, repeating this process until the stone is covered with batter. After baking, the wafers are folded and stored, and when they become dry and flaky they can be crumbled and served in flake form with milk or cream and sugar.

See also: BREAKFAST.

References: Chalmers. *The Great Food Almanac.* 1994; Fantasia. "Time Line of Food Products and Lifestyle Changes from More Than a Century." 1995; Fussell. *I Hear America Cooking.* 1986; Wyman. *I'm a SPAM Fan.* 1993.

CHALLAH

A Sabbath bread served on Friday nights in traditional Jewish homes, challah, or hallah, is usually braided but may come in a variety of shapes and is commonly topped with poppy seeds. The ritual of eating this classic bread dates back more than 3,000 years to the time when Moses led the Israelites out of Egypt into the Sinai Desert where the Jews wandered for 40 years. According to legend, the Israelites were doomed to starvation but were saved by a food called "manna" in the form of coriander seed that came from the heavens. The manna fell during the night on dew, which encased and protected the seeds until morning when they could be gathered and ground into flour, which was used to bake a sweet bread. A double portion of seeds fell on Friday so that there was enough to bake bread for that day as well as for Saturday, the Sabbath, when no manna fell.

The meaning of the word *challah* comes from the practice of making a bread offering to Temple priests, who had no farmland to grow their own food and devoted their lives to study and worship. Although the practice ended long ago, a portion of prebaked dough—challah— may be set aside for a special blessing, and today Jews in North America who follow traditional practices believe that hallah is

essential for Sabbath celebrations. In some Jewish homes two loaves of hallah on the table represent the double portion of manna that fell in the Sinai Desert on Friday. Cloths covering the breads symbolize the protective dew.

Although the Sabbath bread ritual varies depending on the country of origin, challah is always blessed with a special prayer, often accompanied by the use of salt, which stems from Jewish law requiring that salt be a part of ancient sacrificial ceremonies. Pieces of challah are usually broken off and served, since cutting the bread with a knife symbolizes violence.

While the braided challah is common for Sabbath celebrations, other shapes are traditional as well. The round challah, for example, represents the hope for a full and abundant year and is the shape most often used in Rosh Hashanah (Jewish New Year) celebrations. A ladder-shaped challah may be baked for Yom Kippur (Day of Atonement) to symbolize prayers ascending to heaven.

See also: BREAD; ROSH HASHANAH; YOM KIPPUR.

References: Berenbaum. *Rose's Melting Pot.* 1993; Roth. *Harriet Roth's Deliciously Healthy Jewish Cooking.* 1995.

CHANUKAH

Oil is an important ingredient in the food prepared for Chanukah, often spelled Hanukkah, the eight-day Jewish Festival of Lights that commemorates the struggle to gain religious freedom 2,000 years ago. In a military conquest, the Maccabees liberated the Jewish Temple from the Assyrians— Syrian Greeks—but as the ancient Jews prepared for rededicating the Temple, only one jar of pure consecrated olive oil was available to keep the perpetual lamps burning. This little bit of oil burned for eight days, long enough for new holy oil to be prepared. That miracle is celebrated today by lighting one candle on the eight-branched menorah, or candelabrum, for each day of Chanukah and by preparing and serving foods that emphasize oil.

Latkes, or potato pancakes, are traditional Chanukah foods throughout North America as well as many other parts of the world. The latkes are made from grated or finely chopped potatoes, onions, beaten eggs, and matzo meal; fried in hot oil until crisp and brown; then served with apple sauce. Depending on country of origin, there are variations on the traditional latke. A French version is made from baked potatoes, and a version from India calls for mashed potatoes shaped into patties and fried.

Potato kugels are another traditional food during this holiday. They are similar to latkes but are baked rather than fried. Deep-fried yeast doughnuts are another popular Chanukah food. They are usually made with honey, which has been the traditional sweetener since ancient times, and are filled with nuts and dried fruit, or with jelly.
See also: DOUGHNUTS; OLIVES AND OLIVE OIL.

CHEESE AND CRACKERS

See CRACKERS AND CHEESE.

CHEESE FESTIVALS

Throughout the history of the United States, communities have produced over-sized cheeses to commemorate great events. In Cheshire, Massachusetts, for example, townsfolk made a massive cheese weighing 1,600 pounds, which they presented to Thomas Jefferson in 1801 on the occasion of his inauguration. On President Andrew Jackson's inauguration, he too received a huge cheese—a 1,400-pound Cheddar, which was displayed in the White House for almost two years while it aged. Jackson finally held an open house and served the cheese, which was consumed in just two hours. A Wisconsin Cheddar cheese weighing more than 17 tons was produced for the 1964–1965 New York World's Fair, and a special glass-sided trailer had to be built to transport it.

Today, the number one cheese-producing state in the United States is Wisconsin, where, in order to promote the product, the Wisconsin legislature once passed a law that required restaurants to serve a minimum of two-thirds of an ounce of cheese with each meal that was valued at over 25 cents. Annual cheese festivals are common in this state. In Little Chute, between Appleton and Green Bay, for example, an annual cheese festival has been held since 1989. The event includes not only the usual parade and activities associated with festivals but also a competition for the best cheese produced in the area.
See also: CHEESE TASTING; CHEESECAKE; CRACKERS AND CHEESE.
References: Brown. *American Cooking.* 1968; Wason. *A Salute to Cheese.* 1966.

CHEESE TASTING

Delis, supermarket cheese shops, and stores that specialize in cheeses customarily provide trays of cheese for sampling. Cheese tasting is also part of cheese festivals and some wine tastings, and it may be done at home—a great number of mail-order companies offer gift packages containing a variety of cheeses for sampling.

Cheese tasting can be an event in and of itself; it may take place at a private party, as a fund-raiser, or as a social group or club activity. Some cheese tasting parties are designed to present cheeses from around the world, although many of the cheeses may actually be copies produced in the United States or Canada. There are thousands of varieties of cheese, and examples of those that might be included for a tasting event are the popular British Stilton, Cheshire, and Cheddar, named for an English village that no longer produces cheese and now one of the most popular American and Canadian cheeses. Gouda of Dutch origin, Bondost from Sweden, French cheeses such as Camembert and Gruyère, Swiss cheese, Italian provolone, and Mexican Tijuana cheese are other possible cheese tray selections, particularly for those tasting events that feature cheeses from around the world. Some traditional American cheeses served at tasting parties

include Monterey Jack produced in Monterey County, California; Vermont Colby; Tillamook from Oregon; longhorn from Texas or Wisconsin; and Wisconsin brick.
See also: APPETIZERS; CHEESE FESTIVALS; DELI FOODS; DESSERT CHEESE; QUICHE; WINE TASTING.
References: Simon and Howe. *Dictionary of Gastronomy.* 1970; Wason. *A Salute to Cheese.* 1966.

CHEESECAKE

In ancient Greece, cheesecake referred to not only a honey-sweetened dessert of molded cream cheese but also a cheese mixture in a crust and hot, cheese-filled pastries served as appetizers. Every Greek province had its own version of cheesecake, but the molded cheesecake chilled in snow was likely the origin of the type of cheesecake that became popular in other parts of Europe and eventually North America. Today, cheesecake is usually made with cream cheese and sometimes cottage cheese, eggs, cream, and sugar. By some estimates, more cheesecake is consumed in the United States than any other nation in the world, and New York–style cheesecake with a rich, creamy cheese mixture in a cookie-crumb crust is considered the model for this type of dessert.
See also: APPETIZERS; DESSERT CHEESE.
References: Simon and Howe. *Dictionary of Gastronomy.* 1970; Wason. *A Salute to Cheese.* 1966.

CHERRY FESTIVALS

Cherry trees seem to grow everywhere in the western part of Michigan, a state known for its fruits—apples, peaches, and grapes are abundant most years. The National Cherry Festival in Traverse City, Michigan, where about three-fourths of the world's red cherry crop is produced, has been celebrated every July since 1926. This event features a vast array of mouthwatering, tangy or sweet cherry desserts from traditional cherry pie to cherry cheesecake to chocolate cherry bars.

Along with the national festival, there are numerous local cherry festivals in Michigan during the summer. Of course cherry pie–eating contests are a part of these festivals in Michigan and in other states that celebrate cherry harvests and food made with the fruit, such as Washington, Oregon, and New York.
See also: APPLE FESTIVALS; CHEESECAKE.

CHERRY SOUP

In rural Pennsylvania and in the Midwest, where many German immigrants settled, cherry soup has been a traditional summer soup since the late 1700s. Made from pitted sweet cherries, dry wine, sugar, and spices such as cinnamon and cloves, it was served as a refreshing lunch during the hot summer days when families gathered fruit from the orchards. The dish has gained popularity since 1993, when it was presented at the annual Food and Wine Festival in Aspen, Colorado. Some versions of cherry soup call for dumplings, with the cherry-and-wine mixture added after the dumplings are cooked. The soup may be served either hot or cold.
See also: CHERRY FESTIVALS.
Reference: Kirlin and Kirlin. *Smithsonian Folklife Cookbook.* 1991.

CHESTERTOWN TEA PARTY

The Chestertown Tea Party, held every Memorial Day weekend in Chestertown, Maryland, is a festival that commemorates a May 1774 event similar to the Boston Tea Party in which colonists protested the British tax on imported tea. Citizens of Chestertown staged their own protest, boarding the British ship *Geddes* and dumping its cargo of tea into the Chester River. A tradition since 1973, the Tea Party Festival includes a parade of horse-drawn carriages, bagpipers, colonial crafts, and food booths offering typical East Coast foods such as crab cakes, fried clams, Maryland fried chicken, and barbecued ribs.
See also: AFTERNOON TEA.

CHESTNUTS, ROASTED

Roasting chestnuts over an open fire was a common activity long before Nat King Cole popularized the practice in his timeless rendition of "Merry Christmas." Street vendors in New York City, for example, have been selling roasted chestnuts for decades. Roasted chestnuts or boiled chestnuts are associated with Christmas and Thanksgiving in North America and are often served as side dishes or used in poultry stuffings. The mealy nuts are almost always cooked and at one time were considered food for the poor. Although chestnut trees were once plentiful in the United States, they were almost destroyed by disease in the early 1900s, and now most of the chestnuts Americans eat are imported from Europe.

CHEWING GUM

Billions of dollars' worth of chewing gum is sold annually, and millions of North Americans indulge in and enjoy the practice of chewing this confection. Gum chewing, however, is sometimes condemned and even outlawed as a bad or uncouth habit. Many schools, for example, forbid students to chew gum during class time, and numerous employers report that they have very negative opinions of job applicants who chew gum during an interview. Dentists warn against the effects of sugar in gum and its potential to cause cavities in teeth.

Before U.S. manufacturers began to produce and market chewing gum in the mid-1800s, many North Americans chewed the resin from various types of trees, such as the sweet gum tree (*Liquidambar styraciflua*), which is native to the eastern and southern parts of the United States. The substance that seeps from the sweet gum tree can be cut off with a knife, and when chewed it has a spearmintlike flavor. Parafin, used to seal jars of jam and jelly, was also commonly chewed like gum in the past. Today, gum chewers have numerous commercial brands from which to choose. Wrigley is the world's largest and most well known producer of chewing

A Chicago street vendor serves up a bag of roasted chestnuts during the 1988 Christmas season.

gum. Founded by William Wrigley in 1892, it sells its products worldwide.

People who chew gum habitually prefer a specific flavor. Some of the most popular flavors are spearmint, peppermint, and wintergreen, all of which were first introduced by Wrigley. Cinnamon and licorice flavors have also been popular for many years. Relatively new flavors include sour apple, cherry, grape, orange, strawberry, and lemon. Various shapes and types of chewing gum are also produced, such as sugar-free sticks, candy-coated squares, bubble gum rolls, and nonstick gum for people with dentures.

Quite often, people chew gum to freshen the mouth and to enjoy the sweet flavor. Gum chewing may help ease nervous tension, especially during a sports competition—sports athletes routinely chew gum (sometimes several sticks at a time) as a substitute for chewing tobacco. Chewing bubble gum and blowing bubbles are rituals with many professional baseball players. People who have stopped smoking or who are on a diet and need something in their mouth (as a substitute for a cigarette or food) chew gum on a regular basis. Gum chewing also helps aid digestion and may relieve queasiness due to altitude sickness or seasickness.

It is common for habitual gum chewers to develop particular ways to chew. Some only chew on the right side of their mouth, while others only chew on the left or transfer the gum from one side to the other periodically as they chew. Some people chew gum for a while and then let it sit at the top or in the corner of their mouth. Many chew gum until it loses the "best" part of its flavor, then they throw it away.

There are even routines for disposing gum. It may be wrapped in a paper and thrown in the trash, stuck under a chair or table, or spit out on the street, sidewalk, or parking lot (the first method being the most accepted). There are also many patterns for saving chewed gum for future enjoyment. At mealtime, some gum chewers may place their gum at the side of their plate, and at bedtime some people stick their gum on the bedpost or on the nightstand until the next day. In some cases, students have been known to stick gum behind their ear, particularly when school rules forbid gum chewing in class and the student does not want to get caught doing so. In order to avoid the consequences of breaking the gum-chewing rule (such as wearing a wad on the nose for the remainder of class), some children swallow their gum—a fairly harmless practice, but not recommended.

See also: BUBBLE GUM.

CHEYENNE FRONTIER DAYS

This Cheyenne, Wyoming, celebration originated in 1897 and is held for a week in July each year to celebrate the area's cattle-raising history. It usually begins with a traditional openrange–style breakfast of pancakes, ham, and coffee served by volunteers. Recently, the pancake batter has been prepared each year in a concrete mixer to feed some 300,000 people who attend.

See also: PANCAKE BREAKFAST.

References: Hill. *Festivals U.S.A.* 1988; Thompson and Carlson. *Holidays, Festivals, and Celebrations of the World Dictionary.* 1994.

CHICKEN À LA KING

Although the origin of the dish is uncertain, one popular theory is that chicken à la king was created in one of New York City's foremost restaurants, Delmonico's, in 1923. Chunks of cooked chicken in a cream sauce served over rice or in a pastry shell with a pimento garnish, it was an elegant ladies' luncheon entree and banquet dish during the first half of the twentieth century. It is still offered on lunch as well as dinner menus in some homestyle restaurants and cafes, and it is also included on some buffet or Sunday brunch tables. In addition, it is a favorite frozen food entree among numerous consumers who prefer what is now considered a traditional American food.

See also: BANQUET; BUFFET; CHICKEN ENTREES; LADIES' LUNCHEON.

Reference: Trager. *The Food Chronology.* 1995.

Volunteers serve a free pancake breakfast on three mornings of the ten-day celebration of Cheyenne Frontier Days. While this event is free, many organizations and communities stage pancake breakfasts as fund-raisers.

CHICKEN AND DUMPLINGS

See CHICKEN ENTREES.

CHICKEN ENTREES

Roast chicken was a special treat, usually reserved for a Sunday or holiday dinner, among many immigrant groups coming to America during the 1800s and early 1900s. A campaign slogan in the 1920s—"a chicken in every pot"—helped popularize the concept of making chicken an affordable everyday food for the majority of Americans, not just the wealthy or those in rural areas who could raise their own supply of poultry.

Until the 1950s, chicken was expensive because infectious diseases confined the raising of poultry to small farmyard animals. Mass production was not possible until the invention of coccidiostat, which helped farmers successfully fight disease in larger flocks. In conjunction with modern breeding techniques, coc-

cidiostat has contributed to a proliferation of huge poultry houses that raise chickens ready for market in just 42 days. Since 1900, there has been a 280 percent increase in U.S. chicken consumption. North Carolina farmers raise a large part of the nation's chickens, and in a recent year they produced 643.5 million chickens, adding up to 3,217,500 pounds of meat that generated $1.062 billion in revenue. Thanks to overproduction, chicken is now far less expensive than it was years ago when inflation factored into the price and only the wealthy could partake.

Today, almost every ethnic or regional cuisine in North America claims some type of chicken dish as its "very own." Chicken and dumplings is associated with southern cooking and with the Pennsylvania Dutch and other German settlers. Actually, a chicken soup or stew with dumplings is a common meal among people of many national backgrounds. Chicken pot pie is a popular, inexpensive, one-dish meal served in many areas of North America.

Southern fried chicken is well known throughout the United States and the world, thanks to the proliferation of fast-food chains like Kentucky Fried Chicken (KFC). Curried chicken is a favorite among Middle Easterners transplanted to North America. Pelau made from leftover chicken and beef and vegetables is a typical Monday meal in the traditions of Trinidad and Tobago. Chicken cacciatore—garlic-rubbed and roasted chicken—is a well-known Italian dish. Obviously, chicken can be used in numerous ways and its versatility has contributed to its overwhelming popularity.

See also: CHICKEN À LA KING; CHICKEN SOUP; POT PIES.

References: Chalmers. *The Great Food Almanac*. 1994; Kirlin and Kirlin. *Smithsonian Folklife Cookbook*. 1991; Mariani. *The Dictionary of American Food and Drink*. 1993, 1994; Rothrock. *"Wing Ding of a Price Surge."* 1995; Trager. *Foodbook*. 1970; Visser. *Much Depends on Dinner*. 1986.

CHICKEN POT PIE

See CHICKEN ENTREES; POT PIES.

CHICKEN SOUP

Almost everywhere in the world some type of soup or stew is given to people who suffer from a cold, flu, or similar ailment. Although beef broth was once the common sickroom remedy in North America, chicken soup (sometimes called Jewish penicillin because it was recommended in medieval times by the Jewish philosopher and physician Moses Maimonides) is now likely to be at the top of the list for feeding a cold or flu. Modern researchers have found that chicken soup indeed contains ingredients that help reduce inflammation. Many people add spices, garlic, horseradish, ginger, red and black peppers, and other seasonings to increase its medicinal value. The added ingredients apparently help loosen mucus in the lungs—red pepper, for example, is chemically similar to guaifenesin, an

ingredient in cough syrup. The vapors of hot soup also help relieve congestion.

Chicken soup is also a popular cold-weather meal, especially if it is hearty soup with vegetables and pasta. Many cooks prepare chicken soup with leftover chicken and vegetables, and, in some households, it is routine for a cook to boil chicken parts and save the broth for use in a variety of dishes.

See also: CHICKEN ENTREES; CRANBERRY JUICE; MEDICINAL FOODS.

CHILDREN'S MEALS

The restaurant industry has developed many ways to attract customers. One of the most popular in eating establishments that cater to family diners is the "pint-size" meal, which is usually ordered from a children's menu. Typically, choices are made among what a restaurant perceives are kids' favorite foods. The assumption is that anyone under 12 years old is not sufficiently sophisticated to appreciate "adult" fare. The meals for children are also priced low so that a family may visit the restaurant without feeling as though they must spend the week's grocery budget on one dining-out experience. Usually simple foods are endowed with cute names and embellished with whimsical graphics on the menu: Pooh's P-Nut Butter and Jelly Sandwich, Hoppy's Happy Burger, The Leaning Tower of Spaghetti are typical. Fastfood restaurants have their own version of this popular promotion, with the most famous being the Happy Meal of McDonald's. For a few dollars, a child can get a hamburger, french fries, soda, and a toy premium that changes weekly.

See also: FASTFOOD.

CHILDREN'S TABLE

In ritual fashion, most American families of any size set up a children's table at major family eating events such as holiday dinners, reunions, christenings, bar mitzvahs, weddings, funerals, or any other functions that bring more family and friends to a dining room table than can be comfortably accommodated. Depending on the size of the family and the distribution of ages, the youngest members of the clan (usually ages 3 to 15) are relegated to sitting at their own table often in another room. While the younger children typically find being away from the parents an exciting and desirable situation, the teenagers in the family cannot wait to make the passage to the "regular" table; they perceive sitting at the children's table as one of the many embarrassing inequalities that they must suffer through as they make the transition to adulthood.

See also: FAMILY DINNER; FAMILY REUNION.

CHILES

Hot peppers—botanically categorized as fruits—may be called by any number of different names, but in North America they are usually known as *chiles* or *chilies*, terms that are common in South America where hot peppers originated (contrary to the popular belief that they came from China or India). Hot peppers are not as popular in the United States as they are in other parts of the world, but Americans who love these fiery fruits eat them—chopped, roasted, fried, marinated, or blended in a sauce—with their meals and in their foods as often as possible, if not daily. One of the most popular sauces made from hot peppers is Tabasco produced in Avery Island, Louisiana, which is now a tourist attraction.

There are at least 1,600 different varieties of hot peppers classified under a number of species. They are produced primarily in India, Thailand, parts of China and Africa, Mexico, Louisiana, and parts of the southwestern United States. Peppers may have a pungency ranging from mild (such as paprika) to extremely hot (such as the habanero that people in the Yucatan enjoy). In the United States, the jalapeño pepper is the most common hot pepper in use, and many people immediately associate hot peppers with this dark green variety. Some more popular varieties include Anaheim chiles, chipotles, and serranos.

Jalapeños and some of the other hot varieties are especially popular in the Southwest where the pepper industry has been growing rapidly. In New Mexico, for example, true New Mexican food is richly spiced with green chiles as well as the fruit of the prickly pear cactus and piñon nuts.

The use of chiles in New Mexican cooking dates back to ancient practices of the many Pueblo Indian tribes that populated the land and prized a wild chile known as chiltepan. Native peoples also made sauces of chiles used on cooked wild game wrapped in cornmeal cakes that resemble today's tortillas. In Mexico, people have been eating hot peppers cooked, or raw, or in combination with other dishes for at least 8,000 years, and many Mexicans today—whether in Mexico or the United States—would not think of eating a meal without peppers. They may even make an entire meal of them. Many Americans who have emigrated from Thailand, Korea, the Szechwan province of China, India, Africa, and parts of Latin America routinely consume hot peppers as well. In fact, Thais are known to eat more hot peppers than any other group in the world, with Koreans not far behind. Those who have carried over traditions from India also indulge in food prepared with various forms of hot peppers—sautéed, powdered, and pureed. North Americans of European ancestry may not be as eager as other groups to consume hot peppers, but the change in immigration patterns and the proliferation of Mexican, Thai, Szechwan, and other ethnic eating establishments have helped spawn increasing interest in foods sparked with pungent peppers.

Chile festivals and backyard chile roasts in the Southwest have also helped promote consumption of hot peppers in their varied forms. The increased demand has in turn spurred production of chile pepper crops, particularly in New Mexico where people of Mexican descent have planted peppers on family farms for generations. About 40,000 acres of peppers were planted during the early 1990s, more than double the amount of acreage planted a decade before.

Capsaicin is the chemical agent in chiles that creates the heat sensation. Many skiers today faithfully observe an old wives' tale, sprinkling cayenne pepper in their socks to keep their feet warm.

See also: BARBECUE SAUCE; CHILI AND CHILI SUPPERS; CURRY; HOT SAUCE; SALSA.

References: Chalmers. *The Great Food Almanac.* 1994; DeWitt and Gerlach. *The Whole Chile Pepper Book.* 1990; Naj. *Peppers.* 1992; Robbins. "Care for a Little Hellish Relish?" 1992.

CHILI AND CHILI SUPPERS

Chili made its first appearance at the San Antonio, Texas, stand at the 1893 World's Fair in Chicago. The basis for chili is a chili pulp made from peppers and a tomato sauce. Cubed and seared beef and pork (or ground meats) are added along with seasonings and sometimes pinto or red kidney beans and simmered to prepare what some call *chili con carne*. Chili, however, can be made without meat or with ground poultry for today's more health-conscious individuals, and authentic Texas chili is never made with beans.

Although chili is commonly eaten straight from the pot, there are local variations on the way that it is served. For instance, a popular way to serve it in Ohio is on spaghetti. In Hawaii it is often mixed with rice. A midwestern favorite is combining chili with macaroni and cheese. Nowhere is this one-dish meal more common than in Texas, where annual cook-offs to determine world champion chili makers have been taking place since 1966. President Lyndon Johnson, a Texan, was primarily responsible for designating chili the official Texas dish, and he was known for his ranch parties at which chili was always served. Chili is frequently served at outdoor events, particularly in the Southwest where there are also many chili cook-offs. In other parts of the United States, a chili supper may be a fund-raising event, a firehouse food, or a routine family meal.

Chili is often used as a side dish or condiment. Chili dogs and hamburgers as well as baked potatoes topped with chili are found on the menus of many casual restaurants across the country. For those people who lack time but enjoy chili, there are canned chili products on the market, giving cooks the option of spicing up their dinner menus with the convenience of a can opener and a saucepan.

See also: CHILES; CHILI DOGS; CHILI POWDER; FIREHOUSE FOOD.

CHILI DOGS

A hot dog smothered in chili is a popular variation of the hot dog in a bun. Hot dog, or frankfurter, stands serving chili dogs are common at baseball parks, food festivals, street fairs, and carnivals. In major cities, workers and shoppers who want a quick lunch or snack frequently buy chili dogs from street vendors.

See also: BASEBALL PARK EATING AND DRINKING; CARNIVAL AND FAIR FOOD; CHILES; CHILI AND CHILI SUPPERS; FOOD FAIRS; HOT DOGS.

CHILI POWDER

Some accounts credit the invention of chili powder in 1835 to an English settler in Mexico's Texas territory, who combined various ground peppers as a convenient way to make Mexican-style dishes. It was German-American cafe owner William Gebhardt, however, who made the first commercial chili powder in 1894 by running bits of pepper through a small meat grinder several times and drying the ground mixture to a powder consistency. He opened a chili powder factory in 1895 with initial production estimated at five cases per week. He sold the chili powder from the back of a wagon. With the introduction of chili at the 1893 Chicago World's Fair, the powdered concoction got an extra boost. It simplified the preparation of chili, which became a popular dish throughout the United States. Gebhardt is also credited with promoting chili when he produced the first canned chili con carne at his factory in 1911.

See also: CHILI AND CHILI SUPPERS.

Reference: Trager. *The Food Chronology*. 1995.

CHIMICHANGA

See TASTE OF . . . FESTIVALS.

CHINESE BUFFET

As fastfood outlets have popped up in increasing numbers all across North America since the 1970s, so have Chinese buffets. Classic family-owned and -operated Chinese restaurants with names like Great Wall, Lotus Flower, Peking Gourmet, and Szechuan Garden have been serving traditional Chinese dishes—sometimes in elegant style—for decades, but the Chinese buffet is a relatively recent concept. Such chains as Manchu Wok and Panda Express, each with at least 200 outlets, have been set up in downtown areas, malls, shopping centers, and airports across the United States. Some Chinese buffet dishes—and Chinese restaurant dishes—are strictly American creations (such as chop suey and sweet-and-sour pork), but customers who want a quick lunch or evening meal can choose from a wide variety of both traditional Chinese and "Chinese-style" foods at these outlets.

See also: BUFFET; FASTFOOD.

Reference: Karnow. "Year In, Year Out, Those Eateries Keep Eggrolling Along." 1994.

CHINESE NEW YEAR

Based on the lunar calendar that marks the movements of the moon circling the earth, the Chinese New Year falls on the second new moon of the winter solstice and is the biggest holiday of the year for people in China and those of Chinese ancestry living in North America. It occurs anytime between 21 January and 19 February, and each new year is given a designation based on the Chinese zodiac (e.g., Year of the Dog or Rat). Sometimes called the Spring Festival, the Chinese New Year celebration has a touch of all the major U.S. holidays, including parades, firecrackers, lavish red decorations (red is considered a good luck color), family gatherings, and certainly traditional meals and foods. Usually edible gifts are exchanged, such as apples, symbols of peace and goodwill, and oranges, which signify good fortune for the coming year.

During this time, families honor their ancestors, settle old debts, and observe centuries-old traditions such as making offerings to the kitchen god. According to custom, the image of the god hangs in the kitchen and members of the household smear his lips with honey so that on his return to heaven he will only make sweet remarks about the family.

Food plays a prominent role during the Chinese New Year ritual. Traditional foods include pan-fried or steamed dumplings with meat, seafood, and vegetable fillings, and perhaps a lucky coin is stuffed inside. According to custom, friends gather the day before the holiday to prepare the dumplings, and only good things are discussed during this time to ensure good luck for the coming year.

Other traditional foods include shark fin soup, an expensive delicacy that is supposed to bring good luck; long-life spinach noodles made with spinach, flour, and eggs and symbolizing, as the name implies, longevity; deep-fried spring rolls (or egg rolls), symbols of gold; sticky rice cakes for great achievement; and meatballs, which signify unity. Some families may follow the custom observed in China, serving a whole fish as a symbol of bounty.

See also: SPRING ROLLS.

References: Cohen and Coffin. *The Folklore of American Holidays*. 1991; Davis. *The Potato Book*. 1973; Lundy. *The Festive Table*. 1995; Simonds. *Chinese Food*. 1990.

CHIPS AND DIP

Serving potato or tortilla chips with a dip is routine at many a cocktail party or during the cocktail hour before dinner at home. This practice has increased over the past few decades along with the growing number and types of dips on the market. Chips and dip became the "ultimate party food" in 1952 when Lipton started printing dip recipes on the back of its onion soup packages. A seemingly endless variety of cheese dips is now available in supermarkets. These may be made with processed cream; cottage, pot, farmer, or aged cheese; or almost any other type of cheese that can be blended and mixed with such ingredients as onions, garlic, caraway seeds, peppers, olives, anchovies, crab meat, shrimp, herring, mustard, and wine. Sour cream or yogurt may be added for smoothness or used as a base for a dip.

Another popular dip is guacamole, an avocado dip available in nearly all Mexican-style restaurants and in deli or refrigerated sections of supermarkets. Dipping tortilla chips in salsa and guacamole is a tradition that began in the seventeenth century with the indigenous tribes of Mexico. Potato chips, however, are a much newer invention. They were created in 1853 by a chef playing a joke on a customer who had complained that the French fries were too thick. The chef shaved the next order paper thin and sent them out to rave reviews.

See also: APPETIZERS; COCKTAIL PARTY; GUACAMOLE; SALSA.

References: Chalmers. *The Great Food Almanac.* 1994; Mariani. *The Dictionary of American Food and Drink.* 1993, 1994; Trager. *The Food Chronology.* 1995.

CHITTERLINGS

See SOUL FOOD.

CHOCOLATE

"The food of the gods" is how the eighteenth-century botanist Carolus Linnaeus characterized *cacao*, the pod-tree source of what is arguably the world's most desired and romantic food. *Theobroma*, the Latin term for chocolate, has a long history and an extensive mythology. The use of the cacao plant's beans originated in the Amazon (present-day Brazil and part of Peru) or Orinoco (present-day Venezuela) basins of South America some time prior to 2000 B.C., when it was used to make a bitter-tasting beverage. This cacao product went through great transformations after European explorers took cacao beans back to their own lands. It became the basis for sweet drinks (chocolate milk and hot chocolate) and confections that millions of people around the world enjoy. In 1828, a machine was invented that extracted cocoa butter from chocolate liquor to make cocoa powder, the basis of many chocolate delights, and the process was perfected during the 1840s.

Chocolate certainly is a favorite food among North Americans. In the United States, for example, an annual chocolate festival held in Burlington, Wisconsin, where a Nestlé Food Company factory is located, celebrates the glories of chocolate. The May event, which began in 1987, features all the usual attractions of festivals but focuses on chocolate treats handed out to participants and a community breakfast that includes pancakes riddled with chocolate chips. Chocolate Festival Park was created by the state of Wisconsin especially for this event, which includes a steam locomotive ride with passengers treated to free chocolates.

Chocolate is literally the foundation of Hershey, Pennsylvania, where Milton S. Hershey established his chocolate factory early in the 1900s and in 1903 built a company town, which is now a famous resort. The Hotel Hershey still serves a traditional chocolate cream pie made from a recipe that has not changed over the years. In Victoria, British Columbia, Canadians and millions of tourists have long enjoyed the "Death by Chocolate Buffet" at the Empress Hotel; varieties of rich chocolate desserts are offered every evening in the hotel's Lobby Lounge.

See also: CHOCOLATE BEVERAGES; CHOCOLATE CANDY; CHOCOLATE CHIP COOKIES.
Reference: Stewart. *Entertaining.* 1982.

CHOCOLATE BEVERAGES

As early as the twelfth century in Europe, a frothy chocolate beverage was used in royal rituals such as marriage ceremonies. Two decades after Christopher Columbus landed in America, Hernando Cortés observed that the Aztec emperor Moctezuma drank from golden cups that contained a bitter, spicy beverage made from the cacao bean. The great chief shared this drink—*xocoatl*—with the Spaniard who noted that it was so precious that even though Moctezuma drank cup after cup, each golden vessel was destroyed after one use. To this day, Mexican tradition that carried over to the United States calls for toasting to good fortune with a sweetened chocolate drink. As an ancient Mexican saying puts it: "O divine chocolate, we grind it on our knees, we beat it with our hands in prayer and we drink it with our eyes lifted to the heavens."

The Spanish were responsible for initiating the use of chocolate in a sweetened drink that came to have such a strong hold on the world's taste buds and psyche. They mixed cane sugar with processed cacao beans and water to achieve a concoction that had all who tasted it crowing about its virtues, real and imagined: it was an elixir, a balm, and an aphrodisiac!

At first, because of the high cost of preparing the sweetened chocolate, hot chocolate was a drink that only royalty and the upper class could afford; the drink became a kind of status symbol. According to one authority, "Aristocratic society preferred to drink its chocolate at breakfast. Ideally it was served in the boudoir, in bed if possible." Drinking it was a ritual of "fluid, lazy, languid motion." When mechanization lowered the cost of producing chocolate, the masses in both the "old" and "new" worlds were able to enjoy the treat. During the nineteenth century in North America, most middle- and upper-class homemakers purchased chocolate sets—covered pitchers or pots (rather like tall teapots) and special china cups with matching saucers—with which to serve cocoa, or hot chocolate. Today, hot chocolate is a common breakfast drink, regardless of the economic or social status of the consumer. Hot chocolate is also a customary drink after such cold weather recreational activities as sledding, skiing, and ice skating.

In Oaxaca, Mexico, where chocolate production has a long history and where the major chocolate company Chocolate Mayordomo is located, hot chocolate is served almost everywhere and at all times of day. (Much of Mexico's cacao is grown in the nearby state of Tabasco.) Hot chocolate is a traditional drink for fiestas and holidays, such as All Souls Day (or Day of the Dead). Traditionally, Mexicans make hot chocolate by pouring boiling water into a cup and then melting an ounce or so of chocolate in the cup, frothing the drink, then dunking chunks of *pan de yema* (an egg bread) into the beverage.
See also: ALL SOULS DAY; BREAKFAST; CHOCOLATE.
References: Boyton. *Chocolate.* 1982; Brownson. "Oaxaca's History Is Linked to Its Luscious Chocolate." 1994; Schivelbusch and Jacobson. *Tastes of Paradise.* 1992; Young. "Chocolate." 1984.

CHOCOLATE CANDY

Chocolate was mostly consumed as a beverage up to the mid-1840s. At that time, extraction of cocoa butter from the ground beans was accomplished as part of the process of developing cocoa powder. The fat, added to ground bean paste and sugar, became the first attempt at a solid product for eating. Refinements continued, and by 1847 the first chocolate candy bar was produced.

In 1875, the Swiss developed solid milk chocolate. Chemist Henri Nestl worked with candy maker Daniel Peter to blend in condensed milk. Later in the United States, Milton Hershey developed an inexpensive process to use whole milk, and today the company he started makes not only candy bars but at least 25 million Hershey Kisses—bite-size chocolates—every day at the plant in Hershey, Pennsylvania.

The popularity of chocolate as a sweet snack food and as a special gift for a loved one is surpassed by no other food in North America. Well over $4.5 billion worth of chocolates is sold each year in the United States as millions of American consumers traditionally buy chocolates to give as gifts for a variety of occasions such as holidays and birthdays. Chocolate candy is also known as a comfort food, because it is often eaten to ease the "blues" or other negative feelings. Special chocolate gifts often carry the names of the great world chocolatiers and sell for up to $25 per pound. These truffles, creams, nougats, cordials, fruits, and so forth are the domain of the venerable houses of See, Fannie Mae, Tobler, Kron, Godiva, and many other boutique manufacturers who guard their recipes as if they were state secrets.

See also: CHOCOLATE; COMFORT FOODS; SNACK FOODS.

References: Chalmers. *Great American Food Almanac.* 1986; Minifie. *Chocolate, Cocoa, and Confectionery.* 1980.

CHOCOLATE CHIP COOKIES

"I mix them up and bake them for every carry-in I attend and I always bake a batch of chocolate chip cookies—we used to call 'em Toll House cookies—to keep on hand in case unexpected company comes." That comment from a 90-year-old woman in the Midwest has probably been echoed countless times across the United States. For years, home bakers have used the recipe on the wrapper for Nestlé chocolate morsels (bits or chips) to create Toll House cookies or what are now generically called chocolate chip cookies.

The Toll House cookie originated with Ruth Wakefield, the co-owner of a historic inn called Toll House, located near Whit-

man, Massachusetts, where a tollgate once stood. As the story goes, Wakefield created the recipe one day when she ran out of nuts to put in butter cookies she was making. She substituted pieces of a Nestlé semi-sweet chocolate bar, and the cookies produced were an instant hit at the inn. Eventually, the recipe appeared on the chocolate bar wrapper and then later on the package of chocolate morsels that Nestlé started producing in 1939.

Today, there are a variety of brands as well as generic packages of chocolate chips, pieces, bits, or morsels, and chocolate chip cookies are a favorite across the land. Frequently, a youngster's first baking experience is creating these cookies—and eating them warm from the oven with the chocolate smearing the fingers and melting on the tongue. Gigantic chocolate chip cookies are popular at cookie bars in shopping malls and at bakeries. Seldom does a community bake sale or bazaar take place without some version of a chocolate chip cookie on a counter or table, and they are sold at many coffee shops, delis, and similar eating establishments.

See also: BAKE SALE; CHRISTMAS BAZAAR; COFFEE HOUSES; COOKIE BARS/SHOPS; COOKIES.

Reference: Wyman. *I'm a SPAM Fan.* 1993.

CHOPPED LIVER

Served on the Jewish Sabbath—Friday night—and as an appetizer for Jewish holiday meals, chopped liver is also a traditional food for buffets and such events as bar mitzvahs. Chicken livers are sautéed with onions and salt and pepper, then they are chopped coarsely or fine, combined with chopped egg, and in the traditional way blended with chicken fat (although today many cooks use mayonnaise). Usually chopped liver is spread on challah, matzoh, or crackers.

See also: APPETIZERS; BAR MITZVAH/BAT MITZVAH; BUFFET; CHALLAH; MATZOH.

CHOPSTICKS

See EATING UTENSILS.

CHOW-CHOW

Pickling is a harvest activity practiced all across North America, although not as extensively as it was when most Americans lived on farms. During the pickling process, some farm folks routinely make a vegetable relish known as chow-chow, consisting of corn kernels, chopped cabbage, bell peppers, onions, and celery; seasoned with salt, mustard seed, and turmeric; and pickled in a vinegar and sugar mixture. Many believe that chow-chow made its first appearance in North America via Chinese laborers working on the railroads of the American West. The Mandarin word *cha* means "mixed." Whatever the origin, the condiment is served with meals throughout the year.
See also: PICKLES.
Reference: Mariani. *The Dictionary of American Food and Drink.* 1993, 1994.

CHRISTENING PARTY

This party takes place after the Christian ritual of baptism—a ceremony for accepting a person into the Christain faith, which includes a sprinkling with water or immersion in water symbolizing spiritual cleansing and/or regeneration. Catholic children are usually baptized within the first six weeks of life, while the baptism ceremony for Protestant children (except Baptists) is usually held within the first six months (although the ceremony can be much later in life). When an infant is baptized, gifts for the baby and a christening party, with family and close friends in attendance, often follow the ceremony. A white christening cake with white icing, a wine punch, champagne, and soft drinks are usually served, and guests toast the christened child.
Reference: Baldridge. *The New Manners for the '90s.* 1990.

CHRISTMAS BAZAAR

About six weeks before the Christmas holiday, many church groups hold a fund-raising bazaar, selling baked goods and other foods as well as handmade craft items for gift giving. Dedicated bazaar-goers usually visit as many bazaars as they can to see and taste what is new or traditional in the food world. One-dish meals like chili or a special lunch may be offered for sale to those who attend.

Bazaars may focus on foods that reflect the ethnic background or national ancestry of the congregation. In a Swedish neighborhood or community, for example, a church bazaar would likely offer foods such as Swedish rye bread, *kottbullar* (Swedish meatballs), *brod grot* (Swedish bread pudding), and *frugt suppe* (Swedish fruit soup). Other bazaars concentrate on baked goods only, offering sweet breads, christmas cookies, and such all-American favorites as brownies and fruit pies. Still others may sell homemade preserves and jellies, pickles, relishes, and similar items.
See also: BREAD; CHILI AND CHILI SUPPERS; CHRISTMAS COOKIES; PICKLES; PUDDINGS.

CHRISTMAS CANDY

In Clement Moore's classic poem about the night before Christmas, he brought forth "visions of sugarplums" and may have been referring to marzipan candies, some historians say. Making marzipan is a holiday tradition in many homes throughout North America. The candy is made with almond paste and sugar or honey and shaped and painted with food coloring usually to look like miniature fruits. These confections probably originated in ancient Persia and were later carried to Europe, where Italians transformed the practice of making marzipan into an art form.

Various types of hard candies are also popular during the Christmas season. One of the most common is the peppermint-flavored sugar, or candy, cane with its red and white stripes. Candy canes in clear wrap are often hung on Christmas trees and stuffed in Christmas stockings.

Chocolates, too, are especially favored at this holiday time. Chocolate-covered cherries, chocolate-covered mints, and many other types of chocolates appear on buffet tables and as after-dinner treats, and boxes of chocolates are also popular gifts. **See also:** CHOCOLATE CANDY; CHRISTMAS COOKIES; MAIL-ORDER FOODS.

CHRISTMAS COOKIES

Although "store-bought" Christmas cookies are now commonplace throughout North America, it is still a holiday custom in many homes to bake holiday cookies and gobble them up in lip-smacking fashion throughout the season, or, if they last, to present them as gifts. Children in some homes still leave a plate of cookies and milk for Santa Claus, a custom that may have had its start in Sweden or Norway but also could stem from the long-ago practice of appeasing gods, fairies, and other supernatural beings that brought good fortune.

Every home baker who makes traditional Christmas cookies has his or her specialty, but some favorites are gingerbread, rum balls, and sugar-and-butter cookies that can be rolled out; cut in star, bell, and other shapes; and decorated with frosting or colorful candies or sugars. Many Americans of German ancestry prepare marzipan cookies, made with a flour, sugar, grated almond, and rosewater dough that is shaped into balls or molded like fruits and colored with vegetable coloring and baked. (A similar type of confection, marzipan candy, is popular in Mexico and among Americans of Italian descent as well.) The sweet and spicy *pfeffernusse*—a ginger biscuit or cookie—is another traditional German cookie popular at Christmastime.

People who follow Norwegian traditions bake seven different kinds of cookies for the Christmas holiday. These include cone-shaped cookies called *krumkakes*, baked on a special iron by the same name; several varieties of butter cookies; and rolled white sugar cookies. Another Scandinavian favorite is gingersnaps—ginger cookies baked in the form of trees, "gingerbread men," animals, and candy canes and decorated with white icing.

It is a custom among Italian Americans to prepare cannoli, pastry-type cookies filled with a mixture of ricotta cheese, sugar, chocolate, and candied fruit, and *pizzelle*, anise- or almond-flavored cookies decorated with elaborate designs. Another Italian favorite is *biscotti*, made from basic ingredients but prepared in a variety of ways and usually rolled and shaped into forms before baking, although *biscotti* for some is more like a cake that after baking may be toasted and then dipped in wine or coffee as it is eaten.

A Mexican favorite is *buñuelos*, fried tortillas covered with syrup. Anise-seed sugar cookies called *biscochitos* are traditional at Christmastime in Native American and Spanish communities of the U.S. Southwest.
See also: CHRISTMAS CANDY; COOKIES.
References: Gerlach and Gerlach. *Food of the Maya*. 1994; Hutchison. *Pennsylvania Dutch Cook Book*. 1948; Malpezzi and Clements. *Italian-American Folklore*. 1992; Nathan. *An American Folklife Cookbook*. 1984.

CHRISTMAS EVE/DAY DINNER

For the majority of North Americans, the Christmas holiday is a time for family and friends as well as a time to indulge. Many celebrate with a Christmas Eve or Christmas Day dinner, which frequently centers on a ham or turkey. What people serve for this meal, though, often depends on a family's cultural heritage. A Christmas Eve meal in the Norwegian tradition, for instance, includes lutefisk—a codfish dish—potato dumplings, meatballs in gravy, vegetable casseroles, a Norwegian flat bread made from mashed potatoes called *lefse*, cranberry relish, and a Christmas bread known as *julekage*, or julecake. Another traditional Scandinavian holiday dish is Christmas porridge made with white rice, milk, sugar, vanilla, and cinnamon. The Danes often plan Christmas dinner around a roasted goose stuffed with apples, prunes, and chopped onion and served with braised red cabbage and caramelized potatoes. In the English tradition, a mincemeat pie with its spicy fruits representing the gifts that the Magi brought to the infant Jesus is the customary Christmas dessert. Cornish saffron cake or bread filled with raisins, currants, and candied fruit are baked for good luck and also for gift giving during the holidays.

Beigli, a Christmas log made of a rolled dough with walnuts or poppy seeds and coated with an egg wash, is on the table for Christmas dinner in almost every Hungarian home. Chocolate-covered candies in rum, walnut, or fruit flavors adorn the Christmas tree or are served after dinner.

A Christmas Eve dinner in the French tradition may be long and leisurely, stretching from around nine at night to about one in the morning. Whether rich or poor, people generally indulge for the Christmas feast, beginning with raw oysters—perhaps a bushel of them—as hors d'oeuvres. The main course may include a turkey with chestnut dressing, escargot, lobster, *boudin* (French sausage), and a variety of cooked vegetables. A traditional French Christmas dessert is *bûche de Noël,* made from a sponge cake batter laced with a cherry liqueur syrup, baked in a jelly roll pan, rolled and shaped like a tree log, and iced with a chocolate buttercream frosting.

Christmas Eve Italian-style is called Fish Night and the dinner features seven kinds of fish, symbolizing the lucky number seven and the seven phases of the moon. The fish and seafood dishes typically include stuffed squid, baked eel, codfish cakes, fried shrimp, fillet of sole, scallops, and smelt. Three kinds of vegetables (broccoli, cauliflower, and artichoke hearts) representing the Trinity in Christian belief are also served. At the Christmas dinner or at any time during the holiday season, Italians might also serve *panettone,* a sweet egg and yeast bread spiked with candied citron and lemon peel, pine nuts, and crushed anise seeds.

For the Pueblo Indians in the southwestern United States, *pasole*—a traditional corn and pork stew with garlic and chiles—is a must for the Christmas Eve meal, which also includes chicken stew, chili, and fry bread. A stew—goat or veal—is also a traditional part of the Christmas Eve or Christmas Day meal among Puerto Ricans. Roast pork and a dish made of rice and green pigeon peas are included as well. Another Puerto Rican favorite during the entire Christmas season is *asopao de pollo,* a hearty chicken soup made with chicken cut into serving pieces along with rice, tomato sauce, diced ham, and peas.

According to Kraft's Holiday Homecoming Survey, 80 percent of Americans make the same holiday meal that they enjoyed as children. This fact keeps many family and ethnic Christmas traditions alive. **See also:** ARTICHOKE FESTIVAL; BREAD; CHILES; CHILI AND CHILI SUPPERS; HAM; LUTEFISK; POTATOES.

References: Betz. *Tastes of Liberty.* 1985; Kirlin and Kirlin. *Smithsonian Folklife Cookbook.* 1991; Nathan. *An American Folklife Cookbook.* 1984; Ortiz. *A Taste of Puerto Rico.* 1994.

CHUCK-WAGON SUPPER

In the southwestern and western United States, chuck-wagon suppers are common fund-raisers. A chuck wagon built to resemble the cook wagons—converted army wagons—that were used on the range to feed cowboys in the 1800s and early 1900s is set up for a community cookout. The wagon may be equipped with a Dutch oven and a variety of other cooking equipment, and the event may be a steak feed, or a savory stew or chili (or both) may be served. Cowboy frying pan bread, made from a baking powder dough, is a traditional accompaniment.
See also: CHILI AND CHILI SUPPERS; FRYING PAN BREAD.

CHURCH DINNERS/SUPPERS

Gathering at a church or religious meeting house for a meal is a long-held tradition in North America. Ever since their arrival in North America during the 1700s and 1800s from Europe, the rural Amish, for example, have taken part in a community meal following a preaching service, which is usually held every other Sunday in a member's home. Urban churches are also sites for numerous communal suppers and dinners. The Abyssinian Baptist Church in New York City, for example, has been serving a home-cooked Sunday dinner since 1923. At Greek Orthodox churches, Roman Catholic churches, most Protestant denominational churches, and many non-denominational churches, people routinely gather together after a Sunday service to share a meal in a church basement or recreational hall. In some churches, the same cooks have prepared meals every Sunday for decades; in others, the cooks rotate duties periodically.

Carry-in meals are also common for such events with fried chicken, meat loaf, sliced roast beef, or stuffed turkey being common main dishes along with vegetable casseroles, green and gelatin salads, and plenty of desserts.

Many church congregations also sponsor communal meals as part of festivals and street fairs that feature ethnic foods or for special holiday celebrations. This is especially true in the ethnic neighborhoods of major cities such as New York, Chicago, and Los Angeles. Communal meals in a church are also traditional events after weddings, funerals, and anniversary celebrations.

References: Hostetler. *Amish Society*. 1968; O'Neill. *New York Cookbook*. 1992.

CIDER

The English word *cider* is derived from the Hebrew *shekar* meaning "strong drink of grain and honey," but cider in North America is usually made from apples. In the apple-growing regions of the United States—New England, parts of the Midwest, and the Pacific Northwest—cider is associated with the fall season, when apples are harvested, milled, and pressed to obtain their juices. It can be served in different ways: as a cooled beverage, in a mixed drink, or as a warmed or hot toddy.

Sometimes it is mulled with spices such as cinnamon, cloves, nutmeg, or lemon rind.

Since malic acid is a major component of cider, the apples used to make cider usually have a higher acidity than eating or cooking apples. In North America, there are two categories of cider: sweet and hard. Sweet cider is the unfermented or partly fermented form of the beverage (under 3 percent alcohol), while hard cider is the more fermented form (3 to 7 percent alcohol). Yeast may be added during the fermentation of hard cider, or the cider may be naturally fermented. Usually the cider is fermented at 12 to 15 degrees Celsius until "dryness" is reached (the point at which all the sugar is converted to alcohol). The beverage may be clarified by filtration and stored in wooden barrels (draught cider), or it may be pasteurized and filtered into aluminum casks (keg cider) or bottled.

Cider-related drinks are made by variations in the fermentation process. If a higher final alcohol content is desired, extra sugar may be added during fermentation. A beverage of over 7 percent alcohol made in this manner is usually known as "applejack." "Ciderkin" is a more dilute drink formed from watered-down second and third pressings of the apples, "cider royal" is cider mixed with brandy, and "stonewall" is cider mixed with rum.

Cider was the most popular drink of the North American colonists. Almost every village had a cider mill to make sweet cider, hard cider, apple butter, and apple sauce. Alcoholic drinks such as hard cider were important because the water supply was sometimes contaminated or undependable. Making a fermented beverage was a way of preserving it. If the cider went "bad," it could be used to make cider vinegar. Although the popularity of cider waned in the nineteenth century when beer became the most popular beverage among adults, today cider is a common fall and winter beverage. Apple harvesting and cider pressings are often part of fall harvest festivals and Halloween, Thanksgiving, and Christmas celebrations. During these occasions, food, cider, and musical and dramatic amusement are combined into a community event.

See also: APPLE BUTTER; APPLE FESTIVALS; HALLOWEEN; HOT TODDY; THANKSGIVING DAY DINNER.

References: Campbell-Platt. *Fermented Foods of the World.* 1987; Mariani. *The Dictionary of American Food and Drink.* 1993, 1994; Neufeldt. *Webster's New World Dictionary of American English.* 1994.

CIDER AND DOUGHNUTS

See HALLOWEEN.

CINCO DE MAYO

A fiesta that marks the victory of the Mexican-Indian Army over the French in 1862, Cinco de Mayo (the fifth of May) is a time for people of Mexican ancestry as well as people of other heritages to enjoy Mexican food and the music of a mariachi band. Corn, tomatoes, beans, squash, chiles, and avocados—foods that originated in ancient Mexico—are the main ingredients in many dishes served. One traditional food served on this holiday is soft tacos with shredded beef. Salsa—a mixture of tomatoes, chiles, cilantro, and onion—is always on the table as an accompaniment.

See also: CHILES; SALSA.

CIOPPINO

A seafood stew, cioppino is a combination of various whitefish and shellfish, such as shrimp, crab, clams, and mussels, in a tomato sauce that has become a ritual meal for the Italian fishing community in San Francisco. Contrary to most traditions, however, the stew is not made the same way each time, because the seafood included depends on what the fishermen catch on a particular day. The other ingredients usually include onions, carrots, tomato sauce, olive oil, white wine, and various herbs and seasonings, depending on the cook. This

seafood stew in all its variations is prepared and enjoyed across the continent today.

References: Brown. *American Cooking.* 1968; Clayton. *Cooking across America.* 1993.

CLAM CHOWDER

Just mention the word *chowder* and people associate it with New England, where fish and seafood soups made with a cream or milk base have been part of many residents' eating patterns—patterns probably carried over from France and England—for hundreds of years. The word itself is derived from the French *chaudiere,* meaning "large cauldron." In the early colonial days, chowder was an inexpensive meal, since the fish and seafood could be found easily along the Atlantic coast. Today, New England clam chowder (using quahog, a particular type of clam) is considered a classic, and travelers to New England usually make it a point to visit restaurants serving this regional specialty.

Another type of clam chowder that many North Americans prefer is made with a tomato base and is known as Manhattan-style clam chowder. It is eaten with near religious fervor—a must for some easterners. In Rhode Island, for example, legislators passed a law mandating that the state's official shore dinner include tomato-clam chowder. Clam chowders are not just East Coast foods, however. They are served in restaurants across the continent and are popular canned or frozen items in grocery stores and supermarkets.

References: Sokolov. "Insects, Worms, and Other Tidbits." 1989; Stern and Stern. *Good-Food.* 1983.

CLAMBAKE

The clambake is a ritual feast that originated with the Wampanoag and other Native Americans long before European settlers arrived in North America. Europeans learned to steam fresh clams and other seafoods along with fresh vegetables, and the custom evolved to become a traditional beach party on North American coastlines. New England clambakes have been annual events since about the mid-1800s, and some, such as the Cape Cod clambakes, probably have even earlier roots dating back to the 1830s. According to one folklorist, Kathy Neustadt, "the clambake is a unique American folk tradition," which often brings family members together in reunions or is a major community celebration. Neustadt traced the history of an annual clambake in Allen's Neck, Massachusetts, describing not only "How They Do It at Allen's Neck" but also the "Food, Ritual, and Festivity" of the event in a book appropriately titled *Clambake* (1992).

Clambakes are, of course, held in other parts of North America, and while clams are an integral part of the fare cooked and offered to the participants, other available shellfish are often included in the feast. Typically, preparation begins the day before a bake, or very early in the morning on the same day, if the food is to be served by the afternoon. First, a pit is dug in the ground, usually at a beach site. In some cases, a concrete slab is used for a clambake. Whether using a pit or slab, it must be lined with plenty of firewood and large, clean rocks. When the fire dies down and the rocks become red hot, a layer of wet rockweed or seaweed is strewn across, and clams in burlap bags or wooden trays (or sometimes loose) are placed on the wet weeds. Then another layer of seaweed might go in with a row of lobsters, crabs, shrimp, and other shellfish. Ears of unhusked corn, small potatoes, and other hardy vegetables are also an option for addition to the pit.

Once the food is arranged, the pit is covered with a last layer of rockweed or seaweed, a layer of canvas, or perhaps sand. At this point the wait and the party begin. The party revolves around the cook pit, with guests typically trading conjectures regarding the estimated time to eat (E.T.E.). The cooking can take one to two hours or more, depending on the size of the pit, the temperature of the rocks, and the amount and type of food being cooked.

When ready for eating, the clams are carefully uncovered and taken out of the pit with a clean shovel and rake. All the food goes directly to the buffet, where the guests serve themselves to a fabulous feast of freshly steamed shellfish.

See also: BUFFET; GRUNION RUN.
Reference: Neustadt. *Clambake*. 1992.

COCKTAIL PARTY

While a cocktail party may include people who know each other well, it is more likely to be an event that brings together mere acquaintances and strangers, sometimes fellow workers. Those who attend a cocktail party usually are served mixed drinks—some form of alcohol combined with other ingredients—over ice. There are hundreds of thousands of possible combinations, but some of the most common concoctions are the martini, gin and tonic, old-fashioned, manhattan, whiskey and soda, daiquiri, margarita, and champagne cocktail.

Party-goers usually consume a variety of appetizers, or finger foods, with their cocktails (or nonalcoholic beverages), taking part in an eating and drinking ritual designed to break down barriers between people.

Many cocktail parties are held in private homes. Others may take place in public buildings, such as restaurants, art galleries, museums, or concert halls. Most are held two or three hours before dinner and on some occasions in the mid-afternoon.

See also: APPETIZERS; HAPPY HOUR; MARTINI.
Reference: Grimes. *Straight Up or on the Rocks*. 1993.

COCKTAILS

Cocktails, or mixed drinks made with several types of spirits and a mixer such as soda or fruit juice, have probably been around since people first learned about fermentation. No one knows the exact origin of the term *cocktail*, but some etymologies declare that the word derived from the French *coquetel*, for mixed drink, or from the English *cock-ale*, a drink of the seventeenth century. Another etymology suggests that *cocktail* as a term might have been invented in the early 1800s to describe a toast after a cockfight, when people raised a drink and toasted the cock with the most tail feathers left. Among the most colorful stories regarding the origin of the term is that of New York barmaid Betsy Flanagan, who had a penchant for decorating the Halls Corner tavern with poultry tail feathers. As the story goes, an inebriated customer asked for a "glass of those cock tails," and Flanagan served him a drink garnished with a feather. Whatever the origin, the term first appeared in print in a Hudson, New York, newspaper in 1806 and was described as a "stimulating liquor, composed of spirits of any kind, sugar, water, and bitters." Today, the cocktail is associated with a variety of social rituals in North America, not the least of which is the cocktail hour or cocktail party.

The manhattan and martini were two of the earliest cocktails to gain popularity in the United States. In the 1920s, demand increased for new and imaginative alcoholic drinks, and mixed concoctions—cocktails—gained widespread popularity. During this period, Henry MacElhone of Harry's New York Bar in Paris invented such drinks as the Sidecar and the White Lady, both favorites of Americans in France. At the same bar, Fernand Petiot is credited with inventing the Bloody Mary. The Ritz Hotel in New York had its share of famous bartenders such as Frank Meyer, Georges Sheuer, and Jean Bernard Azimont, and the Ritz was the origin of such drinks as the Mimosa.

Later, when American interest shifted to more "tropical" rum-based drinks, the daiquiri was invented in and named after a village near the original Bacardi distillery in Cuba. Trader Vic (Victor Bergeron), a well-known restauranteur, later took advantage of the "Polynesian-style" fad, and created such famous drinks as the Mai Tai, the Fog Cutter, and the Scorpion.

Bartenders continue to create specialties, and there is no way to predict which mixed drinks will gain widespread acceptance in the future.

See also: COCKTAIL PARTY; MARTINI; MINT JULEP.

References: Funk. *2,107 Curious World Origins, Sayings, and Expressions.* 1993; Grimes. *Straight Up or on the Rocks.* 1993; Mariani. *The Dictionary of American Food and Drink.* 1993, 1994; Trager. *The Food Chronology.* 1995.

COFFEE

The term *coffee* appeared in English around 1600 and may have derived from the Turkish word *kahveh*, which actually means "a wine tonic that restores the appetite." Another theory says that the word *coffee* originated from the province of Kaffa in Ethiopia, where coffee trees have been growing wild since ancient times. Coffee has a long, illustrious history as a drink that has been both praised and damned and has also been celebrated in song, art, politics, and even religion.

Coffee's caffeine content produces an "eye-opening" effect for many. This stimulating effect is one reason that people tend to drink coffee in the morning or at times when they would like to eliminate sleepiness. In North America, coffee has long been a popular breakfast drink, often served with milk or cream and sugar. Coffee also has been consumed throughout the day in many homes and businesses, where people often keep a pot of coffee warm on the stove or brewer, ready for drinking during the routine coffee break.

Coffee has always been a vital part of the rations issued to America's armed forces, and pioneers carried tins of coffee with them on their treks from the East to the American West. It has also been a staple for modern-day travelers, whether traveling over the road, by train, or in the air. Many Americans ritually carry a cup of coffee in a mug to drink on their drive to work, or they buy coffee-to-go for a commuter trip to the job. North Americans, like people in many other parts of the world, have also used coffee in food, adding it to gravies and using it as flavoring for cakes, chocolate candies, ice cream, and coffee liqueurs.

See also: COFFEE BREAK; COFFEE HOUSES; ESPRESSO BARS.

Reference: Rolnick. *The Complete Book of Coffee.* 1982.

COFFEE BREAK

One of the most common drinking rituals in the United States is the coffee break. In most businesses, factories, stores, shops, and institutions, employees take a break from the work routine and relax with a cup of coffee or some other "social lubricant." During leisure activities or while taking part in volunteer work, people often stop for a coffee break, too. Not only is this a way for individuals to unwind, but in many instances provides a means for socializing.

The custom of taking a coffee break probably originated centuries ago when coffee houses were established in Arabia. Between the twelfth and fifteenth centuries, coffee drinking was popular throughout the entire Middle East, and by the sixteenth century, coffee's popularity had spread to Europe, although only the wealthy could afford the drink prepared for a morning and evening ritual.

See also: CAFES; COFFEE HOUSES; ESPRESSO BARS; KAFFEEKLATSCH.

COFFEE HOUSES

During colonial times in North America, coffee houses were popular meeting places for political leaders and others who wanted to discuss current events. Today, small family restaurants, roadside cafes, fastfood restaurants, pastry shops, and delicatessens serve that purpose. In rural areas, for example, farmers often gather after chores are finished, meeting in country restaurants to discuss politics, local affairs, crop prices, weather conditions, and other matters of concern. Urban workers may meet fellow employees, retirees,

or friends for "morning coffee" and take part in the ritual of passing judgment on world affairs over coffee before going on to take care of daily business.

See also: CAFES; COFFEE BREAK; ESPRESSO BARS; FASTFOOD; KAFFEEKLATSCH.

COLESLAW

Shredded raw cabbage served as a cold or hot dish is traditional among numerous ethnic groups in North America and is a common carry-in dish for an American potluck, a typical accompaniment at a barbecue or picnic, and a side dish at numerous fastfood outlets. Although cabbage has been eaten since prehistoric times, cabbage slaw or coleslaw, as it is most often called, apparently was introduced to colonial America by the Dutch, who made a hot slaw—simmering shredded cabbage in a butter, vinegar, and water mixture with seasoning. They called the slaw *koolsla* (meaning "cabbage salad served either hot or cold"), but Americans assumed the term was *cole* or *cold slaw,* thus the typical American coleslaw is a cold salad. There is, however, no single coleslaw recipe that could be labeled all-American. Many slaws are made with not only shredded cabbage but also shredded carrots and perhaps diced green pepper and celery. Sometimes apple or pineapple chunks are added to the slaw. In the southwestern and western United States, slaw may include finely shredded jicama, a crisp potatolike tuber indigenous to Mexico and a popular ingredient for numerous salads, relishes, and salsas.

See also: BARBECUE; PICNIC; POTLUCK.

References: Fussell. *I Hear America Cooking.* 1986; Pyles. *The New Texas Cuisine.* 1993.

COMFORT FOODS

Some people believe that certain foods can alleviate their individual problems, easing the stress of everyday life. People may routinely eat special foods to soothe distress, to calm fears, and to relieve countless other types of apprehension or uneasiness.

Although comfort foods vary with individuals' tastes, some general rules seem to apply to the foods that are categorized as such: they are usually highly caloric, are often called junk foods, and are eaten in large quantities. Some examples would be ice cream—in particular the brands Häagen-Daz and Ben and Jerry's and the Dove Bar—pizza, french fries, nuts, cookies and milk, chips and dip, or anything made with chocolate. Ironically, eating these foods often leads to guilt feelings; the very food that is supposed to provide comfort can easily become "forbidden."

See also: CHOCOLATE; CHOCOLATE CANDY; CHOCOLATE CHIP COOKIES; ICE CREAM; SNACK FOODS.

Reference: Mariani. *The Dictionary of American Food and Drink.* 1993, 1994.

COMMUNAL DINING

Even though the number of communes and communal societies in North America is relatively small, those that do exist follow an eating ritual that has probably been practiced since prehistoric times when people first formed in protective groups. Long before the arrival of Europeans on American soil, members of ancient indigenous groups lived, worked, and ate communally, and, when European settlers came to the New World, some immigrated primarily to follow religious practices that included communal living—a way to maintain beliefs and a particular life-style. Among such settlers were several Anabaptist groups from Austria, Switzerland, and Moravia (people who followed a doctrine of adult baptism, established in the early 1500s), such as the Amish, Mennonites, and Hutterites.

In spite of persecution, the Hutterites have maintained at least 370 colonies in the Great Plains areas of the United States and Canada. From 85 to 100 people live in each colony and, except for the young children, share three meals every day in a communal dining room. Most of the food is grown on cooperatively owned land, and colony members share the labor of harvesting, preserving, and preparing food. Certain types of food are served on particular days of the week, and the weekly schedule is repeated throughout the year, although the menu does reflect the change in seasons. For example, after harvesting potatoes and making sausage in the fall, soups made with potatoes and sausage are common. Other agrarian communal groups—which may or may not have been established because of religious beliefs—follow similar eating practices.

See also: AMISH FOOD FESTIVALS.

Reference: Kant. *The Hutterite Community Cookbook.* 1990.

COMMUNION

See EUCHARIST.

CONTINENTAL BREAKFAST

Following a European-style practice, numerous hotel restaurants and cafes in North America offer their patrons continental breakfast, which usually consists of coffee, tea, or hot chocolate; sweet rolls, doughnuts, bagels, or muffins; and fresh fruit or fruit juice. During the 1990s, the practice has become a well-established promotional effort in many motels and hotels across the United States. Travelers can help themselves to free continental-style breakfasts served in motel lobbies. Some of the breakfasts simply consist of coffee, doughnuts, and juice, while others are more elaborate, offering a range of breakfast foods, from cold cereal to hot toast, which lodgers might prepare themselves. This type of breakfast benefits people on the go and those who generally eat light.

See also: BAGELS; BED AND BREAKFAST; CAFES.

CONVENIENCE STORE FOODS

Aptly named, the convenience store has become increasingly popular among Americans who want quick, easy ways to buy food and beverages such as bread, milk, soda pop, and snacks, along with cigarettes and other nonfood items. Since about the 1960s, convenience stores in many cases have replaced the rural grocery store and the corner grocery, a small mom-and-pop store that was near at hand for people in a city neighborhood.

One of the most well known convenience store chains is 7-Eleven, a name that once indicated the usual hours for the store to operate. Today, however, many convenience stores operating under a variety of franchises are open 24 hours, never closing except on an occasional holiday. Every major truck stop along the U.S. interstate highway system includes a convenience store of some kind, and other such stores are located within or near gas stations and other businesses that line state and national highways. Along with truckers, tourists and other travelers frequent convenience stores to buy snack foods, prepared sandwiches, soups, and other foods that can be heated in a microwave on the premises; cold drinks; coffee; and other foods and beverages that are consumed while "on the road."
See also: TRUCK STOP FOOD.

COOKIE BARS/SHOPS

Baking cookies for various holidays is a tradition in many American homes, and family members enjoy sampling the goodies fresh out of the oven; however, a great many consumers buy their freshly baked cookies at supermarkets, mall cookie bars or shops, or at community or neighborhood bakeries. As the number and size of malls has grown over the past few decades, so have cookie bars or shops, which usually bake cookies (from commercially prepared batter) on the premises, emitting a sugary aroma that tempts shoppers to take a shopping break and buy a snack.
See also: COOKIES; SNACK FOODS.

COOKIES

Cookies are a staple in most American homes, according to food marketing

experts and the giant cookie producers such as Nabisco and Keebler. While freshly baked cookies sold in supermarkets and malls are popular, they are only a small portion of the total cookie market. The vast majority of cookies are prepackaged and purchased at the supermarkets and are eaten as snacks. Cookies and milk or a juice drink are routinely served to children as a snack or dessert, and cookies with coffee are a favorite adult snack.
See also: CHOCOLATE CHIP COOKIES; COOKIE BARS/SHOPS; CREME-FILLED SANDWICH COOKIES.

CORN DOGS

Hardly a carnival or county fair takes place without a stand selling corn dogs. Hot dogs are dipped in a cornmeal batter and quickly deep fried, then served on a stick with mustard or some other condiment. This unexpected treat first appeared at the 1942 Texas State Fair after Dallas vaudevillians Neil and Carl Fletcher perfected their recipe and called the result the "Fletchers' Original State Fair Corny Dog."

Street vendors in New York, Chicago, and other major cities across America also sell corn dogs, which are a customary snack or lunch for many shoppers and workers. Corn dogs also are popular at baseball games, and packaged batter mixes are available in most supermarkets for those consumers who want to make their own corn dogs at home.
See also: BASEBALL PARK EATING AND DRINKING; CARNIVAL AND FAIR FOOD.
Reference: Mariani. *The Dictionary of American Food and Drink.* 1993, 1994.

CORN FOODS AND FESTIVALS

Corn is the "king crop" in North America, and corn festivals pay tribute to this essential food and its many by-products. One corn festival has been held in La Habra in southern California since the 1940s. Since only small quantities of corn grow in La Habra, the festival did not begin as a harvest celebration; instead, it started as a way

Cookies served with milk for dipping make for a popular snack. Many people develop a particular ritual for dipping.

for a civic group to raise funds and has continued for that purpose. Each year in August, tens of thousands of people gather for a two-day event that includes a parade and preparation of thousands of ears of corn for butter-dripping consumption.

While corn festivals vary, they are common celebrations in most parts of the continent, particularly among Native American tribes. Perhaps as long ago as 7,000 years, Indians of ancient Mexico were beginning to domesticate the wild grain that they called *maize*. This early corn, a primitive grass relative of wheat and oats, grew as a tiny four-rowed ear. Over the next 1,000 years, however, the industrious Mexican farmers crossbred to increase the size and to develop all of the basic strains of the plant. By the time Europeans arrived, Native Americans had perfected the processes of drying, storing, and cooking this very adaptable staple, and the knowledge had spread from those early experiments in the region of (what was to become) central Mexico down throughout the Southern Hemisphere and at least as far north as the rocky soil of New England.

American colonists at first adapted Native American recipes such as succotash, cornmeal mush, and corn bread. Later, particularly in the South, they created corn-based foods that have become classics, such as hush puppies and fritters. Colonists began to use milk products, which were not common among indigenous people, in corn recipes to create foods that became part of the daily fare such as corn chowder and more moist corn breads and muffins.

Today, the average American ingests three pounds of corn each day in the form of meat, butter, milk, and cheese because approximately $10 billion worth is fed to cows, pigs, and chickens. Even the American dog and cat kibble is substantially cornmeal. So dependent are Americans on corn (the grain is used in everything from new fuels to biodegradable disposables such as eating utensils) that it is no wonder corn harvests are widely celebrated.

In Mexico, the eating of corn in its many forms is even more pervasive than in the United States. Most corn foods begin with shelled corn that is soaked in lime water (or cooked), softening the kernels and causing them to swell and double in size. Called *nixtamal,* the softened corn may be cooked with pieces of beef or pork and eaten, creating a traditional food used to counteract a hangover. *Nixtamal,* however, usually is ground to make tortillas used for a variety of Mexican foods, such as tamales, masa dumplings, posole, and hominy dishes that originated from the recipes and preparations of the ancient farmers. One or more of them are still consumed almost every day by a vast majority of the population in Mexico and by the new Latino immigrants in the United States.

See also: CHOW-CHOW; CORNMEAL MUSH; FRITTERS; GREEN CORN FESTIVALS; HUSH PUPPIES; NATIVE AMERICAN FEASTS; POPCORN; THANKSGIVING DAY DINNER.

References: Fussell. *The Story of Corn.* 1992; Rhoades. "Corn, the Golden Grain." 1993; Rozin. *Blue Corn and Chocolate.* 1992; Schwartz. "The Great Food Migration." 1991; West. *Mexican-American Folklore.* 1988.

CORN ROAST

A corn roast is often part of harvest festivals, especially those that celebrate the corn crop, and it is a component of many backyard barbecues and picnics. While backyard cooks often wrap corn-on-the-cob in foil and roast it on the grill, some insist on the roasting method that Native Americans have used for centuries in which cobs of fresh corn are left in their husks, soaked in water for several hours, then roasted on a grill or dropped into hot ashes, where it is steamed anywhere from 15 minutes to an hour, depending on the heat of the fire or ashes. Usually roasted corn is served with melted butter or a butter substitute and various seasonings.

See also: BARBECUE; CORN FOODS AND FESTIVALS; NATIVE AMERICAN FEASTS.

CORNED BEEF AND CABBAGE

See NEW ENGLAND BOILED DINNER; SAINT PATRICK'S DAY.

CORNED BEEF HASH

The word *hash,* meaning "fried odds-and-ends dish," came into English in the mid–seventeenth century from the old French word *hacher,* meaning "to chop." Corned beef hash—a dish traditionally made of chopped corned beef, onions, potatoes, and seasonings—probably has its origins in being a palatable combination of leftovers. In the nineteenth century, restaurants serving inexpensive meals—precursors to today's diners—became known as "hash houses" or "hasheries." By the early 1900s, corned beef hash was a common menu item in these places. Sometimes called "cornbeef Willie," corned beef hash is a popular breakfast entree, often served with home fries, toast, and fried eggs on top.

See also: BREAKFAST.

References: Mariani. *The Dictionary of American Food and Drink.* 1993, 1994; Simon and Howe. *Dictionary of Gastronomy.* 1970.

CORNMEAL MUSH

Mush is often called a pioneer food, and a bowl of steaming cornmeal mush served with butter and milk has long been part of hearty breakfasts in many rural areas of North America. During colonial times and later on the frontier, mush was sometimes called "Indian pudding," "hasty pudding," or Italian polenta. The term *hasty pudding* used during the 1700s was a misnomer; for, until the advent of fast-cooking methods such as the use of microwave ovens, making a thick mush of cornmeal required slow cooking in a double-boiler or over a low flame. The term, however, was immortalized prior to the American Revolution in a verse of the song "Yankee Doodle," which described a campground filled with men and boys as "thick as hasty pudding." Cornmeal mush was also a favorite of soldiers fighting in the War of 1812 and a staple food among Native Americans, enslaved Africans brought to North America, and groups of people with European ancestry such as the Pennsylvania Dutch, as well as people in the southern United States.

Today, many varieties of mush are prepared and served. One cafe in Bellwether, Oregon, for example, serves 27 different varieties of mush, including corn, barley, wheat, rye, sweet pea, and oatmeal—a house blend made from an original pioneer recipe.

See also: BREAKFAST; POLENTA; PUDDINGS.
Reference: Fussell. *The Story of Corn.* 1992.

COTTAGE CHEESE

Cottage cheese is a moist, soft white cheese made from skim milk. A daily lunch ritual for countless Americans—especially those on a weight-loss diet—is eating a serving of cottage cheese, usually the low-fat and low-calorie variety. Often the cottage cheese is accompanied by fruit or a seasoning such as chives, or it is part of a salad. The Pennsylvannia Dutch enjoy "summer cottage cheese," which is thinned with cream and flavored with various seasonings.

One of the most unusual lunch rituals was that of President Richard Nixon who ate his daily cottage cheese with ketchup. Apparently, he did not like cottage cheese but thought it was a good source of protein and an important food in helping to control his weight. Thus, he forced himself to eat it, smothering it with ketchup to make it more palatable.

COTTON CANDY

This sweet, puffy confection is made of sugar and coloring spun at very high speed in a large tub. It first appeared in 1900 at the Ringling Brothers and Barnum and Bailey Circus, where snack vendor Thomas Patton began experimenting with the common practice of caramelizing sugar. He boiled the sugar on a gas-fired hot plate that spun then, using a fork, formed long threads—a "cottony sugar floss."

Cotton candy is still popular at carnivals, circuses, county and state fairs, festivals, and on boardwalks. In fact, for many people part of the fair-going or amusement park ritual is eating cotton candy. The standard color of the confection is pink; however, blue, purple, and even yellow cotton candy may be found. It is traditionally served spun around a paper-cone "stick" and is eaten by pulling away bits of the spun candy fluff. Although packaged cotton candy is available for candy stores, it is rarely seen.

See also: CARNIVAL AND FAIR FOOD.
Reference: Mariani. *The Dictionary of American Food and Drink.* 1993, 1994.

CRAB FESTIVALS

Feasting on crabs is a common activity in North America, and over 3,000 pounds of fresh cracked crabs may be served at a single crab festival. There are over 4,000 species of these crustaceans, ranging in size from the tiny pea crab (less than 1 inch across, from leg tip to leg tip) to giant crabs weighing 25 to 30 pounds. Two of the most common edible crabs in North America are the Alaska King crab (*Paralithodes camtschaticus*) found along the Pacific coast and the blue crab (*Callinectes sapidus*) found along the Atlantic and Gulf coasts.

A crab festival includes a crab boil in which crabs are cooked in a huge pot over an open fire. When they are done, they are piled on a table—usually a long picnic table where people have gathered to eat. Cooked crabs are soft and easy to manage with dexterous fingers, so they can be easily pulled apart and dipped in butter and/or a sauce made with horseradish, lemon juice, ketchup, and Tabasco. They are usually served with corn-on-the-cob, boiled new potatoes, coleslaw, and ice tea or beer—sometimes home-brewed. One man who regularly attends crab festivals wherever he travels in the summer explained his style of eating: "I find myself a table or good spot on the ground, put down some newspapers, pile the crabs and corn on the papers, and take my shirt off to prepare for eating—it can get messy. Then I go for it! There is not a lot of meat on crabs

Cotton candy, sugar spun onto sticks or paper cones, is a popular treat at fairs, carnivals, and circuses. This little girl, the 1,776th child to see the Ringling Bros. and Barnum & Bailey Circus in 1976 received an outlandish sized cloud of cotton candy during a performance in San Antonio, Texas.

so I usually eat the whole thing, spitting out the bits of shell or leg now and then."

Not all crabs are eaten at crab festivals; some are used for other activities. In the United States, one focus of a festival may be crab races, a tradition that dates back to the time when local fishermen would take the fastest crabs from their catch, place them in the center of a circle, and bet on which crab would reach the outer edge of the circle first. The "winning crab" would then be released back into the ocean or kept for later races. Boat-docking contests, soft shelled crab–cutting contests, fireworks, and music are all part of the entertainment, too.

One major American crab festival is the World Championship Crab Races, held in Crescent City, California, in February. Nine- to eleven-inch Dungeness crabs are raced down four-foot runways, with prizes awarded to the owner of the winning crab. Another famous crab festival is the National Hard Crab Derby, held in Crisfield, Maryland, over Labor Day weekend. Its traditional "circle-style" races have been held annually since 1947, and entries from all over the United States race to be winner of the Governor's Cup Race, which occurs on Saturday.

See also: CRAWFISH BOIL; LOBSTER BOIL.
Reference: Thompson and Carlson. *Holidaqys, Festivals, and Celebrations of the World Dictionary.* 1994.

CRACKERS AND CHEESE

Crackers and cheese (especially hard cheeses) are both foods that are well suited for long-term storage; hence, the eating of the two together stemmed from necessity rather than from gastronomic exploration. The earliest Europeans in America probably ate crackers and cheese, since these foods were taken on long sea voyages. It has been a long-standing practice in Vermont to make a meal of crackers crumbled in milk eaten with a hunk of cheddar cheese. Across the United States, crackers and cheese are often eaten as snacks, as appetizers, or as cocktail party food.

The most common combination is a type of hard cheese such as Cheddar and dry, puffy wheat crackers such as saltines. The cheese may be sliced and placed on the crackers as is or melted on top. Another popular combination is soft cheese or cheese spread and crunchy, fibrous crackers. North Americans also like to snack on cheese-flavored crackers, which is a handy substitute for the traditional combination of cheese and crackers. The cheese ball—semisoft cheese molded into a ball and covered with chopped nuts—served with crackers is practically ubiquitous as an appetizer at many types of North American parties.
See also: APPETIZERS; COCKTAIL PARTY; SNACK FOODS.
References: Cahill. *Olde New England's Sugar and Spice and Everything.* 1991; Mariani. *The Dictionary of American Food and Drink.* 1993, 1994; Stern and Stern. *GoodFood.* 1983.

CRACKLINGS

During the eighteenth and nineteenth centuries, when lard rather than vegetable-based shortening was the primary fat used in cooking and baking, farmers rendered pork fat into lard and referred to the browned connective tissues that remained as cracklings, or cracklins. Cracklings were mixed with other food ingredients to prepare flavorful dishes and were eaten as snack foods. Today, cracklings serve the same purpose, but they may be made from various pork products, such as bacon rind, fatback—the rind of a joint of pork,— or the crisp browned skin of roast pork. Fatback must be cut into pieces and fried, roasted, or baked crisp.

Cracklings have long been used to make cracklin bread—baked cornmeal batter with cracklings mixed into it, which is a popular food item among many rural people, particularly those in the southern and southwestern states. Cracklin bread is commonly served with collard greens, a combination that routinely appears at black family reunions. Cracklings are also used to season soups, gravies, or vegetables.

As a snack food, cracklings are often referred to as "pork rinds," which reportedly were a favorite of former President George Bush. Although cracklings have been popular snack foods throughout the United States, consumption of cracklings has been in decline because of the increasing focus on reducing fat in the diet. **See also:** SNACK FOODS.

CRANBERRY FESTIVALS

Cranberry festivals most likely originated during the 1800s when entire communities gathered together to harvest cranberries. An important part of the traditional Thanksgiving feast, cranberries are generally harvested in late September or early October. Although the highlight of a cranberry festival is the harvest, it is often accompanied by craft shows, flea markets, beauty contests, and musical entertainment. Food-related events such as cranberry pie–eating contests, cranberry baking contests, and a variety of games are popular as well.

Local volunteers usually organize and run cranberry festivals, which are common events in Massachusetts, where two-thirds of the cranberries in the United States are grown. New Jersey and Wisconsin are other states known for their cranberry bogs. The largest of all the cranberry festivals is held every autumn in South Carver, Massachusetts. Called the Massachusetts Cranberry Festival, it began in 1949 with the support of Ellis D. Atwood, founder of the Edaville Railroad, and Robert Rich, founder of Ocean Spray Cranberries (now Ocean Spray). On the average, 10,000 people attend the festival annually.
See also: THANKSGIVING DAY DINNER.
References: Shemanski. *A Guide to Fairs and Festivals in the United States.* 1984; Thompson and Carlson. *Holidays, Festivals, and Celebrations of the World Dictionary.* 1994.

CRANBERRY JUICE

For generations, some women have used a folklore antidote for bladder infections: drinking a glass of cranberry juice daily for a period of several weeks. Until recently there was only anecdotal evidence that there was any correlation, but in 1994 Harvard researchers concluded a small study that scientifically indicated that cranberry

Cranberry growers in Massachusetts harvest cranberries by flooding the bogs in which cranberry vines grow. Called wet harvesting, growers use a motorized contraption to beat the berries free and then herd the floating berries with booms and rakes to conveyors and trucks. The fruit is packaged raw, crushed for juice, and even made into wine. Fall festivals on Cape Cod celebrate the harvest.

juice was effective in preventing (not curing) bladder infections. Still, the findings may be challenged. Whatever its health benefits, cranberry juice is a traditional and festive nonalcoholic cocktail, usually served just before dinner, in numerous households. In some instances it may be mixed with ginger ale, soda water, or other carbonated drink. It also serves as a colorful base for holiday punches.

See also: COCKTAILS; PUNCH.

CRAWFISH BOIL

"One of the best things about living in Louisiana is that you get to go to crawfish boils," according to Emeril Lagasse, chef and owner of an award-winning restaurant and author of a cookbook titled *Emeril's New New Orleans Cooking*. In his words, crawfish (or crayfish) boils "are usually raucous parties where the centerpiece is a huge vat of boiling crawfish and spices."

Heaps of crawfish and corn-on-the-cob are featured at a Louisiana backyard crawfish boil. Crawfish or "mud bugs," as some Cajuns call crawfish, are smaller, freshwater cousins of lobsters.

Usually the vat also contains corn-on-the-cob and new potatoes. When everything is cooked, the crawfish, which are fresh-water crustaceans that are sometimes mistaken for lobsters, are dumped on tables covered with newspapers, and people eat the crawfish "with a lot of noisy sucking and chomping."

Although a great variety of people attend and enjoy annual spring crawfish boils, they are a central part of Cajun culture in southwest Louisiana, a region that includes New Orleans and is known as Acadiana because it was settled by people of French-Canadian ancestry who were forced to leave Acadia, Canada, in the 1700s. Many Acadians, or Cajuns (an altered form of *Acadian*), and their descendants in Louisiana have earned their living by farming, fishing, or trapping, and for generations they caught crawfish in the swamps and streams, where there was a plentiful supply.

Until about the 1950s, many people outside Acadiana considered crawfish inedible—an unclean "poor people's food." Today, however, crawfish are fairly expensive and are symbolic of Cajun foodways or customs that have become increasingly popular over the years. In fact, the town of Breaux Bridge, Louisiana, in the heart of Acadiana where more than 90 percent of Louisiana's crawfish farms are located, is known for restaurants and cafes featuring traditional Cajun cooking and is the site of a crawfish festival that has been held annually since 1960. A May event, the crawfish festival attracts up to 100,000 people and includes not only a crawfish boil but also other popular foods ranging from a crawfish stew to a crawfish hot dog.

While crawfish boils are associated with New Orleans and the state of Louisiana, they are not limited to that region. They are popular wherever crawfish are found, and they are similar to seafood boils or bakes in New England.

See also: CLAMBAKE; LOBSTER BOIL; MARDI GRAS.

References: Gutierrez. *Cajun Foodways*. 1992. Lagasse. *Emeril's New New Orleans Cooking*. 1993.

CREAMED CHIPPED BEEF ON TOAST

Some food historians say that the frugal meal of processed beef in a hot cream sauce poured over toast originated with the Pennsylvania Dutch. It has been popular with many American families since the days of the Great Depression. Creamed, chipped, or dried beef on toast has also been known as *shit-on-a-shingle* or *SOS,* terms attributed to the U.S. Army and troops who obviously disliked the military version of creamed chipped beef on toast that was served to them during World War II. The terminology stuck and today many diners, truck stops, and small cafes across the United States feature SOS on their menus as a blue-plate special. Even though people may disparage and joke about this rather plain food, it is routinely served—perhaps once a week or once a month—as a breakfast, lunch, or supper item in many homes, and many people even consider it a comfort food.
See also: COMFORT FOODS; MILITARY CHOW.

CREME-FILLED SANDWICH COOKIES

There are a number of different brands of sandwich cookies held together with a vanilla creme filling, but one of the best-known and top-selling brands is Oreo made by Nabisco. Although the brand has been a favorite with consumers for decades, part of its popularity stems from a 1990s advertising campaign focusing on the way people eat these chocolate sandwich cookies. Surveys show that 50 percent of those who buy Oreos routinely twist them apart, then either lick off the creme or scrape it off with their teeth. After that, each half is eaten separately. Whether people eat the Nabisco brand or choose those made by Keebler, Sunshine, Barbara's, or some other competing firm, they are likely to add one more component to the eating ritual—a glass of milk. Some people like to dip these biscuit-type cookies into milk to soften them before eating, or they take a bite of cookie and then a sip of milk to form a mushier morsel before swallowing. There are those who habitually eat their sandwich cookies without any pomp and circumstance; their only routine is to pop the whole sandwich cookie in their mouth, crunch it up, swallow, and reach for another.

See also: COOKIES.

Reference: Wyman. *I'm a SPAM Fan.* 1993.

CREPES

Originating in France, crepes were once made and served almost exclusively in fine restaurants or special crepe shops in North America. Today, however, home cooks as well as chefs in many types of eating establishments prepare crepe dishes from a batter that is similar to the mixture of flour, eggs, milk, and oil used to make pancakes and waffles. The trick for making crepes is using only a couple of tablespoons of batter, spreading the batter thinly and evenly over a preheated crepe or fry pan (there are pans that are specifically designed for making crepes), cooking for only a minute on one side, and flipping and cooking the other side for about 30 seconds. Flipping the crepe with dramatic flair is one of the rituals expert crepe makers develop.

Once crepes are made, they are spread or filled with almost any food mixture a cook can imagine, from fruit and yogurt to vegetable and cheese combinations. They are then rolled and served at almost any meal and are popular Sunday brunch dishes or dessert items at buffet dinners. Crepes filled with baked chicken or turkey slices and served with a sauce make a popular light meal.

See also: BUFFET; SUNDAY BRUNCH.

CROISSANTS

One of the most popular breads in North America, the buttery croissant is often the bread of choice for sandwiches served at lunchtime, and croissant sandwich bars are popular in malls and shopping centers in many large cities throughout the nation. Croissants with fruit, custard, or other fillings are also routine breakfast items for many Americans.

No one knows the exact origin of the croissant, but one legend declares that it was invented in the late 1600s, when the Turks invaded the city of Vienna (Austria). The Turks were driven out, and to celebrate their victory, Viennese bakers made crescent-shaped pastries patterned after the crescent moon emblem on the Turkish flag. By eating the crescent roll, the Viennese could show they had "swallowed up" their enemies. Eventually, Marie Antoinette, an Austrian princess who became queen of France in the 1700s, introduced the roll to French bakers. They created their own version—a light and flaky roll made with thin layers of dough—and called it a croissant. It became a favorite throughout much of Europe and eventually in America, where it has become a familiar and traditional bread among much of the population.

See also: BREAD; SANDWICHES.

Reference: Coutelle. *The Perfect Croissant.* 1983.

CROQUETTES

Croquettes are primarily made of shredded chicken, salmon or other fish, or ground veal. The meat is mixed with spices and held together with eggs and rice, then it is shaped into cones, dipped in egg batter, rolled in bread or cracker crumbs, and fried quickly in hot fat to a golden brown. (Another common croquette is made from mashed potatoes.) Traditionally, croquettes are served with a hot cream sauce or milk-based gravy, and, during the 1940s and 1950s, croquettes were one of the most popular foods served at ladies' luncheons and were common fare for some family dinners. Although not as common as they once were, they are still on the menu in some diners and family restaurants across the United States and may be prepared and served at home in the form of cakes or patties rather than in cone shapes.

See also: LADIES' LUNCHEON.

References: Stern and Stern. *GoodFood.* 1983; Stern and Stern. *Real American Food.* 1986; Williams. *Savory Suppers and Fashionable Feasts.* 1985.

CROUTONS

Before cubes of dried, baked, or fried bread were commercially packaged and sold as croutons, thrifty Americans routinely saved stale bread to break or cut up and use in stewed vegetable dishes (such as stewed tomatoes), in dressing, and in bread pudding. Sometimes the bread was dried and then crushed to make bread crumbs for a variety of uses. While this is still a common practice in some North American homes, consumers now demand food items that are ready to use from the package, and croutons—plain or spiced with herbs— have joined the many other convenience foods on grocery store shelves.

Croutons (the word is derived from a French word meaning "crust") are rarely eaten alone, but instead are either ingredients in or garnishes for other dishes. They are sometimes added to soups, a practice related to the bread soups found in some cultures. Herbed croutons are especially popular as garnishes for green salads, adding texture, color, and flavor. Croutons may also be used as a major ingredient in turkey stuffing, a traditional item in Thanksgiving meals.

See also: BREAD; GARNISHES; THANKSGIVING DAY DINNER.

CRUISE SHIP DINING

Formal and elegant dining aboard ship has been a practice ever since the 1800s, when British steamship lines began to stress service and comfort as a means of increasing the number of passengers on ocean pleasure voyages. Today, most passenger ships offering ocean or inland waterway cruises main-

tain several dining rooms where formal meals are served, plus deckside cafes, alternative restaurants, and spas. There is almost always a great diversity in the foods served. Reflecting the current focus on healthful eating, most American cruise ships offer vegetarian, low-fat, or other alternative items to their standard fare. Some ships also appeal to different groups of passengers by providing more family-oriented fare with "fun foods" for kids, as well as meals reflecting the cuisine of every port on their itinerary.

Although cruise ships offer diversity in dining, they maintain some standard practices, such as providing afternoon teas (a tradition carried over from the British) and large food buffets, which are most often served in the main dining room for breakfast, lunch, dinner, and sometimes midnight meals. Although these buffets tend to serve mainly American food with a few European and Asian contributions, there are occasionally "theme nights" in which the focus is a single type of cuisine.

See also: AFTERNOON TEA; BREAKFAST; BUFFET; CAFES.

CURRY

As an increasing number of ethnic restaurants and ethnic food booths and shops appear in North America, more of the U.S. and Canadian populations are being "turned on" to curry spice and curried dishes. While in other countries the word *curry* refers to any number of elaborate freshly ground combinations of spices, herbs, and seeds, in North America it generally refers to a jarred mixture (containing ground cumin, turmeric, coriander, black pepper, fenugreek, red pepper, ginger, celery, and cardamom, and sometimes allspice, anise, bay leaves, capsicum, caraway, cinnamon, chili, cloves, mace, poppy seeds, and saffron).

According to food expert Dave DeWitt, North Americans tend to associate curry with India more than any other country. In fact, the term *curry* derives from *kari*, the name for the curry tree in India. Although the leaves of the tree may

Elegantly prepared and presented meals are a tradition on cruise ships. Waiters aboard a Princess cruise ship display (left to right) beef Wellington, fish, and desserts. Cruise companies serve diverse menus to accommodate low-fat diets and vegetarians.

be used in creating curry flavoring, the other spices are more prominent in most curry dishes, which are actually a combination of ingredients resembling stew. Although the sauce, or gravy, for the "stew" varies from north to south in India, it basically includes chile peppers, black pepper, coriander, cumin, cinnamon, and turmeric in a base of coconut milk or yogurt. In other countries such as Pakistan curries may also contain nuts and dried fruit. Traditional Thai dishes are prepared with a curry sauce or paste that is very spicy. Curried dishes worldwide may include vegetables and/or seafood, pork, beef, or chicken, and they are almost always served with rice.

References: Chalmers. *The Great Food Almanac.* 1994; DeWitt and Pais. *A World of Curries.* 1994.

DANISH DAYS

Founded by Danes in 1911, Solvang, California, is the site of a food and cultural festival known as Danish Days. Held over a weekend in mid-September each year, Danish Days call attention to the village's architectural heritage (many of its buildings represent those found in Denmark), its arts, crafts, music and dances, and one of Denmark's most famous authors, Hans Christian Andersen. Traditional Danish foods are featured in Solvang all year long, but during Danish Days visitors can enjoy an authentic Danish breakfast of *aebleskiver* (small round pancakes) and *medisterpolse,* a lunch or dinner of a typical Danish dish such as meatballs served with red cabbage, and Danish pastries for dessert.

DATE FESTIVAL

In February each year, date harvests take place in Indio, California, and the surrounding Coachella Valley where 95 percent of the dates consumed in the United States are grown. For miles along the state routes through the valley, there are groves of date palms and roadside stands that sell date products, including date pies, chocolate-covered dates, date shakes sweetened with honey, date butter spreads, date cakes and cookies, and gift packs of various types of dates, some of which come from palms that are offshoots of plantings imported from Morocco early in the 1900s. Indeed, the valley climate is similar to that of the Sahara Desert and the date-growing regions of North Africa and the Middle East. As date palms took root in the California desert, so did Arabic influence with towns named Mecca and Oasis, Moorish-style buildings, streets named Arabia and Deglet Noor, and city signs written in Arabic script.

Since 1921, the National Date Festival has been held at the Riverside County Fairgrounds in Indio each February, and several hundred thousand visitors attend the ten-day event. While date-based products are an expected part of the festival events, so are camel and ostrich races and townspeople dressed in Arabian costumes. **See also:** CHOCOLATE CANDY; COOKIES.

DELI FOODS

"You don't have to be Jewish to enjoy our food" is how the owner of Al's Deli in a Chicago suburb greets newcomers. Although not all delicatessens (or delis, as these stores are usually called) specialize in Jewish food, Jewish immigrants were among the first to establish such shops

Powdered sugar dusts Danish aebleskiver, *which is served with jam as a dessert during Danish Days in Solvang, California. Danes from the American Midwest founded Solvang in 1911 to preserve their heritage and to enjoy the moderate climate of the Santa Ynez Valley.*

during the late 1800s and early 1900s in New York City, selling prepared foods, many of which were kosher.

The term *delicatessen* derives from the German *delikatesse*, meaning "delicacy." As Jews immigrated to the United States, they set up *schlact*, or "butcher shops." As they began to add a variety of foods for sale, the *schlact* became known as *delicatessen*, which was later shortened to *deli*.

Today, there are numerous Jewish delis in New York and other eastern cities as well as in major urban areas across North America. Many of these delis are neighborhood stores, and residents routinely frequent them for hearty soups and sandwiches (corned beef, roast beef, pastrami, pepper beef, turkey, brisket, salami, chicken salad, chopped liver, and egg salad are some of the popular varieties) or for other carry-out items ranging from potato salad to cheesecake and strudel.

Delis serving other types of food are also popular. Some Italian restaurants, for example, maintain a deli section, offering pasta salads, sandwiches, breads, and other items for carry-out. Vegetarian delis are common in natural food stores, and most supermarkets maintain a deli section where shoppers can order prepared foods to eat on the premises or to take home. Some of the most popular items in such delis are salads, barbecue chicken, and lunch meats. **See also:** CARRY-OUT FOODS; SANDWICHES; VEGETARIAN EATING.

DESIGNER WATER

The general concern for leading a healthier life-style that began in the 1980s fueled an incredible increase in the consumption of bottled waters. Grocery stores, mini markets, and liquor stores now stock an amazing array of waters. Bars and taverns are promoting a "bottled water breather" between alcohol rounds as a measure to ward off intoxication. There

Delicatessen (deli) patrons enjoy corned beef on rye sandwiches, a specialty of shops that serve soups, sand-wiches, salads, and baked goods. Irish runner Marcus O'Sullivan, left, and American Steve Homan, right, visit the Carnegie Deli in New York in 1995.

are even bottled water bars springing up in some of the tonier locales. The multi-million dollar business of selling designer bottled waters is driven by advertising that speaks to the obsession for physical perfection and optimal health.

Drunk for their supposed health-producing properties in Europe for many years, brands like Evian, Perrier, Vichy, and Peligrino were said to contain minerals that would ameliorate all sorts of chronic problems. These same brands have recently attracted North American consumers. Water "bottled at the source" and marketed as seltzer, mineral water, bubble water, or spring water is now the beverage of choice for many who are looking for an alternative to the overly sweet soda pops or the alcoholic beverages that have become the accepted liquid refreshers over the past 100 years.

In response to the increased interest, American and Canadian bottlers have begun to fill the shelves with domestically produced products as well. Clearly Canadian, Poland Springs, Calistoga, Talking Rain, and Sparkletts are just a few of the companies that market bottled water, most of which is carbonated. Some of these sparkling waters are flavored with fruit.

Some mineral waters are gaseous at the spring, but the commercially available bottled products have gas added at the plant, using the carbonic acid process that was first perfected by Joseph Hawkins in 1809, when he received the first U.S. patent for the process. It, however, took John Matthews to make "belch" water a part of Americana. In 1839, his company began an advertising campaign that may have been the first to link sexual pleasure with the consumption of a beverage. "Youth as it sips its first soda, experiences the sensations which, like the sensations of love, cannot be forgotten."

See also: SODA POP.
References: O'Neill. *New York Cookbook.* 1992; Root. *Food.* 1980.

DESSERT CHEESE

Serving cheese along with fruit and/or an after-dinner drink as a dessert course following an elegant dinner is a European custom that has carried over to North America. Cheeses used for dessert are usually soft and delicate in flavor and go well with fruit, a liqueur, or sweet wine, although stronger cheeses may also be served. Some popular dessert cheeses include Stilton, Edam, Camembert, and Brie. Frequently, the cheeses are presented on a cheese board or tray accompanied by such fruits as grapes, strawberries, and cherries and apple, pear, pineapple, or melon slices. Strong, dark-roasted coffee, such as espresso, is also routinely served with dessert cheese.

See also: APPETIZERS; CHEESE FESTIVALS; CHEESE TASTING; CHEESECAKE;.
Reference: Wason. *A Salute to Cheese.* 1966.

DESSERT TRAY

It is a custom in many fine restaurants to present a dessert tray to diners after they have completed a meal. The tray includes individual servings of pies, cakes, puddings, and so on. A primary purpose of the dessert tray is to promote a restaurant's elegant cakes, pastries, and other desserts, but many diners like the opportunity to see samples of what they may order rather than selecting from a menu listing.

DEVILED EGGS

Deviled eggs are one of the most common carry-in foods, frequently appearing at church suppers, family reunions, potlucks, or picnics. Since the 1800s, "deviling" has meant using mustard, chiles, or other seasonings to make a "hellishly hot" dish, and Stephan Pyles's *The New Texas Cuisine* even calls deviled eggs "hell's eggs." To prepare the eggs, they are first hardboiled and shelled, and then they are "deviled"; the hard-cooked yokes are carefully removed

Diners aboard a cruise ship end an elegantly presented dinner with coffee and dessert selected from a tempting dessert tray.

from the whites, mashed, and mixed with mayonnaise, mustard powder, and spices and spooned back into the egg white. Deviled eggs are usually garnished with sprinkled paprika.

See also: CHURCH DINNERS/SUPPERS; FAMILY REUNION; PICNIC; POTLUCK.

References: Mariani. *The Dictionary of American Food and Drink.* 1993, 1994; Pyles. *The New Texas Cuisine.* 1993.

DÍA DE LOS MUERTOS

See ALL SOULS DAY.

DIETS

Since the 1970s, weight-loss diet plans, such as Weight Watchers, and health food fads have proliferated in the United States. Americans seem obsessed with trying to find "magical" ways to lose weight and stay healthy. Dieters have followed plans that include solely liquids or certain foods such as grapefruit, ice cream, or popcorn on a daily basis, and there are even no-diet diets and "think-yourself-thin" programs.

Concern about the high levels of heart disease has led to increased medical research on how high cholesterol and fat in foods effect the cardiovascular system, and numerous "heart smart" diet plans have been developed. One early example is the Pritikin Diet, which became popular in the mid-1970s. Developed by Nathan Pritikin at the Longevity Center in Santa Barbara, California, the low-fat diet and sustained exercise plan was touted by numerous Hollywood stars and other celebrities and was featured on the television show *60 Minutes.* When the plan was published in book form, it quickly became a best-seller, and it is still in print. Another popular diet plan of the 1970s was the weight-reducing

Scarsdale Medical Diet developed by Herman Tarnower. In addition to these plans, numerous diets based on natural foods (rather than prepared foods) became popular as a way to maintain good health.

During the 1990s, with heart disease still the top American killer, consumers have continued the low-fat diet trend—but at an accelerated pace. The government has even stepped in to advocate healthy diets. A national Health Mark program has been set up to indicate on restaurant menus those items that fit into the health-conscious diet, so that people do not have to make an exception when they dine out. Foods of the Mediterranean region, where inhabitants enjoy low rates of heart disease and cancer, have become particularly popular. This type of diet includes plenty of olive oil, which along with canola oil is a monounsaturated oil that can help lower levels of the low density lipoprotein (LDL) in blood cholesterol and raise levels of the high density lipoprotein (HDL), which helps carry cholesterol away from the arteries. Some researchers believe that the low incidence of heart disease in Mediterranean countries is due to the use of olive oil in place of animal fat and to the emphasis on grains (primarily in pasta), fresh fruits and vegetables, beans, and wine. Some U.S. health officials, however, are concerned about recommending wine because Americans are not as likely as Europeans to drink just a glass or two of wine with a meal. (Of the 87 million American alcohol drinkers, at least 1 out of 12 has a drinking problem.) Although not all experts agree that the Mediterranean diet is a heart-healthy diet, this way of eating and other low-fat diets will probably be popular with millions of Americans well into the twenty-first century.

See also: CANOLA OIL; FASTING; PASTA; VEGETARIAN EATING.

DINING BY RAIL

Dining by rail is an experience that takes diners back to the days of luxury trains and offers scenic travel as well as an elegant meal—a brunch, a luncheon, or a full-course dinner. Passengers board refurbished dining cars of the early 1900s and dine at tables covered with white

Passengers in a refurbished railroad dining car roll through California's Napa Valley on the run between Napa and St. Helena.

linen cloths. Waiters in formal attire serve them the meals, which are usually prepared on board.

Dining by rail has become especially popular during the summer and fall seasons in the Northeast and the Midwest. Luncheon and dinner trains carry passengers along routes with spectacular views. A Michigan train called the Wine Country Dinner Train, for example, takes passengers through vineyards as well as orchards, woods, and wetlands of western Michigan. A four-course dinner is served and a wide selection of wines is available.

In the Napa Valley region of California, the Wine Train offers passengers a way to celebrate holidays or special occasions and tour California's famed wine country. For example, on Thanksgiving chefs present a gourmet feast as the Wine Train winds its way through the renowned Napa Valley vineyards.

Some dinner trains plan meals around a murder mystery. Passengers aboard the train watch an acting troupe perform a murder mystery drama, sometimes taking part in the drama that unfolds and helping to solve the mystery. In some areas of the country, Santa Trains offer excursions to tree farms where families can cut their own Christmas trees and have them delivered to the train for the return trip, which usually includes snacks of potato chips, sandwiches, or other items and beverages such as hot chocolate, cider, and coffee.
See also: CIDER; WINE TASTING.

DINING ON DELIVERY

Pizza is one of the most popular hot food dishes delivered to homes. Along with pizza chains, many other restaurants (such as ethnic food chains) and food stores have gotten into the meal delivery business, responding to the increasing demand of those who want a meal without much fuss in the kitchen. Some small companies have been established as well to deliver specially ordered meals from local restaurants to customers, and numerous vendors deliver

proportioned frozen meat products, hors d'oeuvres, and other food items for preparation at home.
See also: FASTFOOD; MAIL-ORDER FOODS; MEALS-ON-WHEELS.

DINING OUT

See EATING OUT.

DINNER PARTY

Since the time of the medieval banquet, people have gathered to eat, drink, and socialize around a sumptuous feast. From about the fifth century through the fifteenth century, lavish dining along with a code of behavior called etiquette evolved to become a ritualistic and pretentious event in well-to-do European homes. The practice carried over to North America and was especially prevalent in the nineteenth century when upper-class Victorian Americans attempted to set themselves apart by their manner of eating, which included dressing for dinner, elaborate service, and exotic and expensive foods and beverages presented to guests.

During the 1800s, formal dinner parties were often held on New Year's Eve or on other holidays, a practice that continues to this day, but modern dinner parties take place at many different times during the year and for a great variety of purposes. While formal attire and ritualistic behavior are still part of some dinner parties, especially those held for high-level government officials or those held to honor well-known individuals in society, the dinner party in general is not the rigid, self-conscious affair it used to be.

Most dinner parties, however, do follow a routine procedure. Usually the event begins with cocktails and appetizers, and then dinner is served. The meal itself may be a sit-down affair or a buffet-style presentation, and it is almost always followed by dessert and after-dinner drinks.
See also: AFTER-DINNER DRINKS; BANQUET; BUFFET.

DINNER THEATER

Going out for an evening of dining and theater is a popular entertainment in many communities. People buy a "package" that includes dinner and a comedy, drama, or musical. In some cases dinner is served at a well-known restaurant and the performance takes place at a nearby theater; however, many dinner theaters that have been established in the United States over the past few decades combine the two, presenting a theatrical show while people dine.

DISCOUNT DINING

Many Americans who want to save money when eating out routinely use restaurant discount coupons printed in local newspapers or sent through the mail as promotions. Usually a coupon offers a discount of $5 to $10 on the purchase of two dinner meals or two meals for the price of one. A variety of discount dining plans offer books of coupons at a set price; the coupons can be used throughout the year for a percentage off on meals at local establishments. For those who dine out often these coupon books provide a tremendous savings. Numerous meal discount coupons are also available for senior citizens, and travelers who purchase guidebooks, maps, and similar materials may also receive discount coupons. Some motels and hotels across North America regularly offer discount coupons for meals in their restaurants or in nearby eating establishments that share in promotional efforts.
See also: EARLY-BIRD SPECIAL.

DIWALI

A vegetarian meal with the whole family in attendance is the highlight of the Hindu Festival of Lights celebrated for a week to mark the beginning of the Hindu New Year in the month of Kartika—an October or November event in North America. This dinner is known as Diwali, or Dewali, and

no one knows when it originated. Along with candles, bright lighting, and firecrackers, new clothing and household goods symbolize a fresh beginning. Cooked lentils, which could include any number of 60 different kinds; rice dishes; and fried vegetable balls with gravy are traditional during this holiday. *Chappati,* an Indian flat bread that is served year round, is also an important part of the meal. For dessert, it is the custom to exchange sweets such as *halva,* made from grated vegetables and/or ground nuts. The ingredients are cooked in milk, combined with sugar and spices, and then fried in ghee, or clarified butter.
See also: GHEE; RICE DISHES.
References: Bragdon. *Joy through the World.* 1985; Hanes. *"India's Chefs Expand Repertoire."* 1991.

DOOR COUNTY FISH BOIL

Except for tourists who travel regularly to Door County, Wisconsin, where Scandinavians settled more than a century ago, few people outside the midsection of the United States had heard of the area until a decade or so ago when descriptions of it were included in several festival guides and travel cookbooks. Today, travelers from near and far would not miss an annual trek to the Wisconsin peninsula to sample a fish boil at White Gull Inn in Fish Creek or one of the other smaller fish boils in communities along Lake Michigan's shore.

A fish boil is a ritual—an outdoor cook-out—that apparently originated with lumbermen years ago, and at the present time is likely to occur nightly or on each weekend evening during the summer. Lake whitefish is the traditional fish used for the boil, but haddock, halibut, tuna, or salmon may also be used.

The boil begins with a wood fire and a large iron kettle filled with water. When the water comes to a boil, a cup of salt is added and small red potatoes and sometimes onions tied in a cheesecloth bag are dropped in to cook until done. Then the pieces of fish wrapped in cheesecloth and another cup of salt, which helps bring the

A master boiler, as the presiding fish boil cook is called in Door County, Wisconsin, tends his iron kettle on an open fire. Fish boils, using whitefish from Lake Michigan, originated among Scandinavian settlers and lumbermen.

fish oils to the surface, join the vegetables. When all the food is cooked, it is time for the grand finale. The master boiler, as the person in charge of the fish boil is called, throws kerosene on the fire, creating spectacular flames and a great surging boil in the pot. Water rushes over the sides, carrying fish oils with it. At the same time, the overboil cools the water so that the food can be removed. It is customary to serve the fish with melted butter and lemon.

See also: CRAWFISH BOIL; LOBSTER BOIL.

References: Clayton. *Cooking across America*. 1993; Hill. *Festivals U.S.A* . 1988; Stern and Stern. *GoodFood*. 1983.

DOUGHNUTS

Doughnuts, or donuts, have been part of American fare since colonial days, and the first were yeast-raised varieties made at home. Many types of fried cakes in a great variety of shapes have been called doughnuts, but some people insist that a ring-shaped cake with a hole in the center is the *real* doughnut.

A machine to mass-produce doughnuts was invented in the 1920s by Adolph Levitt, who became the American doughnut king, not only selling doughnut machines to bakeries across the United States but also setting up a chain of doughnut shops. There are now hundreds of varieties of cakelike doughnuts made of flour, sugar, shortening, eggs, milk, leavening, and flavorings ranging from vanilla and chocolate to peanut butter and bacon-and-eggs. Doughnuts are cooked in hot fat, then topped with icings and nuts or candies and/or filled with jellies, custards, or other ingredients. Although the chocolate and plain varieties are very popular, the glazed doughnut (made of yeast dough and topped with icing) is the favorite among customers of Dunkin' Donuts, a chain outlet that sells 4 million doughnuts worldwide every day.

In spite of the variety in shape, size, and flavor, doughnuts are served and eaten in routine ways. They are part of countless coffee breaks in North America; they are served traditionally with cider during Halloween and other fall celebrations; they are eaten for breakfast and for midday and midnight snacks, often with a glass of milk; they are featured at fair and festival booths; and often they are fed to the homeless. In the past, doughnuts were a special treat for military personnel serving in World Wars I and II; the Salvation Army prepared and distributed them at U.S. train stations where troops stopped and also on or near European battlefields.

Since the 1930s, doughnuts have been celebrated in songs, poems, and legends and in Broadway shows and movies. One legend says that the ritual of dunking doughnuts in coffee was popularized by actress Mae Murray, who was in the famed New York restaurant Lindy's (known for its cheesecake) having coffee and doughnuts with a friend. Mae accidentally dropped her doughnut in her coffee and her friend deliberately "dunked" a doughnut mimicking Mae as if it were a routine way to eat these sweet, round cakes. Others claim that dunking originated during the Civil War when soldiers dunked their hardtack in coffee in order to soften it; dunking doughnuts was just a natural carryover.

However the dunking practice came about, doughnuts dunked in coffee spawned a National Dunking Association in the 1930s that established rules for dunking: no splashing or getting one's fingers wet while dunking! Most people today, however, have their own particular way of dunking. Some will just barely dip the doughnut in coffee or milk; others will nearly submerge the doughnut; still others will break the doughnut in half and gingerly or aggressively dunk each of the halves before eating them. So popular is dunking, that Dunkin' Donuts has capitalized on it with a chain of doughnut shops by that name, selling at least 52 flavors of doughnuts, one for each week of the year.

The shops as well as other doughnut makers also sell doughnut holes, the portions punched fron the dough, fried, and sugared or left plain. Dozens of other chains also specialize in doughnuts that are sold individually or by the bag or box and often shared at the routine coffee break and as part of refreshments served at meetings and social events.

See also: BREAKFAST; HALLOWEEN; SNACK FOODS.

Reference: Steinberg. *The Donut Book.* 1987.

DRINKING TOASTS

"Wassail! wassail! all over the town/Our bread is white, and our ale it is brown/Our bowl it is made of the maplin tree/So here, my good fellow, I'll drink to thee." This verse from an anonymous seventeenth-century drinking song was in part a toast to someone's good health (the Old English *Waes hael* means "to your health") and also a song associated with a spiced ale served during Christmas and New Year holidays in old England.

From ancient times to the present, people all over the world have raised their cups or glasses filled with wine, beer, or spirits to toast good health or good cheer before downing their drink. Toasting is probably linked to the universal concept of thanking the gods for the basic necessities: food and water. It is a common practice in North America today, and a toast is often prompted when congratulations are in order for someone's good fortune or a special event. Drinkers in a bar or lounge frequently toast one another's good fortune; diners often toast before dinner; wedding guests toast the bride and groom; sports fans toast winners of ball games, horse races, tennis matches, and the like; and toasts are common at birthdays, anniversaries, holidays, and other festive occasions. Some popular toasts are "Here's lookin' at you," "Cheers," "Skoal," and "Salut."

People usually clink their glasses together when making a toast. This ritual is said to stem from ancient practices—during times when it was common to poison one's enemies. Usually the poison was put into the potential victim's wine or other drink. In order to avoid being poisoned, people would switch drinks with each other, but, over the years, the practice changed, and people merely clinked their glasses together, indicating they meant no harm to one another.

See also: BEER DRINKING; BOILERMAKER; SHOOTERS.

References: Baldridge. *The New Manners for the '90s.* 1990; Digby and Digby. *Inspired by Drink.* 1988; Gay. *Keep the Buttered Side Up.* 1995.

DYNGUS DAY

Although Dyngus Day is a popular event in some Polish communities in the United States, it is not a well-known celebration. It stems from an ancient Polish custom observed on the Monday after Easter, but some historians say it may actually be German in origin. Apparently *dyngus* (roughly translated as "to douse" or "to pester") once was related to the Christian ritual of baptism, but it became a kind of playful tradition as buckets, pans, pots, glasses, and cans of water were tossed on unsuspecting females.

Today, Dyngus Day is more a social and political event. One modern version in South Bend, Indiana, began in a Polish neighborhood but became a citywide celebration and a day for parades, socializing, and meeting politicians. Halls, clubs, bars, and restaurants serve kielbasa—a Polish sausage—and beer or other beverages, and such foods as sauerkraut and strudel.

See also: ETHNIC FOOD TRADITIONS.

Reference: Knab. *Polish Customs, Traditions, and Folklore.* 1993.

EARLY-BIRD SPECIAL

A popular marketing scheme for restaurants, the early-bird special has been used for at least two decades, and a number of variations on the concept exist today. Many eating establishments open their doors for dinner at 5:00 or 5:30 P.M., hoping to attract customers during the earlier part of the evening as the kitchen prepares to handle the typical rush period, which usually occurs any time after 6:00 P.M. Typically, only one server is employed to wait on these "early-bird" customers and to take care of a good deal of set-up preparation, since management does not usually expect the customer load to be too heavy during this time.

As the competition for business began to increase in the last decade, restaurant managers began to rethink this "prerush" period in their establishments. Some studied the traffic that was coming in an hour or more before the traditional dinner hour, and they noticed that most of those patrons could be best described as senior citizens. Seniors, as a group, generally rise earlier in the morning and retire earlier in the evening. Naturally, their dinnertime falls much closer to 5:00 P.M. than the 7:00 or 8:00 P.M. dinner of the younger diner. As a rule, seniors tend to eat smaller portions so are not willing to spend large sums on a

meal. Using this data, restaurants have created special limited menus to draw more of this identified group into their establishments. For example, the residents of Leisure Village, a retirement community in Camarillo, California, board the bus every weekday afternoon at 4:30 P.M. to make the trip to Giovanni's Restaurant for a special low-priced offering. Similar plans catering to seniors have been used in other states, such as Arizona and Florida, where there is a large population of retirees. Early-bird specials also appeal to families with small children and to those who have plans for later in the evening. "Two for One," "50 Percent Off," and "Complimentary Desserts" are some of the offers made to attract more business during the early-bird hours.

See also: DISCOUNT DINING.

EASTER

Coloring and decorating hardboiled eggs and hunting for Easter eggs are common rituals during the spring celebration of Easter, which, in the Christian religion, commemorates the resurrection of Jesus Christ. The egg, like the celebration itself, symbolizes new life. Although Easter eggs are prepared more for decorative purposes and for games than for eating, the hardboiled eggs are also peeled and consumed on Easter. Usually they are chopped fine and used in dips, sandwich mixtures, or in various types of salads. The most popular type of edible Easter eggs, however, are candies—chocolate-covered creams, nuts, fruits, and jellies. Chocolate rabbits—Easter bunnies—are even more in demand by both adults and kids, and many chocolate lovers remember the mixed reactions of revulsion and salivation associated with biting off the head of a favorite chocolate bunny. Just one candy company in the United States produces at least 75 million chocolate bunnies for each Easter season.

Other popular Easter confections that also symbolize new life are colorful jelly beans, which usually line the nests of Easter baskets, and marshmallow candy chicks. Easter breads and cakes baked in lamb shapes and covered with frosting and coconut are also traditional.

Meals served on Easter are customarily family or even community affairs and may begin with sunrise breakfast as in the Moravian tradition. As part of a dawn service, Moravian churches conduct a love feast as an expression of unity, serving love feast buns, which are lightly sweetened, Moravian sugar cake made from a sweetened yeast dough, and coffee, which is traditionally served by the men in the congregation. Most family Easter dinners are planned around lamb or ham, although poultry is another popular main entree, and these dinner celebrations may be served in the home or consumed in a restaurant. The families that do dine out help make Easter one of the busiest days of the year for restaurants in the United States.

Those who celebrate the Russian Orthodox Easter mark the day by the Julian calendar, established in 46 B.C. by Julius Caesar. Like its replacement, the Gregorian calendar, the Julian calendar is based on a solar cycle, but it is almost two weeks longer than the Gregorian version. Thus, Eastern churches that abide by the Julian calendar celebrate Christian religious holidays later than do Western churches. Eastern Orthodox usually begin the season with a week of fasting. In the Ukrainian tradition, people prepare a large basket of foods to take to the church on the night before Easter. Some of the foods include smoked meats, hardboiled eggs, Easter breads, and a dish called hrin (horseradish and beets). After the priest blesses the food baskets at midnight, the food can be taken home for the Easter feast. Foods served on an Orthodox Easter Sunday may include such dishes as cabbage rolls stuffed with ground meat and seasonings; egg balls made of slowly cooked eggs, milk, sugar, salt, and vanilla; and a garnish of grated horseradish and red beets.

An Easter dinner in the Greek tradition would likely include spanokopetes (phyllo dough pastries filled with spinach and feta cheese), spit-roasted whole lamb and/or roast chicken, roasted potatoes sprinkled with lemon juice, Greek-style green beans, orzo (rice-shaped pasta), and certainly *lambropsoma*, a special Easter bread baked with hardboiled eggs and sprinkled with sesame seeds. Rich butter cookies called *kourabiethes* would be served for dessert.

A Polish Easter dinner might include such traditional foods as cold beet and cucumber soup, cucumbers in sour cream, kielbasa (Polish garlic sausage) with sauerkraut, and an egg bread with raisins.

See also: GREEK FOOD FESTIVALS; HOT CROSS BUNS; UKRAINIAN FESTIVALS.

References: Betz. *Tastes of Liberty.* 1985; Borghese. *Food from Harvest Festivals and Folk Fairs.* 1977; Davis. *The Potato Book.* 1973; Pavlik. "Even without the Memories, You'll Enjoy These Ukrainian Dishes." 1993.

EATING EXPRESSIONS

Dozens of common English sayings include references to food or to eating and drinking customs. Some of the expressions allude to the importance of obtaining food for survival. "Manna from heaven" is a well-known example, referring to a windfall, a great blessing; the saying stems from the biblical story of the hoar frost on the ground that provided sustenance for Jews escaping bondage in Egypt. When people say they will "keep the pot boiling," they use a phrase that once referred to what was in a container—pot usually meant meat. So, to keep the pot boiling refers to keeping enough food, or other necessities, available to survive.

Some eating expressions refer to status. "Eating high on the hog" suggests that one can afford to buy the best cuts of an animal for meat. To "eat humble pie" is easily understood but probably stems from a misunderstanding: umble pie was an English pasty, a dough filled with edible animal intestines, considered in some cases to be "poor food." But "umble" became humble with later use. "Eating crow" refers to a similar humbling, if not debasing, experience, but it originated from an incident during the War of 1812 in which a soldier was forced to eat a crow as a form of punishment.

References to food, although not necessarily eating, appear in some English expressions that are in common use today. "Polishing the apple" is familiar to anyone who has taken a highly polished apple to the teacher in order to gain favor in her or his eyes. To "pick a bone" with someone is to try to settle a dispute or complaint. Anyone (or anything) "not worth a hill of beans" was of little value since beans were not highly regarded in early England. On the other hand, to be "worth one's salt" reflects the fact that salt was valuable in ancient times; Roman soldiers who "earned their salt" were paid a small allowance to buy this commodity.
See also: PASTY; SALT.
Reference: Funk. *2,107 Curious World Origins, Sayings, and Expressions.* 1993.

EATING OUT

The practice of eating in establishments where food and beverages are served at a cost dates back thousands of years. Ancient travelers were able to buy food and drink in open kitchens along their routes or at countryside monasteries and convents. At most seaports of old, there were usually

places to obtain meals and beverages for a price. In Europe during the 1700s, taverns, coffee houses, or public houses served well-to-do travelers or politicians and traders.

Modern dining establishments in North America have some association with earlier European establishments. Since the late 1800s, however, as an increasing number of people have been able to pay the cost of eating out, restaurants have catered to a growing number and range of customers. For some, eating in a particular restaurant is a way to "be seen"—to show that one is part of an elite group, but for the vast majority of today's diners, eating out is a form of socialization or entertainment as well as a way to satisfy a basic need for sustenance.

According to some estimates, North Americans on average eat at least one or perhaps two meals outside the home on a daily basis. People who habitually eat out have a great number of choices, and sometimes those choices are determined not so much by preferences in food but by preferences in atmosphere and how they feel about a place. Some might routinely go to a bar, pizza place, or other fastfood restaurant after a sports event because the atmosphere is informal and is conducive to boisterous activity. Others may establish a ritual of eating at a fine restaurant after a concert, theater, or other performance to complete an elegant evening out. Gourmet diners and foodies might like to experiment when eating out, checking out a new type of restaurant (often ethnic) once a week or once a month. Another type of diner may habitually go to restaurants that offer a great view of a waterway, of the mountains, or of another naturally beautiful setting. Some frequent a restaurant where she or he has established a rapport with a server or the owner. Businesspeople may routinely select a favorite restaurant (usually one with "character" or "class") to entertain clients or customers.

There are so many choices in eating establishments that most major newspapers carry regular reviews of restaurants, including not only the type and quality of the food but also descriptions of the ambiance, decor, service, and cost. Numerous books and travel and tourist guides also include such information. People use these resources as well as recommendations from friends, relatives, and associates to find restaurants that satisfy diverse needs, not the least of which is to be part of a ritualistic way of eating—in a social setting.

See also: EATING/DINING CLUBS; GOURMET FOODS.

Reference: Finkelstein. *Dining Out.* 1989.

EATING TRENDS

The restaurant industry in North America frequently sets eating trends throughout society. The popularity of a particular type or style of food changes periodically in direct relation to the size of the crowds going out to eat. As diners become sated on a particular food fad, a new one will appear. Certainly, cultural changes and new health-related concerns have driven some of the trends, but even these are turned into marketing opportunities through commercial food service initiatives.

"Nouvelle cuisine" is a prime example. What began in French culinary circles as a revolutionary change in the traditional preparation techniques (less butter and cream, smaller and more artistic portions, unusual combinations, for example) was hyped on the West Coast in the early 1980s as "California cuisine." Food gurus such as Alice Waters and Wolfgang Puck began the trend toward fresh, locally grown, and simply prepared foods. Their ingredients involved such exotic-sounding items as fiddlehead ferns, sundried tomatoes, baby vegetables, and edible flowers. The ingredients were expensive, the portions were small, and meals were usually costly. Chefs and restaurant owners became superstars in this era of rising demand and conspicuous consumption. People wanted to be seen at the rising number of trendy places. With the economic recession of 1991, however, the luxury of the $100 dinner was no longer affordable, and many of the tonier places began initiating a new trend, removing the white tablecloths, introducing

"comfort foods," lowering the prices, and retro-decorating in the 1950s cafe style.

Other recent trends have centered around ethnic cuisines. For example, Cajun food dishes are served in diners, four-star restaurants, and even fastfood places. Carribbean island cuisine is popular in some areas. Sushi and other Japanese delights have been served in many eating establishments, even in some Jewish delis. There is also a trend to combine two or more ethnic cuisines, such as Chinese-Cuban or Mexitalian. Some restaurants create egg rolls filled with pizza ingredients or chicken fajitas in pita bread.

Country cooking once again is prominent in numerous restaurants, perhaps because plainer food is a kind of antidote for the more complex ethnic foods. Although diners overall are not necessarily eating more red meat, those who do eat red meat are eating more expensive cuts, such as steak. Indulging in the best cuts when eating out may be a way to recall the days when fat and high cholesterol were not considered major health problems.

See also: MEAT AND POTATOES; MEAT LOAF.

EATING UTENSILS

For thousands of years people have used their hands as eating or drinking utensils, and continue to do so in many parts of the world. Food may be served in a huge cooking pot or bowl or on a large piece of flat bread or palm leaf, and individuals gather around to take portions with their fingers, sharing the communal dish.

Sharpened sticks and flint knives (which were also used for many other purposes) were the first eating tools, then spoons and chopsticks appeared. Forks, patterned after a forked stick used to roast meats and designed as a two-pronged eating tool, were not common eating utensils until about the 1700s in Europe, and not until the 1800s in North America.

Most Americans now use the familiar knife, fork, and spoon while eating a meal, although chopsticks are the traditional utensils of choice in homes and

Chef Wolfgang Puck displays pizzas in his Los Angeles restaurant. Puck and fellow Californian Alice Waters began a trend during the 1980s of using nontraditional foods, such as fiddlehead ferns and edible flowers, in their cooking.

restaurants that follow Chinese, Japanese, or other Asian eating customs. Whatever the utensils, they have been used for centuries in ritualistic ways, whether during everyday meals or during formal dining. People who use chopsticks, for example, often follow the traditional Chinese practice of picking up a bowl of rice and bringing it chin-high in order to scoop rice with the chopsticks into their mouth. When diners using chopsticks finish a meal, they usually place their utensils across a bowl to indicate that they have had enough to eat.

The rituals connected with knives, forks, and spoons can be quite complex, particularly during formal dinners. Special utensils are provided for specific foods, such as a soup spoon, a long-handled parfait spoon (which might also be used for a tall drink such as iced tea), a salad fork, a dinner fork, a cheese knife (that looks more like a two-pronged fork), or a butter knife. Tongs for sugar cubes may even be on the table. Large serving spoons or ladles and forks might also be provided to use with dishes that are passed from person to person.

These eating utensils are placed on the table in a traditional fashion. Chopsticks are set to the right or just below a plate. The American custom is to place the knife to the right of the plate and the spoon to the right of the knife; the fork goes to the left of the plate. At a formal dinner with numerous courses, the more specialized knives, forks, and spoons may be included with each place setting, arranged according to use. Two forks on the left, for example, may indicate that the first in order is for the salad and the second (nearest the plate) for the main course.

It was once common for people in the United States to use eating utensils in a manner different from European custom. During colonial days it was the practice to hold food on the plate with a spoon in the left hand, while cutting and eating with a knife in the right hand. When forks became common household utensils in the late 1800s, people used the fork as a holding tool, cutting with a knife, then laying the knife on the plate or table in order to transfer the fork to the right hand, considered the "proper" hand to hold an eating device (although left-handed people are likely to argue this point). The European practice, which numerous Canadians and other North Americans follow today, is to cut food with the knife in the right hand, use the knife to slide the pieces to the back of the fork (held in the left hand), which is then used to transfer the food to the mouth.
See also: FINGER BOWL; TABLE MANNERS; TABLECLOTHS.
References: Paston-Williams. *The Art of Dining.* 1993; Visser. *The Rituals of Dinner.* 1991.

EATING/DINING CLUBS

Eating or dining clubs are called a variety of names including gourmet clubs, but they all have one main purpose: members get together to eat or dine (the term used depends on the formality of the club). Such ritual events were common in Europe a century ago, when wealthy men gathered at a well-known restaurant and spent the entire evening eating a multicourse meal and drinking numerous bottles of wine and champagne. That practice was continued in North America, particularly at prestigious universities such as Princeton in New Jersey. In the late 1980s, however,

courts ruled that all-male dining clubs were discriminatory and ordered them to admit female members.

Outside the academic setting, dining clubs composed of singles or couples form to try out restaurants in their local area or within a 50- to 70-mile radius. One person is usually designated to determine the restaurant where members will meet, socialize, and order their meals from menu selections. In other cases, members meet in individual homes, bringing dishes that are prepared to fit a particular theme, such as a Mexican turkey mole dish (turkey in a rich sauce made with chiles and chocolate) as a contribution to an all-chocolate dinner. A dining club in the Washington, D.C., area once held an all-lemon potluck dinner; guests brought a range of lemon-flavored or lemon-garnished dishes, including lemon butter for artichokes, a spinach-lemon dip for appetizers, lemon-flavored salad dressing, green beans with lemon and herb flavorings, lemon-chicken casserole, and desserts such as lemon torte, lemon mousse, and lemon cookies.
See also: DINNER PARTY; PROGRESSIVE DINNER.

EDIBLE FLOWERS

Eating the blooms of plants and using them to make tea have been common practices for centuries. Roses, for example, have been grown especially for making jelly or tea. Carnations and violets are also popular flowers for tea making.

In the mid-1980s, experiments to obtain the latest "new" ingredients for the California cuisine craze brought edible flowers back into the cookbooks. Any restaurant that wanted to compete at that time was garnishing its plates with baby nasturtiums or violet buds. Customers were learning to acquire a taste for the new "vegetables."

The flower of the green or yellow zucchini has been used as a vessel for various fillings for a long time. Either filled or plain, the large blossoms are battered and deep fried to become one of the frittered flower varieties. Some of the other blos-

soms that will hold up as fritter fodder are yucca, lilac, pumpkin, and elderberry.
See also: EATING TRENDS.

EGGNOG

The traditional drink of the Christmas season, eggnog is a richly sweet milk and egg concoction that is now found in a carton in almost any grocer's cold case by Thanksgiving. While some commercial products are quite passable, they pale in comparison to the homemade nogs created over stoves by all of those cooks entertaining family and friends on Christmas and New Year's Eves. In many cases, the holidays would not be the same without a toast with the eggnog cups. The word *nog* is an Old English term for "ale," and many people would cringe today if their eggnog did not have a bit of the old spirits. In fact, most homemade eggnogs have a very high alcohol content.

True eggnog is the result of slowly heated milk, cream, and sugar stirred constantly to avoid scalding. Toward the end of the process, which usually takes place in a kitchen that is ideally filled with festive revelers and Christmas decorations, beaten egg yolks are delicately blended into the pot. Rum, brandy, and/or bourbon is usually added, and the mixture is quickly poured into a silver or crystal bowl. Beaten egg whites are dolloped on top, and freshly grated nutmeg completes the heavenly picture.

It is very easy for a party crowd to consume too much of this heady brew. It is sweet, warm, and luscious and packs a decidedly powerful wallop, depending on the alcohol content. Many a Christmas and New Year's Day hangover has been blamed on eggnog that was "too good."
See also: CHRISTMAS EVE/DAY DINNER; DRINKING TOASTS; NEW YEAR'S DAY; NEW YEAR'S EVE.

EGGS BENEDICT

Stories about the origin of this dish attribute it to several Benedicts. One story says that Lemuel Benedict, a Wall Street stockbroker, came up with the idea; another says that Mr. and Mrs. LeGrand Benedict, who were regular customers of the famous Delmonico's Restaurant in New York City, were the inventors. Wherever it originated, eggs Benedict has been popular since the late 1800s or early 1900s.

Arguably the most favorite Sunday brunch order, this rich and wonderful dish is packed with cholesterol, but those who indulge push guilt aside. Two toasted English muffins make a bed for slices of grilled Canadian bacon, which are in turn topped with two perfectly done poached eggs. The whole affair is then covered liberally with a ladle of Hollandaise sauce and the lightest garnish of truffle, paprika, or parsley. During the 1980s, this dish was so popular with customers at Voilá Cafe in Ventura, California, that out of the 90 to 120 brunches typically served on a Sunday, 50 to 60 included eggs Benedict.

An interesting variation of this dish is the Royal Wedding. In place of Canadian bacon, a piece of lightly sautéed filet mignon is placed on the muffins. After the poached egg is laid on, Bearnaise sauce substitutes for the Hollandaise, creating an absolutely decadent dish. This is, indeed, what eating Sunday brunch in a restaurant is all about.
See also: SUNDAY BRUNCH.

EINTOPF

Originally a "poor-man's food," or peasant meal, *eintopf* is a traditional German soup or stew, a one-dish meal cooked in a pot over low heat or in a slow oven. It is usually made with a meat or poultry stock, potatoes and other vegetables, and rice or barley. For vegetarians or those watching their weight, an all-vegetable *eintopf* is popular. These one-dish meals are served at many German festivals or family gatherings throughout North America.
See also: ETHNIC FOOD TRADITIONS; OKTOBERFEST.

ENCHILADAS

A common food in the southwestern United States, enchiladas are made with corn or white flour tortillas, which are layered with cheese, onions, salsa, and meat. While the enchilada is not a national dish in Mexico, it is Mexican in flavor and is one of several popular foods that combine American and Mexican cuisine. Chicken and beef enchiladas are especially popular in the United States and are featured at many restaurants serving Mexican-style food. Various types of enchiladas are special features at folk festivals celebrating Mexican culture and at food fairs across the Southwest. In fact, the Whole Enchilada Festival has been held in Las Cruces, New Mexico, each October since 1980. The weekend festival in 1993 highlighted an enchilada that was 8 feet in diameter, with each tortilla weighing 25 pounds. It was layered with 175 pounds of cheese, 60 gallons of salsa, and 50 pounds of onions, and it cost around $6,500 to make, according to a restaurant owner who donated the ingredients. Some 8,000 of the 200,000 festival goers received portions of the enchilada.

See also: CHILES; HUEVOS RANCHEROS; MEXICAN FIESTAS.

EPIPHANY FEAST

From the Greek word *epiphaneia* meaning "appearance" or "revelation," Epiphany celebrates several major events in the life of Jesus—the visit of the Magi to the infant Jesus (commemorated as All Kings Day in Mexico), the baptism of Jesus, and the first miracle of transforming water into wine. Epiphany is observed on 6 January, marking the last day of the Christmas season, but the entire 12 days of Christmas are a time for festivities in parts of the United States and Canada. Many Catholics begin celebrating after the Christmas Eve midnight mass on 24 December. They continue to celebrate with much eating, drinking, gift giving, and visiting until Epiphany.

A Twelfth Night celebration, usually held on the evening of 5 January if Christmas is counted as the first day of the period, includes a Twelfth Night cake. The cake and the customs surrounding Twelfth Night stem from an ancient Roman custom that carried over to England. A huge cake was baked with a pea and a bean inside, and when the cake was cut and served, the male receiving the slice with a bean was crowned king for the night and the female whose slice contained the pea became queen.

Grand balls and huge parties were typical Twelfth Night celebrations in the British colonies of North America, but over the years the festivities became less elaborate and today are remembered with a buffet table, including meat and fish dishes, pastries, nuts, candies, a wassail bowl, and the Twelfth Night cake made with a rich egg batter, raisins, currants, candied fruits, nuts, and spices. For ceremonial purposes and entertainment, the cake is still likely to include the bean and the pea.

See also: ALL KINGS DAY; WASSAIL AND WASSAIL BOWL.

Reference: MacDonald. *The Folklore of World Holidays.* 1992.

ESPRESSO BARS

Espresso is a type of coffee and a method of brewing. It begins with dark roasted coffee beans that are ground very fine and hot water held in the tank of an espresso machine. The water is forced under pressure through tightly packed grounds. (Most other coffee is brewed by allowing hot water to percolate over or drip through loose grounds.) At most espresso bars and upscale coffee shops, espresso is made one cup at a time, and it is usually served in a preheated demitasse cup accompanied by a sugar cube or lemon twist—a tiny slice of lemon that when squeezed over the coffee provides just a dash of lemon juice to "cut" the bitterness of the brew.

Originating in France during the 1800s, the first espresso machine brewed large pots of coffee, but around the early 1900s, Italians began to develop espresso machines to produce single cups of coffee. Most Europeans drink a form of espresso called cappuccino, which is about one-third coffee and two-thirds steamed milk, served in a 5-ounce heated cup and topped with frothed milk. Although not a European custom, cappuccino in North America is often garnished with sprinkles of chocolate, cinnamon, or nutmeg.

Commonly served in European-style restaurants in North America, both espresso and cappuccino became popular in a wide variety of eating establishments after World War II. In the 1980s and early 1990s, an increasing number of espresso bars and upscale coffee shops serving espresso as well as other coffees were established across the continent, and more are cropping up in the late 1990s. Mobile espresso/cappucino bars—espresso carts—are also common, particularly in Seattle and other West Coast cities, and espresso/cappuccino bars are frequently part of catered events, such as dessert parties, open houses, and receptions.

Wherever espresso is served, variations of the brew are usually offered. These include cafe latte (from the French *cafe au lait* and the Spanish *cafe con leche*), which is a double serving of espresso with steamed milk served in a bowl-shaped cup; espresso ristretto (meaning "restricted") in which the flow of water is stopped at about 1 ounce to produce a more dense brew than the normal espresso; and espresso lungo, a diluted or milder form of espresso.
See also: COFFEE HOUSES.
Reference: Davids. *Coffee.* 1987.

ETHNIC FOOD TRADITIONS

Throughout North America, ethnic food traditions are maintained in countless homes. People who emigrated from Europe, Asia, Africa, and South America, as well as from island nations, brought with them food customs that have been preserved in cookbooks, passed on by word of mouth, or maintained just because people have followed traditional patterns of eating and drinking in their own homes. People of Italian heritage, for example, may routinely prepare eggplant dishes,

pasta with a tomato and meat sauce or pasta with olive oil, perhaps *pasta e fagioli* (pasta and beans), and Italian pastries.

Among the Scandinavians whose ancestors immigrated in the early 1900s and settled primarily in the Midwest and in such states as the Dakotas and Washington, foods such as cured salmon, herring salad, liver pâté, a creamed potato-onion-anchovy dish called Jansson's Temptation, and lutefisk are common. The British may enjoy such dishes as steak and kidney pie, welsh rarebit, and perhaps trifle—a dessert made of several alternate layers of sponge cake, fruits, and custard, sprinkled with brandy or sherry, garnished with whipped cream, and refrigerated before serving. People of French extraction may routinely eat dishes such as onion soup, ratatouille (eggplant casserole), bouillabaisse (fish stew), scalloped potatoes, and, of course, French bread. Russian favorites include beef stroganoff and borscht—a hearty soup of stew meat, cabbage, and beets garnished with sour cream, and *blinis* (pancakes) served in a stack wrapped in a cloth to keep them warm and accompanied by a variety of spreads such as mashed sardines, smoked salmon, and hardboiled eggs. At a Serbian home or gathering such as a picnic, some traditional foods are roasted meat with plenty of garlic, spinach pies, and *palatchinke,* a rolled pancake filled with cottage cheese or fruit preserves.

Paella, a saffron rice dish made with seafood and chicken, is a favorite Spanish dish, as is gazpacho. Jamaicans who have settled primarily in New York City and Miami also enjoy these foods and are likely to serve such dishes as ox tail stew flavored with plenty of allspice or curried goat or lamb. A dish of rice and beans is a traditional accompaniment to most Jamaican meals.

Among Middle Easterners, some traditional dishes include a fine-grain wheat dish called couscous and a type of "salad" called tabouleh—a mixture of cooked bulgur wheat, parsley, chopped red bell peppers, onions, celery, tomatoes, and mint tossed with olive oil, lemon, and various spices.

Many Asian groups—Cambodians, Chinese, Japanese, Thais, and Vietnamese among them—have maintained some eating customs of long standing. For example, a popular Korean dish is kimchee, spicy pickled cabbage. Traditional Japanese meals include miso, a fermented soybean paste that is used to make marinades, to make soups, and to flavor other foods. Sake, a rice wine, and sushi are traditionally Japanese as well.

Wherever these and many other ethnic dishes originated, they have become familiar and are part of the American way of life because they have been served at ethnic restaurants, food shops, festivals and fairs, and street-vendor carts and kiosks. Ethnic food festivals also help introduce people to traditional foods from other lands. In the San Francisco Bay area, for example, a two-day October ethnic food festival has been conducted since the 1940s by the St. John's Armenian Church and features full-course dinners as well as take-out food. For the 1994 festival, cooks prepared 5,000 grape leaves for a rice roll called sarma and 1,000 pounds of lamb for shish kebab and kufta—a type of meatball.

See also: AMERICAN FOLKLIFE FESTIVAL; ATLANTIC ANTIC; BASTILLE DAY; CHINESE NEW YEAR; CHRISTMAS EVE/DAY DINNER; CINCO DE MAYO; DANISH DAYS; DIWALI; DYNGUS DAY; FEAST OF SAN GENNARO; FIESTA FILIPINIANA; GREEK FOOD FESTIVALS; GREEN CORN FESTIVALS; LAS POSADAS; MEXICAN FIESTAS; NATIVE AMERICAN FEASTS; UKRAINIAN FESTIVALS.
References: Algren. *America Eats.* 1992; Betz. *Tastes of Liberty.* 1985; Simon and Howe. *Dictionary of Gastronomy.* 1970; Smith. *The Frugal Gourmet on Our Immigrant Ancestors.* 1990.

EUCHARIST

A sacramental ritual, the Eucharist, from the Greek word *eukharistos* for "gratitude" or "thankful," has been performed since early Christian times. According to New Testament accounts, Jesus Christ inaugurated the ritual when he met with his disciples at the Last Supper before his crucifixion and declared, in symbolic terms, that bread represented his body and wine his blood. He instructed his disciples to continue to partake of the bread and wine in remembrance of his death. Celebration of the Eucharist, which may be called the Holy Communion, the Lord's Supper, or the Mass, has been part of Christian worship ever since. At first it was only celebrated on Easter, then in the early days of the Christian church it was observed each Sunday or on a daily basis, depending on where Christian groups were located. Today, most Christians in North America and around the world observe the sacrament by partaking of a bread cube, cracker, or wafer and wine or grape juice as an expression of their faith and remembrance of Christ's death.
See also: EASTER.
Reference: Parrinder. *World Religions.* 1983.

EXECUTIVE DINING

In the 1980s, one of the desirable perks of higher management was access to the executive dining room, which was common in corporations that could afford to treat their top people like the chosen few. Companies set up an on-site kitchen and dining room where chefs and waiters would turn out a spread fit for the gentry. Guests would be wined and dined in sometimes extravagant manner. Lunches could be two or three hours on special occasions; the tab was always picked up by the company. In recent years, downsizing has taken a toll on this practice. Top-heavy management structures are falling away. The distribution of decision making has broadened to include many more workers in a corporation, and even the time-honored tradition of separate lunchrooms for management and workers has lost favor. Now, if executives even stop for lunch, it is frequently in a cafeteria or similar lunchroom to eat with the "common folk."
See also: CAFETERIA DINING.

FAMILY DINNER

Formal family dinners were very much a part of nineteenth-century American life, especially for those who could afford a meal of several courses. Those dinners, according to historian Susan Williams, "began with either soup or fish and appetizers. A roast or some other form of meat or poultry accompanied by assorted vegetables followed, and the meal ended with something sweet." Croquettes made of veal, chicken, or fish were also common fare at family dinners, as were mashed potatoes and gravy. Usually the final course was a pudding or pie—considered the most common American dessert.

The ritual of having formal family dinners continued throughout the early part of the 1900s, and advertising, magazine photographs, plays, movies, television shows, and other media frequently depicted family members gathered around a formal dining table. The customary gathering, however, is fading among modern North American families, as members scatter in various directions during evening hours when dinner or supper is usually served. In fact, one home economics teacher in the Washington, D.C., area reported in 1993 that many of her students never ate a meal with their families, and even when in the home at dinnertime they usually went to separate rooms to eat.

Younger children, the teacher noted, often had to be taught to sit down to eat, since the children were used to such informal eating situations as eating carry-out food while walking down the street.

Nevertheless, the traditional family meal, with all in a household gathering to eat together, whether at breakfast, lunch, or supper/dinner, is still observed by numerous Americans. Some families attempt to share an evening meal most days of the week; others may set aside only one time during the week, such as Sunday morning or Saturday night, for family meals. Still others may manage a family meal just on special occasions such as birthdays or holidays. A family meal that brings together many extended family members as well as the nuclear family is also a common occurrence at birthdays, anniversaries, and holiday celebrations.

See also: FAMILY REUNION; SUNDAY DINNER.
References: Visser. *The Rituals of Dinner.* 1991; Williams. *Savory Suppers and Fashionable Feasts.* 1985.

FAMILY REUNION

The gathering of the clan, or a family reunion, is one of the most traditional events in North America. Extended families

Family-style dinner in the kitchen with the television family of Cliff and Clair Huxtable (Bill Cosby and Phylicia Rashad) of "The Cosby Show."

gather each year in a park pavilion, conference room in a hotel or motel, or in some other public place or private home to "eat, drink, and be merry" as members catch up on births, weddings, deaths, and other information about one another's lives. Some family reunions are held in rural areas where extended family members live close by, although it is not unusual for people to travel hundreds or thousands of miles to attend a family reunion.

The Anderson family reunion in Illinois, for example, has brought people from all parts of the United States. It began in 1923 in the village of Donovan, Illinois, with the third generation of descendants of Swedish immigrants who came to the United States in the late 1800s. Anderson reunions have been held ever since, primarily in rural Donovan but also in other Illinois sites, on the first Sunday of August each year to celebrate the family history and ancestors. Family members usually gather in a park and share a noon meal that includes traditional carry-in dishes such as gelatin molds, potato salad, baked beans, Swedish meatballs, fried chicken, corn-on-the-cob, various types of vegetable

casseroles, and desserts ranging from brownies to homemade fruit pies.

Since its inception in Washington, D.C., in 1986, a huge gathering called the Black Family Reunion for the Southeast has been held annually in various cities, such as Atlanta, Cincinnati, Chicago, Memphis, Los Angeles, and Philadelphia. The event has drawn between 5,000 and 6,000 people to celebrate the strength of the black family. Initiated by Dr. Dorothy Height, president of the National Council of Negro Women, the reunion emphasizes family values and spirituality. Although no special foods are associated with the reunion, a community breakfast has become a routine part of the celebration.

The family *boucherie* is a type of family reunion among people of Cajun ancestry in south Louisiana. It is an old-fashioned meat-butchering event at which a hog is slaughtered, cleaned, cut into parts, and shared with participants. Cracklins are usually made at the time and are served as snack foods. Another common Cajun food, *boudin*, is made at the butchering as well. By custom, women usually make the *boudin* by cooking the bony parts of the butchered hog and pulling the meat from the bones to grind and mix with seasonings and cooked rice. The mixture is then stuffed into sausage casings. Besides these foods, rice dishes and such pork dishes as backbone stew and hogshead cheese are made and served.

See also: CASSEROLE DISHES/MEALS; CRACKLINGS; FAMILY DINNER; RICE DISHES.

Reference: Gutierrez. *Cajun Foodways*. 1992.

FASTFOOD

An estimated 16 to 20 percent of total food purchases in the United States now go to fastfood establishments. The gross amount spent on going out to eat at these restaurants approaches $64 billion annually. There is no doubt that the convenience of no wait, inexpensive, and ubiquitous fastfood has had a major impact on the economy and the culture of the Western world. It is not uncommon to find this American innovation in the far reaches of Europe, Africa, Australia, and Asia. To cite two examples, there is a McDonald's on the Champs Élysée and a Kentucky Fried Chicken (KFC) in Moscow.

For many people around the world, fastfood is a defining segment of American life, and it would be difficult to argue that it is not. Competing enterprises take up retail space on all of the key intersections in most cities and towns in the United States. McDonald's, one of the first franchised fastfood chains, started in the 1950s and quickly popularized its concept for preprocessed and precooked food.

The consuming public has come to expect their food immediately: hot and convenient, and, in the vernacular of just one of the pervasive advertising campaigns, they want to "have it their way!" Choices for fastfood establishments are seemingly endless. Burger King, Wendy's, KFC, Jack-in-the-Box, Pizza Hut, and Taco Bell are just a few of the multinational players who have refined the concept of the "centralized kitchen," where all of the product is prepared, packaged, and other-

wise readied for delivery to the retail store outlet. Once there, the portions are cooked (usually fried) and ready for sale in less than five minutes.

The giant chains, however, do not have a monopoly on the concept. Many of the finer restaurants, which traditionally would never even open a can to prepare their gourmet meals, have instituted the practice of purchasing premade frozen entrees, desserts, and so on from vendor companies. These "gourmet" products are heated in the microwave, dressed up, and served to unsuspecting patrons who are more than willing to continue to pay the high prices that they paid for fresh foods.

The convenience and speed of popular restaurant chains are promoted through television advertising. The budgets for the fastfood industry's campaigns are astronomical, and they are keyed to current special events taking place in society. The latest trend has been tying in a popular movie with on-site promotions and packaging of products at the fastfood chains. Whatever the scheme, the goal is to get the masses to visit the food outlets more than once every week. For some, the fastfood restaurant has become a "destination" or "hangout," where they can socialize with friends.

FASTING

In the epic *Hiawatha*, Henry Wadsworth Longfellow tells readers that Hiawatha "prayed and fasted in the forest" not for triumph and renown "but for profit of the people, for advantage of the nations." Longfellow's hero, like so many others of legend throughout the ages, used the technique of fasting to cleanse his spirit in order to reach an apex in physical well-being and/or spirituality. Hiawatha saw visions and fought three times with "the Master of Life descending, . . . the friend of man, Mondamin." In the end, his purity and heightened awareness led him to victory over the spirit, which in turn gave his people a bountiful harvest of corn. In the present time, fasting is usually related to a health or weight concern, but increasingly it is recommended (as it has been throughout history) as an ascetic meditation, or a means to get in touch with other levels of consciousness.

The practice of completely or partially abstaining from food for long or short time periods is centuries old. Most of the world's great religions include a fasting element: Yom Kippur in Judaism, Ramadan in Islam, and Lent in Christianity are examples. Hindus of India frequently fast, sometimes to honor a deity, to prevent evil, or to obtain a reward. Prayer is a critical element in this spiritual ritual wherein the adherent abstains from a normal lifestyle to atone for sins and transgressions of the preceding year.

Recent scientific research suggests that fasting may have physical and mental benefits that were heretofore only promised by gurus and other spiritual advisors. Always a tool of the alternative medicine community, the therapeutic fast is now finding its way into the repertoire of mainstream health practitioners. Based on studies done in Sweden, many medical doctors and nutritionists are prescribing specific fasts for patients who are overweight, cancerous, arthritic, or complaining of a whole range of common maladies.

The theory is simple. In the process of aging, diseased, dead, and dying cells take up room in the bodies of all of us. The accumulation of too many of these useless cells leads to any number of symptomatic complaints and general ill health. By fasting, or eliminating 100 percent of the normal diet and replacing it with specific foods and juices, the experts believe that the body will be free to eliminate the dead matter from its system.

Many people now regularly fast at least once per year. A group of Californians, for example, gets together in the spring each year to take part in The Master Cleanser or as they call it, "The Master Blaster" fast. The first few days of weaning from regular food can be difficult for most people. Usually the main complaint is of headaches due to caffeine withdrawal, but the pain subsides by the second or third day. The social interaction and commit-ment of the California group goes a long way toward supporting all of the participants as they get through the more trying manifestation of "doing without." The group meets at a different house each night for ten days to tell tales, commiserate, and share hints about the experience, and they all drink their glasses of the concoction that is sustaining them for the duration—distilled water mixed with fresh lemon juice, grade C maple syrup, and cayenne pepper. By the fourth or fifth day, almost all of the participants report feeling no hunger and a substantial increase in their energy levels and spiritual well-being.

For those who have never tried to do without food for an extended period of time, this practice may seem very contradictory to attaining physical health; when one is fasting in this culture, it is very difficult to find a sympathetic or knowledgeable voice within a group of peers or relatives. For this reason fasting with a partner or with a group is a popular alternative for those who believe there are benefits in the practice.

See also: DIETS; EASTER; LENT; RAMADAN; YOM KIPPUR.

References: Airola. *Are You Confused?* 1971; Burroughs. *Healing for the Age of Enlightenment.* 1976; Farb and Armelagos. *Consuming Passions.*

FEAST OF SAN GENNARO

The Feast of San Gennaro has been called New York City's most famous street fair. It is an 11-day event that started in 1925 and continues to attract millions of people. Indeed, the feast or festival has been described in numerous festival guides and food books, and it draws tourists from across the United States as well as many residents from other New York neighborhoods. There is no doubt that it is a special social event that includes a great amount of robust and ritualistic eating and drinking. Held each September in Little Italy, the oldest Italian quarter of New York City, the festival honors the patron saint (San Gennaro, or St. Januarius) of descendants of immigrants who came from Naples, Italy, to North America during the late 1800s and early 1900s.

While solemn religious ceremonies are part of the festival, the event also focuses on traditional Neapolitan foods, which are served from outdoor wagons or booths. Attendees often dine al fresco fashion, sampling one food item after another. The offerings include calzone, a type of turnover made from a yeast dough that is stuffed with cheeses and ham, or any other type of filling the cook prefers, and deep-fried. Sausage sandwiches with hot peppers and onions, mini pizzas, eggplant, and various seafoods such as oysters and clams are other popular foods. For dessert, most festival goers try an Italian ice or some type of Italian pastry such as *zeppole,* a deep-fried pastry flavored with mace and covered with powdered sugar. Regardless of the choice, dessert is likely to be accompanied by a shot of espresso coffee.

See also: ATLANTIC ANTIC; NINTH AVENUE FOOD FESTIVAL; TASTE OF . . . FESTIVALS.
References: Borghese. *Food from Harvest Festivals and Folk Fairs.* 1977; Davis. *The Potato Book.* 1973.

FIESTA FILIPINIANA

Philippine independence is celebrated on 12 June, the day Filipinos declared their independence from Spain in 1898. In southern California, where there is a large Filipino population, the two-day independence celebration features ceremonies giving thanks for the harvest. Traditional Filipino food is served, such as mung beans with pork; lumpia, a Filipino version of an egg roll made with chopped pork, shrimp, cabbage, green beans, scallions, and bean sprouts, rolled in lumpia wrappers, and cooked in hot oil; and Filipino ponsit, a rice noodle dish with pork, sausage, garlic, onions, leeks, and fish sauce.

See also: ETHNIC FOOD TRADITIONS; TASTE OF . . . FESTIVALS.

FINGER BOWL

The finger bowl is rarely seen in North America today except at some formal dinners. If used, this utensil, which is a glass bowl of water with a floating flower or lemon slice, is presented just before dessert to each diner, who fastidiously rinses off sticky fingers. Stories have been told of diners who are unfamiliar with this practice and have mistaken the finger bowl as some type of soup or beverage, picking it up and drinking the whole thing.

At some informal dinners, a finger bowl is useful when foods must be picked up and eaten with the hands—corn-on-the-cob, lobster, barbecued ribs, and clams, for example. As an alternative to finger bowls, guests at a dinner party may be presented with steaming towels to wipe their fingers and hands.

See also: EATING UTENSILS; TABLE MANNERS.

FIREHOUSE FOOD

Traditionally, members of a platoon working a shift at a fire station share a communal lunch or dinner, and someone on duty has the job of cooking the meal. The cook either volunteers to prepare all the meals or to serve on a rotation basis. At one time firehouse meals were the meat-and-potatoes variety washed down with soda pop or coffee, but now fire fighters are more health conscious. It is not unusual for a large salad and plenty of fresh cooked vegetables to be on the table. Soups and hearty stews are popular because they can be left simmering on the stove if the platoon has to race out to a fire.

In large cities, fire station meals may be based on the ethnic traditions of a neighborhood where the firehouse is located since it is common practice for firehouse cooks to buy groceries from nearby stores. In towns and cities across the United States, fire fighters also make it a practice to help out with community events that feature food, perhaps flipping pancakes for a fund-raising breakfast, preparing huge

kettles of chili, or barbecuing chicken or ribs to be sold at a fund-raiser.
See also: COMMUNAL DINING.

FISH AND CHIPS

Pub food from England, fish and chips are deep fried and traditionally served in a basket lined with paper. "Chips," on the other side of the Atlantic are what North Americans call french fries. Haddock and cod, and other firm white fish are thickly breaded and cooked in hot oil. Done correctly, neither the fish nor the chips should taste greasy.

Many eating establishments throughout Canada and the United States specialize in this dish today. Sometimes fish and chips is nothing more than a fastfood specialty, but in places like Victoria, British Columbia (the most Anglicanized city outside of the United Kingdom), the English descendants have remained true to the authentic British fare. It is still possible to pick up an order of fish and chips, topped with the traditional malt vinegar and wrapped in newspaper.
See also: FASTFOOD.

FISH FRY

The fish fry is a popular way for nonprofit groups to raise money. Throughout North America, groups such as the Veterans of Foreign Wars (VFW), the Kiwanis, the Elks, school districts, and churches in towns of various sizes hold an annual fish fry. Typically, the fare is very simple and inexpensive and is served on paper plates. Local club members or organizers are usually the ones who are in charge of the preparation, promotion, cooking, serving, and clean up duties.

An annual May fish fry that is an integral part of the Rhododendron Festival of Port Townsend, Washington, is typical of many such dinners held all over the continent. The "Rhody Fish Fry" is held in the basement of the VFW Hall after all of the parades, dances, and shows of the festive

week are completed. For the occasion, many banquet tables are covered in red-and-white checkered tablecloths, and all who attend sit together, family-style. The menu includes a surprisingly tasty deep-fried white fish, corn-on-the-cob, homemade coleslaw, bread, and beverages. Proceeds from the dinner are used to pay for the expenses of putting on the festival each year.

On the third weekend in June each year, a major fish fry called the Festival of the Fish is held in Vermillion, Ohio, a historic fishing community on the shores of Lake Erie. Although, like with other festivals, there are many attractions, the focus is on fried fish, usually served with french fries and coleslaw or a vegetable.
See also: CATFISH FRY.
Reference: Schulz. *Celebrating America.* 1994.

FLAVORED COFFEE

Before the introduction of flavored coffee, those who did not like black or strong coffee had to rely on the traditional additives of cream and/or sugar to moderate the taste. The preference for and aggressive marketing of flavored coffee apparently began in the 1960s when powdered instant coffees were mixed with vanilla, chocolate, or spices. Consumers who routinely bought these coffees usually served them for special occasions.

During the 1970s, flavorings were injected into the coffee bean itself, and gourmet flavored coffee was born. Many people who only had an occasional cup of coffee before have found favorite flavors for certain meals or occasions. Americans in their twenties have made this a very profitable market in the 1990s, opening businesses specializing in coffee drinks—coffee shops and espresso bars—where coffee lovers can enjoy a favorite cup of coffee any time of day, such as after work or the theater.

The most popular coffee flavors—according to sales figures—are chocolate, vanilla, and nut, but choices on grocery shelves seem almost endless. Some of the recently marketed flavors are: Irish creme, hazelnut, chocolate cherry, cinnamon vanilla, cookies and cream, macadamia nut, and raspberry creme. These coffees, like their plain forefathers, are also sold in the decaffeinated form.

Nearly all flavoring additives are artificial, but there is a growing demand for natural ingredients. Organic chemists are working with coffee bean plants and DNA, with the hope of someday growing beans with a natural flavor already included. For now, however, natural flavoring is accomplished by inserting such ingredients as coconut or chopped nuts into the bag with the beans.

See also: COFFEE; EXPRESSO BARS.
Reference: Pool. "Flavored Coffee Has the Taste of Success." 1994.

FLAVORED ICE

The flavored ices consumed in North America come in a variety of forms such as Snow Cones, slushes, and Slurpees. They are made with shaved ice blended with a sweet, flavored syrup and may be dispensed from machines in convenience stores or purchased from street or mall vendors. They are also part of the traditional items sold from booths at fairs, festivals, and amusement parks. These icy drinks (some of which literally have to be slurped) are actually variations of sorbets and crushed ice with flavoring that have been popular food items in Europe for centuries.

They may stem from an old practice of mixing snow with honey and fruit or other flavorings. During the first signs of spring in North America, when the sap begins to run in the maple trees, people in maple syrup–producing areas (parts of Canada, New England, and the Midwest) still prepare and consume "sugar on snow"—maple syrup poured over freshly fallen snow. Other types of flavored ices include smoothies that are popular beach drinks made with blended fruits and shaved ice, pure fruit ices that are a blend of pureed fruits and unsweetened fruit juices and sometimes beaten egg whites, and Italian ices made with shaved ice and sweetened fruit syrup.

See also: SORBETS AND GRANITAS.
References: Stern and Stern. *Real American Food.* 1986; Tarantino. *Sorbets!* 1988.

FLAVORED LIQUOR

Aquavit, gin, rum, vodka—these are some of the spirits that have taken on new flavors since the 1980s and have become popular in North America. These liquors include vodka flavored with fruit, herbs, or pepper; spiced rum and tequila; and lemon-flavored gin. Flavored liquors may be prepared commercially or at home, and they are usually used in mixed drinks or are served straight or over ice as cocktails.

See also: COCKTAILS.

FLAVORED NUTS

Cinnamon-glazed almonds, chile hot cashews, honey-roasted mixed nuts, peanuts flavored with cheese and garlic, and walnuts stir-fried Chinese-style are just a few of the treats that have become standard gifts during the Christmas season. When flavored nuts are prepared as homemade gifts, they are usually presented in decorative glass jars, bowls, or other fancy containers. They are also routinely served at cocktail parties and are popular snack foods.

See also: NUTS AND SEEDS; SNACK FOODS.

FLAVORED OILS

Flavored oils are always popular as gifts, and they have been used in the kitchens of gourmet cooks for years. Highly aromatic herbs such as garlic or rosemary work very well as infusers of their particular flavors when placed in a container filled with a good quality oil. Normally used as a replacement for regular oil in a salad dressing recipe, the flavored varieties can be used to add a distinct taste to lightly sautéed foods, too. Annatto or achiote

seeds, usually used as a yellow coloring for cheese and butter, are often added to oil not only for color in sautéeing but also for subtle flavoring. An infusion of cilantro in olive oil is yet another possibility for flavored oil. Often, a flavored oil will be paired with a complementary flavored vinegar as a homemade gift during the Christmas season.
See also: FLAVORED VINEGAR.

FLAVORED VINEGAR

The trend in the last few years is to eliminate as many sources of fat from the traditional diet as possible. As an alternative to high-fat, oil-based salad dressings, vinegars that have been infused with the subtle flavors of various herbs and spices are now very popular. Any good wine vinegar, red or white, is the perfect vehicle for a flavored product. While now found on the grocer's shelf, the best vinegars are usually obtained in the home adding the freshest ingredients available. Garlic, raspberries, strawberries, blueberries, thyme, basil, oregano, rosemary, and whole red chiles are popular flavorings for vinegars. Many imaginative cooks buy decorative bottles and fill them with visually pleasing herbs or fruits and a fine vinegar. Sometimes they even decorate the bottles with a bow. After curing for at least two weeks, the vinegar may be used for creating culinary delights, or it may become a highly prized gift for the holiday season, a housewarming, or another festive occasion.
See also: FOOD BASKETS; OIL AND VINEGAR.

FONDUE PARTY

During the 1970s, one of the most popular food fads was "fonduing"—serving hot melted cheese from a fondue pot along with bread cubes, which were speared with two-pronged, long-handled forks and dipped into the hot melted cheese. (The term *fondue* comes from the French verb *fondre*, meaning "to melt.") This ritualistic eating pattern soon went out of style, however, and today many fondue pots end up at garage sales or hidden away for posterity. Yet during the 1990s, some people have begun to try to revive the fondue custom, and fondue recipes are reappearing in many cookbooks.
See also: CHEESE TASTING.

FOOD BASKETS

Almost every supermarket and gourmet shop plus some restaurants specializing in ethnic or natural foods offer decorative baskets filled with prepared and/or fresh food items for holiday (especially Easter and Christmas) gift giving. By far, most food baskets are given—and their contents consumed—during the Christmas season, and baskets with fresh fruit and nuts or cheeses, ham and other preserved meats, and wine are the most traditional. Many food baskets, particularly those from gourmet stores and restaurants, contain freshly baked cookies, fruit-filled cakes, chocolate candies, crackers and breads, flavored vinegars and oils, chutneys, jams, and jellies. Oil and tomato sauces that are specialties of the house are common gift basket items in Italian restaurants. Mail-order firms also offer a great variety of food-and-beverage baskets and boxes, which are sold all year but are particularly popular during the holiday seasons.
See also: BREAD; CHOCOLATE CANDY; COOKIES; FLAVORED NUTS; FLAVORED OILS; FLAVORED VINEGAR; GOURMET FOODS.

FOOD COURTS

The food court is a concept unique to the shopping mall experience in America. Modern shopping malls are designed for optimal accessibility and efficient traffic flow. This is done, of course, to ensure a maximum revenue for all of the businesses that have leased space therein. The placement of particular types of stores is all a part of the scheme. Large department stores are the "anchors," but food courts may even be more important to keeping the customers on the property.

Anywhere from two to ten (or even more) food outlets, often located around a common eating area of tables, chairs, and occasionally a central depository for utensils, napkins, and condiments, sell a broad array of consumables. Stuffed baked potatoes, Orange Julius drinks, pasta dishes, pizza, tacos, Chinese buffet food, lemonade, cinnamon buns, popcorn of many flavors, cookies, muffins, candy, espresso, coffee, sushi, Thai food, smorgasbords, and frozen yogurt are just a few of the foods displayed for sale out of these highly efficient fast feeders. Some food purveyors have enough drawing power to actually have their own "courts." McDonald's, Burger King, Pizza Hut, and Kentucky Fried Chicken (KFC), all fastfood giants, can corner a whole section in some malls. Inclusion of these restaurants in shopping destinations where hundreds of retail outlets are located has helped fuel the establishment of a new shopping tradition in North America. Many people find the mall to be a mainstay of their week. Shopping is not done to procure goods only. It is very much an entertainment, a diversion. One need not even leave the confines of the mall to have a bite of food from an incredible diversity of sources.

See also: AIRPORT DINING/DRINKING; CHINESE BUFFET; COOKIE BARS/SHOPS; EXPRESSO BARS; FOOD EVENTS; FOOD FAIRS; SUSHI AND SUSHI BARS; TACO BARS AND RESTAURANTS.

FOOD EVENTS

A step above food festivals or food fairs, food events are held annually in North America and are usually lavish weekend affairs often featuring talks and demonstrations by award-winning chefs and cookbook authors. One annual event in Hawaii called Cuisines of the Sun each year spotlights a particular kind of food, such as hot and spicy dishes made with chiles. The Aspen Food and Wine Classic is another food event that features chefs' creations from such diverse locales as Spain, Singapore, and Texas. Food buffs as well as culinary professionals attend such food

events, which include cooking seminars and classes on marketing and successful service. Some food events are held at resorts where a specific cuisine and prominent guest chefs are featured along with activities that promote healthful living.

FOOD FAIRS

They are known by such names as Bit of Seattle, Taste of Chicago, Taste of Orange County, Pennsylvania Dutch Food Festival, Gourmet Food and Wine Festival, Farmer's Market Fest, Ethnic Food Fair, and dozens of other terms, depending on the location in North America. Although called different names, festivals have much in common. Most are annual celebrations that local people as well as tourists attend in the summer and early fall.

Based on an old tradition of buying food at outdoor festive events (as in the central plaza of Mexican towns during fiesta days), food fairs tend to key on a central theme to help bring in the crowds. In many places, especially rural areas, one can still find community-based events like harvest days, wooden boat festivals, road races, and so on where the reason for the celebration is not necessarily the food, yet the food booth area is usually a major attraction. Almost universally, *food, drink, fun, and celebration* are terms that belong together.

Wherever food fairs are held, merchants or nonprofit organizations are invited to sell the results of a favorite recipe that uses the theme food. In large cities, festivals enlist hundreds of restaurants, taverns, hotels, caterers, wineries, and breweries (any business that deals in food or beverage service) to help make the affair a success. A professional event planner is normally hired to oversee almost every aspect of the execution, setting up a site that includes hundreds of mini restaurants, all requiring electricity, refrigeration, cooking facilities, and water. The event planner must also set up for the thousands, sometimes over hundreds of thousands, of people who visit a site for one or more days.

The 1991 International Boston Seafood Show a popular food event attracted jovial Chef Paul Prudhomme, owner of a well-known New Orleans, Louisiana, restaurant.

Those who attend food fairs usually get into the spirit by arriving early, paying admission, and then buying groups of tickets that are redeemed for food samples available throughout the festival grounds. One of the favorite activities of the adult attendees is to intersperse the tasting of wines and beers with the foods. By the end of the day, many are looking for the espresso and cappuccino booths.

See also: AMERICAN FOLKLIFE FESTIVAL; APPLE FESTIVALS; ARTICHOKE FESTIVAL; ATLANTIC ANTIC; BLUEBERRY FESTIVALS; CHEESE FESTIVALS; CHERRY FESTIVALS; CORN FOODS AND FESTIVALS; CRAB FESTIVALS; CRANBERRY FESTIVALS; DATE FESTIVAL; GARLIC FESTIVALS; GREEK FOOD FESTIVALS; NATIVE AMERICAN FEASTS; OYSTER FESTIVALS; PEACH FESTIVALS; PECAN FESTIVAL; PINTO BEAN FIESTA; SALMON FESTIVALS; SHRIMP FESTIVALS; SOUTHERN FOOD FESTIVALS; STRAWBERRY FESTIVALS; TASTE OF . . . FESTIVALS; VIDALIA ONION FESTIVAL; WATERMELON FESTIVALS.

FOOD SAMPLING

One of the most popular marketing techniques in the United States in recent years involves the practice of offering appetizers at no cost to patrons of bars and cocktail lounges. In saloons of a bygone era, this practice was known as the free lunch. Today, the availability of free food buffets in local bars centers around a time known as happy hour. Typical sample foods at happy hour include buffalo wings (spicy chicken thigh and wing pieces), mini quiches, mini tacos, pizza rolls, stuffed mushrooms, nuts, and pretzels. Specialty restaurants with bars provide foods keyed to menu items that they expect patrons to order at full price on subsequent visits. The concept is to instill loyalty and to get people to order more alcoholic drinks.

During the 1980s, it was customary for friends and coworkers to meet at particular bars after the workday to partake in the free food, which would become their only evening meal. Single folks on a tight budget found the promotional displays and low-priced drinks very attractive, and it was not uncommon to find some patrons at the establishment every day of the week. As the bars saw a diminishing return from the offer (revenues were not increasing), and as law enforcement agencies began to apply pressure to limit the promotion of "half-priced" or "two-for-one" alcoholic beverages, this type of food sampling began to die out in some areas of the United States.

Another form of food sampling has gained popularity in supermarkets, gourmet grocery stores, and buyers' discount club establishments. Especially on the weekends, a shopper entering one of these places can be overwhelmed by the smell of cooking food. At the end of many of the aisles, a customer will be greeted by a smiling employee whose job it is to hand out freshly prepared samples of food or beverage products that are being promoted that day. Crab salad, spicy hot dogs, cakes and cookies of all varieties, cheeses, quiches, juices, soft drinks, bits of doughnuts, candies, cereal, and pasta are all possible in the larger stores. Like the bar promotions, the idea of free food tends to bring in those who just want the free lunch. Individuals and groups have been known to visit several sites in one day to partake of enough samples to fill their stomachs, creating a sort of food grazing sport of the 1990s.

FOOD TABOOS

For centuries, numerous religious and some secular groups have lived according to dietary practices that include taboos against eating certain types of food. Many North Americans still adhere to food taboos. The dietary laws of Orthodox Jews and Muslims, for example, forbid consumption of pork. Some Hindus and Buddhists avoid meat of any kind in their diet, which stems from a common practice among many early peoples who venerated

the life cycle and refused to eat animals or animal products, although such taboos were ignored when there were major food shortages. Among some people of Asian ancestry, dairy products are considered taboo, a practice that probably is based not on religious belief but on the fact that many Asians lack the enzyme lactase needed to digest milk and milk products.

There are few food taboos among Christian groups, although some Catholics avoid meat on Friday as a form of fasting and ritually fast during Lent. Many Protestant groups studiously avoid alcoholic drinks, considering alcohol an abomination. Tea and coffee fit the same category for such groups as Seventh-Day Adventists and Mormons. These groups, especially Adventists, also avoid meat and advocate a vegetarian diet for health and spritual well-being.

Even though certain foods and beverages may not be specifically forbidden by religious doctrines, North Americans by custom avoid a number of foods that people in other parts of the world may enjoy and may even consider a delicacy. Insects are one example of such foods. Common garden snails are seldom eaten, but large numbers of Americans enjoy expensive escargots, which are of the same species as the garden variety. Horse meat, camel meat, and the meat of such domestic animals as dogs and cats, for example, are considered taboo among most Americans but are relished by those whose culture regularly includes such foodstuffs.

See also: CANNIBALISM; FASTING; INSECTS; KOSHER FOOD; LENT; VEGETARIAN EATING.
References: Cook. *Diet and Your Religion.* 1976; Farb and Armelagos. *Consuming Passions.* 1980; MacClancy. *Consuming Culture.* 1992; Parrinder. *World Religions.* 1983.

FOODIES

During the 1980s, *foodies* became a popular term throughout the United States, referring to people whose hobby—or passion—is to learn all they can about food and beverages, collecting and studying cookbooks and trying a great variety of restaurants, particularly ethnic restaurants. Many are almost addicted to cooking classes and have become virtual experts on food and cooking, sharing their favorite recipes by electronic forums established on services such as CompuServe and Prodigy and also through Internet mailing lists. Foodies also have a penchant for food catalogs and are likely to indulge in mail-order foods, ordering items ranging from Brie and catfish pâté to popcorn and fresh fruits.

Like members of eating/dining clubs and gourmet societies, some foodies gather in groups to eat out, trying many different restaurants that serve similar foods, such as those specializing in the cuisine of India. Foodies, however, tend to be quite fickle, and after trying a particular cuisine a few times may turn to another—for example going from Cajun cuisine to restaurants featuring meat loaf and homecooking.

One of the most important rituals for foodies, however, is to "discover" a new restaurant. Foodies often are on the scene waiting for the doors of a new restaurant to open, and after a meal they provide word-of-mouth reports about the quality of the food and drinks served. The critiques may be shared in newspaper columns if a foodie is a restaurant reviewer, but most are not professionals and pass on their opinions—some of them rather "catty"—to friends, relatives, and coworkers.
See also: EATING/DINING CLUBS; MAIL-ORDER FOODS.

FORTUNE COOKIES

Although the fortune cookie is strictly an American invention, the concept behind the fortune cookie had its origin in ancient China, when Chinese rebels exchanged secret messages hidden inside buns. David Jung, a Los Angeles noodle manufacturer, is credited with inventing the first modern fortune cookie in 1916. Today, they are made and sold by the billions each year and served in most Chinese restaurants in North America. Customers expect the meal to end with fortune cookies, usually placed

atop the check. Only recently has the ritual been copied in China. Won Ton in Brooklyn, New York, one of the world's largest makers of fortune cookies, made arrangements in 1992 to build and operate fortune cookie plants in China, for the first time providing these cookies on a large scale to the Chinese people.

Until just a few decades ago, fortune cookies were made by hand, and bakers and their helpers, using chopsticks, inserted fortunes while flipping and folding the cookies just after they were baked. During the 1960s, Edward Louie, cofounder of the Lotus Fortune Cookie Company in San Francisco, invented a machine that automatically inserted the slips of paper into the cookies. Louie died in 1990, but today, at the Lotus company and in other plants where fortune cookies are made on a large scale, nearly all operations are performed by machines. Large mixers blend the flour, sugar, vegetable oil, vanilla, and yellow food coloring into a cookie dough that is pumped onto small griddles circulating through ovens. The baked cookies look somewhat like pancakes, and while they are still hot and soft, they go through a folding machine that also inserts pieces of paper with messages on them.

Years ago, some messages in fortune cookies were simply a repeat of the wise words of Confucius, the wisdom of Benjamin Franklin, or maxims of Aesop. Most present-day messages are written by employees of companies like Cosmos Enterprises of Westboro, Massachusetts, which has compiled a computer database of thousands of sayings printed in English, Chinese, German, Hebrew, French, and other languages. Many messages are bits of philosophy or advice, such as "In quiet and silence the truth is made clear" or "If you don't determine your own fate, it will be determined for you." Sometimes, though, there will be a prediction such as "The current year will bring you great happiness," "You will make a profitable investment," or maybe "You will take a chance on something in the near future."

A take-out restaurant in Portland, Oregon, serves "unfortunate" cookies that contain such messages as "You are well liked despite your table manners," "Your charms will persuade others to screen their calls," or "You are in your own way, please stand aside." While most customers reportedly like the jibes, a few have been so insulted they have refused to return to the restaurant.

Some fortune cookie makers produce cookies in a variety of flavors, such as barbecue. Some are dipped in chocolate, and colors are added to cookies for holidays, such as red and green for Christmas. There are fortune cookies for weddings and bar mitzvahs. A fairly recent innovation is putting "lucky" lottery numbers inside fortune cookies. Some companies even make cookies with sexually suggestive messages and produce special orders for those who can afford to buy (and give away) cookies stuffed with jewelry or money. Most cookie makers also provide cookies with promotional messages for various companies to use in their advertising campaigns.

References: Gay. *Keep the Buttered Side Up.* 1995; Trager. *The Food Chronology.* 1995.

FRANKFURTERS

See HOT DOGS.

FRENCH TOAST

Pain perdu to the French was a dessert invented to use up "lost bread," that is, older stale brioche or other bread was soaked in milk, dipped in eggs that had been beaten with sugar, and then fried. It was especially popular as an Easter treat. The idea of using up leftover food was not unique to the French, though; in fact, some sources suggest that, in North America, this dish was actually referred to as German bread until 1918.

French toast is on almost every U.S. restaurant breakfast menu. The recipes vary slightly from the original French version, but the effect is mostly the same: older pieces of bread are soaked in an egg mixture (which may actually contain a liqueur),

toasted until browned on both sides, and dusted with powdered sugar. It is often smothered with butter and maple syrup or fruit. This breakfast is traditionally a favorite of children who accompany their parents to Sunday breakfast or brunch at restaurants. It is also a special breakfast treat in many North American homes.
See also: BREAKFAST.
Reference: Trager. *The Food Chronology.* 1995.

FRIED GREEN TOMATOES

Long before the 1991 movie *Fried Green Tomatoes* made green tomatoes famous, farm folks in the United States were creating this simple dish, slicing green tomatoes; seasoning the slices and dipping them in cornmeal, flour, or egg batter; and frying them. The practice of preparing tomatoes in this manner probably began as a way to use up a hefty crop of tomatoes or the underripe green tomatoes left on the vines in the fall when the growing season ended in the colder climates. Fried green tomatoes, seasoned with black and cayenne peppers, are commonly served at Cajun-style restaurants in New Orleans and are a traditional part of many southern meals. Other common seasonings for this dish are oregano and Parmesan cheese.

FRITTERS

Some type of fritter is a traditional food in almost every ethnic or regional cuisine in North America, and fritters of all kinds have been popular since ancient times, perhaps because the combination of fat and carbohydrates can be very comforting. The term *fritter* refers to a food coated with batter and fried, or, alternatively, the batter may be used as the main ingredient, as in doughnuts and hush puppies. Fried corn fritters have been a staple in New England and the U.S. South. They are made by dropping spoonfuls of cornmeal batter into hot fat and frying them on both sides until golden brown. Fritters may also be bits of batter-fried meats, cheeses, fruits, or vegetables. In Puerto Rico, fritters are also a staple in the diet and may be meat or fruit turnovers, but the most common and best known are those made with plantains (blended and fried) and those made with rice flour, cheese, eggs, and milk.

At various times, tempura vegetables, fried eggplant, fried mozzarella, breaded zucchini, and other fritter varieties have been the rage in restaurants and at parties as appetizers. In many restaurants and at home parties, fritters continue to be served as appetizers. They can also be a meal in themselves, a side dish for a meal, or a sugar-coated after-dinner treat. Some fritters made with meat or cheese are served with a sauce for dipping. Apple or other fruit fritters are popular as breakfast or brunch items. Countless varieties of fritters are possible, since the batter and ingredients used often depend on tradition and available foods.

See also: EDIBLE FLOWERS.

FROZEN JUICE BARS

Once a special treat for children prepared by a thoughtful parent, frozen juice bars are now a very popular commercially prepared alternative to the overly sweet Popsicle, a trademark product that made its debut in the 1920s. During the 1950s and 1960s, Mom (the parent most often in the home at that time) used to take a concentrated juice—lemonade, grape, or apple—and mix it with slightly less water than was recommended on the side of the container and pour it into ice trays or a plastic mold that was especially designed for this procedure. Several hours later an inexpensive, healthy sweet was unmolded.

The commercially available juice bars are very popular for the same reasons that homemade bars were once a hit. They are refreshing, low in fat, and much healthier than ice cream bars and most other frozen confections. As the large juice corporations manufacturing these frozen juice bars have extended the range of flavor varieties, the demand has steadily increased.

FROZEN MEALS

In 1954, frozen meals called TV dinners, packaged by C. A. Swanson and Sons of Omaha, Nebraska, were introduced to American consumers, and they soon became part of the American way of life. The first Swanson package carried a picture of a television screen showing a compartmentalized aluminum container holding ingredients for the frozen meal. The original package was placed in an exhibit at the Smithsonian museum in Washington, D.C., which is testimony to its place in American culture.

After its initial sales of 5,000 meals in 1954, Swanson sold 10 million frozen dinners in 1955 and by 1993 had sold 85 million of these convenience meals. Other companies such as Banquet, Stouffer, and Le Menu have also marketed millions of frozen dinners, entrees, and specialty items.

Eating a heated frozen meal in front of the television set quickly became a ritual in millions of American homes during the 1950s. Television was a new phenomenon, and whole families gathered around this large piece of living room furniture to watch their favorite programs in the late afternoon and early evening. Since this was about the time when dinner was usually prepared and eaten, families enjoyed the convenience of being able to pop a meal into the oven, serve it on specially designed "TV trays," and eat while watching television.

By the 1960s and 1970s, an increasing number of women were working outside the home, which brought more demand for frozen food items. Microwave technology developed in the 1980s and 1990s has contributed even further to the enhancement of the frozen food packaging industry. It now takes much less time to heat up a complete meal. In addition, there is a great variety of frozen meals available today, from diet meals to gourmet-style foods.

See also: MICROWAVE COOKING.

FRUITCAKE

In spite of the old joke that there is really only one fruitcake in the whole world and it never gets eaten but passed from person to person, fruitcake remains part of the traditional Christmas ritual. Every year it is given as a gift to relatives or friends. Most fruitcakes are commercially prepared, but some families pass down a particular recipe through the years, and some even pass down the cake! Since fruitcakes are butter cakes, loaded with candied or dried fruit and nuts and usually saturated with a sweet liqueur and sugar, which are preserving agents, some have survived over 25 years.

While fruitcake is still a popular gift item and cooks still like to show off their traditional recipes, this artificially colored, fruit-dotted brick has lost much of its charm in recent years. Many other types of loaf cakes or breads, such as banana, pumpkin, or zucchini bread, seem to be more widely enjoyed. In an attempt to find out if anyone really eats what Charles Dickens called "a geological homemade cake," researchers asked 1,000 adults what they did with fruitcake. They found that 38 percent gave it away, 28 percent ate it, 13 percent used it as a doorstop, 9 percent fed it to the birds, 4 percent threw it away, and 8 percent could not recall.

See also: BREAD; ZUCCHINI BREAD.

References: Chalmers. *The Great Food Almanac.* 1994; Dailey. "Best Quality Ingredients Give Fruitcake a Shelf Life That You Can't Laugh Off." 1990.

FRY BREAD

See NAVAJO FRY BREAD.

FRYING PAN BREAD

In the United States, true southerners traditionally bake their corn bread in a cast-iron frying pan. They consider any other way of making corn bread a poor substitute and the bread hardly worth eating, and most do not believe "Yankees" can make real corn bread. Cast-iron pans are used for two reasons: (1) tradition and (2) results. Although modern cookware is certainly functional enough to get the job done, cast-iron skillets have been passed down

through so many generations of southerners that it is virtually unthinkable to use anything else. Bread made in these pans bakes to a golden brown, crispy finish; the result in other types of pans literally pales in comparison. A well-seasoned cast-iron pan also lends flavors to the bread that no other pan can replicate.

One southern recipe calls for heating a cast-iron frying pan in the oven with a stick of butter. After the butter melts, most of it is incorporated into the corn bread mixture. Then the batter is poured back into the hot black pan and returned to the oven to bake. It comes out crisp, rich, and "correct" according to southern tradition.

A western version of frying pan bread originated with pioneers who moved west across the plains and cowboys who rode the range to care for cattle. When these people set up camp, they often made a quick bread dough inside a flour sack, mixing baking powder, sugar or syrup, oil, and water into the flour. The dough was then spread across the bottom of a long-handled frying pan and cooked over an open fire or over hot coals. In some parts of the West, this method is still used at community cook-outs and some food festivals.

See also: CHUCK-WAGON SUPPER.

FUDGE

Some of the earliest American fudge making has been traced back to the beginning of the twentieth century, when it was commonly associated with New England women's colleges. Each institution had its own version, which was named after the school—Smith College Fudge, Vassar Fudge, etc.—and was often blamed for the infamous "freshman fifteen" (extra weight gained by new students).

Until recent times, it was a common practice to cook up a batch of chocolate fudge on a cool evening, allowing the warm, sugary, and chocolatey aroma to fill the kitchen. As the mixture boiled, it was periodically tested by dropping a half teaspoonful in a cup of cold water to see if the fudge had reached the "soft ball" stage—when it was crystallized enough so that it could be removed from the stove. It then was beaten until stiff, spread in a buttered pan, and left to cool, forming a crusty coating around a soft center just right for melting in the mouth.

Seldom do modern home cooks take the time to make fudge "from scratch," although many use prepared mixes to make a quick fudge from the traditional chocolate to peanut butter or butterscotch flavors. Still, it is one of those decadent chocolate candies that is a very popular item for fund-raisers and bake sales. Fudge is also a traditional confection sold at circuses, carnivals, and amusement parks. And some candy shops found in malls, at shopping centers, at airports, in resort towns, and at tourist attractions such as historical villages make and sell "homemade" fudge to customers who eagerly buy it because it is a favorite sweet treat that induces nostalgia.

The town of Solvang, California, is typical of a site that can boast at least one great fudge shop. A tourist town based on a Danish theme (because so many Danish immigrants settled in the area), Solvang attracts hundreds of thousands visitors every year, and certainly most of these people have stopped by the candy factory to see the brightly clad chocolatiers pour out and knead their many varieties of fudge. Little bites or many pounds of fudge—dark with almonds, light with macadamias, or white with walnuts—are available for purchase.
See also: CHOCOLATE CANDY; DANISH DAYS.
Reference: Mariani. *The Dictionary of American Food and Drink.* 1993, 1994.

FUNERAL FOOD

After most funerals in North America, it is customary for bereaved family members and friends to gather and share a meal and sometimes alcoholic beverages. Frequently, such meals are "carry-ins," dishes prepared by volunteers. Dining tables may be set up in temple or church halls, and food may be served family- or buffet-style. While there is no specific American "funer-

al food," fried chicken, roast beef, ham, and a variety of pasta and potato dishes are typical.

Members of some ethnic groups serve special foods at funerals. People of Greek ancestry, for example, may serve *koliva,* an ancient food symbolizing the cycle of life. Made from boiled wheat, cinnamon, nuts, and pomegranate seeds, the mixture is pressed into cakelike forms and covered with powdered sugar. During mourning, Armenians prepare a traditional dish called *herissah,* a porridge made from wheat and mutton or chicken. Among the Pennsylvania Dutch, raisin pie is considered a traditional "funeral pie," since farm women used to bake a number of these pies as well as other types of pastries and sweets and store them in cool cellars until they were needed for such occasions as wakes, weddings, and other family gatherings.
See also: ALL SOULS DAY.
Reference: Nathan. *An American Folklife Cookbook.* 1984.

FUNNEL CAKE

This favorite treat among the Pennsylvania Dutch is made with a sweetened egg-and-flour batter that is dripped through a funnel into a skillet with hot oil, swirled to form a spiral design, and fried until lightly browned on both sides. The cakes are dusted with sugar and eaten warm or cold any time of the day, but they are often served with syrup or molasses as a breakfast food or mid-morning snack with coffee. Funnel cakes are also routinely sold at folk and food festivals and are popular carnival and fair foods throughout the Midwest.
See also: AMERICAN FOLKLIFE FESTIVAL; AMISH FOOD FESTIVALS; CARNIVAL AND FAIR FOOD; TASTE OF . . . FESTIVALS.

GARLIC BREAD

Bread sticks coated with a garlic spread or thick slices of toasted Italian bread with a garlic spread are usually served with meals in many Italian restaurants. Both bread and garlic are staples in Italian cuisine. Commercially prepared garlic bread is found in frozen food sections of supermarkets across North America and is regularly purchased as an accompaniment to all types of American meals, although many Americans often make their own garlic bread at home. In Italian tradition, authentic garlic bread is made by rubbing toast with a raw garlic clove, but many people now use garlic powder or chopped garlic.

See also: GARLIC FESTIVALS.

GARLIC FESTIVALS

There is little question that garlic grows in the fields near Gilroy, California, which calls itself the Garlic Capital of the World. The smell of garlic permeates the area for miles around, since this is where much of the garlic is grown in the United States. To celebrate the garlic harvest in July, Gilroy has hosted an annual garlic festival, which draws about 150,000 people each year. Other garlic celebrations are held in the

Bay Area—around San Francisco—where restaurants feature garlic dishes and foods seasoned with garlic.

Garlic celebrations are certainly not unique to North America. They have been going on for thousands of years in such countries as India, Greece, and Egypt, and these festivals often focused on the medicinal as well as the culinary uses of garlic. Such harvest celebrations still take place in the Mediterranean and in France. As in these countries, Americans honor the "stinking rose" with garlic-laden foods. At the Gilroy festival, dozens of food booths set up by civic clubs and other groups offer servings of garlic scampi, garlic-spiked calamari, stir-fried vegetables with garlic, garlic-marinated sirloin, garlic pasta, mountains of garlic bread, and even garlic ice cream.

See also: GARLIC BREAD.

GARNISHES

In fine restaurants and for festive dinners at home, it is customary to serve many dishes with decorative and usually edible garnishes, especially greens such as lettuce, colorful cabbage leaves, and parsley. For years, cooks have garnished beef and pork roasts with glazed carrots and whole

Braids of garlic festoon a display at the annual Gilroy Garlic Festival. Learning to braid garlic is one of the many events at the festival in Gilroy, California, which touts itself as the "Garlic Capital of the World."

browned new potatoes, presenting these vegetables in decorative fashion as side dishes on a meat platter. Mushrooms garnish many meat dishes, and pineapple slices and whole cloves garnish as well as flavor a baked ham. Croutons and chives are common edible garnishes for soups and salads. Desserts are often topped with decorative frostings, whipped cream, nuts, or glazed fruits or garnished with edible flowers. Grapes are also a colorful garnish for numerous dishes, from the main course to dessert.

A garnish is also used on many beverages, such as iced tea, which may be served with a lemon slice, and fruit drinks, which may be served with an orange slice. Garnishes are an integral part of some alcoholic drinks: the martini is served with an olive or lemon twist, the Bloody Mary is garnished with a celery stalk and lemon wedge, the old-fashioned is decorated with an orange slice on the glass and maraschino cherry in the drink, eggnog is topped with nutmeg, and coffee-and-liquor drinks are topped with whipped cream.

GAZPACHO

This cold, tomato-based soup was first concocted in Spain, where, before refrigeration, it was held in caves for cooling until just prior to service. Today, in the United States, it is a great warm-weather alternative for a lunch or dinner first course. Vegetarians like the dish because it is full of vegetables, and a vegetable stock can be substituted for a beef or chicken stock that is a traditional ingredient. There are actually many versions of the soup depending on personal taste and local vegetables. It is important that all ingredients be very fresh, and the finished recipe must sit for several hours so that the flavors mingle correctly. Some cooks speed this process by running the chunky vegetables and broth through a blender. The finished soup is then thicker and less chunky, but no less a gazpacho.

120

GELATIN MOLD

Gelatin is made from animal bones, hooves, and other cattle parts and is the basis for desserts that became very popular in the 1890s. A few decades later, mechanical refrigeration made gelatin desserts an American staple. Gelatin is still one of the leading thickeners used in powdered desserts, ice cream, cheese spreads, and yogurt. Jell-O, a trademark name for a flavored gelatin dessert made by Kraft General Foods, is such a popular brand that most Americans think of it as a generic term, a household word synonymous with the word *gelatin.*

The Jell-O brand first came on the market in 1897 with sales increasing almost every year thereafter. As of the early 1990s, U.S. consumers bought approximately 600,000 boxes of Jell-O per day in flavors that include black cherry, lemon, orange, lime, mixed-berry, strawberry, and even watermelon. A few flavors—coffee, celery, apple, and cola—were once marketed but did not meet customer approval and were withdrawn. According to Kraft General Foods, strawberry is the all-time favorite, with cherry and raspberry not far behind.

Jell-O and other gelatin desserts can be served alone (with nothing added) or they may include fruit and nuts and served with whipped cream on top. Salads made with gelatin and shredded carrots and other vegetables as well as fruits are also popular. Americans serve gelatin salads, desserts, and snacks (in fun forms that kids enjoy) for just about any occasion, but traditionally gelatin molded in shapes such as bells, castles, turkeys, and trees have been part of carry-in meals, festive family dinners, and many other occasions that center on eating and drinking. Gelatin molds are the most popular during holidays such as Thanksgiving and Christmas, with lime flavor in demand at those times.

Although gelatin desserts and salads are part of the menu at many cafeterias and other types of family restaurants, an unusual restaurant selling primarily gelatin—specifically Jell-O (oh)—opened in 1994 in Atlanta, Georgia. The shop features gelatin parfaits, salads, and other creations concocted from some of the 400 recipes the owner, Charles Shamoon, has in his files. Shamoon began his operation in his hometown of Greenville, Mississippi, calling his shop "Hello . . . I'm Jell-O," but he had to change the name because of trademark restrictions. He now calls his business places "Hello . . . I'm Gellatin," and he plans to expand with franchises.

References: Mariani. *The Dictionary of American Food and Drink.* 1993, 1994; Shapiro. "No Time To Make Dessert?" 1994; Trager. *Foodbook.* 1970.

GERMAN POTATO SALAD

This hot potato salad is made with a dressing of vinegar, wine, sugar, onion, and bacon. It is frequently served at German food festivals and appears in numerous Pennsylvania Dutch and German cookbooks. Although this dish is most often associated with people of German heritage, potato salads are common at picnics and family reunions all over the continent.
See also: OKTOBERFEST; POTATOES.

GHEE

Ghee is the clarified liquid that is left after the milk solids, water, and salt are removed from butter, and it is a key ingredient in much of Indian cooking. For example, *halva,* a sweet treat served at Indian celebrations like Diwali, is fried in ghee along with sugar and flavorings.

Ghee imparts a distinctive taste—some say a nutty flavor—to foods that cannot be obtained by using other vegetable oils or butter as substitutes. Ghee also stands up well when subjected to very high temperatures; thus, it can prevent burning when foods are sautéed or fried. In traditional French cooking, clarified butter is a necessary ingredient of emulsified sauces such as Hollandaise.

Some people trying to cut their fat intake have erroneously surmised that ghee is lower in fat content. Like any oil, however, it is 100 percent fat.
See also: BUTTER AND OTHER SPREADS.

GIFT BASKETS

See FOOD BASKETS.

GINGERBREAD COOKIES/HOUSES

Cookies made with ginger—a spice from the root of a plant native to Asia but now grown in many tropical areas—has been part of North American cuisine since the days when English colonists brought this spice with them to the "New World." According to food historian Waverly Root, ginger cookies (hard cookies) were part of the standard rations for American soldiers during the Revolutionary War, and a soft ginger "cake," or gingerbread dough, cut in a variety of shapes has been made since colonial days.

A traditional Christmas activity in many American homes is baking gingerbread cookies, which are cut in human shapes (like miniature men and Santa Claus), stars, houses, bells, trees, and canes. After baking, the cookies are decorated and hung as ornaments on Christmas trees or eaten. Some families also "build" gingerbread houses from baked cookie dough that is adorned with frosting and other confections.

In the small community of Buchanan, Michigan, a Palmisano family tradition that began in the early 1980s includes baking and building a gingerbread and sugar cookie village, which is on display at the family bakery, the Palmisanos' Cake House, during the Christmas season. The gingerbread village, which covers an area of about 8 feet by 15 feet, is a replica of the downtown area of Buchanan. Its two- and three-story houses have frosting-covered roofs and are bedecked with candies and gumdrops used for windows and street lights. Candy canes and cookie people complete the display.
See also: CHRISTMAS BAZAAR; CHRISTMAS COOKIES.

GIRL SCOUT COOKIES

They have names like Golden Nut Cluster, Do-Si-Dos, Thin Mints, Trefoils, Tagalongs, and Samoas, and collectively they are known as Girl Scout Cookies, sold and consumed every year by the millions. The tradition began in the 1920s when Girl Scouts in Philadelphia sold home-baked cookies by the dozen as a fund-raiser. In 1936, the Girl Scout organization began to sell the first franchised commercially baked and packaged cookies, and consumers in every part of the United States have been gobbling them up ever since. The cookies are only sold once a year, with girls taking orders in late January and early February, sometimes going door to door but more often today setting up stands in supermarkets and other public places. Orders are delivered in March, and more than 170 million boxes of these cookies are consumed annually, creating a kind of spring rite since the cookies cannot be purchased any other time of the year.
See also: COOKIES.

GLOGG

A traditional yuletide drink for people of Swedish ancestry is glogg, which is made with red wine, raisins, sugar, cinnamon sticks, cardamom seeds, and whole cloves. The ingredients are mixed and heated slowly (but not boiled) for about an hour, and left to sit for 24 hours before the drink is consumed. It is poured through a sieve to remove the spices and raisins, slowly reheated, and served, sometimes with spirits such as aquavit or vodka and with raisins or blanched almonds in the bottom of the cup.
See also: HOT TODDY.

GOLD LEAF

First used at least 600 years ago, gold leaf is the ultimate display of decadence in eating. It has been popular in France, Italy, and the Middle East. In North America

Girl Scouts deliver boxes of cookies to the master of the SS Nieuw Amsterdam, *docked in New York in 1964. The Girl Scout cookie sale has been a spring event since the 1920s when Girl Scouts in Philadelphia began to sell home-baked cookies as a means of raising funds.*

today, specialty chocolate houses will apply gold leaf to their confections as an expensive novelty. Caterers and restaurants will also apply the precious metal to various desserts or sprinkle bits of gold flake on dips and sauces: all for the show. Is it edible? Apparently gold leaf will do no harm when ingested in minuscule amounts. The inert quality of the metal means that it will not interact with the digestive system, and it passes through in a day or two.

See also: GARNISHES.

GOULASH

Originally a shepherd's dish in Hungary, goulash (or *gulyas*) is a rich stew or soup flavored with paprika (the Hungarian national spice) that is on the menu in most U.S. restaurants featuring Hungarian cuisine. Usually goulash is made with boneless beef, potatoes, noodles, tomatoes, and green pepper plus seasonings, but the dish, which is one of the most well known contributions to North America's international cuisine, has been adapted in so many different ways that almost any type of thick stew made with a tomato base may be generically labeled goulash.

See also: ETHNIC FOOD TRADITIONS.

References: Biro. *Flavors of Hungary.* 1973; Simon and Howe. *Dictionary of Gastronomy.* 1970.

GOURMET FOODS

A gourmet is a person adept at choosing fine food and wine. He or she is one who knows how to live in "high style" as it pertains to consuming foodstuffs. Used as an adjective, as in "gourmet food," the term *gourmet* refers to any product that would be chosen as superior by one with good taste and special sensibilities in the area of food. As the consumption of better foods and more exotic preparations has broadened to include the masses, however, the term *gourmet* has lost much of its impact.

In all of North America, *gourmet* has become the term of choice for promoting products in the marketplace. Attaching the term to any type of consumable is intended to impart some sense of class, prestige, and superiority to the product. A whole new category of high-priced foods has been created, allowing consumers a choice of products ranging from gourmet coffee, gourmet wine, and gourmet cheese to gourmet cat and dog food. In a world where the individual desires to stand out from the crowd, this Madison Avenue appeal to snobbery and cultural elitism allows many consumers to feel a part of the "in crowd," the knowledgeable few. It is also a way that people can reward themselves for living through another tough day, particularly if a "gourmet burger" provides more pleasure than a regular hamburger.

There are a few eating and drinking societies that attempt to maintain the high standard and true definition of *gourmet*. Swimming against the tide of commercialization, these eating and drinking clubs are made up of people who have a true interest in seeing that the ritual of fine dining is maintained. Full service china, crystal, and silver are often used at their special meal gatherings, which also serve as educational opportunities for all involved. The art of eating, while truly snobbish in some circles and probably archaic to most observers, is the province of the true gourmet.

See also: EATING/DINING CLUBS; FOODIES.

GRANOLA BARS/CEREAL

Since the 1970s, the term *granola* has been widely used to describe cereal products. Always around in North American rural kitchens, where whole grain cereals have been a tradition, the granola of today has come to symbolize healthful eating. The back-to-the-land movement that began in the late 1960s had a lot to do with the growing popularity of granola. Post-hippies were eschewing everything processed or artificial, and there was a real effort made at the time to become self-sufficient in as many aspects of life as possible. Granola, like macrame, yogurt, and compost, were key elements in this social movement.

Granola is a whole class of breakfast cereals or snacks that include foods such as oatmeal flakes, wheat flakes or grain, rye flakes, nuts, seeds, raisins, dried fruits, and coconut. The homemade varieties, baked at low heat with little added honey or sugar, can be truly wonder foods providing high protein, low fat, and plenty of roughage. Unfortunately, like most commercially produced versions of whole foods, the packaged granolas found on most supermarket shelves are over processed, over sweetened cereals that have very little to recommend them over the "pops" and "smacks" they sit beside. The companies market the health aspects of "granola" and "natural cereals," but their goal is to sell products to consumers looking for a quick fix to improved eating. The granola bar is a perfect example of the quick-fix phenomenon. Cross a whole, natural food product (granola cereal) with one of America's favorite snack foods (the candy bar) and you have a sugar rush with the extra added attraction of increased bulk in the diet; however, sugar is sugar and fat is fat, whether it is in ice cream or a snack marketed as a healthy treat.

See also: CEREAL, COLD.

GRAPE FESTIVALS

See WINE FESTIVALS.

GRAPE JUICE

In the United States, grape juice is a familiar fruit juice that has been a common snack beverage and birthday party drink for children. Grape juice, however, is also an adult beverage, used for religious ceremonies such as the Eucharist in churches that forbid wine because of its alcoholic content. In fact, Thomas Bramwell Welch, who founded the now well known juice company Welch's, got his start in 1869 after preparing grape juice as a nonalcoholic communion beverage for his church. He gathered Concord grapes growing near his New Jersey home and squeezed the juice through cloth bags (a common method for preparing homemade grape juice that continued well into the 1900s). The juice was bottled, sealed with a cork and wax, and lowered into a vat of boiling water, which killed yeast and prevented fermentation. Welch's company eventually became the world leader in the production of Concord grape products ranging from juices to jams. This brand-name juice plus others on the market are frequently used as a base for nonalcoholic punch served at holiday parties and other festivities.

See also: PUNCH.

GRATED/SHREDDED COCONUT

"I was only 4 years old when I had my first piece of coconut cream pie topped with fresh, grated coconut; 60 years later I can still remember the warm, inviting aroma and the delicious taste of that wonderful dessert!" Such a memory is typical among people who enjoy the flavor of coconut, whether in coconut cream pie or some other dessert or confection made with grated coconut or coconut milk. Shredded coconut and coconut milk are used in a variety of Hawaiian dishes, including haupia (coconut pudding), and, among African Americans, grated coconut is a favorite ingredient for foods ranging from fruit salads to cakes.

While long favored as a delicacy in Latin America, the Pacific islands, and parts of India and Asia, coconut was first introduced to North America in a most unusual way in 1895. Franklin Baker (founder of Baker's Coconut Company) accepted a cargo of fresh coconuts as payment for a consignment of flour that had been shipped to Havana. He tried, without success, selling the whole coconuts. After developing methods for opening and shredding the fruit, Baker found a prosperous future in marketing the delicacy. American shoppers can now find canned, dried, and frozen varieties at their local supermarkets. With increasing interest in ethnic foods in the 1990s, coconut is now being used to prepare main dishes as well as the traditional desserts.

References: Lee. "Give Winter Dishes a Taste of Tropical Climes with Coconut." 1995; Trager. *The Food Chronology.* 1995.

GRAZING

Grazing is a tradition that started on the Iberian peninsula, especially in Spain where late afternoon crowds go from bar to bar tasting sherries. As an added attraction, local bars began providing *tapas* (little dishes) as appetizers to tide customers over until dinner, traditionally served late in the evening. The practice of going from bar to bar (or restaurant lounge to restaurant lounge) to sample hors d'oeuvres carried over to North America and became a popular ritual in the 1980s.

Grazing (sometimes called noshing) has also become popular at such social events as receptions, open houses, buffets, and even some types of potlucks. A host, hostess, or caterer sets up food "stations" on tables scattered around the site, each one featuring a different type of food. Placing very small plates at each station encourages the guests to take a few bites from one grouping, sit, eat, talk, then go back for a try at another group of foods.

See also: APPETIZERS; BUFFET; OPEN HOUSE; TAPAS.

GREAT MONTEREY SQUID FESTIVAL

West Coast residents and tourists who have spent time in northern California are familiar with the Monterey Bay Aquarium, which has gained fame as one of the largest aquariums in the world, but perhaps not so well known is the squid festival held on Memorial Day weekend at the Monterey Fairgrounds. The event began in 1984 and draws more than 20,000 every year. As with any festival, there is plenty of entertainment during the two-day event, but it is primarily a celebration of the squid industry in Monterey, the main port for squid fishing where it is not unusual for fishermen to catch over 50 tons of squid every night. In addition to films, videos, and demonstrations showing how squid are caught, cleaned, and prepared, there are food booths offering squid that has been fried, broiled, sautéed, marinated, or barbecued in Italian, Cajun, Mexican, or Greek style. Squid is presented in such dishes as pizza, fajitas, and chowder plus many other squid delicacies.

Reference: Bernardino. "Squid." 1987.

GREEK FOOD FESTIVALS

Whether in South Bend, Indiana; Aurora, Illinois; New Haven, Connecticut; Brockton, Massachusetts; or in other communities where there are people of Greek heritage, a Greek food festival is often a fund-raising event held annually in or on the grounds of a Greek Orthodox church (or it may be connected with a community fair). In Tarpon Springs, Florida, an annual festival celebrates not only Greek food but also Greek sponge and shrimp fishermen and their catch. Wherever the festival is held, people come to enjoy food and entertainment such as Greek music and dances with performers in traditional costumes.

National foods are, of course, featured at a Greek food festival. There are bound to be such items as moussaka, shish kebab, and *gyros* (Greek for "a turn")—sandwiches made with shaved lamb that has been roasted on a turning spit. A Greek dinner menu may include Greek-style string beans, which are braised in olive oil, garlic, and tomato paste; fried marithes (smelt) accented with lemon; flaming saganaki; *spanakopetes,* small phyllo pastries filled with spinach and feta cheese; *loukoumathes,* cinnamon pastry puffs covered with honey; and baklava, a dessert made of phyllo leaves lined with lots of nuts and honey. Other traditional dishes are baked lamb shanks with tomato sauce, meatballs, and a Greek stew called *stefado* made with beef, veal, or rabbit. The stew is traditionally topped with feta cheese and walnuts.

GREEN CORN FESTIVALS

Corn soup is one of the main dishes served at annual green corn festivals, a traditional and sacred Iroquois celebration that honors corn, an essential crop. Only five of the Iroquois nations (Cayuga, Seneca, Oneida, Onondaga, and Mohawk) still sponsor such festivals, and one of the most famous is held in late August each year at the Onondaga Indian Reservation near Nedrow, New York. As is the custom at many other festivals, games, songs, and dances are all part of the activities, but most of the events at the Green Corn Festival have spiritual significance. The Green Corn Dance, for example, is a sacred ritual that is performed at the festival, although it is usually conducted in private.

This public festival, held since 1930, is a fund-raising effort to support the volunteer fire department on the reservation. Participants can sample traditional Iroquois foods, beginning with a corn soup that is basically more like a chowder or stew. Although there are many variations, depending on the cook's preferences, the main ingredients are kernels of corn or hominy, beans such as kidney or lima, squash or turnips, and meat (usually pork, but venison may be used if available) or fish. With salt and spices added, the combination is simmered in water until the meat or fish is cooked. The corn soup is usually served with ghost bread—so named because it never browns—another typical food at Native American feasts. Additional offerings that are customary include corn bread, corn pudding, hearty stews, and wild duck.

See also: CORN FOODS AND FESTIVALS; NATIVE AMERICAN FEASTS.

References: Borghese. *Food from Harvest Festivals and Folk Fairs.* 1977; Davis. *The Potato Book.* 1973.

GREENS AND POTLIKKER

In many parts of the United States, green leafy vegetables such as collard, mustard, and turnip greens and spinach, kale, watercress, and the leaves of dandelion plants are prepared as hot vegetable dishes. The greens, as they are collectively known, can either be boiled or sautéed with olive oil, garlic, and red pepper, or cooked with ham hocks, bacon fat, or cracklings. The potlikker—the liquid left over from cooking the greens—was once a staple among rural people in the U.S. South as well as among people of southern European heritage. Today, those who enjoy potlikker consume it in a ritualistic way—using pieces of corn bread or other bread to "sop it up" or pouring it over bread slices.

See also: CRACKLINGS.

GRITS

In the southern United States, most people do not consider breakfast complete without grits (sometimes called hominy grits), once a staple among Native American tribes who taught colonists how to hull corn, dry it, and grind it into a coarse white meal for gruels, pottages, or puddings. Sometimes the hulls were cracked by pounding the kernels in hollow log mortars, as described in a familiar folk song line, "Ginny cracked corn and I don't care . . . ," or the hulls were removed by boiling kernels in water with a handful of hardwood ashes, a lye that helped soften the hulls.

Today, in commercial processing corn kernels are treated with lye in order to loosen and whiten the hulls, but the lye is removed before drying and grinding. To make grits, the ground meal is poured into slightly salted boiling water and simmered until soft and smooth.

Grits usually accompany, eggs and/or bacon at breakfast. Some folks enjoy this dish with a little butter and sugar and a piece of toast. Others will sweeten it with syrup. For lunch and dinner, it can take the place of a vegetable or a starch; sweetener is not used, but cheese is often added. Leftover grits can be placed in a loaf pan for keeping overnight. By morning, they set up (à la polenta) and can be sliced into pieces for frying in bacon fat. A favorite southern meal includes golden brown fried grits with strips of bacon and fried green apples.

See also: BREAKFAST; CORNMEAL MUSH.

References: Fussell. *I Hear America Cooking.* 1986; Fussell. *The Story of Corn.* 1992; Mariani. *The Dictionary of American Food and Drink.* 1993, 1994.

GROCERY STORE AND SUPERMARKET MEALS

For years, some small grocery stores in rural areas of North America have offered a limited number of hot prepared foods for sale and provided tables for eating on the premises. Vegetarian food markets have also been likely to have a small cafe set up on the premises. A more recent trend, however, is for an increasing number of convenience stores and supermarkets to include a restaurant or deli service. Customers—whether grocery shoppers, store workers, or employees from nearby businesses—can order prepared food for almost any meal. They put together their choice of ingredients from a salad bar, serve themselves from a selection of hot soups, order hot barbecued chicken or ribs or some type of cold sandwich, or get a sweet treat from an in-store bakery, ice cream vending machine, or yogurt bar. In some areas, fast-food outlets are under the same roof as major supermarkets. All of these eating places within a grocery or supermarket reflect the ever-increasing American demand for convenience. People want to eat where they are rather than having to travel a long distance for a meal.

See also: DELI FOODS; DINING ON DELIVERY; EATING TRENDS; FASTFOOD; SALAD BAR; VENDING MACHINES.

Reference: Woods and Styler. *Sylvia's Soul Food*. 1992.

GRUNION RUN

This southern California tradition celebrates the "run" and capture of small smelt-like fish, *Leuresthes tenuis*, when they move ashore to spawn along stretches of wet, sandy beaches from Point Conception to the Baja peninsula. After most new and full moons, for up to three nights, party-goers gather on the beach after sunset and wait for the high tide to recede. They build fires, drink, eat, and generally amuse themselves until the silvery fish show up on the beach. Then, with the aid of flashlights or torches, they scan the shore for the reflections of the creatures who are now wiggling into the sand to deposit their eggs. The "sport" is to run along the surf, snatching up as many of the grunion as possible, depositing them in buckets and baskets, and then displaying the catch to compatriots back at the bonfire. This activity can last for several hours. Typically, the fish are prepared for eating by breading and deep-frying. However, grunion is not a popular fish to consume, and most captured creatures are reintroduced to the briny.

GUACAMOLE

In Mexico, *guacamole*, which is an Indian word that means avocado mixture, is a standard food in most households. Since the seventeenth century, this classic avocado dip has been made with mashed avocado combined with minced chiles and chopped cilantro, onions, and tomato. Traditionally, the mixture is blended with a mortar and pestle, and even today it is never mixed in an electric blender because guacamole is supposed to be somewhat chunky or coarse in texture. Some people add a bit of lemon or lime juice or olive oil to prevent the avocado from darkening when exposed to the air. Guacamole is usually served family-style with a large bowl of tortilla chips or as a topping for tacos.

Until about the 1960s or 1970s, serving guacamole was primarily a southwestern practice in the United States, but has spread throughout North America with the increasing number of Mexican restaurants that have appeared from coast to coast. The availability of commercially prepared avocado dips that are sold in supermarkets and other grocery stores also helped to popularize the practice. Guacamole is commonly served in the United States with chips as an appetizer before dinner or at cocktail parties.

See also: APPETIZERS; CHIPS AND DIP; SALSA.

Reference: Weiner and Weiner. *World of Cooking*. 1983.

GUMBO

Contrary to the popular notion that *gumbo* originated from a French term, it stems from an African word for okra. Enslaved Africans brought okra to the West Indies and then to American shores and cooked it in a variety of ways, often in a stew or soup. Acadians in Louisiana learned to use okra and began making gumbo with not only available vegetables but also with portions of meat, seafood, wild game, or poultry. This hearty soup or stew is now considered a traditional dish in the U.S. South and is especially linked with New Orleans and a Cajun style of eating. Various types of gumbo, such as seafood gumbo and okra and tomato gumbo, are also popular soul food dishes.

See also: MARDI GRAS; SOUL FOOD.

Reference: Angers. *Cajun Cuisine*. 1985.

HALLOWEEN

A variety of foods and drinks are traditionally consumed during Halloween, which derived from the pagan festival of Samhain, a Celtic rite that marked the end of the year, and from All Hallow's Eve, the Christian night prior to All Saints Day when it was believed that the dead walked the earth. All of the ripening fruits and vegetables of late autumn are associated with this holiday, such as apples, nuts, squash, and, in the United States especially, the pumpkin squash.

Usually pumpkins are hollowed out and carved into scary figure heads called jack-o-lanterns, which were thought to be will-o'-the-wisps as in "The Legend of Sleepy Hollow." The pumpkin flesh may be eaten in the form of pumpkin pie or pumpkin bread, and the pumpkin seeds may be roasted and salted for snack food.

School Halloween parties usually include treats such as cider and doughnuts, caramel apples, and various types of candies. Halloween night activities for children center on the tradition of "trick-or-treating." Youngsters dress up in costumes emulating monsters and other eerie creatures or favorite characters or celebrities. They then pass from neighbor's house to neighbor's house, rapping on the door and calling out "trick or treat." Traditionally, this mild form of intimidation meant that a person had to offer a "treat" in order to protect her or his property from the evil forces—a nasty "trick." Treats often include candies, homemade cookies, popcorn balls, fudge, and fresh apples and nuts.

In recent times, this tradition has changed somewhat, adapted to protect children from the senseless adulteration of foods. Numerous stories have been told of unsuspecting children finding foreign objects such as pins and razor blades in their treats. Thus, some frightened parents have forbidden neighborhood canvassing and have organized private parties with safe food and activities such as bobbing for apples, costume contests, and pumpkin carving.

See also: CANDY AND CARAMEL APPLES; CIDER; DOUGHNUTS.

HAM

Baked, boiled, roasted, or fried, ham is served on numerous special occasions, and baked ham is associated with such holidays as Easter, Christmas, and New Year's Day. A roasted ham coated with spices then baked in a pastry is common for Easter Sunday celebrations in many parts of the U.S. South. A stuffed ham is a Maryland

Easter specialty. For this dish, the ham is slit to form pockets for such stuffings as cabbage, kale, onions, peppers, and seasonings. It is placed in a cloth bag and simmered in water for several hours, cooled, refrigerated, and served cold.

Kentucky ham, which is a country-cured or salt-cured and smoked ham, is baked to serve at parties and other events during the Kentucky Derby Festival in May. Since ham is as much a Kentucky food as whiskey is a Kentucky beverage, Ham Days are celebrated every September in Lebanon, Kentucky. Every year since 1969, Ham Days have included a country breakfast with red-eye gravy and biscuits, eggs, and fried apples.

At folk and food festivals in Georgia, a popular way to prepare a country ham is to soak it in beer, tea, and molasses for several days and then glaze it with brown sugar, mustard, and ketchup. In states where maple syrup festivals are held, a ham baked with maple syrup is a common dish.

A number of different types of hams, including canned Danish hams and other imported hams, as well as those prepared in North America, are included in food baskets or presented as gifts in and of themselves during the Christmas holiday. One of the most prestigious of these hams is the Smithfield processed in Smithfield, Virginia, where hams and bacons were first exported to England in the mid-1700s. Smithfield hams, or their imitations, are processed from hogs that are fed nuts in the woods and peanuts and corn in the fields. Once butchered, they are dry-salted, spiced, heavily smoked, and allowed to mature for a year.

See also: BISCUITS AND GRAVY; EASTER; FOOD BASKETS; KENTUCKY DERBY FESTIVAL.

References: Borghese. *Food from Harvest Festivals and Folk Fairs.* 1977; Fussell. *I Hear America Cooking.* 1986; Mariani. *The Dictionary of American Food and Drink.* 1993, 1994; Simon and Howe. *Dictionary of Gastronomy.* 1970; *Southern Heritage* editors. *The Southern Heritage Celebrations Cookbook.* 1984; Thompson and Carlson. *Holidays, Festivals, and Celebrations of the World Dictionary.* 1994; Trager. *Foodbook.* 1970.

HAMBURGERS

Considered a United States original, hamburger sandwiches (simply called hamburgers)—cooked patties of ground meat on buns—have been made and served for more than a century. The term for the sandwich probably derived from Hamburg, Germany, where ground meats were popular and where citizens sometimes enjoyed a popular Russian dish of shredded raw meat (known today as steak tartare). Before ground meat became hamburger in North America, however, it was eaten as Salisbury steak, named for J. H. Salisbury, a physician who recommended ground steak for a variety of ailments. By the early 1900s, Americans were preparing "hamburg steak" (a ground beef steak) in kitchens and later at backyard barbecues and picnics, but the hamburger did not become widely popular until the proliferation of fastfood chains beginning about the 1930s.

White Castle was one of the first hamburger chains to be established, beginning as roadside restaurants in Witchita, Kansas, in the 1920s and spreading to city neighborhoods and college towns. Many Americans growing up in the 1930s and 1940s are partial to White Castle hamburgers, affectionately known as "sliders," primarily because they were (and still are) small in size and quickly consumed in two or three bites, or even whole in some cases. White Castle fans indoctrinated their children in this particular hamburger culture, and some of them today will drive up to 50 miles to a familiar white building shaped like a castle for a bag of the sandwiches. These products are also frozen and sold by the box in most supermarkets across the United States, but, in the words of one White Castle fan, "they ain't the same!"

McDonald's hamburger chains first came on the scene in the 1950s when Ray Kroc started the franchise in Des Plaines, Illinois (although the original McDonald's restaurant had been opened more than a decade earlier in San Bernardino, California, by Richard and Maurice McDonald). By the 1960s, McDonald's hamburgers were so popular that the familiar golden

Served on a sesame bun, hamburgers are an American classic. Standard accompaniments, or fixings, may include mustard, mayonnaise, and ketchup with the works on the side: lettuce, tomatoes, pickles, and onions.

"M" sign included a changeable number indicating how many million hamburgers had been sold. Other hamburger chains soon appeared on the scene, some starting as a single restaurant.

In 1969, Dave Thomas founded Wendy's Old Fashioned Hamburgers in downtown Columbus, Ohio, naming the restaurant after his daughter and selling quarter-pound hamburgers and bowls of chili. With award-winning advertising, Wendy's grew from a single restaurant to a worldwide chain of nearly 4,400 restaurants and sales totaling $4 billion annually in 1994.

Whether purchased at a chain restaurant or made at home, hamburgers vie with hot dogs as the top all-American food, and all-beef patties no longer are the only choice. Instead, a patty may be made of anything from ground round to a substitute meat made of soybeans, the latter often called a "veggie burger." Crab, buffalo meat, fish, pork, turkey, lamb, and even duck can be used to make burgers. Nevertheless, the beef hamburger will probably continue its long time popularity not just in North America but worldwide, since McDonald's, Wendy's, and other chains have been established in numerous countries.

See also: BARBECUE; BOXED MEALS AND HELPERS; CHILDREN'S MEALS; MEAT AND POTATOES; PICNIC; STADIUM AND ARENA EATING AND DRINKING; TRUCK STOP FOOD.

References: Mariani. *The Dictionary of American Food and Drink.* 1993, 1994; Trager. *The Food Chronology.* 1995.

HANUKKAH

See CHANUKAH.

HAPPY HOUR

Usually a weekday event occurring between 5:00 and 7:00 P.M., happy hour is similar to a cocktail party except that it is held in a commercial establishment. Drinks coupled with free appetizers are offered as a way to lure customers into a drinking establishment. This common promotional technique has been used by many bars, cocktail lounges, and restaurants across North America.
See also: APPETIZERS; COCKTAIL PARTY; FOOD SAMPLING.

HEALTH/NATURAL FOOD RESTAURANTS

In the late 1960s and early 1970s, it was rare to find a restaurant in the United States dedicated to serving what was known then as "health food." At that time such a restaurant was usually an outgrowth of a back-to-earth cooperative organization. Patrons referred to as "hippies" found that food cooperatives and the natural food restaurants that often accompanied them were some of the few places where there were like-minded souls (these long-haired, free-thinking vegetarians in the United States and Canada often experienced discrimination for the life-style they chose).

As understanding about vegetarianism grew, there was also a growth of alternative eateries. "Macrobiotic," "Zen," "meatless," and "whole food" became common descriptions for the new restaurants. They often served such foods as tofu, brown rice, whole grains, unrefined sugar, raw foods, and exotic juice and herbal tea blends. Today, there is more widespread understanding that consuming too much fat, meat, and processed and otherwise adulterated food is not the best regimen for health. As a result there are any number of natural and health food establishments that are catering to a much broader cross section of the dining public. Chefs in some establishments that may be called "gourmet" have incorporated the whole food philosophy into their cooking; thus, these foods are making inroads onto the regular restaurant menus.

See also: GRANOLA BARS/CEREAL; VEGETARIAN EATING.

HEAVENLY HASH

This is a common carry-in dessert for church suppers and potlucks in many parts of the Midwest. One version calls for layers of vanilla wafers and whipped cream chilled for several hours before serving. Another popular version of heavenly hash is routinely made with a mixture of fruits (often canned fruit cocktail), marshmallows, sometimes nuts, and whipped cream.
See also: CHURCH DINNERS/SUPPERS; POTLUCK.

HERBAL TEA

Herbal teas have been consumed for centuries. These infusions of dried or fresh leaves, roots, or fruits in hot water have been used as traditional cures for most ailments of the body. Chamomile, peppermint, and elderflower were especially popular among early American colonists from England. One special herbal favorite was Oswego tea made from dry flowers of wild bergamot (bee balm). After the Boston Tea Party, when imports of real tea (that is, the dried leaves of the shrub *Thea sinensis* grown primarily in China and India) were forbidden, Liberty teas made with blends of such ingredients as mint, balm, rosemary, and sage became popular as substitutes.

Chinese or Indian tea packs a large dose of the chemical compound caffeine in each cup. For this reason, many people who have decided to eliminate caffeinated beverages from their diet and those who want to eliminate additives like the dyes used in regular tea have turned to the more subtle tastes of herbal teas. Most are naturally decaffeinated and, purchased in bulk or from a reputable commercial packager, are likely to be free of chemical adulteration.

There are hundreds of herbs that can be used to make a pleasant-tasting infusion, and many aficionados have their own favorite teas and times to sit and sip them.

Dried herbs and fruits steeped in hot water have long been a part of diets around the world. Trading on the 1960s American awareness of nutrition and desire to use products with fewer preservatives and additives, Celestial Seasonings, a company in Boulder, Colorado, created a line of herbal and fruit teas.

Such a ritual is associated with "mu tea," which is made from 16 different herbs and is often consumed in the middle of the day. This tea acts as a very satisfactory stimulant, and its unique taste has been likened to the flavor of light beef broth. Often people will use chamomile infusions at the end of an evening for its relaxing effect.
See also: AFTERNOON TEA; HEALTH/NATURAL FOOD RESTAURANTS; MEDICINAL FOODS.
Reference: Marcin.*The Complete Book of Herbal Teas.* 1983.

HIGH SCHOOL CLASS REUNION

The centerpiece of the high school class reunion is traditionally a Saturday night banquet or dinner served in a hotel or motel dining area, community hall, or similar facility. Sometimes members of the class hosting the reunion invite out-of-town members to a cocktail party prior to the main event, which includes a formal program, a group photo session, and a dance. Usually a class reunion is held on a weekend during the summer or early fall, and a picnic or brunch may be on the agenda the day after the formal reunion.
See also: FAMILY REUNION.

HIGH SCHOOL GRADUATION PARTY

Across the United States, graduation from high school is a rite of passage that prompts numerous festive events. Parents often host a picnic, barbecue, buffet, or evening party to honor their graduates. Numerous graduates also plan their own parties—usually all-night affairs held in hotels or private homes. Unfortunately, many of the student-initiated parties have become drunken brawls, and some parties have resulted in injuries and deaths from gang violence and alcohol- or other drug-related accidents. Because of these tragedies, some parent and student groups and school systems in the United States have joined together to establish another type of party tradition.

Since the late 1980s or early 1990s, cooperative adult-student groups have been holding chaperoned all-night events, which typically run from about 9:00 or 10:00 P.M. until about 6:00 A.M., at a high school gym or auditorium, an amusement park, a sports arena, or a similar facility where only nonalcoholic beverages are served along with a variety of sandwiches and snack foods.

All-night bashes with such names as Late Night or Graduation with Pride sponsored by parents and the schools have included a raffle for a new car and other prizes, and such activities as basketball, volleyball, short musical plays, magic shows, disc jockeys, karaoke, and plenty of food. In some cases, a bus may transport students to various events, such as a comedy act or bowling competition. At some schools anywhere from 75 to 95 percent of the senior class attends, which bodes well for a continuation of this ritual.
See also: PROM NIGHT.

HOG ROAST

Perhaps one of the most widely known hog or pig roasts is the Hawaiian luau, but it is traditional practice in many other cultures to roast a pig or hog for a holiday or feast day. During the days when most people in the United States lived in rural areas, a special event would be celebrated with the butchering and roasting of a young calf, sheep, or hog.

For festive occasions, Mexican families frequently roast small pigs in their ovens. Preparation of this dish requires plucking out the eyes and then lowering the eyelids again prior to roasting. The finished product is served on a large platter covered with greenery, and the finishing touch is an apple stuck in the animal's mouth, a variation on an old European practice in which a lemon, considered a symbol of plenty, was placed in a boar's or pig's mouth.

Hogs are also cooked outdoors on a spit over a fire, an activity that can be the focus of almost any type of festive event. People gather to socialize and watch and comment on the cooking process—the animal cooks for the better part of a day before it is ready to serve at an outdoor feast.
See also: FAMILY REUNION; LUAU.

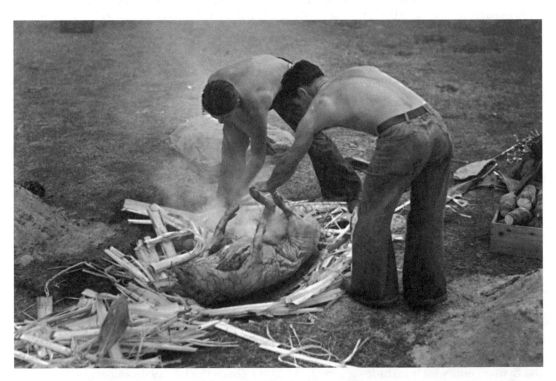

Hawaiians prepare the main feature of a luau, a roasted hog. Wrapped in ti leaves and cooked in an imu, a covered pit, the pig will steam for hours.

HOT CROSS BUNS

Many attempts have been made to establish the origin of hot cross buns and trace their historical path. According to some historians, the cross on the bun originated with ancient Greeks, who marked bread-like cakes with a horned symbol and offered them to the goddess of love and fertility. Others say the practice of marking bread with a cross stemmed from early Christian culture and the ritual ceremonies for remembering Christ's crucifixion. Whatever the origin, European bakers have for centuries marked a cross in bread dough before baking, believing the symbol would protect not only the bread but also the household from evil. Today, hot cross buns are part of meals served from Good Friday through Easter.

See also: BREAD; EASTER.

HOT DOGS

In some parts of North America, they are called frankfurters, named for Frankfurt, Germany, one place where sausages originated. In other areas, they are known as red hots, hot dogs, foot-longs, or wieners. The latter name derived from Vienna, Austria, another origin of sausages. The most popular term *hot dog* most likely originated with a Chicago cartoonist, who, in 1916, depicted a vendor at a baseball park selling a dachshund in a bun.

However they are labeled, these sausagelike products are all made of ground, precooked meats (usually beef and/or pork) inserted into casings, and they are commonly served in buns, shaped and sized to fit the meat. They are sold at such eating places as street stands in major cities; booths at beaches, country fairs, athletic events, train stations, airports, and various types of food festivals; and fastfood shops and delis. For many folks, a barbecue or picnic is hardly complete without hot dogs, and a summer wiener roast is common in many parts of the United States. At least 95 percent of all Americans serve hot dogs at one time or another in their homes.

There are numerous variations in what constitutes a hot dog on a bun. They may be all-beef kosher hot dogs or they may be made with a combination of veal, ham, and beef and called white hots. The hot dogs may be cooked over charcoal fires or split and fried on a griddle, or they may be boiled frankfurters called Sabrett's, which are sold by street vendors in New York City. According to Jeff Smith, the popular Frugal Gourmet chef and cookbook author, Chicago has more hot dog stands than New York City—4,000 of them—more than any other city in the United States.

Countless sports fans would enjoy the game less if there were not red hots available to munch on and wash down with an ice cold beer. At the first basketball game of the 1994–1995 season at Gund Arena in Cleveland, Ohio, for example, fans gobbled up about 3,000 hot dogs ranging in variety from kosher and Polish dogs to the Cleveland Dog—an all-beef hot dog topped with fried purple cabbage, cheddar cheese, diced onions, tomato, dill pickle, and Cleveland's own authentic stadium mustard.

While the traditional hot dog has been the beef or pork variety, many of today's consumers prefer turkey or chicken franks, which are touted as low-fat. These have become staple fare for people with dietary concerns. No matter what the fat content of the hot dog, seldom do Americans simply eat the hot dog plain in a bun. It is usually accompanied with sauerkraut, chili, hot sauce, or other condiments. Most consumers top their dog with mustard or ketchup or both, relish of some sort, onions, and perhaps diced tomatoes. Each person has her or his own way of garnishing a hot dog, which in itself may be a ritual, for example, placing a wiggly mustard stripe over the frank, tucking in the relish "just so" along the side of the bun, and topping it off with chopped or sliced onions. Most hot dog lovers eat their sandwich with chips or french fries and usually a beer or bubbly soft drink.

One noneating ritual that focuses on hot dogs is the annual appearance in many U.S. cities and towns of one of Oscar Mayer's wienermobiles. First developed in

1936, the wienermobile was obviously created to be an advertising vehicle in every sense of the term, and each of the mobile units manufactured since has been similar to the original—designed like a huge bun with an Oscar Mayer wiener nestled inside. The wienermobiles have become part of parades; they travel to baseball parks and country fairs; and they navigate the parking lots at malls and shopping centers. Promoters traveling with the wienermobiles give away wiener-shaped whistles to children and adults who gather to see this giant, mobile dog-in-a-bun roll by.

See also: BASEBALL PARK EATING AND DRINKING; BEANS AND FRANKS; CHILI DOGS; CORN DOGS; SANDWICHES.

References: Brallier. *The Hot Dog Cookbook.* 1993; Smith. *The Frugal Gourmet Cooks American.* 1987; Stern and Stern. *Real American Food.* 1986; Wyman. *I'm a SPAM Fan.* 1993.

HOT SAUCE

Some people are addicted to hot sauce and use it on almost any kind of food. People who enjoy hot, spicy food often keep a bottle of hot sauce not only in the kitchen for "spiking" food while cooking but also on the table for additional boosts of heat and spice. Although many other varieties are routinely used, one of the most widely used is Tabasco, made from a tropical red pepper, salted and mashed and aged for three years, then blended with vinegar and bottled. Tabasco is a common ingredient in such mixed drinks as the Bloody Mary and the Bloody Caesar, a Canadian alcoholic specialty made of tomato and clam juice.

See also: CHILES.

References: DeWitt and Gerlach. *The Whole Chile Pepper Book.* 1990; Henderson. "The Tabasco of Louisiana." 1994.

HOT TODDY

A hot toddy has been used for centuries as a cold or flu remedy. It is also frequently served at parties or after outdoor activities on chilly or cold days. One of the most common forms of a hot toddy is a mix of hot water, sugar, and a single spirit such as rum, brandy, whiskey, or gin. Another type of hot toddy is made with a coffee base—for example, Irish coffee. Hot cider and apple schnapps, glogg, and hot tea with amaretto are other types of toddies.

See also: CIDER; GLOGG; IRISH COFFEE; MULLED WINE.

HUEVOS RANCHEROS

A traditional breakfast in the southwestern United States, huevos rancheros consist of fried eggs on a tortilla with a covering of salsa. Although the breakfast is a regular item on menus at many restaurants in California, Arizona, New Mexico, and Texas, huevos rancheros are also served in numerous Mexican-style eating establishments across the United States.

See also: BREAKFAST.

HUSH PUPPIES

Traditionally, hush puppies have been served with fried catfish but now routinely accompany many types of fish meals. These fried puffs are made with a batter of cornmeal, flour, baking powder, eggs, milk, and chopped onions dropped by the spoonful into hot fat. Almost every southern state has claimed to have invented the name for this cornmeal biscuit or bread. According to one oft-repeated story, fishermen used to fry this batter at the same time that they fried their catch for the day, and the savory smells would set their hungry dogs pacing and barking for food. So the fishermen would throw out some of the cornbread with the admonition "hush, puppy." Of course, the dogs were appeased and became quiet, but the name stuck to the pone, or corn bread.

See also: BREAD; SPOON BREAD.

Reference: Funk. *2,107 Curious World Origins, Sayings and Expressions.* 1993.

ICE CREAM

"I scream, you scream, we all scream for ice cream" is an old verse with which most people worldwide would agree. This frozen confection probably evolved from the ancient Greek and Roman practice of flavoring ice or snow with wine or fruit juices. Today, however, it is much richer than ice. Heavy cream is the main ingredient, and sugar and various flavorings such as chocolate or fruit complete the recipe.

Ice cream is celebrated during a dairy festival every July in Elsie, dairy capital of the state of Michigan. During the three-day festival, which began in 1986, competitions in ice cream eating and milk drinking (from a baby bottle) are major attractions.

Throughout the United States, over 1 billion gallons of ice cream are produced annually, and the average person consumes about 15 quarts each year. Ice cream consumers can select from hundreds of flavors. Baskin-Robbins, a major producer and franchiser, claims to have developed 548 flavors of ice cream thus far, with vanilla being the all-time favorite.

One of the customary ways to eat ice cream is in a wafer or sugar cone or as a bar covered with chocolate or other coating. These frozen dessert treats are popular with young and old alike and are traditionally consumed at outdoor events such as fairs, festivals, picnics, parades, races, and beach outings. During the summer months when children are out of school, the ice cream truck travels through towns and city neighborhoods, playing a familiar recorded tune over a loudspeaker system and calling youngsters out to buy their favorite ice cream or other frozen treat.

Ice cream sundaes—scoops of ice cream in a dish with syrup (such as chocolate, strawberry, caramel, or butterscotch), usually topped with whipped cream and nuts—are also traditional desserts served at home or in restaurants. Another customary way of eating ice cream is in a milk shake, a thick blend of ice cream, milk, and flavoring, often ordered to go with a fastfood item or just as a refreshing drink. It is common for all members of a family to go to the nearest ice cream shop or stand on a regular basis for an afternoon or evening treat.

Because of the widespread concern about excess fat and calories in the diet, dozens of low-fat substitutes for ice cream have been developed and sold in the United States in recent years. Usually these products are made with skim milk and may be sweetened with a chemical sweetener rather than sugar or corn syrup. People who habitually consume these frozen desserts may do so because of heart disease, diabetes, or other health problems, because they are following weight-loss programs, or simply because they believe such foods are "healthier."

Yet, people who love and crave ice cream seldom are satisfied with substitute products. Perhaps that is one reason ice cream companies like Ben and Jerry's are so successful. Their rich, creamy, and flavorful ice creams are not only appealing but are also a "must" for some consumers who say they habitually include "real ice cream" in their weekly eating patterns.

See also: FLAVORED ICE; ICE CREAM AND CAKE/COOKIES; ICE CREAM CONE; ICE CREAM SOCIAL; MILK SHAKE.

Reference: Dickson. *The Great American Ice Cream Book.* 1972.

ICE CREAM AND CAKE/COOKIES

A birthday party nearly always includes a traditional birthday cake served with ice cream, and ice cream seems a natural accompaniment almost any time pieces of cake or cookies are served, whether at home, at a banquet, community dinner, or similar event. In restaurants, a cookie may be used as a decorative top for a dish of ice cream, and whenever ice cream is the main dessert after a home meal, a plate of cookies is usually on the table.

See also: ICE CREAM; MILK SHAKE.

ICE CREAM CONE

The ice cream cone is a favorite treat for kids, and countless adults love to snack on them. In fact, the ice cream cone became an American institution not long after it was introduced in the early 1900s. By 1924, sales of ice cream cones totaled 245 million per year.

Food historians cite a number of different origins for the ice cream cone. Some say it originated in France where ice cream was sold in paper cones during the early 1900s. In the United States, debates over who invented the ice cream cone have been going on since 1954 when the International

Association of Ice Cream Manufacturers was holding a convention in St. Louis. The two-day event honored Ernest A. Hamwi, who 50 years earlier had been at a World's Fair in St. Louis selling a wafflelike Persian pastry. His stand was next to an ice cream vendor who sold his product by the dish, but when the ice cream dishes ran out, Hamwi rolled up one of his pastries to use as a container. The ice cream cone was sold at the fair from then on and became an instant success. Although other vendors were also at the World's Fair and claimed to have created an ice cream cone, Hamwi is the man most often credited with the feat.

See also: ICE CREAM.

Reference: Dickson. *The Great American Ice Cream Book.* 1972.

ICE CREAM SOCIAL

During the late 1800s and early 1900s, an ice cream social was a popular way to entertain in the United States. Guests were invited to a home or community center to make ice cream in an ice-filled, hand-cranked freezer (the Peerless Freezer was just one of many brands manufactured at the time), a task usually shared since the cranking could be exhausting. After the mixture of cream, eggs, sugar, vanilla or other flavoring, and pieces of fresh fruit (such as strawberries and peaches) had frozen, the ice cream was ready to be served, usually accompanied by home-baked cookies and cakes. To re-create such an event, a Victorian Ice Cream Social has been held each July since 1975 at the historic President Benjamin Harrison Home in Indianapolis, Indiana.

Ice cream socials with handmade or store-bought ice cream are common fund-raising events today for schools, religious and civic groups, clubs, and other organizations. Cakes, cookies, and pastries are donated for the social, and funds collected help pay for such things as recreational equipment, library books, or special service projects.

See also: ICE CREAM; ICE CREAM AND CAKE/COOKIES.

ICED TEA

Since it was created at the 1904 Louisiana Purchase Exposition in St. Louis, iced tea has become one of the most popular beverages in the United States. It is consumed almost any time of day for almost any event, although iced tea, especially "sun tea"—bags of tea steeped in a jar of water placed in the hot sun—is a traditional summer drink. Today, over 127 million people in the United States drink iced tea, and in 1994 ready-to-drink tea was one of the fastest-growing product categories in the supermarket, according to *PR Newswire* (May 1994). Lipton, the leading trademark in tea, now markets a ready-to-drink variety. Another popular brand, Snapple, founded in 1972, produces a real-brewed iced tea as well as fruit drinks and sports drinks for distribution all across the United States. And in 1994, Veryfine Products, a Boston-based fruit juice and fruit drink maker, entered the booming business of flavored iced teas and lemonades.

In recent years new technology has enabled manufacturers to bottle tea without having to add preservatives, which were needed in the past. Thus, there has been a dramatic improvement in the taste of bottled teas, but iced tea is not only popular for its great taste. It offers potential health benefits as well. Many of the components found in tea, such as polyphenolic antioxidants, may help decrease the risk of cancer and heart disease. Research shows that tea may increase the metabolic processes in the liver that detoxify environmental toxins and carcinogens, according to the American Health Foundation.
See also: AFTERNOON TEA; SPORTS DRINKS.

INDEPENDENCE DAY CELEBRATIONS

One of the most important holidays in the United States, Independence Day is celebrated on 4 July, marking the adoption of

The 200th anniversary of the signing of the Declaration of Independence is celebrated in grand style at the nation's Capitol. Here, a National Archives staff member wields a ceremonial saber to slice a birthday cake while an actor in colonial wig and frock coat stands by to read the Declaration of Independence.

the Declaration of Independence on 4 July 1776. A day of patriotic parades and speeches, fireworks, boat races, fairs, and carnivals, it is also a time for community or family picnics in a public park, backyard barbecues, clambakes, and fish boils. Some of the traditional foods consumed on this day include fried chicken, barbecued ribs, coleslaw, potato salad, and watermelon. An old-fashioned ice cream social also is a common Fourth-of-July event.

See also: BARBECUE; FAMILY REUNION; ICE CREAM SOCIAL; PICNIC.

INSECTS

About 80 percent of the world's population eats some insects as food, a practice stemming from ancient times. Ancient Greeks and Romans, for example, relished the larvae or grubs of beetles, and, according to biblical accounts, the tribes of Israel ate locust. For centuries, people in China have harvested crickets for food, and in Mexico people have long eaten insect eggs, larvae, and pupae—sometimes toasted or ground up in tamales. Locust too have long been part of the Mexican diet. The practice of eating insects, however, is not popular in the United States or Canada. In fact, the majority of Americans find the very thought of insect eating repulsive.

Nevertheless, some U.S. entomologists and naturalists in different parts of the nation have held annual parties or receptions to introduce people to the concept of insects as food, pointing out their nutritional value as well as how to prepare them. After an entomologist introduced outdoor author Robert H. Boyle to the idea of edible insects during the 1970s, Boyle reported that he learned to enjoy the practice and one of his favorite treats was grubs, which he washed, fried, and served on toast.

Tom Turpin, a professor of entomology at Purdue University in Indiana, and his wife, Chris, conduct a taste-testing of "bug treats" about 50 times a year. The Turpins' specialty is called "chocolate chirpy chip cookies," which are made with crickets (legs and wings removed) instead of

chocolate chips. After tasting "buggy" desserts or appetizers made with insects, some unbiased individuals say that such culinary treats as highly spiced pan-fried mealworms, chocolate-covered crickets and ants, waxworm corn fritters, cricket and vegetable tempura, and sugar cookies spiked with assorted insects are tasty—even delicious.

See also: FOOD TABOOS.

References: Boyle. "The Joy of Cooking Insects." 1992; Sokolov. "Insects, Worms, and Other Tidbits." 1989.

INSTANT FOODS AND BEVERAGES

The convenience trend that started in the 1950s spawned hundreds of commercial food products that were quick and easy or "instantly" available, in the hyperbole of the day. Although Jell-O, the brand name for flavored and sweetened gelatin, had been on the market for more than 50 years, many more instant foods became available during the 1950s and 1960s. Tang, an orange powder that became an orange juice substitute with the addition of tap water, was first developed for astronauts, and it has been a popular instant drink for several decades, as have a variety of chocolate powders to mix with milk for instant chocolate milk. The widespread demand for these products prompted the development of even more instant foods, such as puddings, cake mixes, frostings, cheese in dispenser cans, sauces, and dried vegetables that can be reconstituted with water. The trend toward using more and more instant food products shows no sign of slowing down, and science fiction stories depicting our future meals as multicolored pills may not be far off the mark, particularly if they provide a balanced diet in one swallow.

See also: GELATIN MOLD; KOOL-AID.

IRISH COFFEE

The custom of pouring a shot of Irish whisky into a cup of hot coffee supposedly began on St. Patrick's Day in 1946 when a bartender in San Francisco experimented with the concoction and liked it. He found that his customers also liked whisky-laced coffee. The bartender shared his new recipe with others, and the practice spread. Although drinking Irish coffee is associated with St. Patrick's Day, it is not a tradition of long standing. Many types of alcoholic beverages as well as other drinks are consumed on that day. Nevertheless, people across North America make and serve Irish coffee at countless social events, with each person preparing the coffee according to his or her favorite recipe. This is a popular drink at coffee bars and houses as well.

See also: COFFEE HOUSES.

JAMBALAYA

Preparing jambalaya, a dish that is traditionally Cajun, is a common way to use up leftovers. It is frequently associated with Mardi Gras, although it is popular in the diet of many residents of the U.S. South. The term *jambalaya* probably came from the African *jomba*, meaning "bundle." West Africans often cooked chopped meat and fish together, combining these ingredients with spices, oil, and nuts. The combination was wrapped in plantain leaves, which were steamed over hot coals. Acadians, who learned about *jomba* from enslaved Africans brought to the Louisiana Territory, substituted rice for the chopped nuts in the combination. Today, jambalaya is usually made with pork or poultry, but shrimp, crawfish, and sausage jambalaya are also common. It is also make with a combination of these ingredients.

See also: MARDI GRAS.
Reference: Angers. *Cajun Cuisine.* 1985.

JERKY

The term *jerky* comes from an ancient Inca word, *charqui*. In fact, the Incas of the Andean region in South America prepared *charqui*, or dried meat, thousands of years ago so that they could preserve and easily transport meat from wild animals killed in the hunt for food. On the Pacific Northwest coast of North America, salmon jerky was the choice among coastal tribes. Europeans exploring the Americas adapted the practice of drying meat and fish, and pioneers on the North American frontier, who learned the practice from Native Americans, carried buffalo, venison, or beef jerky along the trails. Today, jerky along with dried meat sticks are common snack foods that are often served at bars as an accompaniment to beer or other drinks. It is also a popular camping and convenience store food.

See also: CAMP/TRAIL FOOD; CONVENIENCE STORE FOODS; SNACK FOODS.
References: Fussell. *I Hear America Cooking.* 1986; Weatherford. *Indian Givers.* 1989.

JOHNNYCAKE

This flat white cornmeal bread may have been named after the "Johnny Rebs" (Confederate soldiers) of the Civil War because they ate so much corn pone, although there also are references to "jonny cake"—a hard, cornmeal-based bread—that was eaten during the American Revolutionary War. Another term common for the bread was *journey cake*, so named, some say, because Johnny is pronounced like journey in New England, but others say it was because it could be prepared easily on a trip. Consisting of cornmeal and water or milk, and the occasional egg, and sweetened with a few tablespoons of sugar, the batter would be pressed into a flat cake and cooked on a board alongside an open fire or on a grill or oven if one was available. One traditional U.S. recipe referred to Johnny Hoe Cake, because it was cooked on a hoe. Today, Johnnycake may be served at a variety of American festivals celebrating historical events.

See also: AMERICAN FOLKLIFE FESTIVAL.

JUNETEENTH

This traditional holiday is celebrated in the middle of June each year by various African American communities in the United States. While there is some argument regarding the derivation of the holiday, it is generally believed that picnics and barbecues are now organized to honor President Abraham Lincoln's Emancipation Proclamation. Although the proclamation went into effect on 1 January 1863, Texas rebelled and refused to emancipate slaves until 19 June 1865 when Union General Gordon Granger landed in Galveston and declared U.S. sovereignty over Texas, announcing that the state's 250,000 slaves were free.

Celebrations within the ex-slave populations of Galveston apparently began in the years immediately following 1865, and eventually the custom spread to other parts of Texas, Oklahoma, and neighboring states as the Galveston population began to migrate. From about 1945 to 1975, many blacks abandoned the celebration because of its ties with past repression, but over the past two decades, hundreds of thousands of blacks across the United States have gathered in various cities and towns for Juneteenth celebrations. In 1980, Texas made Juneteenth a state holiday. Although not all the events are held on 19 June, the gatherings have a common purpose: to reaffirm African American heritage and bring families and whole communities together to share cultural, historical, and social events. The festivities are centered around community picnics and sharing summer foods.

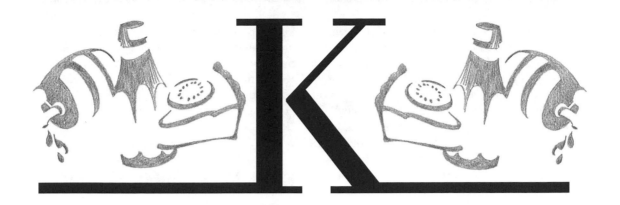

KAFFEEKLATSCH

In North America as in Europe, the kaffeeklatsch has been predominantly a social event, usually more formal than meeting for coffee in a cafe or other restaurant. Because women were excluded from early coffee houses and the ritual of coffee drinking wherever it was practiced, German women originated the kaffeeklatsch, which included both men and women. The practice carried over to North America and is now often referred to as "a coffee." Having "a coffee" is a popular way for politicians to meet voters and may be a means of fund-raising for an organization or group. **See also:** COFFEE HOUSES.

KEG PARTY

Kegs of beer have been around for years, and this was the accepted method of beer storage in the centuries prior to decent refrigeration and the general availability of glass or cans. In some cases, finishing off the brewing process in a particular type of wooden keg is important to the taste of the finished product. Most beer drinkers say that brew from a keg, even those that are now made from aluminum or steel, tastes better than beer in cans or bottles.

Most experts place the beginning of the modern keg party in and around the college campuses of the 1960s. Although campus parties always have included heavy beer consumption, the introduction of the "kegger," as they have been called, gave party-goers a real activity: getting the beer out of the keg. There is something exciting about the process, to which only those who have experienced the pleasure can attest. Tapping, pumping until the foam is drained off, and drinking the first cool, smooth swallow of malt liquid are the important rituals of a keg party.

Usually the cost of beer is lower in a keg, so more volume can be obtained for those truly dedicated to enjoying every drop of brew. This larger quantity leads to the final rites of the keg party: vomiting, passing out, and missing a day of classes due to a hangover. Unfortunately, the college keg party with binge drinking seems to be on the rise, leading to injury and even death.
See also: BEER DRINKING; SPRING BREAK.

KENTUCKY DERBY FESTIVAL

Although the famous Kentucky Derby race held at Louisville's Churchill Downs on the first Saturday in May each year only lasts a few minutes, the festivities go on for at least a week beforehand. Prederby parties and other types of entertainment are common, and Kentucky bourbon or the milder mint julep are usually served at most social events. Mint juleps may also accompany Derby Day breakfasts, which are events in and of themselves—rituals that include such staples as eggs, country ham, and biscuits. Depending on the weather, picnics on the day of the horse race are also part of the ritual on the grounds or just outside of the racetrack. People gather on the meadows and grassy areas near the track, as they have been doing ever since the first Derby in 1875, carrying hampers or coolers full of food and drinks and sharing in a community event that today draws people from all across the continent.

See also: HAM; MINT JULEP.

KETCHUP

In the United States it is hard to imagine food without ketchup (from the Chinese term *ke-tsiap,* a spicy sauce), or catsup, as it is often spelled. Backyard barbecues and picnics would not be the same without this condiment. Each year people in the United States consume at least 68 million gallons, more than a quart for every man, woman, and child in the nation.

While most people think of ketchup as a tomato-based condiment, it was not always so. According to historians, pioneers of the 1800s (who believed as did most North Americans that tomatoes were poisonous) made a sauce called ketchup from such foods as mushrooms, gooseberries, grapes, peppers, anchovies, oysters, or walnuts. A pepper ketchup, for example, was made from red bell peppers, vinegar, brown sugar, and spices. The mixture was cooked to a pulp, put through a sieve, then bottled. Walnuts and vinegar cooked to a pulp was also a popular ketchup. These and other sauces were used to cover the foul flavor of overaged meat. When tomatoes were finally used to make ketchup, commercial varieties were labeled "tomato

ketchup" to distinguish them from the other sauces referred to as ketchup.

See also: HOT DOGS; MEAT LOAF; SCRAPPLE.

References: Funk. *2,107 Curious World Origins, Sayings, and Expressions.* 1993; Rice. "Pioneers' Ketchups Avoided Tomatoes." 1994.

KEY LIME COOKIES AND PIE

Along the south Atlantic coast, many stores offer tins of key lime cookies for sale, and these tangy sweets frequently are given as special gifts to those living outside the region. The area, however, is better known for its key lime pie, which originated on the islands off southern Florida—the Keys—where true lime trees were first grown in the early 1800s. (Most other lime trees in the United States are actually hybrid lemon trees.) By the 1850s, someone discovered that key lime juice mixed with sweetened condensed milk and eggs would make a wonderful custard—tart, smooth, and refreshing. Although key lime pie is probably best known on the southeast coast, the dessert is a staple at some chain restaurants that specialize in fish and seafood.

Reference: Sokolov. *Why We Eat What We Eat.* 1991.

KINGS CAKE

See ALL KINGS DAY.

KOLACHES

Traditional Czech sweet buns, kolaches are made with an egg and yeast dough and are filled with preserves, poppy seeds, or cottage cheese. They are served by the dozens at the annual Kolache Festival in Prague, Oklahoma, held in May. In fact, along with kielbasa, a Czech sausage, the sweet buns are a must at every Czech festival, such as the annual event in Wilson, Kansas, with a population of less than 900, where the Czech After-Harvest Festival is celebrated each July. A similar July folk festival in the small town of Traer, Iowa, focuses on the Czech heritage of its residents, who share not only traditional foods like kolaches and kielbasa but also Czech music and dances with the many visitors who attend.

References: Clayton. *Cooking across America.* 1993; Hill. *Festivals U.S.A.* 1988.

KOOL-AID

A trademark of Kraft General Foods, Kool-Aid is the top-selling kids' soft drink in the United States. This beverage, which is made from a highly sweetened fruit-flavored powder that is mixed with water, is also popular with many adults. During the 1950s, sales of Kool-Aid soared due to one of the first marketing triumphs in the realm of children's food and instant foods. At a time when speed and convenience at a competitive price were of paramount concern, Kool-Aid commercials featured a mother in heels and a pleasant spring dress, standing in her perfect kitchen, sprinkling the Kool-Aid powder into the glass pitcher of water. With a quick stir it became the kids' favorite beverage. In a dual promotion, the Tupperware company created plastic molds with removable handles that allowed Mom to freeze the Kool-Aid to create a frozen treat.

See also: INSTANT FOODS AND BEVERAGES; LEMONADE STAND.

KOSHER FOOD

In a strictly ethical sense, *kosher* is a term that refers to a type of food preparation in accordance with Jewish dietary laws, known in Hebrew as *kashruth.* Those religious laws not only require cleanliness but also represent an affirmation of faith. Pork, for example, is not a kosher food because in ancient times the pig was often used for so-called heathen sacrifices and, therfore, considered unfit for human consumption. As in the past, kosher rules today forbid eating other animals once used for sacrificial purposes, such as the camel, donkey, and horse. Kosher dietary laws allow consumption of meat only from animals that are herbivorous, chew their cud, and have cloven hooves, as is written in the biblical books of Leviticus and Deuteronomy. In addition, only fish with fins and scales are allowed while scavenger shellfish are forbidden. Kosher laws apply also to the way food is prepared in the kitchen. They require separating meat and dairy foods; using separate pans, bowls, and utensils for each type of food; and separating the meat and dairy containers and utensils for washing and storing.

See also: FOOD TABOOS.

References: Cook. *Diet and Your Religion.* 1976; Nash. *Kosher Cuisine.* 1984.

KWANZAA

Celebrated between 26 December and 1 January, *Kwanzaa,* or *Kwanza,* is a cultural event that pays tribute to the heritage of Americans of African ancestry. In Swahili, *Kwanzaa* means "first fruits," and the festival signifies the harvest traditionally celebrated by agricultural groups in Africa. It began in 1966 in the United States and is now observed by more than 13 million people across the nation. *Kwanzaa* is based on seven guidelines for daily living: (1) unity, (2) self-determination, (3) collective work and responsibility, (4) cooperative economics, (5) purpose, (6) creativity, and (7) faith.

A basket or table centerpiece of fruits and vegetables is one important symbol of the holiday, as are ears of corn, one representing each child in the family. Those who celebrate the holiday share food and drink with family, friends, and neighbors. On the evening of 31 December, the *karamu* (feast) that culminates the holiday includes a special program focusing on music, dance, and other cultural performances. A feast follows, featuring a variety of dishes, such as baked fish, fried chicken, rice dishes, plantains, and yams. In a spirit of cooperation and community, those attending *karamu* bring in their favorite foods for the meal.

References: Cohen and Coffin. *The Folklore of American Holidays.* 1991; McClester. *Kwanzaa.* 1993.

LABOR DAY

The first Labor Day was celebrated in 1882 when 10,000 workers gathered at Union Square in New York City to hear speakers call for better working conditions and fair wages for laborers. President Grover Cleveland established Labor Day as a national holiday in 1894. Today, Labor Day weekend not only honors workers but also signals the final burst of summertime activities, and in many parts of the United States people watch parades, take part in tournaments, and attend street fairs or other social events. Family or community picnics and barbecues are common during this weekend, as are ethnic festivals, such as the IrishFest, which has become an annual celebration at St. Xavier University in an Irish neighborhood in Chicago. The festival includes Irish music, dancing, genealogy presentations, and plenty of traditional Irish food, such as lamb stew and colcannon, a potato and cabbage dish.
Reference: Schulz.*Celebrating America*. 1994.

LADIES' LUNCHEON

This social affair began in the late 1800s and early 1900s with society women who gathered to chat and organize charitable or cultural initiatives. Today, the practice of coming together to work on a common goal over a noon meal is still very much *en vogue*, but the projects may now concentrate on business, political, or environmental causes since women have moved into positions of power in the culture. One also may see more than a sprinkling of male faces in the banquet rooms where a luncheon is served.

The agenda for these meetings seems to run a typical course. Beginning usually before noon and running for one and one-half to two hours, the first order of business is finding a place to sit and then going through the buffet line, if that happens to be the style of service. More often a restaurant or country club staff serves lunch to guests at their tables. Menus are normally set, with no choices, and the main dish is some variation on chicken.

During the first course, it is customary for the chairperson to welcome the participants and introduce a guest speaker or the program for the afternoon. Through lunch, the presentation is made, and during dessert and coffee, there is typically a question-and-answer period.
See also: BANQUET; BUFFET; CHICKEN ENTREES.

LAS POSADAS

In Mexico and in many cities in the south-western United States, a festival called Las Posadas (The Inns) is held for a week in mid-December each year. The festival marks the period when Mary and Joseph of Nazareth traveled to Bethlehem. Public processions of Las Posadas players drama-tize the couple's search for shelter, a cus-tom dating back to the 1700s. Groups of costumed "travelers" also go from house to house in some neighborhoods, asking for admittance. They are refused at first, but finally they are welcomed and offered cookies and cider or traditional Mexican fare, such as guacamole and chips. In some cases, a dinner is held.

See also: MEXICAN FIESTAS.

References: Schulz. *Celebrating America.* 1994; *Southern Heritage* editors. *The South-ern Heritage Celebrations Cookbook.* 1984.

LATKE

See CHANUKAH.

LEFSE

See LUTEFISK; SMORGASBORD.

LEMONADE STAND

The lemonade stand is the symbol of the child entrepreneur. On a hot summer day, along many side streets throughout the United States, children as young as five years old set up their lemonade stands to make a little money and entertain them-selves for hours. Parents help their kids make the stand, the sign, the lemonade, and possibly cookies to go with the drinks. Popularized in comic strips, stories, and films, the lemonade stand has been shown with a sign that reads, "Lemonade 5¢," although that price has probably doubled or tripled in some areas. In some cases, Kool-Aid is substituted for the traditional lemonade sold.

See also: KOOL-AID.

LENT

Observed since the fourth century, Lent in the Western Christian church begins 40 days before Easter, excluding Sundays. In the Eastern church it extends over seven weeks, excluding both Saturdays and Sun-days. At one time, the faithful in North America and all of the Western world were directed to eat no more than one meal per day and to avoid all animal products for the duration of the fast. The fast originated as a spiritual preparation for Easter and represents the sacrifices of Jesus Christ. In common practice today, most church mem-bers who observe the tradition choose a favorite food (or even an activity) to give up until Easter Sunday arrives. Many choose sweets, alcohol, or red meat as their vehicle of self-sacrifice. After attending church services, the fast is broken with the traditional Easter feast.

See also: EASTER.

LIGHT EATING

Since about the 1970s, American con-sumers because of health concerns have increasingly and routinely bought pack-aged foods labeled "light" or "lite," under the assumption that these labeled products are low in fat, cholesterol, sodium, sugar, and calories. Some so-called light foods (and those labeled "low-fat," "lean," or "extra lean" or with phrases using words such as *reduced, less,* or *free*), however, have been little more than advertising claims, and people have been misled. Products such as "light" vegetable oils, for example, often have been merely light in color and a "light" dessert may have been only light in texture.

In 1993, the U.S. Food and Drug Administration (FDA) and the Food Safety and Inspection Service of the U.S. Depart-ment of Agriculture issued new food label-ing regulations designed to ensure more credible food labels. Today, the nutrients and fat, sodium, and sugar content of foods must be stated as accurately as possi-ble. When terms like *reduced* or *light* are

A golf enthusiast attending the U.S. Open in Rochester, New York, purchases lemonade from the "3 Princesses" in 1989. Lemonade stands flourish during the summer on neighborhood street corners and may serve as youngsters' first entrepreneurial endeavor.

used, the claims for the products must be compared to a similar reference food, that is, low-fat potato chips must be compared with regular potato chips. According to the FDA, *light* or *lite* on a label must mean "that a nutritionally altered product contains one-third fewer calories or half the fat of the reference food. If the food derives 50 percent or more of its calories from fat, the reduction must be 50 percent of the fat." In addition, the sodium content of a food product labeled "low-calorie" or "low-fat" must be reduced by 50 percent.

Numerous other FDA regulations require accurate labeling when using comparative terms such as *less* and *reduced* and claims for "higher" nutritive values. The new labeling laws provide the information that many health-conscious consumers need and at the same time help maintain the light eating trend.

See also: EATING TRENDS.
Reference: Stehlin. "A Little 'Lite' Reading." 1993.

LOBSTER BOIL

Eating lobster is frequently an event—for many it is the ultimate eating experience. A lobster boil is a common outdoor feast on the Atlantic Coast, and many tour groups from other parts of the United States and Canada often include a lobster boil in their itinerary, especially if they visit Maine where many annual lobster festivals are held. Rockland has conducted the four-day Maine Lobster Festival each August since 1948.

The traditional method of cooking this regal and rich crustacean is by boiling. Purists insist that the lobster be alive (for ultimate freshness) and plunged into a giant pot of rapidly boiling water kicking and clawing. A top is immediately placed on the cooking vessel, and it is not removed for about ten minutes. At that time the lobster shell will be a bright red and ready for cracking.

In areas where the lobster boil is a tourist attraction, the uninitiated receive "How To Eat a Lobster" instructions. A diner is advised to:

1. Tie a large bib around your neck.
2. After the lobster is cooked and served, twist off the claws.
3. Use a nutcracker to crack each claw.
4. Separate the tailpiece by arching the back until it cracks.
5. Break the flippers off the tailpiece and insert a fork inside the body where the flippers broke off.
6. Pull the back from the body, and open the remaining part of the body by cracking sideways.
7. Finally, eat the meat inside and suck the meat from the small claws.

Many people will eat only the tail and the claw portions, but experts insist that the liver (green section) and the roe (red if it is there) are superior eating, too. Black bean sauce or a little clarified butter are common accoutrements to this decadent feast, but there are some who say that the meat should be consumed without any sauces.

LOLLIPOPS

Hard candies on a stick—lollipops or suckers—are a favorite with children and were celebrated in song during the 1930s with Shirley Temple's rendition of "Good Ship Lollipop." In the United States, these candies gained in popularity during the 1980s, partly because of the increasing number of young children who created the growing market for these confections.

Lollipops are frequently given to kids as a reward for good behavior or an accomplishment. They are also popular on Valentine's Day, when many schoolkids give and receive cherry-flavored, heart-shaped lollipops. Many adults also enjoy the taste of lollipops and feel free to indulge themselves since compared to many other types of candies on the market they are low in calories.

See also: VALENTINE'S DAY.

Armed with nutcrackers and nutpicks, bibbed diners break apart boiled lobsters at a New York restaurant.

LONG-LIFE SPINACH NOODLES

See CHINESE NEW YEAR.

LOX

Lox is the Jewish-American version of smoked salmon. Uncooked and cold-smoked, it is a staple in Jewish delis, restaurants, and markets throughout North America. Although the term *lox* is associated with the Yiddish word *laks*, it is virtually unknown in Europe and Israel. A breakfast of lox and bagels is traditional in many North American Jewish homes, and many people enjoy an egg omelet with onions and lox for breakfast.

See also: BAGELS.

LUAU

Almost everyone who has ever heard or read the term *luau* knows that it is associated with a feast and stems from a Hawaiian eating ritual that began long before Hawaii ever became part of the United States. Many vacationers and other visitors in Hawaii attend at least one luau. The word *luau* actually means "taro leaf"—a frequently used ingredient in luau dishes. Foods at almost every luau are served outdoors whenever possible—buffet-style on paper plates.

The main attraction at a luau is roast pig, or the kalua pig, which at a traditional luau has been steamed for hours along with sweet potatoes, bananas, and bread-

fruit in an underground imu, or oven, lined with the lon, narrow leanes of the ti shrub or tree. Other basic luau dishes would include poi, which is crushed taro root and was once the mainstay of early Hawaiians. Laulau (which is sometimes a substitute for the kalua pig when underground roasting is impractical) is a traditional steamed dish that consists of ti leaves wrapped around a stuffing of boneless pork and salted fish, taro or spinach leaves, sweet potatoes, bananas, and taro shoots. Lomilomi salmon is one more luau dish. The term *lomilomi* means "massaged," and salted salmon is massaged, or rubbed, with a combination of tomatoes and onions and then marinated and chilled for hours before serving. Another mandatory part of the feast is chicken luau, which consists of chicken pieces cooked along with taro or spinach leaves in coconut milk. Pineapple spears, baked sweet potatoes and baked bananas, and haupia, a coconut pudding, would be served at the luau as well.

See also: POI.

Tourists are serenaded by a guitarist as they anticipate the beginning of a luau. Hawaii's traditional feast, the luau features fish, pork, and chicken steamed in an imu, a covered fire in a pit.

LUNAR NEW YEAR

For many Asian cultures, the New Year is the most important holiday celebration of the year, and many people of Asian ancestry now living in North America celebrate the beginning of a year based on the lunar calendar. The Chinese New Year, for example, is a well-known celebration, but other Asian groups—Cambodians, Koreans, Thais, and Vietnamese among them—also observe a lunar New Year with special dances, games, foods, giftgiving, and ceremonies to show respect to elders. One custom among those of Korean ancestry is to celebrate the New Year with a feast that includes *bulgogi* (barbecued beef) and *kimchi* (pickled cabbage). In Vietnamese communities during Tet (short for Tet Nguyen Dan, meaning the "Feast for the First Day"), a customary Vietnamese New Year food is spring rolls with fish sauce.

Cambodian and Thai groups celebrate the New Year for three days in April, the hottest month in Cambodia and Thailand when the harvest has been completed and people can set aside time for relaxation. During the New Year celebration in the United States, Cambodians and Thais visit Buddhist temples and share food with one another. Some traditional Thai dishes served are likely to be deep-fried fish and shrimp cakes, stir-fried chicken in red curry sauce and coconut, or a whole chicken simmered in water with herbs, lemon grass, chiles, and fish sauce.
See also: CHINESE NEW YEAR; SPRING ROLLS.

LUNCH

"Let's do lunch" became the phrase that defined the Hollywood business community (and by extension, all business movers and shakers) for most of the world in the 1980s. Popularized by movies, television, magazines, and books that portrayed members of the show business community as the "beautiful people" who were defined as much by where and with whom they were seen as by their last theatrical release, lunching became the way to meet and deal with one's peers.

Business was (and still is) conducted at the most prestigious places: Spago, Ma Maison, and whatever is the current favorite of the elite in Los Angeles. Highly visible to others in the industry, or to those that want to be, the "let's-do-lunch" crowd feeds on more than the food offered at these toney establishments. They are also sustained by the exposure and the perception that they are players in the most important game in town: making big money in the world's most glamorous business.

The business lunch is a staple of the more mundane industries, where time and close working relationships are important. Lunching is also a key social event for friends and acquaintances who just need to keep up with the latest happenings and gossip, and anyone can feel glamorous and more important by "doing lunch" on occasion.
See also: LADIES' LUNCHEON.

LUTEFISK

Lutefisk is of Scandinavian origin and is a Norwegian food specialty of the most cherished kind. It is a traditional Christmas dish in Norway and in some Scandinavian communities in North America, particularly in the Midwest, where large numbers of Norwegians and Swedes have settled. Madison, Wisconsin, for example, calls itself the Lutefisk Capital of the World.

In Scandinavia, it is a custom to make lutefisk, or lye fish, from dried cod that has been soaked in water, skinned, soaked in a lye mixture, then soaked in water again—a process that takes six to nine days and preserves the fish through the winter months. The fish can be cut into pieces, boiled with salt, and served with potatoes and peas. Although lutefisk was once commonly made in Scandinavian homes, today it is commercially processed—not with lye but with caustic soda—and it is sold in specialty food stores for special occasions. Minneapolis, Minnesota, claims to be the world's largest processor of lutefisk.

In spite of its ties to Scandinavian food customs, lutefisk is not universally appealing to North Americans of Nordic descent. There does not appear to be any middle ground on the opinion of lutefisk. Either people rave about its qualities or hate its very name and the experience of eating it. Antilutefisk people believe that the dish is inedible—"a Norwegian horror," "a Yuletide atrocity," "a mess that you would not set in front of your worst enemy," and "one of the main reasons that the Vikings left Norway!" One Scandinavian humorist, John Louis Anderson, likened the texture of lutefisk to that of a jellyfish slithering over his tongue. He noted that his mother used a "special kettle for boiling lutefisk. She bought it cheap at a garage sale, and thus had no qualms about ruining it. She refused to cook anything else in it, claiming that the lutefisk's oil, or aura, or karma, or something, had so permeated the kettle that it was unfit for any other culinary purpose."

Lutefisk lovers, on the other hand, have no such animosity toward this codfish dish. Rather, they often serve and eat lutefisk with wine on festive occasions, and they have helped preserve an ethnic tradition with lutefisk suppers, usually held in the fall in a Norwegian church. These suppers are likely to include lefse, a kind of pancake made with cold mashed potatoes that have been combined with milk and flour, rolled thin, and baked.

See also: CHRISTMAS EVE/DAY DINNER.

References: Algren. *America Eats*. 1992; Mariani. *The Dictionary of American Food and Drink*. 1993, 1994; Vanberg. *Of Norwegian Ways*. 1970.

MACARONI

For most of North America, the word *pasta* is synonymous with *macaroni* or *spaghetti*. The former term has been in existence for centuries and was used as a reference to many things. It was an Italian dumpling in the 1500s. The English have used the term to refer to a fashionable person. This usage, some believe, is the derivation of a verse from American Independence Day's favorite song, "Yankee Doodle." One version began: "Yankee Doodle went to London, just to ride a pony. Stuck a feather in his hat, and called it macaroni." Originally the song was an English ditty, made up to ridicule the colonists in their fight against the realm. The use of the word *macaroni* might have been a pun on a "noodle as a head" and/or the "affectation of foreign manners," which was one of its definitions of the time. It is almost impossible to say with any certainty at this point. One fact is irrefutable: Americans took the term and the reference to heart and made it their own. The song became the battle cry for the revolution.

Certainly, in the modern era one of the basic comfort foods is macaroni and cheese. A popular potluck dish, it is usually made with a variation of American cheese and elbow noodles. Real cheese is not necessarily a prerequisite for this dish,

as the most popular variety comes from a box containing a packet of dehydrated cheese powder, which reconstitutes into the familiar creamy-orange sauce. Kraft Foods has fed many families with this staple throughout the years.

Macaroni also is typically used as the main ingredient in salads. Hot summer evenings, picnics in the park, and buffet tables at informal luncheons seem to demand the traditional macaroni salad. This custom started when women's magazines of the 1950s and 1960s popularized the use of macaroni as a quick and easy option for the harried housewife.

See also: CASSEROLE DISHES/MEALS; CHURCH DINNERS/SUPPERS.

MADRIGAL DINNER

During the Christmas season, numerous communities in North America plan a madrigal dinner designed to re-create the pageantry of an Elizabethan Christmas. The celebration, which originated on college campuses in the 1930s, is named for madrigals—songs—based on tales or fables and written with parts for several voices. Brought to England from Italy in the sixteenth century, the songs were first sung without the accompaniment of musical instruments and were performed in the castles and homes of gentry. The lord and lady of a manor invited guests for an annual feast, and madrigal singing became part of the entertainment, eventually carrying over to English celebrations of the Twelve Days of Christmas.

Today's madrigal dinners follow some of the old customs and usually include a posted list of rules for the guests, which come from *Ye Olde Booke of Curtasye*. Among the rules of etiquette: "Gueysts myst have nayles cleane; myst aboyd quarrelying and makying grymaces; myst not stuff theyre mouths; should not pyck theyre teethe at the table with a knyfe, strawe, or stycke; never leave bones on the table—allways hyde them under they chayres; myst not tell unseemly tales at the table, not soyle the clothe wyth theyre knyfe, nor reste theyre legs upon the table; myst not leane on the table with theyre elbows, nor dyp theyre thumbs in theyre drynke; myst retain theyre knyfes or they shall be forced to grubbe whyth theyre fingers."

A college or high school cafeteria or a community center decorated to resemble a great royal hall is a common site for a madrigal dinner. Jesters, plays, and singing are all part of the event, which usually begins with a wassail toast led by madrigal singers wearing brightly colored costumes of velvet, brocade, and tapestry. In Elizabethan times, people drank to one another's good health, downing an alcoholic punch, but the wassail today is more likely to be a nonalcoholic spiced cider.

One of the oldest madrigal feasts in the Midwest has been held at South Suburban College in South Holland, Illinois, each year since the late 1960s. The madrigal singers are primarily community volunteers who stroll from table to table as diners enjoy a feast of six courses, including soup, salad, roast beef, chicken, and dessert. Since 1972, St. Mary's College in South Bend, Indiana, has held an annual madrigal dinner complete with the traditional centerpiece, a boar's head (or suck-

The lord and lady of the fictional Bracebridge Manor, center, sing for their supper during an annual dinner with madrigals, carols, and dancing during the Christmas season at the Ahwahnee Hotel in Yosemite National Park, California. The hotels re-creation of an Elizabethan Christmas has been an annual event since 1927. Participants dress in Elizabethan costumes and dine on courses of fish, pie, beef, plum pudding, and a wassail. The event is so popular that reservations are by lottery.

ling pig's head) that is purchased from a local meat-packing plant and roasted. At Valparaiso University in Indiana, the boar's head used for the madrigal dinner has been around since the early 1980s—after each performance the head is frozen.

Most madrigal dinners served today do not include a roast pig for eating; rather, more contemporary foods and dishes such as cornish hens, ham, and roast beef are common fare, and side dishes include potatoes and green vegetables. Although the traditional plum pudding is on the menu at some dinners, the dish is not always well accepted by diners, so other desserts such as pumpkin pie and cheesecake may be available.

MAIL-ORDER FOODS

Increasingly, North Americans have turned to mail-order companies—many of them small family businesses—for special foods that they want to include in their weekly meal plans. Ordering foods by mail is also a convenient way to shop for ethnic foods or regional foods that may not be available locally. Many small farms produce cheeses such as aged Cheddar or creamy fresh chevre or Camembert, and their products are mailed directly to consumers. Vermont cheese; Nauvoo blue cheese from the Nauvoo Blue Cheese Company in Nauvoo, Illinois; and Tillamook cheese from Tillamook County Creamery Association in Oregon are well-known cheeses offered in mail-order catalogs. Consumers also routinely order special coffees, condiments and sauces, pecans and other nuts, fresh and dried fruits, breads, pastas, and salad dressings by mail.

In recent years, another trend in mail-order foods has appeared: a growing number of corporations and businesses have purchased mail-order foods as Christmas and Chanukah gifts for customers and employees. Everything from gallon-sized cans of popcorn to barbecued ribs are chosen as gifts. The popularity of mail-order food gifts stems from the fact that food is "gender neutral" and can be

given to virtually anyone on a holiday shopping list. In addition, the growing popularity of food gifts has prompted a boom in new mail-order houses, so today there is a greater variety of food and beverage items than there was just a decade ago. Sending food gifts by mail is also simple and convenient to do, and prices are reasonable. As a result, gourmet and specialty food items have been among the most popular business gifts in the 1990s. **See also:** FOOD BASKETS.

MAPLE SUGARING/FESTIVALS

When the sap in hard or rock maples and a few other species of maple trees begins to run in the spring or just before the spring season each year, thousands of North Americans make plans to tap trees for the sap or to attend some type of maple sugaring festival. Indigenous people in North America have celebrated sap gathering and sugar making from maple trees for centuries. Except for dried berries, maple sugar was the only concentrated sweetener known on the continent until honey bees were introduced to the colonies in the 1630s.

The ritual of tapping the maple sap flow is as important as the preparation and consumption of the syrup. European settlers in North America learned the techniques of maple sugaring from such native tribes as the Algonquins, Iroquois, and Ojibways, who usually notched trees and drove in wooden sticks to allow water and sap to flow into containers made of bark. Colonists later began making small holes in maple trees, fitting in spouts made of metal or wood, and hanging buckets from the spouts to capture the sap.

After sap is collected it must be boiled to bring impurities to the top of the liquid, where they can be skimmed off. The sap is usually boiled until it reaches a desired density and color. Between 30 and 40 gallons of sap are needed to make 1 gallon of syrup. Maple sugar is made by boiling the syrup at a high temperature and allowing it to cool and crystallize. Slow cooling usually forms large crystals, while rapid cooling makes finer crystals.

While maple sugaring may be conducted the "old-fashioned" way as part of maple syrup festivals or by those who own just a few trees, the process has been mechanized by commercial maple sugar and maple syrup producers, most of whom are in New York and Vermont and in some provinces of Canada. Power drills may be used to tap trees, and tubing may be attached to carry sap from trees to a holding tank. The boiling process is carefully monitored to control the sugar concentration. True maple syrup is just that—made from the sap of maple trees—but most syrups on grocery store shelves or on tables in the majority of pancake and waffle houses are made with corn syrup and maple flavoring.

At some restaurants and sugar houses (informal cafes often connected with a maple farm) in the northeastern United States, however, the real thing is served. Maple syrup may be used not only as the traditional sweet topping for pancakes but also as flavoring for a variety of foods from baked bean dishes to muffins, or it may be poured over freshly fallen snow or shaved ice to create a dish called "sugar on snow."

At maple festivals true maple syrup is in abundance. Usually festivities begin with hearty breakfasts that include sausage and pancakes drenched in syrup. Maple syrup is also used to make a kind of chewing gum called jackwax or lockjaw, which is made by pouring boiling syrup in a circular fashion over crushed ice or fresh snow (if available during festival time). The syrup quickly cools and hardens for chewing. Maple sugar candies, ham baked in maple syrup, and drinks made with maple syrup are other items available during annual maple festivals.

See also: PANCAKE BREAKFAST.

References: Borghese. *Food from Harvest Festivals and Folk Fairs.* 1977; McGee. *On Food and Cooking.* 1984; Stern and Stern. *GoodFood.* 1983.

MARDI GRAS

Fat Tuesday (*Mardi* is French for Tuesday; *gras* is fat) is the last day of the Winter Carnival season closing out the Christmas holidays. Originating in France, the festival was first celebrated in the New World on 3 March 1699 in what is now New Orleans. At that time a French explorer established an outpost on the Mississippi River, calling it Point de Mardi Gras to commemorate the French holiday that took place on that date. Mardi Gras flourished under the French, but the festival was outlawed by the Spanish who took control of New Orleans. Revived for a time in the early 1800s, Mardi Gras did not become an established celebration in North America until the latter part of the century.

Today, Mardi Gras is the traditional final day of feasting, drinking, and celebration before Lent (the 40-day period of reflection and sacrifice among Catholic and other Christian religious groups) in New Orleans. People travel thousands of miles to take part in the festivities, which include colorful parades, dances, and other performances. The holiday is also celebrated in other cities throughout North America with restaurants featuring Cajun and Creole foods, which are so much a part of New Orleans culture.

Contrary to popular opinion, Cajun and Creole cuisines are two different types of American cooking. *Cajun* is a term that refers to Acadians, a people who originated in southern France and moved to Nova Scotia and eastern Canada. About 6,000 were driven out by the British in the 1700s and migrated to Louisiana. Food, in the Cajun style, is an integral part of the tradition and culture of these very independent people, and Cajun cooking is an old style of food preparation with roots in the French country tradition, as well as a blend of Spanish, Native American, and African cuisines. Fresh ingredients, local sources, and simple techniques are the building blocks, with hefty doses of herbs and spices to enhance flavors. Raw materials include sea or freshwater fish and crustaceans such as crawfish, plus game meat, chicken, and smoked pork. Rice is basic to almost every meal.

Some typical Cajun dishes are jambalaya, bouillabaisse, and gumbo. Blackened redfish is a common dish linked with Cajun cooking. It is prepared by dipping a fillet of redfish (a species found in the waters off the coast of Louisiana) in melted butter; covering both sides with a seasoning blend of paprika, salt, onion powder, garlic powder, cayenne pepper, black pepper, thyme, and oregano; and then placing it in a very hot iron skillet. The dish gives off plenty of smoke (and possibly flame) as the seasonings "blacken" for about two minutes per side.

Creole cooking was born and bred in the city of New Orleans, which differentiates it from Cajun cooking. Another difference between Cajun and Creole cooking, according to one Acadian authority, is that much less fat is left in a Cajun dish than in a dish prepared the Creole way.

There are some similarities between the two cuisines, however. Like the older Cajun cuisine, Creole cooking relies on fresh local foods in season. During the crawfish season, for example, a traditional meal would probably include crawfish étouffée, a stewed dish, and a bread pudding. The beginnings of the Creole style, like the Cajun style, are rooted in many cultures. The French and every other subgroup that resided in New Orleans added something to the pot. These groups included Italians, Africans, Spaniards, and Native Americans.

Chef Paul Prudhomme, of the famed K-Paul's restaurant in New Orleans, explains the beginnings of Creole thus: "Seven flags flew over New Orleans in the early days, and each time a new nation took over, many members of the deposed government would leave the city; most of their cooks and other servants stayed behind. . . . Those cooks, most of whom were black, would be hired by other families, often of a different nationality . . . [and] would have to change their style of cooking. Over a period of time, they learned how to cook for a variety of nationalities, and they incorporated their own spicy, home-style way of cooking into the different cuisines of their employers."
References: Angers. *Cajun Cuisine.* 1985; Prudhomme. *Chief Paul Prudhomme's Louisiana Kitchen.* 1984.

MARGARITA

Since the 1980s, this cocktail has become one of the drinks of choice at bars all across America. Prior to that time, the margarita was a specialty primarily in Mexican restaurants or Mexico where its main ingredient, tequila, is the favorite alcoholic beverage. As the popularity of Mexican food has expanded, and as the population of Latinos has spread throughout North America, the use of tequila has exploded.

The best margaritas are a blend of tequila, triple sec, lime juice, a syrupy lemon-lime mix, and a splash of orange juice. Most are served as a "frozen" drink—the ice and liquid are blended into a slushy consistency and poured into a special high stemmed glass with a straw. It is common to serve the drink with salt on the rim of the glass. Purists, however, will call for their favorite tequila (or preferably a mescal) and have their margarita made and served "on the rocks."
See also: TEQUILA.

MARINADED FOODS

The English version of the Spanish word *marinada* (sea) became *marinade*, or *marinate*, during the 1600s, but the meaning has not changed much over the years. Marinades originally were made of salt (sea salt primarily), which was a way to preserve foods in the days when there was no refrigeration. Today, though, people routinely use a marinade to tenderize meat or to enhance the flavor of meat, fish, or poultry and vegetables. For many backyard barbecues, this is a ritualistic method of preparing food—soaking it in a mixture of cooking oil, seasonings (such as garlic, hot pepper, mustard, and/or Worcestershire sauce), and an acidic

ingredient like lemon or other fruit juice, wine, vinegar, or soy sauce. Beer and bourbon are also common ingredients for marinades. Some foods, such as round steak or other fibrous meats, are usually marinaded overnight, but others such as fish and various vegetables need only a couple of hours of marinading.
See also: BARBECUE.

MARSHMALLOW

The marshmallow is a confection once made from a plant that is part of a family of plants commonly known as mallows, including not only the marsh mallow but also hundreds of other plants, shrubs, and trees (among them okra, hollyhock, and hibiscus plants). The process of extracting the sticky sap of mallows became too expensive; thus, since the early part of the 1900s, marshmallows have been produced from a mixture of gelatin, water, sugar, egg whites, corn syrup, and various flavorings whipped together and dried. The confections are cut into cubes or other shapes and dusted with powdered sugar. Marshmallows often are melted on top of sweet potatoes to create a traditional Thanksgiving dish. They also are used in a number of desserts such as heavenly hash or flavored gelatin. A popular ice cream sundae is made using marshmallow creme topping. Miniature marshmallows are frequently special snack treats, and some cold breakfast cereals with marshmallows are also popular with children.
See also: CEREAL, COLD; HEAVENLY HASH; MARSHMALLOW ROAST; THANKSGIVING DAY DINNER.
References: Root. *Food.* 1980; Trager. *Foodbook.* 1970.

MARSHMALLOW ROAST

For millions of American families, the marshmallow roast is almost a mandatory ritual while on a camping trip or after a backyard barbecue. It is an activity that is usually included at scouting and summer camps. Most roasts are conducted at night when the campfire is burning. Each person who takes part in the roast puts a marshmallow on a long stick or skewer and toasts it over an open fire until crispy brown on the outside and melting (mouthburning hot) on the inside. Families also take part in this popular activity when fires are lit in home fireplaces.
See also: CAMP/TRAIL FOOD.

MARTINI

"Human invention has launched untold thousands of cocktails, but only one has developed a genuine mystique: the martini," wrote William Grimes in his book on the cultural history of mixed drinks. According to Grimes, no one knows how the martini got its name, but apparently the drink made its appearance in the United States some time in the late 1800s, although even the date of its origin is in question. Early martinis were sweeter than the martini that is popular today.

For the traditionalist, the martini is a combination of gin, dry vermouth, and an olive, but the amount of vermouth ranges from one tiny drop in the gin to equal parts of vermouth and gin. The least amount of vermouth produces the "driest" martini, and some prefer that only the bottle of vermouth pass over the cocktail glass, thus only gin and an olive make up the drink. Some martini drinkers insist on two olives in their cocktail or a particular type of olive—a stuffed variety, for example. Others prefer a twist of lemon with their cocktail rather than an olive. Whatever the combination, the drink is often mixed in a chilled martini pitcher or shaker and served "straight up" in a chilled martini glass or "on the rocks"—over ice in a low cocktail glass. Each drinker swears that his or her combination is the "perfect" way to make a martini.

Until about the 1980s, when businesspeople began to cut back on two-martini lunches because of health and financial reasons, the martini was a status drink and the official cocktail for the U.S. business community. The martini also is closely tied with the "cocktail hour," and martini drinkers frequently refer to the hour or so before dinner when cocktails are served as "martini time."

Within the past few decades, some traditional martini drinkers have switched to vodka instead of gin as a basis for their drink. However, the rest of the ritual—from the amount of vermouth used to the way the drink is served—remains fairly constant.

See also: BARTENDER SPECIALS; COCKTAIL PARTY; COCKTAILS.

Reference: Grimes. *Straight Up or on the Rocks.* 1993.

MARZIPAN

See CHRISTMAS CANDY; CHRISTMAS COOKIES.

MATZOH

A thin, unleavened bread, matzoh (also matzah or matzo) is the traditional bread of Passover, the Jewish holiday that commemorates the time Jews fled from bondage in Egypt and had no time to let their bread rise. During the eight-day Passover observance, no foods with leavening agents can be eaten, thus matzoh is often served, although it may be eaten at any time of year and its consumption is not confined to those of the Jewish faith.

Because of the time limitations today, matzoh is not usually made at home. Instead, most consumers buy a commercial product. All commercially produced matzoh is made by two companies in the United States: Streits in New York City and B. Manischewitz in Jersey City, New Jersey. These companies also must follow a tradition: the matzoh must be produced within 18 minutes, from the mixing of ingredients to the baking and final product. It is usually sold perforated so that it can be easily broken apart.

See also: SEDER.

References: Borden. "Matzoh and More." 1994; Mariani. *The Dictionary of American Food and Drink.* 1993, 1994.

Children share matzoh, a crisp unleavened bread, served during the Jewish Passover celebration. Tradition dictates that the bread must be mixed and baked in 18 minutes or less.

MEALS-ON-WHEELS

For several decades a national volunteer program called Meals-on-Wheels has created not just a traditional meal service but also a basic necessity for the elderly and physically challenged who cannot leave their homes. The Expanded Elderly Nutrition Act, which evolved from the 1972 Older Americans Act, added this delivery component, and Senator Edward Kennedy authored the legislation.

Civic clubs, religious organizations, and retired people usually provide the volunteer service. In some cities and towns several hundred to several thousand meals are prepared and delivered each day to the homebound. In the Los Angeles area, for example, St. Vincent's Meals-on-Wheels program delivers 2,000 meals daily.

Either the clients who receive the meals or their relatives, friends, or charitable organizations cover the cost. The meals are usually prepared by a hospital or other institution and include some that are prepared for special diets, such as diabetic or low-sodium.

See also: DINING ON DELIVERY.

Reference: Senuar et al. "Food Trends and the Changing Cuisines." 1991.

MEAT AND POTATOES

Eating meat and potatoes for a main meal is such an entrenched habit in the United States and Canada that, until recent decades, virtually every cook has planned a meal around the meat dish of beef, pork, or lamb. Typically the meal has included a side dish of starch, usually some form of potato. Some common meal combinations include pot roast with potatoes and carrots; steak and baked potato; hamburger and french fries; roast beef with mashed potatoes and gravy; corned beef with cabbage and boiled potatoes; and steak, eggs, and hash browns.

For many people in the United States, a meal is not a meal without meat and potatoes. Serving a hearty meal based around meat stems from rural customs.

People working on midwestern farms must usually spend long hours in hard, physical labor—often in cold weather—so they want substantial meals for strength. Rural folks often butcher their own cattle and hogs as well, thus meat is readily available. Because the meat-and-potatoes meal is customary, it is not unusual to hear midwesterners describe themselves as "a meat-and-potatoes girl" or a "guy whose gotta have my meat at every meal!" That meat usually is beef.

In the 1980s, beef was the king of meats. Dinner out for adults on a Saturday night usually meant consuming some sort of beef steak—a filet, New York strip, or sirloin—served with a baked potato, hash browns, or fries. Teenagers or youngsters who stayed home were likely to have beef hamburgers or a convenience meal with Hamburger Helper. Sunday dinner was commonly a beef roast.

Because of all the data about the health hazards of fat and cholesterol in the diet, there has been a movement away from a heavy emphasis on meals focusing on beef and starch as the main ingredients. This trend is apparent in the data collected by the U.S. Department of Agriculture: before 1977, the average per-person consumption of beef in the United States was 78 pounds per year. In the early 1990s, the average was 67 pounds. Many consumers have turned to chicken and turkey, perceiving poultry as lower in fat and more economical and convenient. From 1984 to 1991, consumption of chicken rose about 30 percent and turkey 67.9 percent. In the 1990s, however, beef producers began responding to consumer demands for leaner meat by decreasing the amount of fat on steak and other beef products in order to improve sales. The traditional combination of a hamburger and fries is still extremely popular among Americans. At least 23 million American households maintain the traditional meat-and-potatoes diet, even though health may be endangered.

See also: EATING TRENDS; HAMBURGERS; MEAT LOAF; VEGETARIAN EATING.

References: Arnett. "Beef Eaters." 1993; Wolf. "A Taste of Tomorrow's Foods." 1994.

MEAT LOAF

An inexpensive meat entree, meat loaf has been prepared and served for generations in North America. Traditionally, meat loaf is made from ground beef, pork, and/or veal held together with bread crumbs, eggs, or another binder and mixed with onions and spices. In the past, meat loaf was frequently the main entree for Saturday night meals, since Saturday was traditional baking day in many homes and the meat loaf went into the oven along with whatever breads, cakes, or cookies the home cook prepared to bake. Although meat loaf fell out of favor for a time and was replaced in some households by "higher status" meat, poultry, and fish entrees, meat loaf today is a comfort food enjoyed by people from all walks of life, and a cold or fried meat loaf sandwich is a popular lunch or snack food.

Variations on the traditional meat loaf recipe abound. Some cooks stuff their loaves with rice, ham, cheese, vegetables, or fruit. Sausage or ground ham also may be added to the basic ground meat. Others mix the meat with hot spices, mushroom soup, or dried onion soup. Meat loaf frequently is smothered in ketchup. It may also be topped with rum sauce, or baked surrounded by carrots, potatoes, and other vegetables. Poultry loaves—made from ground turkey or chicken—and vegetarian loaves made from ground soybeans or other ground vegetables and cooked grains are also favorites in some homes.

Reference: Kaufman and Woods. *The Great American Meatloaf Contest Cookbook.* 1994.

Baked meat loaf and potatoes are basic American fare. Recipes vary and are limited only by the cook's imagination or what's on hand in the kitchen. Generally, meat loaf starts with ground beef, pork, veal, turkey, or chicken and is mixed with bread crumbs, rice, or oatmeal and eggs, to which onions and other vegetables may be added.

MEDICINAL FOODS

Throughout history, herbs, spices, and other foods have been consumed to maintain health or to treat a vast number of ailments. In North America, as in other parts of the world, people who have had little or no access to medical practitioners use home remedies, ranging from the legendary chicken soup antidote for the common cold to cabbage juice for healing ulcers. Today, the growing belief in alternative medicine techniques and the holistic approach to healing have given rise to a renewed interest in "medicinal foods."

Practitioners of the ancient curative arts, especially among the indigenous peoples of North America, have kept alive the rituals and recipes for herbal medicine. Tea brewed from the bark of a willow tree, for instance, was a common remedy for headache; willow bark contains salicin, which converts in the body to salicylic acid, an ingredient found in aspirin.

Although a serious illness nearly always requires sound medical advice and treatment, many people who have tried various home remedies and techniques for common complaints have reported successful results. Some have used burdock root tea as a blood purifier. Raw potato is said to be effective on hemorrhoids. Peppermint is soothing on a sour stomach. Aloe vera is said to be a wonder "drug" and is used externally for insect bites and burns and internally for digestive problems. These and many other traditional aids, however, pale in comparison to the claims for the plant genus *Allium*—onions and garlic.

Recent tests of onion and garlic have indicated that phytochemicals called allylic sulfides in these foods appear to provide protection against stomach cancer. Other foods such as broccoli, Brussels sprouts, cauliflower, kale, soybeans, tomatoes, and turnips apparently also contain phytochemicals that act as anticarcinogens. Rigorous testing of garlic in particular has proven what every culture from ancient times to the present has known through experience: garlic is an effective treatment for disease. Thirty compounds in garlic have been observed to have an effect on metabolic functions, and a researcher for the National Cancer Institute has likened garlic to a virtual drugstore. To date there is data to show that it has a positive effect on cancer deterrence, the cardiovascular system, the process of aging, and detoxification from poisonous chemicals and metals.
See also: CHICKEN SOUP; CRANBERRY JUICE.

MEMORIAL DAY

Celebrated on the last Monday in May each year, Memorial Day, which originally commemorated those who died in the Civil War, now honors all members of the U.S. armed forces who have died in war. Most towns and cities hold memorial services and patriotic parades. In Indiana, the celebration begins the preceeding day with a Mayor's Breakfast as a prelude to not only memorial activities but also the well-known Indianapolis 500 automobile race. For many people, this is also a time for the first picnic or backyard barbecue of the summer season. In some communities food booths or stands are set up in a public square or park. Among the most popular foods for the outdoor events are barbecued or fried chicken, hamburgers, hot dogs, macaroni, and coleslaw.

MENUDO

This tripe and hominy stew is traditional in Mexico and other areas of Latin America, and its use and popularity have spread to many parts of North America as Latin immigration has expanded. While the stew probably originated as a way to use some of the lowlier parts of the cow (tripe is stomach lining) and a popular corn product, its value as a curative is now legendary. Many people claim that they have to eat menudo to help recover from a bout of heavy drinking the night before.

On special occasions, holidays, and most Sundays, it is very common for a member of a Mexican family to go to a local Mexican restaurant for menudo-to-go. Usually that person carries along an empty covered pot to retrieve the hot, tomato-based soup and the accoutrements. Family habits vary, but bowls of the flavorful mixture are generally served with a condiment tray of chopped raw onion, hot peppers such as jalapeños, dried oregano leaves, lemon wedges, and corn tortillas. Much like a Sunday morning tradition of waffles or pancakes for breakfast in other cultures, menudo is the food of choice for many in Latin communities.

MEXICAN FIESTAS

Food and feasts are an integral part of the celebrations of life that Mexicans call fiestas. Weddings, birthdays, christenings, Christmas, All Kings Day, the Day of the Dead, Easter, Cinco de Mayo, Las Posadas, and Mexican Independence Day are all important events in the lives of the people who have carried on the traditions and passed down the special foods for centuries. The ritualistic ceremonies and feasts, along with song and dance and decorations, are the ways that Mexicans remember and honor the important events and people of their past.

Naturally, families will create their own variations of the foods and drinks that are customary for each fiesta, but festivities are enjoyed almost universally among the population. On 15 and 16 September, for instance, it seems as if all of Mexico goes out into the central plaza in every town and city throughout the nation to celebrate Independence Day. This popular celebration is substantially more important than Cinco de Mayo (Fifth of May) in Mexico, and it commemorates the actual establishment of an independent state. During these two days, people dress in traditional costume, make lots of noise, throw streamers, shoot off fireworks, and eat food from the booths established all around the public squares. Green enchiladas, barbecued goat meat, tacos, and *arroz con pollo*, a saffron-flavored chicken and rice dish, are favorites for this fiesta. Such foods plus beans with chiles, jicama salad, and mar-

garitas may also be part of Mexican-style fiestas in the United States.

See also: ALL KINGS DAY; ALL SOULS DAY; CINCO DE MAYO; LAS POSADAS.
References: Davis. *The Potato Book.* 1973; Quintana and Haralson. *Mexico's Feasts of Life.* 1989.

MICROWAVE COOKING

Introduced around 1950, the microwave oven has become the quintessential cooking appliance of the 1990s. There is one found in 90 percent of American homes, particularly in busy households where convenience and efficient use of time are top priorities. For many, the microwave has meant expanding the possibilities of the quickly prepared menu. Commercially prepared frozen or dried meals are now universally packaged in "microwavable" containers, making chicken noodle soup or turkey pot pie or "gourmet" meals readily accessible to millions. Microwave cooking is popular in many college dormitories, especially for heating up leftovers or preparing late-night snacks. Increasingly, convenience stores, gas stations, motels, and hotels have provided microwaves so that customers can prepare packaged meals or snacks. On the job, too, the choices in hot meals have been expanded by the presence of the microwave appliance in the office or factory lunchroom.

See also: BROWN BAG LUNCHES; CONVENIENCE STORE FOODS; FROZEN MEALS.
Reference: Chalmers. *The Great Food Almanac.* 1994.

MILITARY CHOW

Feeding more than 1 million people daily is both a ritual and routine task undertaken daily by the U.S. military. Personnel in the U.S. Army, Navy, Air Force, Marines, and Coast Guard as well as patients in veterans hospitals have to be fed, and the procedure requires at least 1,700 people worldwide just to buy, manage, and transport the food, not to mention hundreds of others

Private Elvis Presley chows down with fellow recruits at a Fort Hood, Texas, mess hall in 1958. The U.S. armed services specialize in feeding large numbers of hungry people quickly and efficiently. When conditions preclude hot meals, individual Meals Ready-to-Eat (MREs) are issued to soldiers in the field.

who have to prepare it. The federal government has set standards for nutritive values of the food and how it should be prepared, and has established a daily ritual for eating meals in base mess halls.

At one time, service people had to take what was dished out and eat, for example, such foods as reconstituted powdered eggs and the much-maligned "SOS"—dried or chipped beef on toast. Today, cafeteria-style mess halls are the norm in the Air Force and on some army bases. Service members can choose what they want to eat and pay for what they take, which prevents much food waste.

In the field, rations are typically a steady diet of perhaps a dozen varieties of Meals Ready-to-Eat (MREs) that consist of heat-and-serve meals, canned and dehydrated foods, and on holidays some fresh foods. While military officials say that members of today's armed services are fed better and tastier food than ever before, complaining about the food is one of the most common rituals associated with mess hall dining.

See also: CAFETERIA DINING; CREAMED CHIPPED BEEF ON TOAST.

MILK SHAKE

"Shake one" was a common way in the 1940s and 1950s to tell a soda fountain attendant in the United States to make a milk shake—a blend of ice cream, milk, and flavoring, usually chocolate unless otherwise specified. Malt was also a common flavoring added to many chocolate milk shakes, so the drink was often called a "chocolate malted" or "malt." Today, milk shakes—or just "shakes"—are frequently made from a so-called soft ice cream product and served from a refrigerated dispenser in fastfood establishments. Although chocolate and vanilla are the most popular flavors, strawberry shakes are widely sold, too, and at festivals celebrating certain foods it is common to find stands selling everything from blueberry to date to watermelon shakes.

See also: ICE CREAM.

MILK TOAST

A traditional comfort food, milk toast is simply warm milk poured over pieces of toasted bread in a bowl, originating perhaps with farm folks as a way to use up dry bread and excess amounts of milk. The bland dish was once a common sickroom food and could have been an inspiration for the name Caspar Milquetoast, a character in the comic strip "The Timid Soul" of the 1930s and 1940s; the slang term *milquetoast* (now often spelled milktoast) is used today to describe a timid person. Milk toast, however, is not always a "retiring" dish and may be given a bit of spark by sprinkling it with cinnamon, nutmeg, or other spice. It has long been a popular snack at bedtime and other times of the day as well. A version of this dish is made with broken soda crackers or graham crackers covered with cold milk.

See also: SNACK FOODS.

MINCEMEAT PIE

According to food historians, mincemeat pie is a traditional Christmas dessert because the spicy mincemeat filling represents the gifts of the Magi. The traditional mincemeat pie was actually made with meat—chopped or ground beef and suet—plus dried fruits, spices, and cider, rum, or brandy, and it was baked in a loaf pan to symbolize the shape of the manger. Although meat is seldom used in mincemeat pie today, in keeping with tradition, the pie has a top crust in a lattice design to symbolize the hayrack above the manger where Jesus was born.

See also: CHRISTMAS EVE/DAY DINNER; PIES.
Reference: Bragdon. *Joy through the World.* 1985.

MINT JULEP

No one knows when the mint julep first appeared, but there is evidence that in the 1700s Virginians put sprigs of mint in silver goblets of brandy or rum and served them as eye-openers before breakfast. Today, however, the traditional mint julep is made with bourbon and has been a ceremonial drink on many occasions, although it is most closely associated with southern hospitality and especially the Kentucky Derby Festival. In Kentucky, the main ingredient is Kentucky bourbon, and many Kentuckians would take issue with anyone who substituted or added another type of whiskey, such as rye. Sugar or syrup and a fresh mint sprig or leaves are added to the drink. There is considerable debate about whether leaves should be crushed or left whole. Some Kentuckians believe that anyone who crushes mint leaves and adds rye to the drink may be less than human. Nevertheless, the mint julep in whatever form is consumed by just about every drinker who attends the famous horse race at Churchill Downs in Louisville. The night before the race, when numerous parties are held, the evening traditionally begins with the mint julep in frosted glasses.

See also: KENTUCKY DERBY FESTIVAL.
Reference: Carson. *The Social History of Bourbon.* 1963.

MOCK APPLE PIE

"We couldn't tell the difference when Mom made mock apple pie. We thought it was the real thing—which was good because it was a cheap dessert and there were twelve of us to feed." That is how a Pennsylvania man who grew up during the Great Depression described his family's experience with what became a traditional dessert in many households of the 1930s. Although the recipe for mock apple pie stems from a pie made with hardtack during the Civil War, the recipe became popular during the Depression because the Nabisco company printed it on packages of its Ritz Cracker products. The recipe calls for crumbled

crackers, water, sugar, cream of tartar, lemon juice, and grated lemon rind. The crackers are formed into a crust, and the other ingredients are cooked in a saucepan, creating a thick syrup that is poured over the crumbled crackers. The pie is sprinkled with cinnamon, dotted with margarine, covered with another crust, and baked until golden brown. During this process, the crackers absorb the flavors, expand, and become similar to apples in texture. As a result, you have a pie that, as the Pennsylvanian attested, tastes "like the real thing."
See also: APPLE PIE; PIES.

MOLASSES

Along with maple sugar and syrup, one of the earliest sweeteners for North Americans was molasses, which was often made at home. Until about the mid-1800s, most people could not afford expensive refined sugar and depended on the low-cost substitute. Several families might plant a crop of sugarcane and in the fall harvest the cane and make syrup, a ritual process that usually supplied enough molasses for all the families until the next season rolled around.

Molasses is the syrup that remains after sugarcane has been boiled down and has crystallized to form sucrose, or sugar. When refined sugar became more affordable for the majority of North Americans, molasses was considered unsuitable except for the poor. Today, however, some families in the South continue the autumn ritual of cutting cane and making molasses, and commercially produced molasses has become more acceptable across the United States. With the trend toward more natural foods, molasses is again being used as a sweetener and has become a staple in many homes. Some cooks, following an old custom, insist on using molasses as the only sweetener (or as the predominant sweetener) when making such desserts as gingerbread, ginger-

bread cookies, shoofly pie, and dishes such as baked beans.
See also: SHOOFLY PIE; SUGAR.
References: Farr. *More Than Moonshine.* 1983; McGee. *On Food and Cooking.* 1984.

MOLE

An integral part of Mexican history and customs, a mole (a term from the Nahuatl people's language that means "sauce") may be any of a variety of thick, gravylike sauces. Many North Americans are familiar with the restaurant staple, *pollo mole,* or "chicken mole." Canned and powder-based moles are available on grocers' shelves, but, as always, the best sauces are those that are made from scratch with the freshest of ingredients.

These types of sauces were made at least as early as Moctezuma's time, with different ingredients finding their way into the pot as new cultures impacted the indigenous people. In ancient times, the moles were not as sweet as those prepared today. Before the arrival of the Spaniards, chiles, seeds, grains, and salt were ground and blended with liquid to form a silky, thick sauce. After the arrival of the European, sugar and fruit became common ingredients in some areas.

The celebration of All Souls Day calls for the creation of many special foods, and *Mole Negro de Teotitlan del Valle* is one of the important ones. This "black mole" is made with chiles roasted with onions, garlic, ginger and other spices, and some sesame seeds, plus roasted tomatillos, tomatoes, avocado leaves, and browned prunes. The ingredients are blended with chicken stock and heated for hours, resulting in a base that is seasoned finally with salt, chocolate, and sugar. Bread crumbs are added as a thickener. The mole is served on chicken, particularly during *Día de Los Muertos* (Day of the Dead).
Reference: Quintana and Haralson. *Mexico's Feasts of Life.* 1989.

MOON CAKES

A small fried dough cake shaped like a moon and stuffed with a paste of pulverized cooked beans (usually soybeans, lima beans, and other varieties), lotus or melon seeds, and egg yolks is the traditional food associated with the Chinese Harvest Moon Festival. This one-day event is celebrated on the fifteenth day of the eighth month of the lunar calendar. Although moon cakes are available throughout the year in many large cities where Chinese bakeries are established, the moon cake is especially significant on the day that venerates the influence of the moon on crops and celebrates the agricultural harvest.
See also: CHINESE NEW YEAR.

MOONSHINE WHISKEY

Since the time the first European settlers arrived on America's shores, people have made their own alcoholic beverages. By the late 1700s, the U.S. government and some state governments were taxing the sale of whiskey. Many distillers deeply resented paying a tax on the spirits they made and refused to turn over any revenue to government officials, selling their whiskey illegally.

Over the years, other government taxes and controls were placed on the production of alcoholic beverages. But some distillers continued to defy government regulations, although seldom with as much daring as was common in the South where some families depended on the income from illegal sales of whiskey. The whiskey became known as "moonshine" because it was made at night, sometimes by the light of the moon. The main reason for making whiskey at night was to prevent government agents ("revenuers") from spotting the smoke from fires needed for the distilling process.

While the whiskey was "cooking off" or going through the distilling process, it had to be tested for alcoholic content, and the only way to test it, of course, was for each person to have a taste. This meant dipping a clear glass jar into the distilled whiskey, holding it up to the firelight, and inspecting

the liquid for tiny air bubbles (low wine), which would tell the "moonshiner" when his whiskey was ready. Usually four or five men sat around waiting for the whiskey to distill, and by the time the first batch was completed and all the testing was done, almost everyone was drunk. Some of the moonshine was called "white lightning" because of its effect on the drinker.

Today, some Americans who continue to make whiskey illegally also follow the old tradition of treating a trusted guest to a drink of moonshine, although "storebought" whiskey is readily available. An old jar or whiskey bottle is given to each person—no one drinks from a glass. The whiskey jug is pulled from its hiding place—under the porch or in a shed. Then the jug is passed from hand to hand, whiskey is poured into each individual's container, and it is "bottoms up" to complete the ritual.

Another traditional event connected with homemade whiskey is the annual Moonshine Festival in Perry County, Ohio, which calls itself the Moonshine Capital. Held on Memorial Day weekend, the festival features a moonshine still, country music, and foods made with moonshine whiskey.
See also: DRINKING TOASTS.
Reference: Hill. *Festivals U.S.A.* 1988.

MOTHER'S DAY

Florists, greeting card companies, long distance phone carriers, and candy companies all see booms in business during the week or two before Mother's Day. It is a time to buy gifts for Mom. However, Mother's Day did not start off as a gift-giving holiday. Instead, it began with Anna Jarvis, a West Virginia schoolteacher, who wanted to honor her mother on the anniversary of her death. The first Mother's Day was a ceremony held on 10 May 1908. More than 400 children and their moms attended, and each mother received a red carnation. Four years later, President Woodrow Wilson signed a proclamation establishing the second Sunday in May as Mother's Day.

Food seems to be the key to the main events of the day. Dads who rarely find their way to a kitchen feel an urge to make Mom breakfast in bed. Children like to make cookies or special treats for her, and most families want to take Mom out to brunch or dinner. No matter what, mothers are not supposed to do any work, including the cooking. Thus, this is one of the busiest days of the year for many restaurants in the United States.
See also: SUNDAY BRUNCH.

MUFFINS

Apple, banana, blueberry, bran, cornmeal, cranberry, oatmeal, orange, pumpkin, zucchini . . . on and on the list could go describing the great diversity of muffins, a traditional breakfast food. Muffins are so popular that many coffee shops, cafes, espresso bars, delis, and fastfood places offer several varieties of hot muffins on their breakfast menus. Muffins—particularly those made with cornmeal or with a wheat flour and cheese combination—are served as a hot, flavorful accompaniment to other meals as well. Although many cooks use package mixes when preparing muffins, these are still some of the easiest hot breads to make from basic ingredients, and favorite muffin recipes are frequently passed on from generation to generation.
See also: BREAD; BREAKFAST; OAT BRAN.

MULLED WINE

A Christmas tradition brought to North America from England, mulled wine is still served at some holiday gatherings in the colder climates. It is a soothing beverage, made by slowly heating a hearty red wine that is infused with mulling spices such as cardamom, allspice, cinnamon, and cloves. Sugar or other sweeteners are also used to make the drink very comforting. Cider can be substituted for the wine if minors are to sample from the bowl. In some neighbor-

hoods, carollers walk past each house singing the favorite Christmas tunes, and it is a pleasant custom to invite them in for a drink of mulled wine. In the past, the wassail bowl held a much headier libation for the same purpose.
See also: HOT TODDY; MADRIGAL DINNER.

MUSHROOM HARVESTS AND FESTIVALS

The ritual of wild mushroom hunting has been going on for thousands of years and has been a practice in North America for as long as people have lived on the land. Mushroom hunts take place all across North America, and nature lovers who regularly participate in the rite have learned how to distinguish edible mushrooms from those that are highly toxic. With about 38,000 varieties of mushrooms, it can be dangerous to eat wild mushrooms unless one is familiar with them.

In early spring, mushroom hunters in the Midwest often concentrate their hunt on morels—the cone-shaped variety that usually appears in late April or early May. Mushroom hunting is primarily a pleasurable outdoor activity for hobbyists, who often indulge in a picnic after an avid hunt. A similar activity is common in many other states, particularly in northern California where flavorful, cuplike chanterelles are plentiful, and in Oregon and Washington where matsutakes, truffles, and many other types of fungi abound.

Harvesting wild mushrooms has become much more than a pleasant hobby; it is a competitive business in the Northwest. Harvesters gather matsutakes, selling them for several hundred dollars per pound. They frequently are exported to Japan where they are highly prized. Along with wild mushrooms, commercially grown mushrooms are an important crop in the United States. Michigan is known for its morels, which are widely marketed, while Pennsylvania grows about half of the U.S. crop of button, shiitake, and oyster mushrooms. These varieties are also important commercial crops in California, where as with other food crops, mushrooms are celebrated in festivals. One example is the Morgan Hill Mushroom Mardi Gras in Morgan Hill, California. Food booths serve such dishes as steak smothered in sautéed mushrooms, spinach and mushroom quiche, stuffed mushrooms, and mushroom and cheese omelets.

Those who prepare mushrooms at home routinely use them in sauces, soups, omelets, or as toppings for steaks and other meats. Sliced or whole mushrooms also are used as garnishes and are common on vegetable trays or stuffed as appetizers. **References:** Lipske. "A New Gold Rush Packs the Woods in Central Oregon." 1994; Margen et al. *The Wellness Encyclopedia of Food and Nutrition.* 1992.

MUSTARD

It is not just a condiment for hot dogs and hamburgers. Mustard is also a processed food sold to enhance all types of sandwiches and other dishes. Since about the 1980s, mustards have become exotic food that can be found in gourmet stores, mail-order catalogs, and supermarkets. These mustards are usually presented as gifts, particularly during the Christmas and Chanukkah seasons.

Basically, mustard is processed from the seeds of mustard plants and was originally developed in the 1700s by an Englishwoman who ground mustard seeds with other spices and sold the fine powder as a seasoning. Mustard is still used in powder form today, but mustard powder is also mixed with other ingredients to produce such combinations as champagne mustard, raspberry vinegar mustard, green peppercorn garlic mustard, smoked barbecue mustard, beer mustard, Chinese hot mustard, honey mustard, and Creole mustard. **See also:** BASEBALL PARK EATING AND DRINKING; BEANS AND FRANKS; HOT DOGS. **References:** Chalmers. *Great American Food Almanac.* 1986; Mariani. *The Dictionary of American Food and Drink.* 1993, 1994; Simon and Howe. *Dictionary of Gastronomy.* 1970.

NATIVE AMERICAN FEASTS

The eating and drinking rituals conducted by indigenous people are based on ancient traditions, which are not well known to the majority of the North American population, yet some of those traditions have been shared in feasts open to the general public. Seneca Indians in upstate New York, for example, have been holding an annual Indian Foods Dinner since 1959. The meal is based on traditional foods and preparation. One basic item on the menu is hulled corn soup. Kernels of white corn are boiled in water to loosen the hulls, which are rinsed off, and then the inner morsels are cooked with salt pork. An important part of this tradition is to use a corn that Native Americans have been planting for centuries, saving seeds after each harvest and planting them during the next growing season.

Ghost bread, which is made from a baking powder dough, shaped like a biscuit, and fried in hot oil, is another traditional food served at the Seneca Indian Foods Dinner as well as at other Native American feasts. In fact, ghost bread is so named because it is part of a feasting ritual for the dead held ten days after a person dies, the time when, according to Native American belief, the soul leaves the earth. At the feast, ghost bread is placed on a plate of food that is left over night for the departing soul. In the morning, an undisturbed plate of food signifies that the person's affairs are in order and that he or she has left the earth in peace.

Other traditional Native American feasts include salmon bakes in the Northwest during the fall and the ancient Cherokee corn festival in Cherokee, North Carolina, in September. Traditional foods are also part of the Great Plains Indian powwow in Bismarck, North Dakota, held in October and the Crow Fair—Northern Plains Indians—celebrated in August. Intertribal events in New Mexico lasting from the spring through the summer are also occasions for celebrating Native American foods.

See also: CORN FOODS AND FESTIVALS; NAVAJO FRY BREAD; SALMON BAKES.

References: Geffen and Berglie. *Food Festival.* 1994; Hill. *Festivals U.S.A.* 1988.

NAVAJO FRY BREAD

Known as sopaipillas or Indian fry bread (or simply fry bread), this traditional fried dough that puffs like a pillow is served at Native American festivals, feasts, and fairs, particularly in the southwestern United States. The dough is made with flour, water, and salt and leavened with baking powder or yeast. When prepared in the traditional way, women use a cutoff broom handle to roll small pieces of dough into circles and punch a hole in the middle of each, and fry the dough in hot oil. (Originally, women used a stick to pierce the dough and to put it into the hot fat.) Once fried, the dough is drained and dusted with powdered sugar. Navajo fry bread may also be served unsweetened as an accompaniment to spicy meals, or it may be stuffed with cheese, beans, or meat fillings and served as a main entree or an appetizer.

See also: NATIVE AMERICAN FEASTS; SOPAIPILLAS.

References: Fussell. *I Hear America Cooking.* 1986; Pyles. *The New Texas Cuisine.* 1993; Schulz. *Celebrating America.* 1994.

NEW ENGLAND BOILED DINNER

Corned beef simmered in a pot of water with potatoes and cabbage and perhaps a few other vegetables is a traditional "boiled dinner," which is really a one-pot meal like a stew that is cooked slowly. Usually called a New England boiled dinner, it may have originated in New England, but the meal is served in many parts of North America. It is a traditional St. Patrick's Day meal, although it is not a national dish of Ireland.

NEW ENGLAND BROILED SCROD

Although frozen scrod can be purchased in most areas of North America, fresh scrod is a typical seafood in New England where codfish are common—scrod is a young cod that has been filleted. Tourists visiting the New England area from other parts of the continent frequently make it a point to order New England broiled scrod when dining out. This regional specialty is usually sprinkled with lemon juice and butter, broiled, and served with a lemon butter and boiled potatoes.

Reference: *American Heritage* editors. *The American Heritage Cookbook and Illustrated History of American Eating and Drinking.* 1964.

NEW YEAR'S DAY

Social events to celebrate the beginning of a new year depend on national origin and cultural background. A basic celebration across the United States includes a gathering of family or friends for a dinner or buffet that usually centers on a meat dish such as ham or poultry. Wines, mixed alcoholic drinks, especially a Bloody Mary, and non-alcoholic beverages may be part of the feast and used to toast the new year.

It is a New Year's Day tradition for French-Canadians and some people in the northeastern United States to prepare and serve *tourtière*, or "pork pie," a meat and vegetable baked in a double crust. Although some pies are made with all pork (ground), others combine both pork and beef. The ground meat is usually mixed with garlic, cloves, and bay leaf and perhaps celery salt and other spices, then it is simmered with a little water. Boiled potatoes and onions are mashed along with the cooked meat, and the mixture is baked in a pastry frequently made with flour, lard, and perhaps a touch of vinegar. *Tourtière* is served with ketchup, pickles, and other relishes and is often accompanied by baked beans.

Some foods served on New Year's Day are said to bring good luck for the year. Pickled herring, some people swear, must be eaten for a "lucky" New Year. Black-eyed peas, cabbage, carrots, and sauerkraut also are considered "lucky" foods for the New Year, and in the southern part of the United States, Hoppin' John is the traditional New Year's Eve dish made with black-eyed peas and rice. An Italian eating custom includes lentils and *cotechino*, a type of sausage, which symbolize money and wealth for the coming year.

See also: CHINESE NEW YEAR; LUNAR NEW YEAR.

Reference: Cunningham. *The Magic in Food.* 1990.

NEW YEAR'S EVE

Toasting the new year at the stroke of midnight on New Year's Eve is common practice throughout North America. Many people celebrate New Year's Eve with a great variety of eating and drinking rituals. Celebrations range from parties that include an elaborate dinner and dance to quiet get-togethers with friends.

Bubbling champagne is a common drink, and such foods as herring, lobster, salmon, caviar, and numerous other foods are often associated with this festive occasion. People of Japanese heritage may follow an old custom of eating *toshidoshi soba*, noodles that represent a long life and wealth, and drinking sake, a traditional Japanese wine.

In many Mexican homes, both in Mexico and in the southwestern United States, a traditional New Year's Eve ritual is to eat 12 grapes at midnight, one at a time, at each stroke of the clock. As one participant in this ritual explained: "The trick is to quickly eat one grape after another without choking, making slurping sounds, or oozing grape juice and skins all over yourself or the person near you." When each person has eaten his or her grapes, the head of the house opens a bottle of champagne or wine and toasts the coming year, the assembled family, and any guests. Then people in the household embrace each other and, amidst laughter and joking, begin to tell about their individual experiences eating and swallowing grapes. Similar rituals are part of New Year's Eve gatherings among people from Spain and Portugal, although they may use raisins or pomegranate seeds.

Many families of Greek ancestry are likely to serve *vasilopita*, a sweet bread shaped like a wreath, baked with a coin inside, and decorated. At midnight, the bread is sliced by the eldest male in the family, and usually he takes special pains to make sure the slice with the coin goes to the youngest child.

A favorite and traditional New Year's Eve food for people of Dutch ancestry is an *oliebollen*. These doughnuts are made from a yeast dough that is mixed with bits of apples and raisins and dropped by the spoonful into a pan of hot cooking oil, where they quickly become plump round balls of goodness. They are then covered with powdered sugar and are ready to eat at the stroke of midnight.

In some parts of the United States and Canada, people of Scotch ancestry celebrate Hogmanay, or "Old Year's Night," on the last day of the year. Traditionally, Dundee cake and black buns—both filled with fruit and nuts—and Hogmanay punch made with apple cider and Scotch whisky are served.

See also: ETHNIC FOOD TRADITIONS; NEW YEAR'S DAY.

NIGHTCAP

Since the eighteenth century, *nightcap* has been a term used to describe an alcoholic drink taken just before going to bed. The warming and soothing effect of the nightcap aids sleep, say many who indulge in this ritual, but not all nightcaps contain alcohol. In North America today, the term now applies to such beverages as hot tea or chocolate, or a glass of milk—whatever may be comforting before bedtime.

See also: BEDTIME SNACK; CHOCOLATE BEVERAGES; COMFORT FOODS; HOT TODDY.

NINTH AVENUE FOOD FESTIVAL

Since 1974, the city of New York and the Port Authority of New York and New Jersey have cosponsored the Annual Ninth Avenue Food Festival. This spring rite held in mid-May is organized by and for the Ninth Avenue neighborhood in celebration of its ethnic roots. All of Ninth Avenue is closed to traffic for part of the day so that residents and visitors can take part in a moveable feast that extends exactly 1 mile. At least 300 booths on both sides offer tasty treats from more than 30 different cultures. The variety of foods includes seafood, hot dogs, 6-foot hero sandwiches, Greek barbecue foods and pastries, swordfish kabobs, Cajun crawfish, kielbasa, homemade pastas and raviolis, shish kebab, area seafood, cotton candy, candy and caramel apples, funnel cakes, and pierogies.

See also: ATLANTIC ANTIC; ETHNIC FOOD TRADITIONS; FEAST OF SAN GENNARO.

New York's Ninth Avenue, closed to traffic, teems with people sampling foods from a mile-long stretch of booths representing 27 countries in 1987. Begun in 1974, the May Ninth Avenue Food Festival celebrates the city's ethnic mix.

NOODLES

A type of pasta, noodles are made from a dough or paste of flour (white, whole wheat, or rice), water, and usually eggs. Preparing homemade noodles is a long-standing ritual in many North American homes. Children often take part in the preparation, helping to roll out the dough on a floured board and cut it into thin strips, which are then dried. Frequently, the homemade variety and commercially prepared and packaged noodles available at most food stores are served with butter and sautéed onions and sprinkled with cheese, or they are used in a soup or casserole dish. One noodle dish common during the U.S. economic depression in the 1930s and still served as a frugal meal today is noodles in broth over mashed or boiled potatoes.

Noodles are a part of many cuisines worldwide, and became popular in North America when German immigrants brought their food preferences with them to the United States during the mid-nineteenth century. Typical German or Pennsylvania Dutch dishes today include egg noodle strips or small dumplinglike *spatzle* (meaning little sparrow) boiled in water or added to a meat or poultry broth. Noodles also are the basis for *mummix*, a Pennsylvania Dutch word (not found in any dictionary) for any leftover food that can be turned into a kind of hash. A noodle and prune *mummix* is made with homemade noodles cooked in salted water and mixed with butter and prunes cooked with lemon juice and sugar. The ingredients are placed in a casserole, dotted with butter, and sprinkled with brown sugar.

Today, North Americans consume numerous noodle dishes, stemming not only from Germany but from many other nations. For example, as with many people of Asian heritage, the Vietnamese include noodles along with rice as staples in their diet, and North Americans of Vietnamese ancestry are likely to serve a noodle soup made with a chicken broth, somen noodles, bamboo shoots, chicken pieces, mushrooms, scallions, and *nuoc mam* (a sauce made from tiny fish) as a full meal or accompaniment to a meal. The noodle soup is a traditional Vietnamese wedding dish.

See also: NEW YEAR'S EVE; PASTA.
References: Davis. *The Potato Book*. 1973; Hutchison. *Pennsylvania Dutch Cook Book*. 1948.

NUTS AND SEEDS

Long before colonial times in North America, indigenous people gathered nuts and seeds for part of their food supply, and they ground them as meal or shelled, toasted, and salted them for nibbling. Today, North Americans consume a great variety of nuts and seeds. Unshelled nuts and shelled whole nuts and pieces are commonly presented as gifts during the Christmas holiday season. Nuts and seeds garnish foods ranging from salads to desserts, and numerous cookies and cakes are made with nuts.

Roasted or toasted nuts and seeds are popular snack foods and are often included in commercial or homemade trail mix. They are also commonly served as an accompaniment to drinks at parties and/or served at bars and lounges.

See also: APPETIZERS; FLAVORED NUTS; SNACK FOODS; TRAIL MIX.
Reference: Fussell. *I Hear America Cooking*. 1986.

OAT BRAN

During the 1980s, oat bran was touted as one of the major health food items of the century, and Americans bought and ate foods with oat bran to add fiber to their diets and to help reduce blood cholesterol, which clogs arteries. As advertisers made claims about the health benefits of oat bran, consumers bought increasing amounts of breakfast foods, muffins, breads, cookies, and other products that included oat bran among their ingredients. Quaker Oats, a major producer of cereal products, increased its sales of oat bran from about 1 million pounds per year between 1984 and 1987 to 2 million pounds per month by 1989. The oat bran ritual became a part of the eating pattern of millions of U.S. consumers; however, a study by Harvard University researchers published in the *New England Journal of Medicine* in January 1990 showed that oat bran by itself is not a panacea for high levels of artery-clogging cholesterol. In the study, if cholesterol was reduced, people usually substituted unhealthy, high-fat foods for healthier complex carbohydrates such as rice, potatoes, and pasta and for foods high in fiber such as fruits, vegetables, and oat bran. The study's conclusion, which has been underscored by many experts in the field, was that a single food cannot solve the problem of high cholesterol.

OBON

According to Buddhist beliefs, the spirits of the dead make their appearance on Earth during July. North Americans of Japanese ancestry mark this event with Obon, or the Festival of the Dead (also called Festival of Joy), usually held in the middle of July (although celebrations could occur almost any time during the summer). Comparable to All Souls Day, this festival almost always is sponsored by a Buddhist temple. Gifts are placed on temple altars and private shrines, and a food bazaar with traditional Japanese foods is part of the event as well.

OIL AND VINEGAR

In numerous North American homes and restaurants, it is a custom to place separate cruets, one of oil (usually olive oil) and one of vinegar, on a table so that diners can mix their own combination of these two ingredients as a dressing for salad—a practice that stems from Mediterranean countries where olives and olive oil are so widely used. Commercially prepared oil-and-vinegar dressings are popular as well, especially among those who maintain low-fat, low-calorie diets. Oil and vinegar also compose a common marinade for vegetable combinations such as tomatoes, onions, and cucumbers, or zucchini, and the two ingredients are essential for such dishes as gazpacho and some pasta salads. **See also:** FLAVORED OILS; FLAVORED VINEGAR; FOOD BASKETS.

OKTOBERFEST

Beer, bratwurst (a German sausage usually called brat), and brass bands are essential to Oktoberfest, a festival that was transported to North America from Germany; it is still celebrated in Munich for two weeks

beginning in late September and lasting through the first Sunday in October. In the United States, the festival is celebrated for a weekend in September or October. It began as a time to drink, eat, and be merry after the fall harvest.

Oktoberfest celebrations are not necessarily rural festivities, however. People in towns and cities across the United States participate in Oktoberfests held outdoors at street fairs or in restaurants. Covington, Kentucky, for example, hosts an Oktoberfest in the historic German village of Main-Strasse, where each year a three-day street

Sausage, or wurst, and beer are standard fare at any Oktoberfest celebration. As the locale where many German immigrants settled during the mid-nineteenth century, Fredericksburg, Texas, continues a tradition that began in the Bavarian city of Munich in 1810 to celebrate a royal wedding.

fair is held and about two dozen booths feature German foods. Cities as diverse as Terre Haute, Indiana; Amana, Iowa; Cincinnati, Ohio; Birmingham, Alabama; Helen, Georgia; Fort Lauderdale, Florida; Fredericksburg, Texas; Bismarck, North Dakota; and San Francisco, California, celebrate this German festival. Milwaukee, home of many German descendants and several famous breweries founded by Germans, is the site of a huge Oktoberfest each year, as are numerous smaller Wisconsin cities and towns. La Crosse, for example, hosts between 100,000 and 150,000 at its annual Oktoberfest.

One of the largest Oktoberfests is held annually in Chicago at two sites—one near Berghoff's, a famous German restaurant, and the other in a Chicago neighborhood, where many residents have German roots. (The neighborhood celebration is technically known as a German-American Fest, rather than Oktoberfest, but the flavor is the same.)

Although the festival in Germany focuses more on beer drinking (7 million quarts are said to be consumed during a two-week festival), the U.S. version of Oktoberfest calls for both beer and brat—bratwurst—or Wiener schnitzel (veal cutlets). Large German pretzels are also in abundance. They are often sold with ribbons that are looped through the pretzel and then around the neck, leaving the hands free to carry beer and brat. Other traditional foods served during the festival include sauerbraten (marinated pot roast), sauerkraut, a cooked red cabbage dish made with beets and apples, hot german potato salad, and a salad made with carrots and celery root. Finally, there is fruit kuchen (a strudel) and old-fashioned *apfelkuchen* (a German custard and sliced apple cake lightly spiced with cinnamon) for dessert. **See also:** PRETZELS.

OLIVES AND OLIVE OIL

No one knows when the olive tree first appeared, but the trees have been cultivated in the Mediterranean for thousands of years, and the benefits of olives have been extolled since the beginning of recorded history. Not only have olives and olive oil been used as food but olive oil also has been prized for cosmetic purposes (among its many benefits, it is said to prevent wrinkles and to soften the skin), for lamp oil, and as an ointment for religious ceremonies.

Although the consumption of olives and olive oil is greatest in the olive-producing regions of the Mediterranean, an increasing number of North Americans are consuming these products. Green olives, which are usually treated with a lye solution to remove the bitter substance known as oleuropein and then cured in brine, and black (or ripe) olives are often used on pizzas, as ingredients in salads and some hot dishes, and are part of appetizer trays for such events as buffets, cocktail parties, and open houses. For many drinkers, a martini would not be complete without the ritual of placing a green olive or two in the drink. Olives stuffed with anchovies, pimentos, almonds, and other ingredients are popular drink and party items.

The trend toward increased use of olive oil in the United States began in the 1980s. At that time, various scientific studies indicated that the use of olive oil and other vegetable oils such as canola, which contain unsaturated rather than cholesterol-producing saturated fats found in animal and dairy products, would help prevent heart disease. Many North Americans now use olive oil for salad dressing and for cooking.

See also APPETIZERS; CANOLA OIL; FLAVORED OILS; MARTINI.

References: Dolamore. *The Essential Olive Oil Companion.* 1989; McGee. *On Food and Cooking.* 1984.

OMELET

Originating either in France or Italy, the omelet (also omelette) is now a favorite dish in North America and one of the most popular choices for people going out to breakfast or to Sunday brunch. Omelets begin with a few beaten eggs. They can be cooked in a skillet until set up, then filled with a hot filling, folded, and turned out onto a plate. The filled omelete may be garnished or covered with a sauce. A flat omelet does not get folded and is turned over in the pan halfway through the cooking. It may be garnished with a choice of toppings and even served cold. For the latter version, flavoring is added to the egg mixture before cooking.

Creating a great omelet, regardless of type, requires mastering a basic technique. Some chefs recommend beating the yolks and whites separately, but others insist that the right pan is the key. There are appliances on the market that attempt to make the process simpler, but fluffy omelets are not generally made at home on a busy morning. They are left to the professionals in restaurants, who may prepare dozens if not hundreds of choices. The Denver omelet (filled with ham, bell peppers, and cheese); omelets filled with mushrooms, cheese, potatoes, seafood, tomatoes, or jelly; the Mexican omelet; the Italian omelet; or the mixed vegetable omelet are just a few of the possibilities.

OPEN HOUSE

The open house is a popular form of entertaining. Usually, but not always, given on or around a holiday such as Christmas or New Year's Eve, this type of party tends to be more informal than other affairs. It also facilitates the visiting of more than one party on nights when people have numerous social commitments. Invitations will specify a time when one is welcome to "drop by" for a quick bite, drink, and conversation. Food might be provided in the form of a buffet or, in more elegant variations, presented on trays by servers in uniform. Drinks can include a full bar set up or passed wine, champagne, or other beverage.

The open house also has become a promotional tool of businesses that want to show off their facilities, new products, or services or that want to extend a thank-you to their best customers. In this case, a caterer will provide food, drink, and service so that the businesspeople can concentrate on their guests.

See also: BUFFET; CATERED EVENTS.

ORANGE JUICE

Even though oranges are grown primarily in California and Florida, drinking orange juice for breakfast is a widespread custom in the United States. Until about the 1950s, people used to prepare fresh orange juice by squeezing the juice from the fruit with a hand-operated or electric juicer, but after World War II, scientists in Florida developed the means for processing oranges to make a concentrate, flavoring it, then freezing it in cans that could be shipped across the land and around the world. Marketing programs to sell "fresh-frozen" orange juice and transportation systems to deliver the product also helped make orange juice a common breakfast drink. Not only is orange juice consumed at home, but it also is offered as a breakfast beverage at nearly all restaurants, cafes, drive-ins, and shops where breakfast is served.

See also: BREAKFAST.

OSTRICH MEAT

Although ostrich meat and eggs were common foods among ancient Romans and Egyptians, the ostrich bird has been considered an exotic animal and was rarely seen in most parts of North America until about the late 1980s. U.S. farmers with the longest experiences in raising ostriches are in Oklahoma and Texas, and an increasing number of ostrich farms have been established in such states as Minnesota, Michigan, and Indiana.

Farmers raise ostriches and sometimes two other members of the Ratitae family—rheas and emus—for breeding purposes and also for human consumption. A breeding pair of ostriches costs between $40,000 and $60,000 and may produce 20 or more eggs annually, but only a few may hatch. Each ostrich yields about 100 pounds of meat, which tastes like beef but is far more

Grilled ostrich offers a lean alternative to beef as a red meat and to chicken. American ranchers, following the practice of South African ranchers, began commercial breeding of the leggy, flightless bird in the early 1980s.

expensive, costing anywhere from $20 to $30 a pound.

Poultry specialists and ostrich farmers from a dozen states have gathered since 1991 for an annual conference to discuss methods for and share experiences in breeding and raising ostriches. At the 1993 Multi-State Big Bird Conference in Indianapolis, Indiana, 300 attendees not only gathered information about the ostrich but also had the opportunnity to taste ostrich for the first time at a banquet. (Because most farmers have raised the ostrich for breeding purposes, they seldom use the bird as meat.) A roast leg of ostrich, a stir-fry, and a chowder with ostrich meat were served.

Because ostrich meat is very lean (less fat than turkey or chicken) and can be a substitute for red meat, farmers hope the potential health benefits of this type of food will prompt consumers to buy it. Researchers have found that ostrich has 2 to 3 grams of fat per 3.5-ounce, or 100-gram, serving. A similar size serving of beef contains from 4 grams to more than 20 grams of fat. In order for consumption of ostrich meat to increase in the years ahead, prices would have to drop, which would require at least 150,000 breeder birds available nationally to produce eggs. At age two or three, ostrich or rhea birds begin laying eggs, producing every other day between March and April and again in September. **References:** Denton. "Ostrich." 1993; Livingston and Livingston. *Edible Plants and Animals.* 1993.

OYSTER BARS

For a large portion of the population living along or near North American coastlines, eating oysters on a regular basis is more than a ritual—it is a way of life. Oyster bars or pubs are popular eating establishments, and they range from New York's famed Oyster Bar with its vaulted ceiling and red tile flooring in Grand Central Station to small down-home "shacks" on piers, whether on the Atlantic or Pacific coast. Raw oysters are one of the specialties at many oyster bars and pubs, but steamed, baked, or smoked oysters and oyster stew are usually featured, too. Some upscale oyster bars may serve souffléed oysters. Most also offer a variety of fresh fish and seafood, from crab cakes to mussels to shrimp.

Oyster lovers may be found just about anywhere in North America, and some make a ritual of going to restaurants that include oyster bars as part of their all-you-can-eat buffets. After all, oysters are expensive for anyone on a tight budget. In northern California, one oyster lover ate so many oysters at a buffet-type restaurant that the management refused to serve him any more, claiming he had devoured 70 oysters. The customer claimed he ate only 40, and he sued the restaurant for limiting his supply. A small-claims court found in his favor, since the restaurant's advertising applied to oyster lovers as well as to those who just gorge on less-expensive pasta. **See also:** OYSTER FESTIVALS.

OYSTER FESTIVALS

In almost any part of North America where oysters are gathered, they also are celebrated with an oyster festival, usually held in late summer or early fall. In Connecticut, for example, the Norwalk Seaport Association has sponsored an oyster festival since 1977, a three-day event held in early September. Like many such festivals, oyster-shucking and oyster-eating competitions are main attractions. An older event takes place the second week in October in St. Mary's County, Maryland. Originating in 1967, the annual St. Mary's festival hosts the National Oyster Shucking Championship, with the winner participating in an international event. Oysters are served raw on the half-shell with sauce, and they are also fried and stewed in a broth based on a recipe that reportedly is 300 years old. **Reference:** Shemanski. *A Guide to Fairs and Festivals in the United States.* 1984.

PANCAKE BREAKFAST

Native Americans introduced colonists to cornmeal cakes as a breakfast food, but pancakes made from wheat (or rice) flour batter are one of the oldest forms of bread and have been a part of every culture. Pancakes also have been served at feast days, such as Shrove Tuesday, so it is not surprising that pancake breakfasts have become community events—often fund-raisers—in North America. The pancake breakfast associated with Frontier Days in Cheyenne, Wyoming, is an example. Many pancake breakfasts are held in the Pacific Northwest, where logging and mining camps first established the practice in the 1800s.

Pancakes are popular foods all across North America and they are typical items served at a Sunday brunch and, of course, are the main menu item at popular pancake houses (chain restaurants) and other eating establishments that specialize in pancakes. Usually a variety of pancakes are available from the fruit-filled to the type topped with eggs. Most pancake houses also offer several types of fruit syrups (blueberry is especially popular) along with the traditional maple syrup. It is common as well to serve pancake breakfasts at children's summer camps, at tourist areas focusing on outdoor activities, and certainly at maple syrup and blueberry festivals.

See also: BREAKFAST; CHEYENNE FRONTIER DAYS; CREPES; DANISH DAYS; MAPLE SUGARING/FESTIVALS; SHROVE TUESDAY; SUNDAY BRUNCH.

PASSOVER FEAST

See SEDER.

PASTA

According to the National Pasta Association, there are 150 different shapes of dried pasta produced in the United States, although some specialty shops selling pasta products may offer over 200 different varieties in flavors ranging from squid to garlic parsley. Evidence of the popularity of pasta-based dishes and meals can be found in the proliferation of Italian restaurants (excluding pizza places), which top all other ethnic restaurants in the United States. Pasta dishes are also popular in other ethnic cuisines—pork paprikash with noodles, for example, is a traditional Hungarian-style dish, and numerous Chinese dishes are served with dried noodles. By the year 2000, Americans will be eating an average of 30.6 pounds of pasta per person annually. Pasta includes the familiar spaghetti, fettuccine, lasagna, and linguine;

twists like rotelle; and a variety of shells and tubes. There are other tiny shapes used in soups or as side dishes. Nearly all pasta, except for vegetable varieties, is made from flour and water and sometimes eggs. Each type, however, may create its own "mouth feel," as the texture is called.

Because pasta is so easy and quick to prepare and is low-fat, nutritious, and inexpensive, it has become a staple in millions of homes. Cooks frequently prepare pasta salads—many tossed with olive oil— and casseroles for picnics, church suppers, buffets, and similar events. Numerous hot pasta dishes are made with tomato sauce, cream sauce, or simply garlic and olive oil tossed with grated cheese. Spaghetti with sauce and macaroni and cheese or macaroni salad are traditional dishes for many Americans. One dish, pasta fazool, is a favorite in many Italian homes. The name is a corrupted version of *pasta e fagioli* or pasta (usually macaroni) with beans.

See also: CHURCH DINNERS/SUPPERS; MACARONI; PICNIC; POTLUCK.
References: Rozin. *Blue Corn and Chocolate.* 1992; Simmons. *365 Ways To Cook Pasta.* 1992.

PASTY

Made with a pastry like crust and filled with meat and vegetables, the pasty is part of traditional cooking among people from Cornwall, England, who settled in the mining areas of Minnesota, Wisconsin, and Michigan. During the mid-1800s, the pasty was a typical miner's lunch. Self-contained, wrapped in a cloth or paper, the meat pie could be carried in a pocket or lunch pail and heated on a shovel over a lamp, then eaten like today's popular pocket sandwiches without utensils.

Although the pasty is considered a Cornish dish, it is part of the customary fare prepared by people from Finland who

Actor Jack Lemmon uses a tennis racquet to strain and rinse pasta in a scene with Shirley McLaine from the 1960 movie The Apartment.

also settled in the northern mining states. According to "serious gastroethnographers," as the cookbook authors Jane and Michael Stern call them, there is a difference in the two types of pasties. Cubes of steak go into a Cornish pasty, while ground beef and pork are stuffed into a Finnish pasty. Apparently, the type of dough distinguishes one pasty from another as well—the "true" Cornish pasty made with flour and beef suet and the Finnish pasty made with flour and lard or commercial shortening.

However pasties are made, they are served and eaten with gusto at many summer festivals throughout the northern Michigan and Wisconsin area. And many people in North America prepare some variation of this meat pie during ethnic festivals, at holidays, or other public events. **See also:** ETHNIC FOOD TRADITIONS; POT PIES. **References:** Kirlin and Kirlin. *Smithsonian Folklife Cookbook.* 1991; Stern and Stern. *Real American Food.* 1986.

PÂTÉ

See APPETIZERS.

PEACH FESTIVALS

June is the month for peach festivals in Georgia, Alabama, Louisiana, and other southern states. A major peach festival is held annually in Peach County, Georgia. Although Georgia is known for its peaches, Louisiana also celebrates the fruit from its orchards, focusing on the state's efforts to "build" a peach better adapted to Louisiana's climate. Peaches are a major crop in the midwestern state of Michigan, too, so peach harvests naturally call for celebration. Since the 1930s, the Michigan Peach Festival of Romeo has taken place over the Labor Day weekend, and daily attractions include carnival rides, art exhibits, sporting events, craft shows, book sales, dances, dinners, car shows, and parades. Other peach festivals throughout Michigan sponsor similar events. Bake sales featuring peach pie and peach-eating

contests are major events in all peach harvest festivals. Peach pound cake, peach preserves and jams, homemade peach ice cream, and fresh peaches are just some of the "peachy" foods sold at numerous stands.

PEANUT BUTTER

In 1990, peanut butter was 100 years old. This nutritious spread was conceived in 1890 by a St. Louis physician who wanted to provide his elderly toothless patients with an easily digestible protein food as a substitute for meat. Although his name is unknown, the physician's ground peanut product has survived countless food fads and is now one of the most popular foods around, primarily because it is convenient, inexpensive, and healthy.

In the United States, at least 800 million pounds of peanut butter are consumed each year. The spread is used in packaged snack foods such as peanut butter filling between cheese crackers, as a filling in hard candies and chocolate-covered candies, and in sandwiches made with peanut butter and jelly or some other combination such as peanut butter and mashed banana. For decades, peanut butter and jelly sandwiches have been a popular lunch and after-school snack for children, and peanut butter spread on apples is a common snack at day-care centers. Many adults love peanut butter as well, and those who regularly consume the sticky product may put it on bagels for breakfast, slap it on bread for a quick lunch, spread it on celery for a snack, or just eat it by the spoonful out of the jar.
 See also: BUTTER AND OTHER SPREADS; PEANUT FESTIVALS.

PEANUT FESTIVALS

Peanut celebrations are common in the U.S. South, and Sylvester, Georgia, which claims to be the Peanut Capital of the World and supplies about half the peanuts produced in the United States, holds an annual October festival honoring its major crop. The festival began in 1964 and in 1987 became known for producing the world's largest peanut butter and jelly sandwich, a huge square measuring 12.5 by 12.5 feet.

A native of South America, the peanut is a type of legume often called a ground pea, although there are hundreds of names for this food. Peanuts probably came to colonial America by way of Africa where Portuguese slavers planted peanuts to feed their captives, who then brought plants with them to America. According to food historian Waverly Root, peanuts were first cultivated in North America during the 1790s. Today, in such southern states as Georgia, Alabama, and Florida, peanuts are a major crop, bringing in $500 million a year in Georgia alone.

Another major peanut event, the National Peanut Festival, has been held each year in Dothan, Alabama, since 1938. (A guest at the first festival was George Washington Carver of Alabama's Tuskegee Institute—one of America's most famous botanists who, during the 1890s, developed several hundred ways to use peanuts.) At this national festival, which is a week long event in November, cooks show off a great number of creative ways to use peanuts—they are boiled, fried, steamed, roasted, pureed, and ground and may be eaten as a spread or added to soups, soufflés, glazes, ice cream, confections, and many other foods. Peanut butter soup made with chicken broth, vegetables, and peanut butter is one of the popular dishes at the festival, as are peanut brittle, peanut butter fudge, and peanut butter cookies.
See also: NUTS AND SEEDS; PEANUT BUTTER; SNACK FOODS.
References: Borghese. *Food from Harvest Festivals and Folk Fairs.* 1977; Mariani. *The Dictionary of American Food and Drink.* 1993. 1994; Root. *Food.* 1980.

PECAN FESTIVAL

While pecans are not as plentiful in the United States as peanuts, they are a widely used product in baked goods, candies, and in the southern specialty, pecan pie. A harvest of pecans is celebrated wherever they

are grown. One pecan celebration has been held annually since 1984 in Okmulgee, Oklahoma, the capital of the Creek nation and the heart of an area where 600 acres of pecan trees are harvested for national markets. The Creek as well as many other Native Americans have made use of nuts and seeds for years and taught colonists how to prepare them.

In 1988, the Okmulgee Pecan Festival featured the world's largest pecan pie, which was 40 feet in diameter and weighed 16.5 tons. Because making the pie was such a tremendous task, the festival now features less-ambitious baked goods such as pecan cookies. A bake-off contest and booths sell a variety of pecan-based foods.
See also: PEANUT FESTIVALS.
Reference: Thompson and Carlson. *Holidays, Festivals, and Celebrations of the World Dictionary.* 1994.

PERSIAN NEW YEAR

Hundreds of thousands of Iranians who live in such North American cities as Washington, D.C., Philadelphia, and Los Angeles (in southern California alone, there are at least 500,000 residents from Iran or of Iranian descent) celebrate the Persian New Year known as Nouruz, No Rouz, Noruz, Nou-Rooz, or Now Rooz. Nouruz begins on the eve of the vernal equinox and extends over 13 days. In some communities, people start the new year by putting on costumes and going door to door for gifts of candy. Throughout the celebration, families and friends gather for visits, and young people receive small gifts from their elders.

In most Iranian homes, a holiday table features Persian New Year symbols, such as garlic to promote peacemaking, goldfish to represent the passage through life's sometimes difficult waves, and sprouting lentils to symbolize the life cycle. The holiday celebration culminates with an outdoor event, since it is considered bad luck to stay inside on Jashnsizdah Bedar—the thirteenth day. The event, which stems from celebrations dating back 3,000 years, is similar to other ethnic festivals with traditional music and entertainment and athletic contests, but families gather to eat traditional foods in picnic or barbecue style. The foods include chicken, beef, and lamb shish kebabs, some marinaded in a yogurt-based dressing or served with *somagh,* a condiment made from sumac leaves; a New Year soup made of noodles, mint, garlic, and vinegar; or a thick meat and bean soup. Throughout the holiday, such dishes as *dolmeh,* vegetables stuffed with meat and rice; the national dish *chelokabab,* grilled lamb served with rice; *albalu pollo,* a rice pilaf of cherries and chicken; fried eggplant in a tomato-saffron sauce; Iranian flat bread called *lavash;* and traditional sweets such as baklava and a variety of candies and cookies are served.

The Persian New Year is also celebrated by Parsi, descendants of followers of the Zoroastrian religion who fled Persia in the seventh century at the time of the Muslim conquest and settled in India, calling themselves "Parsi" after the ancient name of Persia. A relatively large community of Parsi live in Los Angeles and San Francisco, California, and they combine both Iranian and Indian traditions at Navroz, as the New Year is called by the Parsi community. Parsi foods served during this holiday include meats prepared in Iranian style and lentil dishes from India. One traditional dish is chutney-coated fish, wrapped in a banana leaf and steamed.

PERSIMMON PUDDING

Few people today grow persimmons or make persimmon pudding, although it was once a popular midwestern dessert. It, however, is featured at the Prairie restaurant in Chicago, where foods from the heartland are specialties. Persimmon pudding as well as other persimmon desserts and persimmon bread and rolls are also mainstays in southern Indiana, particularly in the town of Mitchell, home of what is believed to be the world's only persimmon-pulp canning factory called Dymple's Delight. Persimmon trees grow wild in southern Indiana and also grow in cultivated orchards, producing a harvest in the fall when the fruit is honored at an annual festival that has been taking place each September since 1947.

In order to use persimmons in puddings and other specialties, the ripe fruit, which is soft and sweet, must be quartered and the pulp scooped out and blended in a food processor. Many people, though, use the canned product, which usually has to be ordered from the canning factory in Mitchell.

References: Borghese. *Food from Harvest Festivals and Folk Fairs.* 1977; Langlois. *Prairie.* 1990.

PESTO

Pesto is a traditional food of families whose ancestry stems from the Mediterranean area, but its appeal has broadened substantially. Technically, it is a ground mixture of fresh basil leaves, garlic, pine nuts, olive oil, Parmesan cheese, and salt. Some chefs will add their own favorite touches such as walnuts, parsley, or even anchovies. Others will make cilantro pesto or oregano pesto, but pesto most usually refers to the traditional basil paste.

Undoubtedly first devised to keep a bumper crop of fresh herbs on the shelf for a longer period of time, the concoction proved to be highly adaptive and useful in many dishes. Restaurants, other than Italian, popularized pesto dishes in the 1980s when the pesto pizza, pesto potatoes, pesto garlic bread, broiled fish with pesto, and pesto cream pastas seemed to be on every menu. Today, commercially prepared pesto is available thoughout North America. The best, however, is usually made in one's own kitchen.

PICKLES

During the early decades of the 1900s, it was common to see a pickle barrel in many grocery stores and delis in the United States. Customers could take their pick from the barrel of cucumbers, which had been preserved in a brine (the most common type of pickle). The cost was usually a nickel. It was also a custom at neighborhood taverns to provide free pickled eggs; customers helped themselves from a jar placed on a bar.

Pickles are still offered at a nominal cost to customers in some delis, and dill pickles (flavored with dill seeds and leaves) and garlic-flavored kosher pickles often accompany sandwiches served in many types of restaurants. Pickles and pickle relishes are in fact condiments that appear at most fastfood establishments and salad bars, and they are certainly staples at picnics.

Pickles also are routinely featured at food fairs, county and state fairs, and harvest festivals throughout the United States. Many of the pickles on display and available for sampling are made from other vegetables besides cucumbers, and some are made from fruits. Pickled artichokes, beets, cauliflower, peppers, tomatoes, and watermelon rind and preserved fruits in a sweet and spicy brine are common.

One unique way to celebrate pickles takes place in Dillsburg, Pennsylvania, named not for a type of pickle but rather for settler Mathew Dill, according to an Associated Press report (30 December 1994). Replicating the New York City ritual when a lighted ball drops in Times Square, residents in Dillsburg await the drop of a 6-foot, papier-mâché pickle, which at the stroke of midnight plunges 80 feet from the top of a ladder. The second annual event was held on New Year's Eve 1994 and included the sale of baked goods with proceeds used for community improvements.
See also: AMISH FOOD FESTIVALS; CHOW-CHOW; WATERMELON FESTIVALS.

PICNIC

North Americans, as a rule, have always enjoyed picnics, which can range from a simple boxed or bagged lunch to an elaborate spread in an elegant setting such as a courtyard at a concert hall or a museum. People carry picnic meals to parks, aboard boats, on bus and automobile tours, to beaches, to the mountains, to sporting events—to just about any place where they might be able to spread out the food and beverages. Some of the most common picnic foods include hamburgers, hot dogs, potato salad, macaroni salad, coleslaw, potato or corn chips, and watermelon. Most people take along a jug of water or fruit-flavored beverage and a cooler of beer and cola drinks. While a picnic can be a spur-of-the-moment event, some picnics are seasonal rituals, such as a "company picnic," an annual family reunion, or a Fourth-of-July celebration.
See also: BARBECUE; CLAMBAKE; FAMILY REUNION; GRUNION RUN; INDEPENDENCE DAY CELEBRATIONS; PICNIC BASKET; TAILGATE PARTY.

PICNIC BASKET

One of the favorite activities of summer—picnicking—is symbolized by the traditional wicker basket filled with warm weather foods and drinks. Families, couples, a parent taking the kids to the beach, all carry a variation of the well-packed basketful of the picnic lunch. Lovers may pack a blanket, a jug of wine, a loaf of bread, and some cheese in their basket before going to a romantic spot overlooking the sea. The picnic lunch in the park for a family includes such favorite picnic foods as coleslaw, potato salad, sandwiches, chips, soda pop, and beer.
See also: PICNIC.

PIEROGIES

Filled dumplings called peirogies are traditional Polish food (although they are also part of the cuisine of many people of Eastern European descent) and are often served at food fairs and ethnic festivals. Several brands of frozen pierogies have appeared in supermarkets during the 1980s and 1990s, attesting to their increasing popularity. At home they are made with a dough consisting of flour, butter, sour cream, and eggs (for a low-fat variety yogurt and egg whites can be substituted for the latter two) that is rolled and cut in rounds for the outer "shell," which is then filled. Mashed potato and cheese fillings are popular as are sauerkraut or cabbage and mushroom mixtures. Pierogies also may be filled with ground cooked meat mixed with egg and seasonings. Once filled, the pierogi dough is folded in a half-moon shape, sealed at the edges, and cooked in boiling water or tomato sauce, or they are sautéed with vegetables and seasonings.

See also: ETHNIC FOOD TRADITIONS; TASTE OF . . . FESTIVALS.

References: Betz. *Tastes of Liberty.* 1985; Smith. *The Frugal Gourmet on Our Immigrant Ancestors.* 1990.

PIES

A dough made of flour, shortening, and water is the basis for a great variety of pastry dishes routinely served in North America, including two-crust dessert pies, turnovers, and open-faced tarts. These foods most often are made with fruit fillings—from apple to strawberry— and are continental favorites. Apple pie has become associated with the American image; in fact, "as American as baseball, motherhood, and apple pie" is an old adage that many use to describe something they consider quintessentially American. One-crust cream, chiffon, and custard pies such as chocolate cream, coconut custard, and lemon chiffon are also popular.

Many dessert pies are associated with specific groups of people—the shoofly pie and Shaker lemon pie are examples of such pies. There also are pies that are associated with specific national holidays, such as the Thanksgiving pumpkin pie and the Christmas mincemeat pie. Some popular versions are associated with geographical regions, such as the Mississippi mud pie and the Florida key lime pie.

Pies, a standard pastry dessert filled with fruit or a more substantial filling of meat and vegetables, provide grist for a pie-eating contest. The rule of "no hands" leads to inelegant headfirst gobbling of a fruit-filled pastry.

Many types of main dish pies or small pastry appetizers made with meat, poultry, or seafood are served in North America. Some of the most popular in the main dish category stem from ethnic cuisines or holiday traditions. The Canadian pork pie is a traditional two-crust pie made with ground pork, celery, onions, and seasonings and served hot or cold at any time of the year; it is popular with the brown-bag or lunch-box crowd. Shepherd's pie, based on British customs, is made with leftover meats and fresh vegetables, as is the traditional Twelfth Night pie. Chicken pot pie is another all-American favorite that has been around for many generations.

See also: APPLE PANDOWDY; APPLE PIE; CHICKEN ENTREES; FRITTERS; KEY LIME COOKIES AND PIE; MINCEMEAT PIE; MOCK APPLE PIE; PASTY; POT PIES; QUICHE.

References: Choate. *The Great American Pie Book*. 1992; Kirlin and Kirlin. *Smithsonian Folklife Cookbook*. 1991.

PIGS-IN-A-BLANKET

This is a very well known "children's food" that has been popular since about the 1960s in the United States. The "pig" is a hot dog that is swaddled in a "blanket," which can be soft white bread or commercial refrigerated, crescent roll triangles. The latter is easier and gives the dish that special aftertaste common to packaged quick-rising dough products. Simply wrap a triangle of dough around the center of the frankfurter, and then bake in the oven. The bread version is a little trickier as the hot dog generally is heated through first; then the bread, which has been flattened slightly with a rolling pin or the palm of a child's hand, is wrapped around the little piggy. Careful broiling toasts the bread and finishes the dish. Variations include slitting or hollowing the hot dog to add cheese or other favorite condiments before wrapping. Choices are usually left to the children who love to take part in the preparation of this meal.

Pigs-in-a-blanket are served on occasion at informal adult meals, such as a barbecue or buffet. Miniature versions, which are available in the frozen food section of groceries and supermarkets, are frequently prepared as appetizers or as snacks.

See also: APPETIZERS; HOT DOGS; SNACK FOODS.

PIÑATA

In Mexico, birthdays and special celebrations such as Christmas Eve are not complete until the breaking of the piñata, a practice that may have originated in China before Marco Polo, who took the idea from the Orient to Italy, where it was borrowed by the Spanish who crossed the Atlantic to conquer Mexico. The Mexican émigré populations north of the border have also brought the exciting ritual to other cultures in the United States.

In many parts of North America, the piñata is a hollow papier-mâché figurine measuring approximately 1 foot in diameter and representing a burro, star, pig, legendary figure, or some other whimsical character. In Mexico, the traditional piñata is a clay cooking pot, decorated to resemble the magical figures with ribbon, streamers, and colored paper.

Regardless of its composition, the piñata is always filled with small candies and toys. Once the party is in full swing, one or more piñatas are hung in a central location. Starting with the youngest guests, all the children take turns using a broomstick to bat at the figure. The smallest children do not generally hit anything, and the older ones are blindfolded and spun around to disorient them. As the spectators clap and sing, each child in turn tries to break the unseen vessel. The adult in charge determines the number of swings the children may use . Finally, a lucky hit is made, and the treasure spills to the floor. Every guest then dives to retrieve the goodies in a good-natured revel.

See also: MEXICAN FIESTAS.

PINTO BEAN FIESTA

In Moriarity, New Mexico, the Pinto Bean Fiesta has been celebrated each October since 1987. Tons of pinto beans are grown, harvested, and shipped from this central New Mexican community. The fiesta includes a pinto bean cook-off; cooks prepare spicy bean casseroles and pot bean dishes as well as breads and desserts for judging. In addition, local bean growers offer a great variety of pinto beans for sale.

PITA BREAD

Originally from the Middle East, this round flat bread has proven to be a favorite food for people in North America. The unleavened product forms a pocket of air in the middle during baking. By carefully slicing and separating the bread, the pocket can be filled with a wide array of foods.

The first popular use of pita was at health-, natural-, and vegetarian-style restaurants where the traditional falafel sandwich was served. Falafel is a ground garbanzo (chick pea), garlic, and herb mixture that is formed into balls or patties and then fried. These are placed into the pita pocket with tomato, shredded lettuce, peppers, and a tahini (sesame seed paste) dressing. It is a kind of Middle Eastern "taco." The nonmeat, complete protein characteristics of this sandwich were a hit with people trying to create alternative eating patterns during the 1960s and 1970s. From these beginnings, the light pita pocket has developed into a holder for many other fillings. It also has been cut and baked into chips, served as the crust for mini pizzas, and generally done yeoman duty in the modern kitchen.
See also: SANDWICHES.

PITCHA

Calves' foot jelly—pitcha or petcha—is a classic appetizer or a traditional Sabbath lunch in Jewish homes and is frequently served at an ethnic buffet. Pitcha is made from slowly simmered calves feet. The meat is pulled from the bones, finely chopped, and cooked further with garlic and spices, then it is combined with a broth and refrigerated until jellylike in texture. Cut into cubes, pitcha is usually served with horseradish.

PIZZA

"Let's get a pizza!" or "Call for a pizza!" are typical beginnings to an informal eating ritual enjoyed by millions in North America. Those who routinely eat pizza often are adamant about the places where they consume this dish or order takeouts and about the type of crust and toppings that make the "best" pizza. Most pizza lovers like to share this dish with friends, relatives, or coworkers for lunch, supper, or an evening snack. Many baseball, football, and basketball fans routinely stop at a chain pizza parlor or restaurant for post-game refreshments. Pizza is also a common party food.

This popular food began in Italy as bread and tomato sauce, but the style of pizza now widely known originated in the United States in New York City's Little Italy district in 1905. By the 1940s, the dish was well on its way to becoming Americanized and many varieties began to emerge. Pizza franchises started in 1954, when Shakey's opened its first outlet in Sacramento, California. Today, pizza is associated with Italian restaurants, pizza parlors, stands, or shops that usually serve a variety of Italian dishes and sandwiches along with their pizzas.

One type of pizza—the deep-dish variety—originated in Chicago in 1942 at Pizzeria Uno, where, it is said, a recently returned World War II veteran suggested that the owner try serving a dish he had discovered while stationed in Italy: bread with tomato on it. This later turned into deep-dish pizza baked in a pie pan to form a thick crust for which Pizzeria Uno is famous.

Many other pizzerias have developed their own kind of pizza, such as stuffed pizza, double-crust pizza, pizza soufflé, and pesto pizza. On the Atlantic Coast, white clam pizza pie—fresh clams, with olive oil, oregano, and garlic, on a crust—is a specialty of some pizzerias. Of course, the standard thick- or thin-crust tomato and cheese pizza is also available in most pizza parlors.

See also: SNACK FOODS.

References: Smith. *The Frugal Gourmet Cooks Three Ancient Cuisines. 1989*; Stern and Stern. *GoodFood.* 1983.

PLANKED FOOD

Planking was once a common way to prepare and serve meals, and the practice has been maintained in a few places in North America. Traditionally, planking is the process of baking a piece of fish or meat on an oiled piece of wood and serving it on the same "plank" surrounded by potatoes and other vegetables. A dinner of planked shad fish cooked over charcoal is featured at the annual Shad Festival in Bethlehem, Pennsylvania, where shad runs and colonial life are celebrated in May each year. In some midwestern restaurants near the Great Lakes, planked whitefish is common, and a few restaurants in the heartland feature planked steak. In Virginia, the Ruritan Club in Wakefield holds an Annual Shad Planking, a cook-out that has taken place since the 1940s. It began as a way for the "good ol' boys" in politics to get together, and although the early cook-out originally excluded all blacks and women, the event was integrated long ago and continues to draw political hopefuls from across the state of Virginia.

Reference: Langlois. *Prairie.* 1990.

PLUM PUDDING

Like the "figgy pudding" of holiday song, plum pudding is one of those Christmas dishes of British tradition that is still made and eaten by some North American families. Even if they are not particularly well liked, "steamed puddings" of this type, as with the ubiquitous holiday fruitcake, seem to be fixtures of the season. This is especially true at holiday parties. Recipes for plum pudding usually include the following ingredients: milk-soaked bread, eggs, brown sugar, orange juice, suet, vanilla, flour, cinnamon, cloves, mace, raisins, dates, candied fruit and peels, and nuts. It is served with a hard sauce or another type of liqueur-infused sauce, and quite often it is "flamed" as a dramatic ending to a Christmas dinner.

See also: FRUITCAKE; MADRIGAL DINNER.

POI

Crushed taro root—poi—was the staff of life for ancient Pacific islanders, and it is traditionally served as a staple on Hawaiian and Polynesian tables. Pastelike in texture and purple-gray in color, poi is a nutritious food. It has been credited with everything from contributing to longevity to healing bee stings, but not everyone likes it. In fact, some people insist it tastes like library paste, while others think it is delicious. To eat poi in the traditional way, one must dip one or two fingers in it and put it in the mouth, using no utensils.

See also: LUAU.

POKEWEED SALAD

"Poke salit," or pokeweed salad, is made from a perennial herb (*Phytolacca americana*) that is native to North America and grows wild in the United States and Mexico. In many parts of the South, Southeast, and Midwest, harvesting wild pokeweed has long been a spring ritual. Although the roots and mature stalks, leaves, and berries that form late in the summer are poisonous, the early spring shoots and leaves are edible. They may be parboiled for a salad or cooked like spinach, turnip, collard, or dandelion greens with salt pork. Pokeweed has also been used as a spring tonic—an emetic—and in the 1800s was considered a cure for venereal disease. Today, pokeweed is celebrated at spring food festivals in some areas of the South where the plant is grown from seed and cultivated.

See also: SALAD GREENS; WILD EDIBLES.

POLENTA

Polenta, an Italian word meaning "pearl barley," is a porridge or mush that was likely made from barley centuries ago, some historians believe. When maize (corn) was brought to Europe from the Americas, northern Italians used cornmeal to make porridge, and this dish became a staple food, as important to the northern Italian daily diet as pasta was (and is) to southern Italians. The custom of making polenta traveled with northern Italians when they immigrated to the United States, and polenta is now a part of family meals in many North American households today.

Like other versions of cornmeal mush introduced to North Americans by indigenous people, polenta begins with cooked cornmeal—boiled in water, or in a beef, pork, or chicken stock, or in a combination of dry white wine and water. Prepared as a breakfast porridge, polenta is simply poured into boiling water and simmered until it is quite thick, then served hot with milk accompanied by fresh bread and butter. After it cools and solidifies, polenta can be sliced, fried, and covered with syrup, honey, sugar, or jelly—another common breakfast item. For lunch or dinner, polenta may be seasoned and covered with a tomato sauce made with garlic, onions, and ground meat or perhaps chicken livers. It is often sprinkled with Parmesan cheese and served with chicken, pork, or sausage.

Since cornmeal mush is a bland food, cooks find countless ways to prepare polenta, and it can be a filling meal in itself or an imaginative side dish or dessert. Polenta is frequently used in a baked dish. For example, after being cooked, cooled, and sliced, polenta can be placed in a buttered or oiled pan, topped with mozzarella cheese, baked until the cheese has melted, and served hot. In the U.S. South, a dish called polenta is made with grits instead of cornmeal. Cooked grits are combined with Parmesan cheese, mild goat cheese, and salt. After the mixture cools, the polenta is cut into squares, covered with tomato sauce, and baked. A traditional Italian recipe for the Christmas holidays is a polenta shortcake made with cornmeal mush combined with sugar, pine nuts, raisins, figs, butter, eggs, fennel seeds, and flour, and then baked.

See also: CORNMEAL MUSH; GRITS.

Reference: Ayto. *A Gourmet's Guide.* 1993.

POOR SOUP

Some of the most important foods among the Pennsylvania Dutch are so-called poor soups, prepared as single-dish meals or meals-in-a-bowl. The Pennsylvania Dutch include religious groups such as the Mennonites, Amish, Dunkards, and Moravians who emigrated from what were called the Low Countries in Europe to the Pennsylvania Colony, where thousands settled. Most spoke German and called themselves *Deutsch* (meaning the Folk), which others translated as "Dutch." In the past and present, the Pennsylvania Dutch put almost any available food in the soup kettle to create a hearty but frugal soup. Many poor soups are made with a milk base and simmered with potatoes and onions or with rivlets, a flour and egg mixture that creates what is popularly known as lump soup. Fresh bread with a crisp buttery crust often is served with poor soup to complete the meal, and hearty soups are common Sunday morning breakfasts among some Pennsylvania Dutch.

See also: SOUP SUPPERS.

References: Hutchison. *Pennsylvania Dutch Cook Book.* 1948; Trager. *Foodbook.* 1970.

POPCORN

Almost everyone who eats popcorn regularly associates this snack food with a leisure activity such as going to the movies, watching television, attending a fair, or sitting in the stands at a ball game. In colonial times in North America, however, popcorn was a breakfast food served with sugar and milk or cream. Years later, hot buttered popcorn sprinkled with salt became a delightful snack for settlers and pioneers moving west in the United States.

After movie theaters were established in the United States, popcorn machines were installed, spreading the practice of eating this snack food. Today, many movie fans cannot separate the ritual of eating popcorn from watching a film—the two activities go together. In the same way, many baseball fans would feel cheated if they could not munch on a box or bag of popcorn while keeping their eyes glued on the plays of their favorite team members. Likewise, many of today's "couch potatoes"—people who spend hours in front of the television set—ritualistically take a break during commercials to "zap" a bag of popcorn in the microwave, to prepare popcorn in a hot-air popper, or pop it in a pan with heated oil on top of the stove.

Popcorn also is celebrated in festivals, especially in the Midwest where such corn is grown. Since 1978, Valparaiso, Indiana, has held a Popcorn Festival, which in 1994 honored a fellow Hoosier, Orville Redenbacher, owner of a major popcorn company that bears his name. The festival includes a parade with floats decorated with popcorn and lots of popcorn to eat. **See also:** SNACK FOODS.

PORTUGUESE HOLY SPIRIT FESTIVAL

Hundreds of thousands of Americans whose ancestors came from the Azores to live in North America—primarily California, Nevada, and Hawaii—observe the Portuguese Holy Spirit Festival. This festival is usually held the seventh week after Easter, but that may vary with each community. Parades with people dressed in traditional Portuguese costumes, Portuguese music and dances, a special Mass, and crowning a queen are all part of the event. The festival stems from Catholic religious beliefs and ancient legends, one of which says that fourteenth-century Queen Isabel, known as a peacemaker and friend to the poor, was able to relieve her people's suffering, especially during a severe famine; thus, part of the festival focuses on a feast.

At a hall or church recreation center, volunteers prepare huge pots of *sopas e carne* (beef soup), which is made from slaughtered cows donated by farmers in the Portuguese community. The beef is boiled for hours with onions, paprika, cinnamon, cumin, tomato, and wine (sometimes cabbage is added). When the soup is served, the broth is poured over French bread and mint sprigs, and the meat is placed alongside. In the spirit of Queen Isabel, the soup is served free to everyone. Throughout the day, other Portuguese specialties such as breads and *tremocos* (boiled lupino beans) are available for sale, and after the meal, an auctioneer sells other homemade items. Proceeds from food and beverage sales help pay the cost of the festival.

Reference: *Sunset* magazine editors. "Join the Portuguese for a Festa." 1989.

POSOLE

A Mexican hominy stew or thick soup usually made with a pork stock (although beef is sometimes used), *posole* is served on Christmas Eve and New Year's Eve or Day, in line with a long-held tradition of using a corn dish as a symbol of thanksgiving for survival. *Posole* is a common dish prepared for Native American festivals and feasts throughout North America, and among some groups it is considered a national dish.

In most instances *posole* is a fairly bland dish, but an American Southwest variation known as pozole, which also contains hominy and pork or turkey, is usually a spicier dish with plenty of chiles. Whether plain or spicy, purists advise using only dried hominy because of its "acidic bite," but some who routinely prepare the dish insist that canned hominy is "the best" because it is more tender and easier to prepare than the dried version.

See also: GRITS; NATIVE AMERICAN FEASTS.
References: Fussell. *I Hear America Cooking.* 1986; Kirlin and Kirlin. *Smithsonian Folklife Cookbook.* 1991; Schulz. *Celebrating America.* 1994.

POT PIES

"Pot pies are homey, comforting, and welcome as a casual dinner in front of the fire, a last-minute brunch with friends, or a made-ahead dinner to be reheated, . . . " wrote Beatrice Ojakangas in her book *Pot Pies.*

A pot pie is basically a one-dish meal, either enclosed in a crust or covered with a crust and baked. The crust may be made of a pastry, phyllo, or pizza dough; cornmeal or cornbread; or mashed potatoes. Among the Pennsylvania Dutch (of German ancestry), however, a pot pie is a noodle dish—squares of noodle dough are dropped into a stew and simmered until done.

North Americans of many national backgrounds consider some form of pot pie a traditional meal. One example is tourtiere, a traditional French-Canadian pot pie made of pork and beef and served on Christmas Eve and New Year's Day. Another is a vegetable Finish pot pie made with vegetables, cheese, rice, and such seasonings as oregano, allspice, and nutmeg. A traditional Greek pot pie is shepherd's pie made with ground lamb, gravy, and a mashed-potato topping. A Flemish beef pot pie is flavored with dark beer, Dijon mustard, garlic, bay leaves, and thyme. A mushroom-and-artichoke pie is traditionally served at Easter in Italy and is also prepared in North America for a variety of occasions. Tamale pie is a Mexican-style casserole dish made with ground beef and pork, tomatoes, corn kernels, cornmeal, black olives, and a topping made of cornmeal, milk, eggs, cheese, and butter.

There are numerous variations on pot pie and some reflect regional preferences, such as a seafood gumbo pie or a salmon-and-rice pie inspired by the availability of fresh shellfish and fish. However, chicken, turkey, and beef pot pies are the most common type made and consumed across the United States. In fact, they were the first frozen meals marketed in the 1950s. Today, these and other pot pies such as vegetable and seafood are popular frozen food items. Cooks often prepare pot pies at home to serve for a daily meal or to take to a potluck, family reunion, church supper, picnic, or other gathering.

See also: AMISH FOOD FESTIVALS; NEW YEAR'S DAY; PASTY.
Reference: Ojakangas. *Pot Pies.* 1993.

POTATO BARS

One of the fastfood trends of the 1980s and 1990s has been the increasing presence of baked potatoes on the menus. In many malls, shoppers are now very familiar with baked potato bars that sell the "spud" (named for the narrow spadelike tool used to dig up potatoes) and various accoutrements almost exclusively. Some people make it a regular practice to try all the possibilities at these bars, starting with a basic Idaho baked potato and filling it with any of the numerous choices for toppings: the traditional sour cream and chives, bacon bits, broccoli and cheddar cheese, salsa and taco meat, shrimp, ham and swiss, or other combinations. The toppings determine the price of a baked potato meal, which can range from about $2 for a "nude" potato to over $6 for the "works."

See also: POTATOES.

POTATOES

North Americans prepare and eat potatoes in numerous ways, as a meal in and of itself such as a baked potato with toppings, as a side dish, or as a main ingredient in soups or stews. One common way to prepare potatoes is to boil them. Small boiled potatoes are usually served whole—with their skins on—and sprinkled with parsley or other garnish. Boiled potatoes are also mashed and served with butter or gravy. Cooked potatoes are, of course, the basis for potato salad, a traditional dish for picnics, church suppers, potlucks, family reunions, and many other gatherings. Potato casserole dishes are popular carry-in foods and are frequently part of family meals.

Frying is another common way to prepare potatoes. Chopped or grated potatoes are fried to make hash browns—side dishes for breakfast, lunch, or dinner—or to make potato pancakes. French fries and potato chips (which are fried or baked) are favorite snack foods.

Many cooks routinely buy dehydrated potatoes, a popular packaged food since about the 1950s. Dried potatoes are reconstituted to make scalloped potatoes, potatoes with cheese sauce, mashed potatoes, or potato pancakes. Dehydrated potato soup, as well as the canned variety, is also popular.

While Americans buy and consume several hundred varieties of potatoes in numerous forms, they are following a practice that stems from ancient times. Potatoes have been cultivated in South America for at least 13,000 years. Some historians say that indigenous people developed at least 3,000 different varieties of potatoes and prepared them in numerous ways. The Andean Incas, for example, often freeze-dried potatoes in the mountain air in order to preserve and transport a product called chuño, which was later ground into meal or used in soups and stews, a practice still followed today. Potato crops as well as corn crops have been called "miracle crops" because, as they spread from native populations of the Americas to Europe and back to the American settlers, they improved the nutrition and health of populations, fed armies, and changed the economies of entire nations.

See also: BREAKFAST; CANDIED SWEET POTATOES (OR YAMS); CASSEROLE DISHES/MEALS; GERMAN POTATO SALAD; MEAT AND POTATOES; POTATO BARS; YAMBOREE.

References: Davis. *The Potato Book.* 1973; Weatherford. *Indian Givers.* 1989.

POTLATCH

Potlatch is derived from the Nootka word *patshatl*, which means "to give." Among the Tlingit and other Native Americans living in the Pacific Northwest, a potlatch is somewhat like a potluck, but it stems from a long heritage of winter events celebrating the ample supply of fish (especially salmon) and shellfish, berries, roots, and other foods gathered during the previous seasons. A tribal leader of early inhabitants along the Pacific Northwest coast—from what is now Alaska through Canada and into Washington State—would hold a potlatch to demonstrate his greatness and wealth. Guests from other tribes were served more food than could be eaten and given a great variety of gifts to show that the host tribe and its leader were of high social status and could afford to give away valuables. In some cases, tribes destroyed canoes, blankets, and other items to show they did not need these things and could replace them easily. Today, a potlatch is not necessarily a demonstration of wealth, but it is still a tribal feast or party celebrating giving, sharing, and interdependence. A salmon bake is a traditional part of a potlatch.

See also: NATIVE AMERICAN FEASTS; POTLUCK; SALMON BAKES.

References: Grant. *Concise Encyclopedia of the American Indian.* 1989; Smith. *The Frugal Gourmet on Our Immigrant Ancestors.* 1990.

POTLUCK

Originally *potluck* was associated with eating "whatever was on hand," and some speculate that the term originated in the West when cowboys contributed various foods to a communal "pot." Today, the term now refers to a type of party or gathering—a very popular way to divide food preparation responsibilities among all of the participants of informal social events. Potlucks are also known as "covered dish suppers," but whatever they are called, the concept remains the same. Everyone brings a dish that can be shared by many others. Depending on the size of the crowd, only a small percentage may get to taste a particular dish.

There are many types of potlucks. Some are structured affairs where a host may assign a dish for a course: "Bobby, you bring that wonderful ambrosia mold, and Jean, a different salad. Can you do a dessert, David? Great, I'll do a main dish, and the others are all set! Ciao." Others might be built around a theme such as an ethnic cuisine or a variety of salads or just desserts.

More typical of these meals, however, is an unstructured call to "bring a dish, we eat at six." That can create some odd and unique food-combining adventures, but grazing at the table is usually a very enjoyable experience.

See also: CASSEROLE DISHES/MEALS; CHURCH DINNERS/SUPPERS; GRAZING; POTLATCH; PROGRESSIVE DINNER.
Reference: Mariani. *The Dictionary of American Food and Drink*. 1993, 1994.

POWERBAR

This trademark sports food is popular among long-distance runners and other athletes who find that the heavy intake of carbohydrates is beneficial in their training regimen, particularly before competition. The food is similar in appearance to a candy bar, but it is a means for sustaining energy over time without the quick burst and subsequent letdown of a sugar-filled treat.
See also: SUGAR.

PRETZELS

Pretzels are commonly associated with people of German heritage, and many historians believe that pretzels—a twisted yeast bread—originated with Germans. This belief was refuted by Martin Elkort in his book *The Secret Life of Food*. He declared that the pretzel originally came from Italy, where in 1610 a monk "baked pretzels in the shape of folded praying arms as prizes for his students who recited their catechism without error." Still others claim that the pretzel is a descendant of breads baked in ancient times, shaped in rounds to honor the sun and twisted to form equal center sections to symbolize the four seasons.

The pretzel may not be as popular a snack as popcorn or potato chips, but this food is commonly served in cocktail lounges and bars, placed on snack trays and tables at parties, packed in lunches, dispensed from vending machines, and purchased steaming hot from carts in cities like Philadelphia and New York. Hot, fat pretzels usually served with mustard also are popular snack items at street fairs, agricultural fairs, carnivals, and sporting events.
References: Cunningham. *The Magic in Food*. 1990; Elkort. *The Secret Life of Food*. 1991.

PROGRESSIVE DINNER

The progressive dinner is a popular form of entertainment in the United States, and it may have been the precursor for the grazing practice so prevalent today. A progressive dinner requires planning and much advanced preparation, because each course for the dinner is held in a different home. Diners taking part gather at the first home for cocktails (if served) and appetizers; then the group travels to another home for the salad course, to still another for the main entree, and on to the last home where dessert and/or after-dinner drinks are served. This is a popular custom with many eating or dining clubs, singles groups, and residents of retirement centers. Some progressive dinners may be held in just one apartment building, in a condominium complex, or in a mobile home park where neighbors share in this eating ritual.
See also: COCKTAIL PARTY; EATING/DINING CLUBS; GRAZING.

Enthusiastic patrons crowd around a popular pretzel vendor at his stand in New York. Pretzels, thought to have originated in Germany, may have been a seventeenth-century Italian creation.

PROM NIGHT

The stretch limousine has arrived and formally clad couples, the girls wearing expensive dresses and corsages and the boys in tuxedos with boutonnieres in place, are about to begin the senior class prom night ritual, a rite of passage that occurs across the United States at the end of the high school year. Although not all prom-goers want or can afford limousine service, nearly all couples spend hundreds if not thousands of dollars on the clothing, latest hairstyles, jewelry, flowers, and other accoutrements of prom night. The festivities include dinner beforehand, a party afterward, and a breakfast or brunch the next morning. Some proms held in hotel ballrooms include a buffet dinner, but more often teenage couples go to fine restaurants for their first experience with "grown-up" dining—an experience that often proves embarrassing because young people are unsure what to order, whether the cost of the meal will be within their budget, or how much to tip. A few restaurants, however, cater to teenage prom-goers, helping them with menu selections and explaining that they will not be served alcoholic drinks due to their age.

Alcohol and drugs frequently have created problems at high school proms and at post-dance parties. Tragically, numerous teenagers have been killed in alcohol- or drug-related accidents. As a result, parents, teachers, and students in some U.S. school districts have joined in efforts to sponsor nonalcoholic celebrations patterned after Project Graduation, which began in Maine in 1980, one year after 12 teenagers were killed in alcohol-related auto accidents on prom night. By 1983, no alcohol-related accidents occurred in Maine on prom night, and the program was launched nationwide.

See also: HIGH SCHOOL GRADUATION PARTY.

PUDDINGS

Many people today think of pudding as a commercial powdered mixture that is combined with milk to make a chocolate- , vanilla- , butterscotch- , banana- , or pistachio-flavored dessert. It can be prepared "instantly" by pouring the mixture into a container of cold milk and shaking it. Alternatively, the mixture stirred into milk can be cooked for a few minutes on top of the stove. For even more convenience, some busy consumers buy pudding already prepared, and routinely include these desserts in brown-bag lunches or lunch boxes. Packaged puddings are also popular snacks.

Because convenience puddings have such broad appeal, it is sometimes easy to forget that pudding is one of the oldest types of desserts (appearing in literature as early as 1577 in England) and that some cooks still make pudding "from scratch." Those basic puddings range from a simple bread or rice pudding to a milk and egg custard to a rich, thick, cakelike dessert.

Hasty pudding—a mush made of cornmeal, milk, and molasses—was a common dessert in colonial America. Although it is not as popular today, it can still be found in some cookbooks.

Bread pudding is a fundamental part of the diet in many households across North America. Generations of cooks from a variety of national and ethnic backgrounds have followed a custom of "recycling" stale bread, using it along with milk and eggs and perhaps raisins to make a baked pudding that may be served warm or cold any day of the week. This dessert may also be part of a traditional holiday meal. In the southwestern United States, for example, people of Spanish ancestry serve *sopa*, a Christmas bread pudding that is made like a casserole with layers of toasted and diced bread, raisins, nuts, cheese, and a syrup made of sugar, water, cinnamon, cloves, and vanilla. It is usually served warm with whipped cream, ice cream, or rum.

Custard pudding is often associated with a warm, homey kitchen and the sweet aroma of baking. Baked custard is a nutritious food that may be prepared as a traditional antidote for a variety of ailments, but it is also a pudding dessert that appears regularly in cafeterias, rural cafes and restaurants, and other "down-to-earth" eating establishments. Like bread pudding, it is basic and routinely served in American households.

Rice pudding is another traditional dessert, which can be prepared as a plain or fancy dish. Jane and Michael Stern, who have written several popular books about American food, say that "serious pudding people [themselves included] . . . are especially persnickety about rice pudding. We don't like it if the grains of rice are still raw and chewy; nor is it any good if the rice is so overcooked that it bloats and loses its texture." Many "pudding people" also insist on only a sprinkling of raisins and spices such as nutmeg.

Indian pudding has been considered a traditional New England dessert, but this slow-baked pudding has been popular across North America. It is made with milk, eggs, cornmeal, molasses (or maple syrup), sugar, raisins, and spices.

See also: PERSIMMON PUDDING; PLUM PUDDING.

References: Nathan. *An American Folklife Cookbook*. 1984; Stern and Stern. *A Taste of America*. 1988.

PUMPKIN PIE

See THANKSGIVING DAY DINNER.

PUNCH

Since colonial times in North America, serving a festive beverage, or punch, in a bowl has been a traditional practice at formal dinners, banquets, receptions, and ceremonies such as weddings and christenings. Punch bowls are common today at numerous festive events, and they are a traditional part of holiday celebrations such as Christmas and New Year's Eve parties. Alcoholic punch is generally brandy- , cognac- , or wine-based; nonalcoholic punch usually begins with a fruit juice base and includes a carbonated beverage and perhaps a fruit-flavored sherbet or fruit slices.

See also: MULLED WINE; SHERBET; WASSAIL AND WASSAIL BOWL.

PUPU PLATTER

See APPETIZERS.

PURIM FEAST

The fourteenth day of the month of Adar—the sixth month of the Jewish calendar—is "a day of gladness and feasting and holiday-making." It is a celebration of the time 2,000 years ago when Persian Jews "got relief from their enemies . . . the month that had been turned from sorrow into gladness and from mourning into a holiday . . . days for sending choice portions to one another and gifts to the poor," according to the biblical book of Esther in the Old Testament. A dramatization or reading of the story of Esther and her role in helping to prevent the massacre of Jews by an evil foe, Haman, is part of the festive day, as are games, costume parades, and gift exchanges. A festive family feast is the highlight of this cultural celebration. People are expected to rejoice on Purim and enjoy all kinds of drinks and delicacies.

Generally, it is the custom to spread a sumptuous feast, light candles, and celebrate from late afternoon into the night; however, if Purim falls on Friday, the celebration starts earlier in honor of the Sabbath. It includes traditional and symbolic foods, such as three-cornered sweet pastries or cookies filled with prunes, raisins, or poppy seeds called *Hamantashen* (Haman's pockets). The pastries are said to represent Haman's tricornered hat as well as his bribe-stuffed pockets. Triangular *kreplach*—a dough filled with cheese or meat and cooked in boiling water—and cooked bean dishes are also traditional. The Yiddish name for this food is said to be derived from the holidays on which it is eaten: Yom Kippur ("K"), Hoshana Raba ("R"), and Purim ("P"). A special Purim challah decorated with raisins is also part of the feast, as are various types of seeds such as pumpkin and sunflower, which symbolize the seeds that Esther ate while living in the king's palace.

See also: CHALLAH.

Reference: Sherman. *A Sampler of Jewish American Folklore.* 1992.

QUICHE

This rich brunch and lunch dish gained much notoriety with the publication of the book *Real Men Don't Eat Quiche* by Bruce Feirstein and Lee Lorenz, which played on the perception that quiche is a gourmet, women's luncheon item, thus not a macho food meant for male consumption. Many real men—and women, too—from all walks of life do eat quiche, which is a classic dish in French cuisine, originating in Nancy during the sixteenth century. Initially made from bread dough, the open tart is now customarily made from an unsweetened pie crust filled with an egg, cream, and cheese mixture. It is a popular vehicle for a surprising array of added ingredients. For example, bacon makes what is known as quiche lorraine, mussels or crab make it a seafood quiche, and broccoli and mushrooms complete a vegetarian option. Quiche may be served as an appetizer, first course, or as a meal in and of itself. Miniature quiches, one- or two-bite treats, have proven popular as a passed or buffet party item.

See also: APPETIZERS; BUFFET; SUNDAY BRUNCH.

RAMADAN

The beginning of the ninth month of the Islamic lunar calendar when the thin crescent of the new moon is sighted marks the holiest time of the year—Ramadan—for a billion Muslims around the world. Millions of Muslims live in North America and join others of their faith in the month long Ramadan rituals, fasting each day from sunrise to sunset in observance of one of the five pillars of Islam. It is a spiritual fast—an attempt to achieve a higher degree of self-discipline, piety, and inner peace and a time to break bad habits, to engage in prayer, and to study the Koran. Many people also spend time visiting friends and family.

The daily observance begins before dawn when Muslims prepare and eat a simple meal designed for its nutritional value and drink plenty of liquids to prevent dehydration during the day. No food or drink is allowed during daylight hours. At sunset, the fast is broken with dates and milk or water and then a slight meal called the *iftaar*, meaning "break the fast."

Every evening congregational dinners are held in mosques and homes. Muslims from different countries gather together, bringing traditional foods to share with others. A traditional lentil soup may be served or *fattoush*, a nine-vegetable salad with chips of toasted pita bread mixed in it.

Children are exempt until puberty from fasting, but at age six or seven they may be trained for Ramadan by fasting for half a day. Those who are ill or too old are also exempt, as are pregnant, nursing, or menstruating women. If possible, Muslims fast at a later time to make up for the fasts that they missed during Ramadan. Those who are physically unable to fast may compensate by feeding a hungry person for each day of fasting missed. Feeding others, especially during the month of Ramadan, is considered a great blessing.

When the new moon of the next Islamic month, Shawwal , is sighted, Muslims break from fasting and begin a three-day celebration, called Eid Al-Fitr, meaning "a time of renewal." It is the most important Muslim holiday, and elaborate dinner parties are common at this time. It is often customary to serve *saveinya* or *sevyan* made with very thin *sevyan* noodles, a milky pudding, milk, sugar, butter, nuts, and raisins. *Halwa*, a rich farina dessert, is also traditional.
See also: FASTING; PITA BREAD.

RATTLESNAKE ROUNDUP

Although animal rights activists have strongly objected to rattlesnake roundups held in such states as Oklahoma, Texas, and New Mexico, the annual spring event focuses on a competition to bag and kill poisonous diamondback rattlesnakes, which organizers say is a way to protect farmers and ranchers from snakebites. Rattlesnake roundups usually are fund-raisers and include the sale of rattlesnake meat at outdoor booths.

Sweetwater, Texas, claims to hold the world's largest rattlesnake roundup. The annual event, which began in 1958, includes demonstrations on how to "milk" snakes—extract the venom for use in medical research and to make antidotes for poisonous snakebites. There is also a rattlesnake meat–eating contest, and each year more than 4,000 pounds of rattlesnake meat is fried and served to those who attend the roundup.

See also: NEW ENGLAND BOILED DINNER.
References: Hill. *Festivals U.S.A.* 1988; Thompson and Carlson. *Holidays, Festivals, and Celebrations of the World Dictionary.* 1994.

RED BEANS AND RICE

It is a Monday ritual in New Orleans, Louisiana. Restaurants serve red beans and rice for lunch. The simple combination is also one of the mainstays of Cajun cuisine: basic food with intense flavors. In this dish the red kidney beans are cooked with ham hocks, onion, bell pepper, and a typical Cajun blend of seasonings: bay leaves, white pepper, thyme, garlic powder, oregano, red pepper, black pepper, and Tabasco sauce. They are then served with a simple well-seasoned cooked white rice in restaurants and homes all around Louisiana.

See also: MARDI GRAS.
Reference: Prudhomme. *Chef Paul Prudhomme's Louisiana Kitchen.* 1984.

RED FLANNEL HASH

A New England favorite, red flannel hash may have gotten its name from the type of underwear New Englanders wore in the winter, or it could have derived simply from the bright red color of this one-dish

meal. Traditionally, it is made from leftovers of a New England boiled dinner: corned beef, potatoes, onions, and other vegetables that are chopped and fried along with chopped red beets that provide the color. This type of hash also has been a common menu item in small family-style restaurants, cafes, and diners in the East and Midwest.

See also: NEW ENGLAND BOILED DINNER.
References: Stern and Stern. *Real American Food.* 1986. Stern and Stern. *GoodFood.* 1983.

RED VELVET CAKE

The story that is associated with this marvelous dessert has become an "urban myth," the kind of tale that is repeated year after year without verification of facts. In most versions of the "The Red Velvet Cake" story, a couple visiting New York City has dinner at the famous Waldorf Astoria Hotel restaurant. After enjoying a splendid meal, they decide to try the house dessert specialty, the Red Velvet Cake, a rich, triple-layered red cake with a butter frosting. They cannot believe that such a wonderful dessert has been concocted, so they ask for the recipe. Their waiter hurries off to speak to the pastry chef and returns shortly with the recipe printed on a sheet of paper. Several minutes later when the waiter presents the check for their meal, they are aghast to discover that they have been charged $250 for the cake recipe in addition to the price of their already expensive meal. They protest, but the manager explains that the recipe is of considerable value to the restaurant and that $250 is a small price to pay for something that they themselves consider the most wonderful cake they have ever tasted. Although angry, the couple pays the bill. Once outside the hotel, they make plans to take their own "sweet revenge." They decide to make thousands of copies of the recipe for broad distribution. As a result, the recipe (printed below) became known nationwide, and the cake has been prepared and served on countless occasions. In some families the Red

Velvet Cake is a traditional birthday cake or is routinely served during holidays. **See also:** BIRTHDAY CAKE.

Red Velvet Cake

1/2 c. shortening	2 T. cocoa
1 1/2 c. sugar	2 1/4 c. plain flour
2 eggs	1 small t. salt
2 oz. red food coloring	1 t. soda 1 T. vinegar
1 c. buttermilk	1 t. vanilla

Cream shortening and sugar. Add eggs. Mix together cocoa and food coloring, then add to shortening and sugar and mix in. Add salt and flour with buttermilk and vanilla. Mix everything well. Alternately add soda and vinegar then fold in carefully so as not to smash the bubbles. Pour into two greased and floured layer pans. Bake at 350 degrees Fahrenheit for 20-30 minutes.

REHEARSAL DINNER

In the United States, the rehearsal dinner is a traditional prewedding event, usually held the evening before a wedding (actually after a rehearsal of the wedding ceremony) and hosted by the groom's parents or close relatives or friends. After members of the wedding party—bride and groom and their parents, maid of honor, best man, bridesmaids, ushers, ring bearers, and so on—have rehearsed their particular roles in the ceremony, they attend a rehearsal dinner that may be served at a home or in a restaurant, club, or community center. **See also:** WEDDING CAKE; WEDDING FOODS.

REUBEN SANDWICH

There are numerous claims about the origin of the Reuben sandwich, one of which states that the combination of sauerkraut, swiss cheese, and corned beef between two pieces of rye bread was invented in 1914 by Arthur Reuben in his New York deli. Other stories, however, credit a Reuben Kulakofsky in the 1930s and a Reuben Kay in the 1950s, both of Omaha, Nebraska, for the creation. Whoever invented the sandwich, the Reuben is traditionally served in delis

and at numerous festivals where sauerkraut is featured. **See also:** OKTOBERFEST; SAUERKRAUT. **Reference:** Schulz. *Celebrating America.* 1994.

RICE CAKES

An ultimate example of health food, these low-calorie, high-fiber crackers are often ridiculed by the uninitiated as "cardboard cakes." They are, however, proving to be very popular in North America, and many companies are following the initial introduction by Chico-San and marketing a version of this healthful food. There are now many varieties, including rice, corn, and popcorn cakes that may be cinnamon-flavored, apple-flavored, cheddar cheese–flavored, salted, or unsalted. They come in the common 4-inch diameter size and the new tiny snack version. Typically, a cake will hover around the 40-calorie mark with zero fat and zero cholesterol; thus, they are attractive food items for dieters and the health conscious. Some people will make a meal out of the naked cakes, while others are partial to toppings such as avocado, peanut butter, or melted cheese.

RICE DISHES

While rice dishes are traditional in some parts of North America, the consumption of rice in the United States has been growing steadily since about the mid-1980s. In 1994, the USA Rice Council noted that 75 percent of Americans ate rice at least once a week, averaging 22 pounds of rice per person annually. That figure doubled the amount of rice consumption a decade earlier.

    Most Americans consume rice in one-dish meals that include vegetables and/or meat or poultry, or in salad combinations. Some classic rice dishes have become popular in North America due to various immigrant groups sharing their cuisine. One such dish is the Spanish paella, named for the round pan in which it is prepared. Paella is usually made from a short-grain rice cooked with seafood and chicken flavored with saffron, peppers, onion, and garlic. A traditional dish among people of many different national backgrounds is beans and rice. A staple among Puerto Ricans is pigeon peas and rice; Jamaicans prefer red beans with their rice; Cubans use black beans. Since rice dishes are low-fat, low-cost, and easy and quick to prepare, the trend to eat an increasing amount of both white and brown rice is expected to continue in North America.

See also: MARDI GRAS; RED BEANS AND RICE.

RICE FESTIVALS

Since the 1930s, farmers, millers, and most townsfolk and visitors have celebrated the rice harvest in southwest Louisiana. The town of Crowley, known as the Rice Capital of America, hosts the annual International Rice Festival, which includes Creole rice-cooking contests with contestants preparing rice and meat, rice and seafood, and rice dessert dishes. Similar activities take place in rice-growing areas around Houston, Texas, and in the Carolinas. Jackson, Mississippi, is the site for the annual fall International Red Beans and Rice Festival.

See also: MARDI GRAS; RED BEANS AND RICE; RICE DISHES.

RIVELS

Made from eggs and flour, rivels are a kind of "instant" noodle for soup. Pinches of the dough can be dropped into a chicken or beef stock or a creamy base such as that for corn soup. The Frugal Gourmet (famous cookbook author and chef, Jeff Smith) method is to roll or rub the dough mixture "through your hands over the soup pot, so that very small lumps of dough fall slowly

into the pot. Stir gently and simmer the soup and rivels for about 10 minutes or until tender." Rivel soup, which is most likely of German origin, has long been a traditional dish in Pennsylvania and is common among rural midwesterners as well.

References: Smith. *The Frugal Gourmet on Our Immigrant Ancestors*. 1990; Stern and Stern. *GoodFood*. 1983.

ROCKY MOUNTAIN OYSTERS

As the name implies, Rocky Mountain Oysters are a food popular in the western United States. This meat dish is derived from bulls' testicles, which may be thinly sliced and deep-fried. A number of western restaurants, particularly in Colorado, offer Rocky Mountain Oysters as a speciality, and this food plus rattlesnake meat and buffalo steaks are frequently presented at culinary events featuring southwestern and western cuisine. This delicacy is a star attraction at the Colorado Rockies' Coors Field, with 500 heaping servings served at the opening game in 1995. Those daring enough to try them insist that they taste something like chicken or pork tenderloin—mild, delicate, a little bit chewy.

As one might expect, myths and legends abound about the origin of this unusual dish. Many of the stories cannot be traced beyond barroom fiction; however, one Denverite, Phil Brainard, recalls his father linking the custom with the annual spring castration ritual on a Cripple Creek ranch at the turn of the century. At the end of the day, the cowboys would throw the results of their work on the campfire and enjoy a special treat. More recent rumor suggests that the Rocky Mountain Oyster serves as an aphrodisiac.

A number of western towns host annual Rocky Mountain Oyster festivals. One of the most popular, The Testicle Festival, started in 1982 in Missoula, Montana. According to the festival organizer, during the first ten years, they sold over 5.5 tons of the product to thousands of people from all over the world.

References: Campagna. "Shuffle Off to Bison." 1996; Dornfield. "Oyster Feed Not for the Faint-Hearted." 1993; Gordon. "Morning Briefing upon Further Review." 1995; Purgavia. "Calling All Meat-Eaters." 1995.

ROSCA DE REYES

See ALL KINGS DAY.

ROSH HASHANAH

The meals and foods served during Rosh Hashanah are an integral part of this deeply religious Jewish holiday, a ten-day observance of the Jewish New Year. It is a time when Jews reflect on the past, attempt to atone for faults, and start anew. Foods symbolize times of sorrow, hope, and renewal. Eating apples dipped in honey, for example, is a way to wish for a sweet new year. Honey, in fact, is a favorite sweetener during the Jewish New Year celebrations and fruit stews called *tzimmes*, or carrots sweetened with honey and honey cakes, also are eaten. One honey and nut dessert is shaped like a stick symbolizing the hope for a good year ahead and also a time long ago in Europe when landlords used long sticks to threaten and beat poor Jewish tenants who were evicted from their homes because they could not pay their rent.

Other Rosh Hashanah foods include the pomegranate with its many seeds and black-eyed peas, both of which symbolize "many" and requests for a special blessing: that the merits of the Jewish people be plentiful. The last day of the New Year celebration is a High Holy Day, which is a 24-hour period of fasting.

See also: FASTING; YOM KIPPUR.

SAGANAKI

Saganaki is a dramatic flaming dish popular at Greek restaurants and at every Greek food festival in North America. The ritual of preparing and serving the saganaki appetizer begins with thick slices of Kasseri cheese that are first placed in ice water and refrigerated for an hour. The cheese is drained and coated with flour, quickly fried in butter until lightly browned, and removed from the heat. Each cheese slice is sprinkled with lemon juice and brandy and set afire. As soon as the fire is extinguished, the saganaki is ready to eat.
See also: GREEK FOOD FESTIVALS.

SAGUARO CACTUS SYRUP

The ritual of making and eating saguaro cactus jam and syrup is probably little known outside the southwestern United States. In fact, the practice is fading among those who began the tradition centuries ago—the Tohono O'odham, whose descendants now live on a reservation along the Mexican border. Those who maintain the tradition harvest fruit from the saguaro cactus that grows on the Sonoran Desert. Harvesttime is usually in late June, which for traditional O'odham was the beginning of a new year when some of the cactus

fruit was used to make wine that was served to the entire village. Today, the wine feasts are rare, but the ritual of cooking saguaro fruit until it becomes a thick syrup or jam still continues. Once prepared, the molasseslike syrup with a hint of fruit taste is a sweet topping for muffins, tortillas, or fry bread.

SAINT JOSEPH'S DAY FEAST

Held on 19 March each year, the Saint Joseph's Day Feast honors the husband of Virgin Mary and foster father of Jesus. It is usually observed among Americans of Italian descent living in major cities such as Chicago, Detroit, Buffalo, and Minneapolis and in various parts of the South. The main focus of the celebration is a family altar to the saint, which is prepared as a gift for a special blessing received or to petition for help. The altar is actually a feast table laden with a great variety of foods, except meat when the day falls during Lent. Some of the altar tables may contain up to 500 different dishes, including pastas, cheeses, fish dishes, numerous fresh and preserved fruits, vegetables, pastries, cakes, nuts, and candies. A blessed bread, *pupa-cu-l'uova*, baked with a hard-boiled egg inside, is a traditional Sicilian Easter food, and lucky beans that are said to guard against poverty are on the table for guests. The altar traditionally must include a large square cake with "Saint Joseph" written on it.

Several days before Saint Joseph's Day, a family presenting the altar sends out invitations for the event, inviting as many people as possible and sometimes opening their home to the public via ads in local newspapers. Community or church celebrations also are held, with many families providing foods for the altar.

References: Cohen and Coffin. *The Folklore of American Holidays.* 1991; Malpezzi and Clements. *Italian-American Folklore.* 1992; Shemanski. *A Guide to Fairs and Festivals in the United States.* 1984.

SAINT LUCIA DAY

In Scandinavian communities throughout North America, some families observe St. Lucia Day, a traditional Scandinavian holiday marking the end of the longest night in the year and celebrating the gradual return of light. The ritual is based on a Swedish folktale about a young girl dressed in white with a halo above her head, offering food to the poor. To symbolize the legend, the day begins on the morning of 13 December with a daughter of the house rising early and dressing in a white gown. She dons a green wreath adorned with lit candles, symbolizing the light, and serves family members their breakfast—coffee and Lucia buns—in bed. Lucia buns are made from a sweetened yeast and egg dough flavored with saffron and laced with currants. In the Norwegian tradition, *pepperkakers*—ginger and cinnamon flavored cookies—also are served. Rather than *pepperkakers,* the Danish offer a cookie filled with a lemon cream or a chewy sugar cookie topped with raspberry jam.

SAINT PATRICK'S DAY

As the old saying goes: "Just about everyone wants to be Irish on Saint Patrick's Day." In fact, this is a festive day for Americans of many different national backgrounds. Parades and social gatherings with feasting and drinking are traditional activities during the day, which celebrates St. Patrick, although no one is sure whether the day signifies his birth or death—or any specific event in his life. Nevertheless, St. Patrick, who is said to have lived during the 400s, is credited with bringing Christianity to Ireland.

St. Patrick's Day is not as festive a celebration in Ireland as it is in the United States, but beer drinking is associated with the event in both countries. People gather in social halls, neighborhood pubs, and saloons. Irish stew, Irish soda bread, and colcannon—a stewlike dish made with cooked cabbage, potatoes, leeks, and buttermilk—are Irish national foods and typically part of Saint Patrick's Day food festivals in Ireland. In some instances these foods have carried over to the United States, but primarily corned beef and cabbage are the foods commonly associated with the U.S. version of Saint Patrick's Day.

See also: CORNED BEEF HASH; NEW ENGLAND BOILED DINNER.

SAINT VALENTINE'S DAY

See VALENTINE'S DAY.

SAKE

Sake is the traditional alcoholic beverage of Japan dating back to 200 B.C. It is a rice wine that has increased in popularity on the other side of the Pacific Ocean as North Americans have become enamored of the Japanese eating style and cuisine. At Japanese restaurants and sushi bars, sake is always presented hot, in a small ceramic pitcher, and patrons are given small ceramic glasses about the size of a shot glass. According to Japanese custom, a person should not pour the wine for himself or herself. Rather, the person who does the honor of pouring for the others at the table allows someone else to fill his or her glass.

See also: SASHIMI.

SALAD BARS

Society's general emphasis on fresh, light, low-fat eating has made the salad bar a natural choice for many diners. Because patrons select and serve their own food, the salad bar takes some of the pressure off service staff, making the salad bar concept appealing to restaurant management. Promotions have keyed into the size of the salad bar ("50 feet of veggies!") or the array of possibilities ("choose from 101 fresh items!"). There have even been "all-you-can-eat" options on many menus. The concept has proven to be an effective way to increase traffic during lunchtime; office workers and others can quickly serve themselves a light and healthy dose of salad and get back to the job in less than an hour.

Although many eating establishments in the United States still maintain salad bars, their height of popularity was in the 1980s when the salad bar seemed to have a place in almost every type of restaurant one patronized. Even some fastfood establishments have had a trial run with this food delivery system. The salad bar has lost some of its appeal,however, probably because today there is an overabundance of them. Experience also has shown that a giant plate of fresh raw vegetables is not necessarily a low-calorie meal. It can easily be turned into another high calorie overdose with liberal applications of salad dressings, bacon bits, chopped egg, and any of the other extras that make salad bars so much fun.

See also: CAESAR SALAD; FASTFOOD; SALAD GREENS.

SALAD GREENS

A green salad is a traditional part of many North American meals, or it may be a meal in and of itself, particularly for lunch. Usually North Americans eat salad before the main course, a custom that may have begun in restaurants as a way to keep customers happy while waiting for the entree to be prepared. Those who follow the European tradition, however, may eat a green salad at the end of a meal or even between courses in order to cleanse the palate.

The bulk of a green salad usually consists of various types of greens, or greenings as they are sometimes called, topped with garnishes from vegetables to nuts and seeds. By far the most popular salad green is lettuce, and Americans eat 8,500 tons of fresh lettuce daily. It is thought that Christopher Columbus brought lettuce to America, and a wild (bitter) lettuce still grows in southern Europe. Cultivated lettuce, however, is seldom bitter unless it is overgrown.

In North America, lettuce was produced only in home gardens until the twentieth century, when salads became a "staple." Today, commercial production of lettuce is a profitable business, and many varieties are grown, including bibb lettuce, Boston lettuce, leaf lettuce, and radicchio—a red lettuce that was first cultivated in the United States in 1981 and became a chic salad ingredient during the 1980s. Iceberg, or Simpson, lettuce, is the most common type for salads prepared and served at home and at family-style, fastfood, or informal-type restaurants.

Many Americans, however, prefer other types of greens for their salads. These greens are the tops of leafy vegetables or the whole vegetable itself and may include the green parts of dandelions, a native Eurasian plant that is now common in North America and is considered a weed. Another green that is commonly used in salads—and also as a hot vegetable—is *arugula* (a regional Italian term for an English herb), which was brought to North America by Italian immigrants of the late nineteenth century; it is still popular among a large number of people of Italian descent. It is also popular in health food stores and elite restaurants across the United States. Chicory, escarole, spinach, and watercress are still other types of greens that become part of salad mixtures. Mesclun is a combination of any number of greens, such as arugula, dandelion, and radicchio, picked young. When these greens are mixed with other greens, a salad is created with different textures, tastes, and colors.

See also: CAESAR SALAD; GREENS AND POT-
LIKKER; SALAD BAR.

References: Chalmers. *Great American Food
Almanac.* 1986; Kump. "Practical Cook."
1994; Mariani. *The Dictionary of American
Food and Drink.* 1993, 1994; Sokolov. *Why
We Eat What We Eat.* 1991; Visser. *Much
Depends on Dinner.* 1986.

SALMON BAKES

Salmon has been part of the diet of northwest coastal Indian nations for centuries,
and a salmon bake is a traditional public
event during summer and fall Native
American festivals in the Pacific Northwest. Salmon bakes for the general public
are also common in Oregon, Washington,
and British Columbia. The salmon is
baked Native American–style on alder-
wood stakes over a fire, or it is barbecued
on a grill. Some common items served
with the meal include potatoes, coleslaw,
fry bread, and berry shortcake.

The Depoe Bay Salmon Bake in September is one of the most popular outdoor
events in Oregon and attracts at least 2,000
people annually. Other salmon bakes (or
barbecues) are held annually in Alaska
and Minnesota and in various locations in
the Northeast.

See also: NATIVE AMERICAN FEASTS; NAVAJO
FRY BREAD; SALMON FESTIVALS.

SALMON FESTIVALS

Various small-time food festivals are held
throughout the Pacific Northwest of the
United States and in the Vancouver Island
vicinity of western Canada. One of the
most interesting is the Wild Olympic
Salmon Festival of Jefferson County, Washington. This biennial event takes place in
Chimacum on the Olympic Peninsula.

"Bring forth your children, your Wild
Olympic Women, your strong men—huc
the timbers and raise the tent—build a big
fire for it is time to celebrate in Joy," reads
the proclamation from the organizers of this

educational and festive fund-raiser. Inside
and outside, in drizzly weather or sun,
throughout the morning and into the night,
traditional arts of the area are available to
all: reading aloud, telling tales, wearing
special costumes, drumming, dancing, and
especially eating salmon. Sliced lengthwise
and butterflied, the fish is attached to two
crossed sticks and barbecued next to an
open fire in the tradition of the native peoples of the area. The S'Klallum, Makah,
Hoh, and Quileute tribes have honored
the salmon as a symbol of life and renewal for ages, and organizers of the Wild
Olympic Salmon Festival build on those
traditions in their efforts to educate the
local population regarding the importance
of the salmon as an integral part of the
ecosystem and the health of all of its
inhabitants.

See also: NATIVE AMERICAN FEASTS.

SALSA

In almost every part of Mexico and in
much of the southwestern United States,
salsa or some type of hot sauce is an
essential part of most meals. It is used on
a great number of foods from eggs to vegetables to meats. The basic ingredients for
Mexican salsas are chiles, onions, garlic,
and tomatoes (tomatillos are used instead
of tomatoes to achieve a green salsa). The
finished salsa may vary considerably,
depending on the heat of the chiles, the
quantities and proportions of the ingredients, and the types of seasonings.

Salsa and tortilla chips are routinely
served in Mexican-style restaurants across
North America. The combination is also
common as an appetizer at cocktail parties and during happy hour at restaurants
and lounges.

See also: APPETIZERS; SNACK FOODS.

SALSA AND CHIPS

See SALSA.

SALT

Common salt has been used for thousands of years, often to preserve fish and to season food. Salt is basic to human existence since it holds body fluids that carry away wastes. The pages of history are liberally sprinkled with stories about the value of salt in commerce. It was often exchanged for other goods, and wars have been fought over salt deposits since ancient times. In the U.S. Civil War, Union and Confederate forces battled for possession of salt fields near New Orleans, Louisiana, and Saltville, Virginia.

Today, salt is a readily available and inexpensive product that most North Americans consume on a daily basis. Except for those on a low-salt diet and some who prefer herbal seasoning instead of salt, people use this substance routinely to season foods served at almost every meal. Many people consider unsalted dishes tasteless and unappetizing, and some individuals practice a mealtime ritual that includes a liberal sprinkling of salt on their food before even tasting it.

SANDWICHES

What North Americans call a sandwich and routinely eat as a quick meal today supposedly began in England with John Montague, the fourth earl of Sandwich and the first lord of the British admiralty during the late 1700s. Although notorious for his corruption in both his personal and public life, he became famous for his association with an internationally favorite food concoction. Legend says that the earl devised the convenient repast while he was playing cards during an all-night session. Because he did not want to leave the game, he asked to be served cold meat between two pieces of bread, making it easier to eat and allowing him to stay at the gaming table. Long before the earl of Sandwich requested a convenience meal, however, the Romans served *offula*, a bread-and-meat sandwich.

Traditional sandwiches are made with a bread product and some type of spread or filling, but both the bread and the filling come in many varieties. The bread may be a sliced sandwich bun, a pita bread "pocket," a folded tortilla or other flat bread, a sliced bagel or croissant, or a long, layered party-loaf sandwich sliced into sections. Sandwiches may be "open faced" with the spread or filling placed uncovered on a single slice of bread. They may be hot with gravy, toasted, grilled, or baked; they may be cold and cut into shapes ranging from rounds and squares to rectangular strips. The possibilities for fillings are endless— cooked and sliced or ground meat, fish, shellfish, or poultry; bacon, lettuce, and tomato (commonly known as BLT); chopped eggs; cheese of all kinds; vegetables and fruits; and spreads from peanut butter and jelly to a meat pâté or a vegetable paste.

The vast majority of Americans eat at least one type of sandwich a day or perhaps two now that the breakfast sandwich is so popular at fastfood establishments. The noon meal is the traditional time for eating sandwiches. Working people and students may carry homemade sandwiches with them to the job or school, but increasingly people buy a quick lunch that is usually some sort of sandwich from a hamburger shop; a hot dog stand; a specialty sandwich (such as a po'boy) stand, a Subway shop, a deli, a pizza parlor, or a taco stand; or some other type of food service, ranging from a catering truck or vending machine to a fancy restaurant. **See also:** BREAKFAST SANDWICHES; CATERING-TRUCK FOODS; FASTFOOD; HAMBURGERS; HOT DOGS; PIZZA; REUBEN SANDWICH; VENDING MACHINES.

SARDINES

Canned sardines (packed in oil or mustard sauce) used to be a customary lunch pail food in the United States until about the 1950s. Since then, the consumption of these small fish of the herring family has dropped as convenience foods have become more and more popular among those who carry their lunch to the workplace. An increasing number of workers also buy their lunch at fastfood chains.

Although many Americans—about 10 percent of the population—still eat sardines directly from the can or in a sandwich for lunch or a snack, sardine production in Maine (where the only remaining sardine packers in the United States are located) dropped from a peak of 3.8 million cases (100 cans to the case) in 1950 to 925,000 cases in 1993, the industry reported. Nevertheless, sardines are still a common and inexpensive source of protein for people in Mexico, and U.S. sardine packers hope to export their product to that market as well as markets in the Caribbean, Latin America, and Eastern Europe.
See also: SMORGASBORD; TAPAS.

A serviceman builds himself a multilayer sandwich. Sandwiches, traditionally a filling between two slices of bread, are standard American lunch fare.

SASHIMI

Japanese restaurants often feature a special chef who has been trained for many years in the ancient art of cutting and presenting raw fish for consumption. The purest form of this art is sashimi. Salmon, octopus, halibut, and many other fish varieties are appropriate for eating raw, and they are normally arranged artistically on a plate and served with pickled ginger and green horseradish paste. The presentation varies from sushi, which is based on rice prepared with seasoned vinegar, formed into bricks or rolls, and served with a great variety of fish, shellfish, or vegetables.
See also: SUSHI AND SUSHI BARS.
Reference: Andoh. *An American Taste of Japan.* 1985.

SAUERBRATEN

See OKTOBERFEST.

SAUERKRAUT

Making and eating sauerkraut (or sour cabbage) are annual harvest events on farms and in communities across the midwestern United States, especially where there are concentrations of Americans of German, Czech, Polish, and other Eastern European ancestries. Home gardeners of varied backgrounds have also established an annual tradition of making sauerkraut: gathering excess cabbage grown on their own plots, chopping it up, and then salting and fermenting it in its own juice.

Sauerkraut is traditionally served at Oktoberfest celebrations, but the food is also honored with its own festivals. One sauerkraut festival in Warren County, Ohio, held in October each year features not only sauerkraut dinners and Reuben sandwiches but also sauerkraut pizza and sauerkraut cookies and bread. Ontario County in the Finger Lakes area of New York claims to be the Sauerkraut Capital of the World, where sauerkraut foods of all kinds are a main attraction in an annual August festival.

See also: OKTOBERFEST; REUBEN SANDWICH; SCHLACTPLAT.
References: Aidells and Kelly. *Real Beer and Good Eats.* 1992; Hill. *Festivals U.S.A.* 1988; Nathan. *An American Folklife Cookbook.* 1984.

SCHLACTPLAT

Most German restaurants, especially those in mid-America, serve *schlactplat,* a traditional dish made with sauerkraut and spareribs or other cuts of pork and sausage. It is also popular at harvesttime when sauerkraut is being made and at German festivals such as Oktoberfest.
See also: OKTOBERFEST; SAUERKRAUT.

SCRAPPLE

Rural folks in the mid-Atlantic region have made scrapple, which literally means "scraps," for years. It was first introduced by German Mennonites in Philadelphia, Pennsylvannia, in 1691 and later spread to other rural communities. During hog butchering, farmers save the remains of the pig—pork shavings—which are mixed with cornmeal and sage and other spices and shaped into a loaf that is sliced and fried. Traditionally, scrapple is served for breakfast, sometimes with maple syrup or ketchup, or it may be the basis for a customary Sunday evening supper.
References: Smith. *The Frugal Gourmet Cooks American.* 1987; Stern and Stern. *GoodFood.* 1983.

SEDER

Passover, a seven-day celebration of spring, renewal, and religious freedom, is one of the oldest Jewish holidays, and it is commemorated by at least 80 percent of Jews in North America. During Passover, a family seder (meaning "order" or "procedure") focuses on the liberation of Jews from slavery in Egypt more than 3,000 years ago. The order of the ceremony is spelled out in the Haggada, a book containing the exodus story, prayers, songs, and the meaning of the symbolic foods included on a seder table. These foods include *maror* (bitter herbs usually represented by horseradish) to symbolize the bitterness of slavery and sweet herbs (usually represented by parsley) to symbolize spring and renewal; *charoset* (or *haroset*, a blend of apples, nuts, cinnamon, and wine), symbolizing the building mortar that the Jewish slaves were forced to make; a roasted lamb bone, symbolizing the original sacrificial lamb; and hardboiled eggs, symbolizing an ancient offering and also renewal. Salt water represents the bitter tears of enslaved Jews.

The most important food during Passover is matzoh (also matzo or matzah), which symbolizes the unleavened bread that the Israelites took with them when they were released from bondage. A piece is wrapped in a napkin and hidden. Children in the family search for the hidden matzoh and the one who finds it receives a reward.

See also: MATZOH.

A Jewish father and his sons prepare to celebrate a seder, meaning "order" or "procedure," at a table set with candles and wine. Food items include a hardboiled egg, symbolizing renewal, and horseradish, which represents the bitterness of slavery. The steps of the ritual are written in the Haggada, held by the boys, which also tells the story of the exodus of the Jews from slavery in Egypt.

SHAKER FOODS

While many religious groups claim special foods that have symbolic meaning, the Shakers—one of the first communal groups in the United States—became known for their simple dishes and their use of spices and herbs. This celibate religious group originated in England and first came to North America in 1774, settling communities from Maine to Kentucky. Because Shaker communities banned sex, they depended on proselytizing—recruiting and converting outsiders—to increase their membership. To do so, they often held picnics, serving dishes that were more highly spiced or seasoned than most American cooking at that time, although basic Shaker cooking, like Shaker living, was fairly unadorned. Some traditional Shaker specialties for picnics were cold pork pie, pickled oysters, and potato salad.

A variety of traditional Shaker foods are still served at the Trustee's House, a former Shaker Inn in Pleasant Hill, Kentucky, where about 500 Shaker residents once lived during the mid-1800s. No Shakers live in the community now, but the inn is open to guests. Some of the typical foods on the menu include a beef stew with dumplings served with basil zucchini muffins and vegetable casseroles laced with herbs. Ohio Shaker Lemon Pie is a traditional Shaker dessert, which differs from the standard lemon pie in that it is made with two crusts and thin lemon slices that have been covered with sugar and allowed to stand for several hours to form their own juice. The bottom crust is lined with the lemon slices and juice, beaten eggs are poured over the mixture, and the pie is topped with another crust and baked. Another traditional dessert is Mother Ann's Birthday Cake named for Ann Lee, the founder of the Shakers. It is a white cake that is served every year on 1 March, Lee's birthday. The batter was originally mixed with peach twigs filled with sap that gave the cake a peach flavor, but that is no longer done.

References: *American Heritage* editors. *The American Heritage Cookbook and Illustrated History of American Eating and Drinking.* 1964; Davis. *The Potato Book.* 1973; Stein. *The Shaker Experience in America.* 1992.

SHAVOUT

A Jewish holiday, Shavout marks the first gathering of the fruits of the season, which in ancient times included wheat, barley, grapes, figs, honey, and olives. The holiday also calls for serving milk, eggs, and cheese that usually are encased in doughs in such dishes as kreplach (a dough filled with a potato and cheese mixture and cooked in boiling water) and blintzes. A cheese blintz made with an egg batter and filled with slightly sweetened farmer cheese is a common Shavout dish that not only symbolizes the spring harvest when the production of dairy products increased but also, according to some explanations, represents the days when Jews left the Sinai and had no time to slaughter animals and kosher the meat.

See also: BLINTZES.

Reference: Nash. *Kosher Cuisine.* 1984.

SHERBET

Sherbet is a flavored ice that is generally served in North American homes and restaurants as a dessert, and it is commonly used in a fruit punch for flavoring and as a decorative touch. Some people insist on differentiating between sherbet and sorbet, others say the two are actually the same thing. As well-known cookbook author Julia Child put it: "I know there is sometimes a distinction made that one [sherbet] contains milk and the other [sorbet] does not. . . . As far as I'm concerned they are one in the same, except that sorbet is contemporary chic-speak." Commercial varieties of sherbet do tend to list milk as an ingredient, but their consistency is very similar to that of sorbet.

See also: FLAVORED ICE; SORBETS AND GRANITAS.

SHISH KEBAB

A traditional Turkish dish, shish kebab (from Turkish terms for chunks of roast meat) was originally pieces of mutton placed on skewers and grilled. In North America, shish kabob (the common English spelling) usually consists of pieces of beef, lamb, fish, or poultry interspersed with onions and other vegetables on a skewer. These are grilled and served at many backyard barbecues, food festivals, and taste of . . . festivals. Shish kebab is also part of many ethnic cuisines. An Armenian-style picnic or a Greek festival, for example, nearly always includes lamb shish kebab.

See also: AMERICAN FOLKLIFE FESTIVAL; ATLANTIC ANTIC; GREEK FOOD FESTIVALS; NINTH AVENUE FOOD FESTIVAL.

References: Ayto. *A Gourmet's Guide*. 1993; Nathan. *An American Folklife Cookbook*. 1984.

SHOOFLY PIE

Reportedly the Pennsylvania Dutch invented shoofly pie, which is made with a crumb or pastry bottom and a filling of molasses, sugar, flour, plenty of butter or lard, and baking soda. This traditional dessert is often served in country restaurants and cafes in the states where Amish, Mennonite, and others of "Deutsch," or German, heritage live. According to one often told story about the origin of the name, cooks used to leave pies on a windowsill to cool, which of course drew flies. So naturally the cook would have to chase off the flies with a shout: "Shoo fly!"

See also: AMISH FOOD FESTIVALS; APPLE PANDOWDY.

Reference: Miller. *Amish Cooking*. 1980.

SHOOTERS

Sometimes called a slammer or tooter, a shooter is either the name for a drink or the name of a drinking ritual that is usually accompanied by cries of "down the hatch!" or other encouraging cries to drink up. The ritual may have stemmed from a tequila drinking routine, which includes licking salt from the back of the hand, tossing down a shot of tequila, then sucking on a lime wedge. Shooters became a bar craze in the 1990s. The drink itself is made with several types of colorful beverages skillfully layered and served in a tall glass accompanied by a shot glass of liquor. After downing a shot, a drinker empties the contents of the glass as a chaser. A variation of this ritual is the oyster shooter. A shot glass measuring 3 ounces or more is filled with vodka, a dash of Tobasco, and a raw oyster. The entire concoction is taken in one drink; it is important that the oyster is not too big or it might cause choking.

Reference: Suffes. *Mr. Boston Official Bartender's Party Guide*. 1994.

SHORE LUNCH

In Canada and the United States, a guided fishing or rafting expedition would not be complete without a *shore lunch,* a term that aptly describes the routine of taking a break from fishing or rafting to prepare a lunch on the shore of a river or lake. Some expeditions are for the day only, while others may last a week. Whatever the case, lunch (or supper) is a simple affair, and it is often a cooperative venture, with some participants gathering wood for the fire, some filleting the fresh fish that will be cooked, and others opening the cans of baked beans and starting the fire. The fish is pan fried over an open fire or cooked in foil on a barbecue grill with onion rings, green pepper strips, bacon, and seasonings. Hash browns, canned baked beans, and coffee are common accompaniments.

SHORTBREAD

A popular Christmas biscuit, but now eaten any time of the year, shortbread is associated with the Yuletide in Scotland. Originally, it was prepared for Christmas and Hogmanay, or New Year's Eve—a time when children go from house to house asking for gifts. Derived from the ancient bannock—a pancake made of unleavened oatmeal or wheat flour, which was notched around the edge to signify the sun's rays—today's shortbread in North America is made with a wheat flour (and sometimes rice flour if available), butter, and sugar mixture formed into a soft dough that is usually baked in rounds or in a shortbread mold. It may be decorated with citrus peel and almonds, or the dough may be combined with caraway seeds. Sometimes baked shortbread is topped with caramel and chocolate. Connoisseurs say that a truly good shortbread is so light in texture that when you put a piece between your lips you can inhale air through it and it seems to melt in your mouth.

SHOWERS, BRIDAL AND BABY

A common ritual before a wedding or the birth of a child is to hold a shower. That is, relatives and friends gather to honor a couple or expectant parents with a "shower" of gifts. Both bridal and baby showers used to be exclusively for women, and that custom prevails in some parts of North America, but since the 1970s there has been an increasing trend to make these events less gender-specific. A bridal shower that was once an afternoon tea party or luncheon now may be an evening event—a prewedding party that includes the bride's male children or stepsons-to-be, the groom, and some of the groom's male friends and relatives. Both the bride and groom receive gifts. In some quarters, the baby shower has become gender-neutral as well with both parents honored at a supper, barbecue, or weekend picnic. While no particular pattern has developed yet for these modern showers, they do tend to be "homey" affairs as has been typical in the past, with only relatives and close friends attending.

SHRIMP FESTIVALS

All along North American coastlines where shrimp are harvested, the shrimp is celebrated with festivals. Amelia Island off Florida's northeast coast, a center of shrimp fishing, has carried on a traditional shrimp festival since the 1960s. This Annual Isle of Eight Flags Shrimp Festival, held in late April or early May, includes a shrimp smorgasbord and an arts and crafts fair, attracting more than 200,000 people to the festivities. Just as large a crowd visits the National Shrimp Festival in Gulf Shores, Alabama. Originating in 1971, this national festival is held every October. A similar October event is the Rock Shrimp Festival in Saint Marys, Georgia.

In the coastal town of McClellanville, South Carolina, the annual Lowcountry Shrimp Festival and Blessing of the Fleet has been held since 1978. Another shrimp festival and blessing of the fleet began in 1937 in Morgan, Louisiana, to revive an old European custom of blessing the fleet of fishing boats before they went out for the catch. Two other sites for shrimp festivals in the South are Biloxi, Mississippi, and Tarpon Springs, Florida, and similar events are common in coastal areas of Texas and California as well as in Mexico. At all of these festivals, shrimp is served in many forms ranging from shrimp cocktail to jambalaya. **See also:** JAMBALAYA.

SHROVE TUESDAY

Shrovetide, a three-day period before Easter, culminates on Shrove Tuesday, the last day before the Lenten period begins (also known as Fat Tuesday). Among some Christian groups, Shrovetide is a time for celebrating and feasting, since the weeks that follow it are marked by some token of abstinence and lead into Easter itself.

In British tradition, Shrove Tuesday was the day of the leftovers that had been set aside. It was a time to use up fats and meats that are supposed to be avoided during the Lenten period. That also meant using up the milk, eggs, and butter, which ended up in pancake batter; thus, the day became known to some as Pancake Day. In North American communities today, as well as in England, pancakes have been the traditional treat on Shrove Tuesday, and although the ritual of making and serving pancakes has waned over the years, it is sometimes the custom for churches to feature pancake suppers or breakfasts, and pancakes are enjoyed in many homes.

A community pancake breakfast attended by thousands marks the beginning of Shrove Tuesday in Liberal, Kansas. Since 1950, the town has sponsored a pancake race in which women compete with their counterparts in Olney, England, checking the results by phone or fax. The tradition stems from a legend about a forgetful fifteenth-century woman who was using up fats and eggs before Lent and ran from her home on her way to church with a pancake in a skillet. Pancake Day runners in Kansas and Olney wear traditional garb of skirts, aprons, and head scarves and carry a frying pan containing a pancake that they must flip twice, once at the beginning of the 415-yard race (the distance from the market square in Olney to the steps of the church) and once at the end.

In Hamtramck just outside Detroit, Michigan, and in other areas where people of Polish descent have settled, Shrove Tuesday is better known as Paczki Day. People indulge in traditional custard or fruit-filled doughnuts known as *paczki*. Tens of thousands of the pastries, which are rich with eggs, sugar, and other delicacies that traditionally are forsaken during Lent, are baked by small Polish bakeries during the days before Shrove Tuesday. Some supermarkets also offer the pastries for sale.

See also: MARDI GRAS.

References: Schulz. *Celebrating America.* 1994; *Southern Heritage* editors. *The Southern Heritage Celebrations Cookbook.* 1984.

SINGLES DINING/DRINKING

Unmarried American adults, many of them divorced, have developed a variety of eating and drinking rituals whose main pur-

Contestants in the 1981 Liberal, Kansas, Shrove Tuesday pancake race fly down the 415-yard course, skillets in hand. Runners must fix pancakes and flip them twice—once at the beginning and once at the end of the course. The contestant with the least time and most pancakes wins.

pose is socializing. During the 1960s, the singles' bar became popular as a place where an unmarried person could meet another single person of the opposite gender. Some people say the term *singles' bar* originated with one of the most widely publicized spots of this type: Maxwell's Plum in New York City, which opened in 1966 and closed unexpectedly in 1994, perhaps reflecting the fact that many singles have rejected the frantic scene at bars and have found many other ways to socialize over food and drinks. One such alternative is to join a gourmet society or eating/dining club. Some singles groups also plan regular potlucks, prepare gourmet meals at individual homes, host wine-tasting parties, or participate in progressive dinners.
See also: EATING/DINING CLUBS; POTLUCK; PROGRESSIVE DINNER; WINE TASTING.

SMOKED SALMON

Smoking was one of the earliest ways to preserve meats and other fresh foods. The process not only cured the food and made them edible for long periods, but the type of wood used in the process imparted a particular flavor to the end product. In the Pacific Northwest of the United States and in many parts of western Canada, alder wood is a traditional favorite for smoking the most famous fish of the region—salmon. The practice was adopted from the indigenous tribes of the region, many of whom still smoke their fish in the manner of their ancestors. The salmon is revered by these groups as a symbol of abundance and a connection to the divine.

Other areas make smoked salmon also, but it is hard to top the taste of the fish, caught and cured in and around Oregon, Washington, Idaho, Alaska, and British Columbia. Many people send the smoked salmon to their friends and relatives for special occasions.

When you mention smoked salmon in the East, the immediate association is with lox and bagels. This combination is a staple at Jewish delis, where traditionally smoked salmon is placed on a toasted bagel with some soft cream cheese, a slice of red ripe tomato, and a thin strip of Bermuda onion. It is customary for many Jewish families as well as countless others to go to a favorite deli on weekend mornings just to partake of this treat.
See also: BAGELS; DELI FOODS; LOX.

SMORGASBORD

A smorgasbord is a Scandinavian buffet, and the term comes from Swedish, Norwegian, and Danish terms meaning "buttered bread." In Scandinavia a smorgasbord is usually a sandwich table or sandwich buffet that includes numerous open-faced sandwiches, often with layered ingredients.

Some of the Scandinavian traditions for a smorgasbord carried over to North America. Since Scandinavians love whole-grain breads, preferably the dark, chewy kind flavored with molasses or other dark syrups, a typical buffet includes a variety of breads, such as thin slices of moist, fragrant rye bread spread with sweet (unsalted) butter. The *smorbrot* (buttered bread) is arranged in a large display, allowing guests to look over the colorful array before choosing their favorite toppings, which could range from pickled fish to canned sardines to sliced ham and other cold meats to a great variety of cheeses and vegetables such as sliced radishes, tomatoes, pickled beets, and chives. *Lefse*—delicate, unsweetened potato pancakes served like bread and frequently filled with cured fish—are also traditional smorgasbord items. A smorgasbord in a restaurant, club, or home is usually a complete dinner, from appetizers to dessert. Coffee and amber or dark beer are the customary beverage accompaniment.

Some people say that the varied and abundant North American smorgasbord stems from a time when people had to travel long distances to attend weddings, christenings, funerals, and annual reunions and every family brought a favorite dish or several dishes to share. Others believe that the smorgasbord has much earlier origins, stemming from an early eighteenth-century practice of using rounds of bread as plates and placing slices of cooked meats and other foods on the bread in order to facilitate eating. Bread rounds were also soaked in meat juices and eaten with the main course or were spread with honey for dessert.

See also: BREAD; LOX; LUTEFISK; SANDWICHES.
References: Betz. *Tastes of Liberty.* 1985; Smith. *The Frugal Gourmet on Our Immigrant Ancestors.* 1990.

SNACK FOODS

In North America, snacking is an entrenched habit, which many food companies exploit by producing and marketing potato chips, pretzels, tortilla chips, corn chips, cheese-flavored corn puffs, nuts, dips, pork rinds, and numerous other products. Just about any type of food or beverage, however, could be considered a snack if it is consumed in a hurry or to ease hunger pangs between meals. A snack might range from chips to yogurt.

Snack food manufacturers have begun to cater to the growing number of consumers concerned about fat and cholesterol in their diets by selling low-fat products. Frito-Lay, the largest producer of snack foods in the United States, offers a variety of low- and no-fat snacks, including fat-free pretzels, reduced-fat potato chips, baked tortilla chips, and most recently baked potato chips, which, according to the company, have less than 2 grams of fat to an ounce of chips (versus 10 grams of fat to an ounce of the regular variety). It also markets a line of no-fat salsas and bean dips.

For many health-conscious North Americans, ready-to-eat raw vegetables and dried fruits, commercially packaged or prepared at home, are favorite snack items. Many Americans drink flavored bottled waters or fruit juices as a snack, and fruit juice and crackers or milk and crackers are popular snack combinations among all age groups.

SODA POP

Drunk at the rate of two to one over vegetable and fruit juices in the United States, soda pop—a sweet, carbonated-water beverage—is a multibillion dollar business. Its consumption is so prevalent throughout all of North American society, in fact, that one could say the custom of "drinking a Coke" or "having a pop" has progressed to that of a habit.

New Yorkers have been drinking "fizzy water" since 1809 when Joseph Hawkins invented a machine to carbonate water. Soda fountains serving sweetened drinks made with seltzer and syrups soon followed, and by the end of the century, they outnumbered bars in New York City.

According to some historians, the first sweetened and flavored soda water was the result of experiments done by a Frenchman who had businesses in Philadelphia in the early 1800s. Eugene Roussel is credited with popularizing the beverage in his perfume shop when he added a soda fountain in 1838. The American public clamored for the new treat, and by 1849 there were 64 bottling plants operating in the country.

Today, over 100 billion bottles of various flavors and recipes are being produced. Five of the top sellers are in the cola category; the term *coke* has been generically applied to these types of drinks especially and, at times, to the entire collection of carbonated and flavored pops. This is the result of the Coca Cola Company's dominance in sales and its historic position as the first cola soda producer in the world. A druggist, John Pemberton, stirred the first batch in his backyard with an oar in 1886.

Numerous college students in the United States and Canada report that they drink a cola of some type for breakfast because it provides caffeine and sugar for a morning eye-opener. Cola drinks (Coke, Pepsi, Dr. Pepper, etc.) are also popular during exam time, when students are up most or all of the night studying for tests.

Along with cola drinks, any of the other hundred-plus brands of soda pop available on supermarket shelves, at the counters of fastfood restaurants, and from

Two girls share an ice cream soda—a combination of ice cream and soda pop— at a soda fountain.

vending machines placed almost everywhere else are widely popular because of the billions of dollars spent to advertise these products. Ad campaigns have been crafted and fine-tuned over the years to create a pervasive impression that the drinking of soda pop will result in a happier, peppier, younger, more exciting, and exhilarating life . . . "UH HUH!," as one cola commercial has emphasized.

See also: DESIGNER WATER.
References: O'Neill. *New York Cookbook.* 1992; Root. *Food.* 1980.

SOPAIPILLAS

A traditional bread of Spain and of the Pueblo and other Native Americans of the southwestern United States, sopaipillas are pastry squares made of a yeast dough and fried in hot oil. The dough puffs up while frying and forms a pocket bread that may be stuffed with meat (such as hamburger) and/or vegetables. Alternatively, it may be sugared like a doughnut and served as a snack or dessert. The bread is a staple at most Spanish and Native American festivals held in the southwestern region of the United States.

See also: NATIVE AMERICAN FEASTS; NAVAJO FRY BREAD.
References: Fussell. *The Story of Corn.* 1992; Nathan. *An American Folklife Cookbook.* 1984.

SORBETS AND GRANITAS

A type of flavored ice, sorbets (from the Italian sorbetto) are made with frozen fruit puree and a sweetener, while granitas (from an Italian term meaning grain) are more granular and are made with chopped fruits, chipped ice, and sometimes a sweetener. Popular in Europe for centuries, sorbets and granitas are now prepared and served in numerous forms in North America. Traditionally, sorbets are served as palate cleansers between dinner courses. Those who entertain in the grand style of French cuisine are likely to serve an alcohol-infused ice between courses of very different foods. For example, after a smoked trout salad, a fruit sorbet with cassia (a liqueur) may be served as a palate cleanser in order to ready the taste buds for the full enjoyment of the meat course that might be a baked leg of lamb simmered in red wine.

Sorbets are also served as appetizers and as dessert ices blended with a liqueur, brandy, cordial, or sweet wine. Sorbets and granitas made with alcoholic beverages are usually served at elegant restaurants, formal home dinners, and festive meals.

See also: FLAVORED ICE; SHERBET.

Reference: Tarantino. *Sorbets!* 1988.

SOUL FOOD

Although there are many variations in the types of dishes labeled "soul food," they all stem from the time when enslaved black Americans were forced to live on limited supplies of food—vegetables grown in a small garden and meager portions of flour, cornmeal, and salt pork or lowly parts of the hog discarded by plantation owners. Black cooks used what they had to create a variety of dishes that are now part of the heritage of many blacks from the American South and are considered traditional soul foods, including such dishes as grits, corn fritters, crackling bread, fried catfish, barbecued ribs, chitterlings, fried green tomatoes, seafood gumbo, potato salad, and sweet potato pie. Soul foods are often served at picnics, community dinners, and other events where people of African ancestry eat together, and they are the featured cuisine at soul food restaurants or cafes across the United States. At Sylvia's, a famous soul food restaurant in New York's Harlem, the owner, known as the Queen of Soul Food, has been serving traditional southern favorites since 1962.

References: Smith. *The Frugal Gourmet Cooks American.* 1987; Woods and Styler. *Sylvia's Soul Food.* 1992.

SOUP AND SANDWICH

The combination of soup and a sandwich is a very popular lunch special at many restaurants, and it is commonly prepared in many home kitchens. Depending on individual preference, there are countless variations on this simple, nourishing meal. Some examples are split pea with a ham and swiss cheese sandwich, chicken noodle with a grilled cheese, and minestrone with grilled peppers and cream cheese on French bread. Whether for lunch or for an evening meal, the soup and sandwich is usually a cool weather choice; it is very comforting on a cold winter evening or when it is raining and stormy outside.

See also: COMFORT FOODS.

SOUP KITCHEN

During the U.S. economic depression of the 1930s, soup kitchens became common in North America, and they are a well-established tradition of many churches, synagogues, charity groups, and civic organizations. Soup kitchens today are familiar sights in major cities and some small towns, where volunteers serve hungry, homeless, and often hopeless people.

There have been protests against soup kitchens in some neighborhoods—residents fear the rise of crime and violence from those served, but to many volunteers and religious leaders, feeding the hungry is considered a special mission. Most kitchens serve at least one free meal a day and often two—breakfast and dinner. Some also have a children's program that runs each day after school; kids take part in numerous activities and are fed snacks such as pieces of pizza, french fries, oranges, cookies, and fruit juice.

SOUP SUPPERS

Hearty soups are traditional one-dish meals with almost every group of people in the world. Among many Americans, soup is not only a common food for lunch, but it is also a supper. In fact, the word *soup* derives from the Old French *souppe,* meaning "to supper," and the English words *sop* and *sip.* Before eating utensils were common, people dunked bread in soups to sop up the broth and to carry meats and other solid foods to the mouth.

Although there are as many varieties of soups as there are cooks who make them, some are associated with specific cuisines. *Gulyas* (goulash), for example, which originated with nomadic Hungarians known as the Magyar, is made with beef or lamb, onions, garlic, green peppers, potatoes, noodles, and Hungarian paprika as well as other spices. Sweet-and-sour cabbage soup is a typical Russian supper. Chorba, a substantial vegetable soup made with lamb and saffron, is a traditional Moroccan dish. People of Scandinavian ancestry have made their version of split pea soup famous through the well-known Andersen restaurant in Buellton, California, where the soup is the main item on the menu.

Many main course soups are made with chicken. Chicken soup with matzo balls makes a hearty supper in many Jewish homes and is a traditional item in Jewish restaurants and delis. Shrimp soups are common suppers, particularly among people of Asian ancestry and among Americans living along coastal areas where shrimp are harvested. Bouillabaisse is a typical French stew or soup made with assorted fish and shellfish. Borscht is a beet and cabbage soup that many people of Eastern European ancestry serve for supper. Seafood chowders, creamed vegetable soups like broccoli and asparagus, and bean soups, such as chili and pasta fazool, are traditional supper soups for numerous Americans. Regardless of the type of soup served, a soup supper also includes hearty breads (some used for sopping) such as cheese breads, Italian and French breads, sourdoughs, and ryes.

See also: CHILI AND CHILI SUPPERS; CLAM CHOWDER; POOR SOUP; SOUP AND SANDWICH; SOUP KITCHEN.

References: Betz. *Tastes of Liberty.* 1985; Biro. *Flavors of Hungary.* 1973; Schwartz. *Soup Suppers.* 1994.

Soup kitchen volunteers serve Thanksgiving dinner to the needy and homeless on the grounds of the U.S. Capitol in 1993. Mobile kitchens set up to dispense simple meals—mainly soup and bread—came to be called soup kitchens during World War I.

SOURDOUGH BREAD

One of the oldest leavened breads is made from sour dough. As its name suggests, the leavening for sourdough bread is a starter made from a flour, sugar, and buttermilk mixture that is allowed to ferment until it is "sour." One legend has Columbus bringing a starter to America on his historic trip. North American pioneers often carried sourdough starter with them as they pushed west from the Atlantic coast, and gold prospectors in the Alaskan Yukon during the 1890s became famous for the sourdough breads they made in their mining camps. Prospectors stopped in San Francisco before going by boat to Alaska, so sourdough bread became a specialty of that city. Many San Francisco residents today include sourdough bread in their weekly meal plans, and some regular visitors to the city routinely go to bakeries to buy loaves of sourdough to take home.

Sourdough bread, biscuits, and hotcakes are also popular at food festivals in the West and Northwest. It is customary for those who prepare the sourdough for such events to bring their own starter, which may have been passed on for generations and may be 100 years old or more.
See also: BREAD.
Reference: Mariani. *The Dictionary of American Food and Drink.* 1993, 1994.

SOUTHERN FRIED CHICKEN

See SOUL FOOD; SOUTHERN FOOD FESTIVALS.

SPAM FANS AND FESTS

I'm a SPAM Fan declared author Carolyn Wyman in the title of her book about America's favorite foods. Although many people have joked about this canned meat product, because it has been served so often in army mess halls, school cafeterias, and summer camps, evidently there are many SPAM lovers across North America (and around the globe for that matter). In recent years, fans have been buying an array of goods with the SPAM logo—hats, T-shirts, underwear, earrings, water bottles, and even golf balls offered by Hormel Foods of Austin, Minnesota, which introduced the product in 1937. In recent times, this company has been selling 122 million cans of SPAM each year. Not only do SPAM lovers broadcast their allegiance to this canned meat product made of chopped pork shoulder, ham, spices, and gelatin, but they routinely eat it—for breakfast, lunch, or dinner. SPAM is also celebrated at cook-offs, eating contests, and a variety of festivals where such dishes as SPAM and eggs and SPAM pizza are featured.
References: "Spamming the Globe." 1994; Wyman. *I'm a SPAM Fan.* 1993.

SOUTHERN FOOD FESTIVALS

Celebrated in various parts of the South during the spring and early summer, southern food festivals usually feature traditional foods served southern style. Black-eyed peas with rice and gravy, crispy fried chicken, corn bread, and collard greens cooked with salt pork or ham hocks, fried okra, and jambalaya are common. Such foods are also popular at gatherings where soul food is featured.
See also: CHITTERLINGS; CRACKLINGS; FISH FRY; HUSH PUPPIES; JAMBALAYA; JUNETEENTH; SOUL FOOD.

SPICED TEA

Spiced teas have evolved from the practice of adding herbs and other flavorings to the traditional cup of tea. Beginning in the early days of colonial America, people have experimented with blends that spiced up their tea-drinking experience. Commercial concerns have taken advantage of the public's fascination with these beverages by making many types of spiced teas available on the supermarket shelves, such as black tea blends with raspberry, mint, orange, cinnamon, or vanilla.
See also: HERBAL TEA.

Hormel Foods Corporation President R. L. Knowlton, right, presented a can of SPAM to Russian President Boris Yeltsin in 1992. Hormel introduced the spiced ground pork and ham cooked in its can to American consumers in 1937.

SPOON BREAD

Spoon bread is a simple corn bread popular in the southern United States and also in Mexico where it is made with chiles and cheese. The ingredients are similar to most corn breads except that after the batter is placed in a pan, milk is poured over the top before baking. The name is derived from the fact that the finished bread is always very crisp on the outside, but the inside is soft enough to require serving with a spoon. Small dollops of the cornmeal mixture fried in deep fat are called hush puppies.

See also: HUSH PUPPIES.

SPORTS BARS

Big-screen TVs, reduced drink prices whenever a team scores, menus with a sports theme (sandwiches named after baseball, football, or basketball celebrities, for example), sports memorabilia, and give-aways are all part of sports bars. As the name inplies, sports bars cater to sports fans who like to watch competitions on television and talk about players and games while they drink and eat. The food served is typical bar food such as sandwiches, pizza, buffalo wings, and boiled shrimp.

A big fad in some sports bars is playing sports trivia games via computer hookups. Patrons at sports bars across North America are linked via modems and use electronic devices to activate an answer to sports trivia questions viewed on a large screen at each of the bars. The bars compete to provide the most correct answers.

Sports bars are found in neighborhood saloons or restaurants, upscale resort hotels, or at off-track betting facilities where customers can watch horse or greyhound races on television. Some sports bars are franshise operations—part of a chain. The concept originated in Washington, D.C., during the early 1980s and quickly appealed to single people in their twenties and thirties. In fact, the sports bar has eclipsed the dance club, which was the favorite nightspot of young single people during the 1970s. Sports bars are also popular with fan clubs of professional sports teams and with alumni groups who gather to watch college games. Although a bar can be crowded at any time of the year, it is likely to be jammed during highly contested games and such events as the World Series and Superbowl Sunday.

See also: SPORTS DRINKS; SUPERBOWL SUPPER.

SPORTS DRINKS

According to the U.S. manufacturers of increasingly popular sports drinks, these flavored beverages are scientifically formulated to balance the body's electrolytes after strenuous exercise. The first and most well known of these drinks is Gatorade,

which was introduced and marketed by the Gatorade Company as a very effective lime green thirst quencher. Other companies followed this lead, and the products are now purchased as substitutes for soda pop by athletes and nonathletes alike.

An unusual custom has evolved from the use of Gatorade at basketball and, especially, football contests. In order to have an adequate supply of the thirst quencher on the sidelines for the team members in these events, the company has provided huge insulated dispensers, which trainers keep filled with Gatorade and ice so that players are able to sample it throughout the game. Players have taken to celebrating victory in a big game such as the Superbowl or other championship by taking the top off of the dispenser, picking it up by the two side handles, sneaking up behind the head coach, and dumping the frigid liquid over

New York Giant Harry Carson dumps Gatorade on coach Bill Parcells near the end of the Giants' Super Bowl victory over the Denver Broncos in 1987. Sports drinks, developed as an alternative to water, replace electrolytes lost through perspiration during heavy exercise.

the head of their mentor. One can imagine the surprise and intense discomfort this must produce: especially on those below-freezing days of NFL play-off games.

See also: STADIUM AND ARENA EATING AND DRINKING.

SPRING BREAK

Hundreds of thousands of college students in the United States and Canada take part in a weeklong spring rite and drinking ritual known as "spring break," which many have called a debauch or rowdy beer bust that explodes on Florida and some Texas, southern California, and Mexico beaches for a six-week period beginning in late February and lasting through mid-April each year. During a midterm break, students come from the northern United States and Canada to soak up the sun, surf, swill some beer, and seek friendly encounters with others of their ilk. Other spring break activities include pool parties, basketball and volleyball contests, aerobics classes, bungee rides, "hot buns" and "hard body" contests, dances, and music.

Florida beaches have been sites for this annual student ritual since the 1930s, but students did not descend on the state en masse until the 1960s. During that decade and the next, a popular MGM movie *Where the Boys Are* and national news stories focusing on arrests for drunkenness, marijuana use, and sometimes riots brought ever more publicity about spring break and helped increase the number of students taking part in the ritual.

Florida cities such as Ft. Lauderdale and Daytona have clamped down on spring breakers since the mid-1980s, encouraging former students and their families to visit. These cities entertain only 10,000 to 20,000 students for the ritual each year rather than several hundred thousand. Other Florida cities, however, have welcomed students. Panama City Beach is one such city, and hordes—an estimated 450,000 to 500,000 students—visit during the seven-week spring break period. Some

businesses offer free beer or sponsor beer-drinking contests as an enticement, since beer drinking is a major part of the ritual. Police, however, do check for underage drinkers—the legal age for drinking is 21. First offenders are likely to have their beer confiscated and dumped, but repeat offenders receive harsher penalties.

SPRING ROLLS

Spring rolls are considered a more authentic and delicate version of egg rolls. The name comes from the Chinese tradition of serving them on the first day of the Chinese New Year, which is also the first day of spring in the lunar year. In North America, spring rolls are usually served as an appetizer in Chinese-style restaurants. Thin wrappers made of an egg dough are filled with chopped or shredded vegetables (cabbage and bean sprouts are common), shrimp, ground pork, or small pieces of beef, and then they are rolled and deep-fried. Miniature spring rolls and egg rolls are popular at cocktail parties and as grazing food at cocktail lounges and bars. Both rolls are among the many traditional foods served at food festivals and are popular carry-out foods.

STADIUM AND ARENA EATING AND DRINKING

Many fans of hockey, baseball, football, or basketball would not think of going to a game and missing the "eating" part of the experience. Children, beginning with their first visits, are shown the rites of stadium or arena food, consuming favorites such as hot dogs and cola drinks in the stands or at stadium food booths. Parents pass on the traditions and customs that make true fans out of the little ones, just like their own parents did a generation before. The amount and variety of foods and beverages consumed are reflected in the statistics from opening night of the 1994 basketball season at Gund Arena in Cleveland, Ohio. Fans feasted on 3,000 hot dogs of all varieties, including kosher and Polish frankfurters and the Cleveland Dog (an all-beef hot dog topped with fried purple cabbage, cheddar cheese, diced onions, tomato, dill pickles, and Cleveland's own authentic stadium mustard). Other foods included 3,000 bags of peanuts, 2,000 soft pretzels, 2,000 personal pan pizzas, 1,500 orders of french fries, 1,000 orders of nachos, 750 deli sandwiches, 600 hamburgers, 500 grilled chicken sandwiches, and 500 Italian sausages. As for beverages, about 10,000 cups of soda, 500 bottles of spring water, and 500 fruit juice drinks were served.

See also: BASEBALL PARK EATING AND DRINKING; SPORTS BARS; SPORTS DRINKS.

STAR DINING

In the heyday of restaurants and conspicuous consumption, a popular pastime of the 1980s was getting a reservation for an eating establishment that was rated highly by a respected food critic. Clubs of foodies especially in southern California, where being seen at the "right" place was and is a priority, would actually set their dining agenda based on these reviewers. A newspaper column, radio bit, or television segment would always contain a shortcut guide to help people rank the restaurant being critiqued. The *Michelin Guide* is the most famous, and it uses a star system to judge its entries: five stars being a highly prized award. Other publications and reviewers use a similar system, but instead of stars they use other icons such as forks, knives, and toques for use in the comparisons. Regardless of the rating method, restaurants can thrive or fail based on the report of a well-known reviewer.

See also: EATING/DINING CLUBS; FOODIES; GOURMET FOODS.

STEAK TARTARE

For some people, steak tartare—minced raw beef—is the epitome of exotic eating. Found only rarely in North America at a cocktail party or as an appetizer on

gourmet restaurant menus, the dish is a traditional preparation in France and Belgium. Originally *à la tartare* referred to any dish that was covered with bread crumbs, broiled, and served with a seasoned sauce. Now it refers to the favorite white sauce for fish or the chopped meat dish. According to purists, the meat used for steak tartare should come from a horse, but whether one uses a horse or a cow, the preparation of steak tartare is simple. Mince or grind the lean meat and add salt, pepper, Worcestershire sauce, and Tabasco. Form a ball and place on the middle of a plate. Make an indentation on the top of the mound and place inside half of an egg shell with a raw egg yolk. Display chopped parsley, shallots, onions, and some capers around the meat.

STICKY BUNS

They are called "sticky buns" in many parts of the United States, but they are also known as pecan rolls or the all-American breakfast rolls. Made with a sweet yeast dough, eggs, milk, and cinnamon, the buns are placed in a pan laced with caramel syrup and chopped pecan meats. The dough is allowed to rise and then baked. When removed from the pan, the caramel concoction becomes the delicious topping that tends to stick to the fingers while eating the rolls. Sticky buns are a favorite breakfast menu item in many restaurants, and they usually disappear quickly, long before the breakfast hours are over.

See also: BREAKFAST.

STIR-FRY COOKING

The popularity of Thai, Japanese, and Chinese styles of cooking has created a taste for stir-fried dishes in North America. First used in some of the more imaginative restaurants as they incorporated these ethnic cuisines into their menus, stir-fry has now moved into the home kitchen. Stir-fried food has three main advantages for contemporary living: (1) it is very quick, (2) it is low-fat, and (3) it retains most of its nutrients. Almost any meat or fish can be stir-fried, and the inclusion of vegetables and rice or noodles makes this an efficient one-pan meal.

To stir-fry, American cooks have had to learn how to use a tool that has been around for centuries in Asian kitchens—the wok, a metal pan with a convex bottom. The wok was difficult to find in the United States until about the 1980s, but it is now available at almost every culinary outlet. The Teflon-coated kind is especially easy to master. Several basic rules apply: make sure that the oil is hot before adding the ingredients, put in each one at the right time, and do not overcook.

STOLLEN

Called one of the most traditional Yuletide breads, stollen is a fruit and nut bread that originated in Dresden, Germany, and is an accompaniment to most Christmas celebrations rooted in German customs.

See also: BREAD; CHRISTMAS EVE/DAY DINNER.

STRAWBERRY FESTIVALS

During the spring when strawberries are harvested in the Midwest, many cities and towns celebrate the crop with a community festival featuring strawberry shortcake. A local restaurant or civic group prepares a gigantic shortcake topped with strawberries and whipped cream, presenting and serving it in a mall, community center, or in a tent or other temporary structure near a strawberry field.

Numerous strawberry festivals are held in California, and they feature such items as strawberries dipped in chocolate,

Cultivated in California, these strawberries may be rinsed and eaten fresh from the field, served atop breakfast cereal, added to ice cream, or served with shortcake and whipped cream. Oxnard, California, the self-proclaimed "Strawberry Capital of the World," holds a Strawberry Festival each May.

strawberry daiquiris, and strawberry milk shakes. One of the largest strawberry festivals takes place in Oxnard, California, which calls itself the Strawberry Capital of the World. Held in May each year, the festival attracts hundreds of thousands of visitors, many of whom make their own individual strawberry shortcakes from ingredients offered at booths. During the festival, growers display their products, with Driscoll strawberries considered top of the line. Restaurants compete in contests to determine the best recipes for dishes ranging from strawberry soup to strawberry desserts.

Another type of strawberry festival is held at Tonawanda, New York, where the Iroquois gather during the strawberry season, usually in June, to hear speeches and take part in ceremonial dances of a spiritual nature. Because the occasion focuses on a message delivered 200 years ago by a Seneca prophet who advised his followers to abstain from liquor, a nonalcoholic strawberry drink is served to participants. After lunch the dessert offered is strawberry shortcake.

Reference: Thompson and Carlson. *Holidays, Festivals, and Celebrations of the World Dictionary.* 1994.

STREET FOOD

The practice of selling food from street carts is an old European tradition that was carried over to the colonies. From the earliest days in the eastern cities of the United States and Canada and all throughout Mexico, vendors pushed carts and hawked hot and cold foods and beverages to people in their homes or to passersby. Since the 1950s, people in the suburban United States have heard the familiar strains of the amplified recorded music of the motorized street vendors who drove their specially equipped trucks through residential subdivisions. The music would alert people to the fact that the Good Humor man was there with all of his frozen confections, and if the children could resist that call, they would be tempted again by the Helm's Bakery truck with its familiar whistle rolling by right after school.

Today, these traditions live throughout North America. Vendors in New York City, for example, have their favorite locations on Manhattan sidewalks. They sell foods ranging from hot dogs to ice cream. In Mexico and in Latin communities of the United States, vendors walk the streets ringing a bell to let residents and workers know that they are passing by with such foods as tamales, tacos, coconut ice cream, and ices.

See also: HOT DOGS; ICE CREAM; TACO BARS AND RESTAURANTS.

STUFFED GRAPE LEAVES

According to food folklorist Joan Nathan, the grape leaf is an Armenian national emblem. An old folktale tells of Noah leaving the ark and immediately planting fast-growing grape vines in the Causcaus Mountains in order to provide his family with grape leaf meals. In North America, one of the mandatory foods at Armenian celebrations from christenings to weddings is stuffed grape leaves. Usually the leaves are lined with a mixture of rice, stewed tomatoes, diced onions, pine nuts, currants, parsley, dill, cinnamon, salt, and lemon. The leaves are covered with water and simmered, chilled, and served cold. Grape leaves also are used in casseroles served at traditional Armenian meals. *Dolmadakia* (or stuffed grape leaves) is also traditionally prepared by Greeks. Similar to the Armenian-style dish, the Greek version includes leaves stuffed with garlic-flavored rice mixed with dill, lemon, olive oil, currants, and pistachio nuts. It serves as an appetizer usually accompanied by plain yogurt.

See also: ETHNIC FOOD TRADITIONS; GREEK FOOD FESTIVALS.

References: Bernbaum. *Rose's Melting Pot.* 1993; Nathan. *An American Folklife Cookbook.* 1984.

An Afghan-born street vendor sells fruit from his stand in front of the New York Stock Exchange in New York City. Street foods range from hot dogs and ice cream to espresso and burritos.

SUCCOT

Called the Jewish thanksgiving, Succot is celebrated for eight days in the fall, usually in October or November. The holiday was first observed in *succahs,* small three-sided buildings that were decorated with bunches of grapes and other fruits, as well as vegetables and grains harvested in the fall. In some Jewish communities, a *succah* is constructed for the holiday meal. Whether in a home or in the traditional *succah,* the foods are the same: stuffed foods and casserole dishes.

SUCCOTASH

A traditional Native American dish, succotash (which derives from a Narraganset word meaning "fragments") has been part of the North American diet for centuries. Before Europeans arrived on the continent, Native Americans planted corn and beans (the shell or green variety or both) together in the same plot, and after harvesting the vegetables, they combined them with bear fat to make a stew or soup that was thickened with ground sunflower seeds or pine nuts. In the winter, dried corn and beans (usually kidney beans) were used to make this one-dish meal, which is a staple at Native American feasts and spring festivals.

When colonists learned to make succotash, they added salt pork, bacon, venison, or other game to the dish, and since the mid-1800s, that has been a customary way in numerous American homes to prepare this stewlike meal. Some cooks, however, simply mix lima beans and kernels of sweet corn with a little butter and serve the mixture as a side dish.

See also: GREEN CORN FESTIVALS; NATIVE AMERICAN FEASTS.

References: Brown. *American Cooking.* 1968; Fussell. *I Hear America Cooking.* 1986; Fussell. *The Story of Corn.* 1992.

SUGAR

Sugar is routinely spooned into coffee and tea. In fact, countless North Americans practice a somewhat formal ritual of carefully measuring out one, two, or even three teaspoons of sugar and stirring it into their hot beverage in a deliberate rhythmic pattern. (People who use packaged sugar substitutes follow similar procedures, ripping open a packet or carefully tearing off a corner and pouring it into a beverage and stirring.) Sugar is also sprinkled over breakfast cereal in a routine manner; it is used as a preservative and included in most commercially prepared foods in North America. So much sugar is consumed in the United States that even though the nation is one of the top producers, it still imported $2 billion worth of sugar in the early 1980s. The quantities of imported sugar have declined as of late, but only because many people have switched to sugar substitutes such as Equal and Sweet-n-Low. Still, the North American sweet tooth keeps consumption high.

Some health practitioners claim that sugar is at the root of many degenerative diseases, behavioral problems, and rampant obesity that is now common throughout North America. But the custom of eating a sweet treat for a snack, dessert, depression, fun, nervousness, reward, low self-esteem, and so on is ingrained in the collective psyche. No rational information about the negative effects of overindulgence seems to make a difference.

Historical reports indicate that people produced and consumed sugarcane as long ago as biblical times. By the sixteenth and seventeenth centuries, the huge plantations operating in the Caribbean and other subtropical locales in South and North America needed many laborers. To maintain a continuous supply of sugar for rum, molasses, and other sweet by-products used in the British colonies and exported to Europe, sugar producers imported thousands of African people as slaves. This economic decision obviously has had a lasting effect on the social structures and cultures in North America.

Some extremists insist that the biological effects of the refined sugar "drug" have had an even more direct influence on the development of society than the economic institutions that were created to produce it. Consequently, they advocate the total elimination of sugar. The legal team defending Dan White in his trial for the 1978 murder of San Francisco councilman Harvey Milk spoke to this proposition by theorizing that too much sugar (and additives) in the diet creates behaviors detrimental to normal life. There is, in fact, some evidence to indicate that peoples' patterns are positively influenced when their diets contain less refined sugar. The difficulty of eliminating refined sugars from the North American diet becomes quite clear when one notes the many sweetened foods and beverages that are consumed regularly in North American eating and drinking patterns.

See also: AFTER-DINNER MINTS; AFTERNOON TEA; BAKED ALASKA; CANDIED SWEET POTATOES (OR YAMS); CANDY AND CARAMEL APPLES; CEREAL; CHOCOLATE BEVERAGES; CHRISTMAS CANDY; CHRISTMAS COOKIES; COMFORT FOODS; FUDGE; GRANOLA BARS/CEREAL; ICE CREAM; MAPLE SUGARING/FESTIVALS; MARSHMALLOW; MOCK APPLE PIE; MOLASSES; PUDDINGS; RED VELVET CAKE; SODA POP.

References: Dufty. *Sugar Blues*. 1975; Mintz. *Sweetness and Power*. 1987.

SUNDAY BRUNCH

Weekend editions of most urban newspapers contain numerous advertisements for Sunday brunch, a ritual event for countless individuals and families across the United States. The custom may have originated during the late 1800s in New Orleans. Apparently, after a rush of business in the early morning hours, business owners would take a meal break and eat a second breakfast. This practice eventually became part of the southern way of life.

Today, brunch is primarily a Sunday affair and a relaxing meal. At a restaurant, brunch foods may be selected from a fancy buffet or a lavish groaning board (a table loaded with food) with items ranging from fresh fruits to hot meats and poultry to elaborate desserts. These foods are often served with champagne and mimosas. Brunch also

may be offered at a cozy cafe serving homemade foods such as freshly baked breads, scones, old-fashioned corned beef hash, granola, omelets, quiche, pancakes, and huevos rancheros. Going out for brunch is popular both on holidays (particularly Mother's Day) and as a post-church event.

See also: BUFFET; HUEVOS RANCHEROS; OMELET; QUICHE.

Reference: Pyles. *The New Texas Cuisine*. 1993.

SUNDAY DINNER

Generations of North Americans have taken part in the Sunday dinner ritual that traditionally has followed church services and usually has included extended family members. In the past, the main course for Sunday dinner frequently was roasted or stewed chicken. Among those of modest means, being able to serve chicken was considered a special treat since only the wealthy could afford to buy a full bird. During the 1920s, for example, politicians campaigned for office using the slogan "a chicken in every pot" as a metaphor for prosperity. The slogan, however, did not originate with American politicians; rather, it was used in the sixteenth century by King Henry IV of France, who hoped to improve France's economy and make it possible for every peasant to enjoy "a chicken in his pot on Sundays."

In North America, chicken has become such common fare that it is not necessarily a special Sunday treat, although it is still a popular food on Sunday and every other day of the week. Sunday dinner has changed in other ways, too, as long distances separate many families. Nevertheless, the Sunday dinner is still observed in cities, towns, and rural areas where relatives live close by and can gather for dinner. Traditionally, one member of a family hosts the dinner, and the meal may be quite lavish, lasting for hours as diners consume numerous courses and enjoy conversation. Others may take part in a family dinner at a restaurant each Sunday, and some families have Sunday dinner at Grandma's one week, Aunt Jean's the next, and

Cousin Bill's the following Sunday, alternating the place but not the ritual of gathering and eating together.

See also: FAMILY REUNION.

References: Malpezzi and Clements. *Italian-American Folklore.* 1992; Visser. *The Rituals of Dinner.* 1991.

SUNFLOWER FESTIVAL

During the last weekend in July each year since 1965, the sunflower and its by-products are celebrated in Altona, a town in southern Manitoba, Canada. The sunflower represents the heritage of the Mennonites, a religious group that emigrated from Europe to North America in the late 1600s. While many Mennonites of German heritage settled on farmland in what is now the eastern and midwestern United States, a group of Russian Mennonites made their home in southern Manitoba, and they were the first to extract and use the oil from sunflower plants. One of the special foods prepared for the festival is a sunflower ice cream.

SUPERBOWL SUPPER

Gathering around the television set to watch Superbowl football has become an annual event in many American homes. The Superbowl is the championship game between the winners of the National Football Conference and the American Football Conference. For many sports fans, watching this game is similar to watching the World Series in baseball, and food is always an integral part of the ritual.

Yet, there is no one specific eating and drinking pattern that prevails. At some gatherings, football fans may simply eat snacks and sandwiches along with their drinks—whether alcoholic or otherwise. Some have buffet-type meals. It is common also for some to order food to be delivered, whether from a local deli, pizza parlor, or Chinese restaurant. Whatever the food, it is usually consumed in an informal fashion with the main focus on the outcome of the game.

See also: STADIUM AND ARENA EATING AND DRINKING; TAILGATE PARTY.

SUPERSTITIOUS FOOD PRACTICES

Since the beginning of recorded history, there is evidence that nearly every kind of food and numerous beverages have at some time been associated with "magical" or superstitious practices designed to bring good fortune or to ward off evil. Some North Americans still engage in superstitious eating and drinking rituals, many of which focus on basic foods such as bread and salt. Some say that accidently dropping a piece of buttered bread face down is bad luck or that cutting off both ends of a loaf before eating the middle forecasts problems with making ends meet—the bills might not get paid. Spilling salt is considered a bad omen, so if salt is spilled many people pick up a pinch of it and throw it over a shoulder (usually the left one) to drive evil away. Some North Americans always fill the salt shaker on New Year's Day to bring good luck throughout the year.

In addition to filling the salt shaker for good luck, New Year's festivities throughout North America include numerous superstitious rituals involving food and drink. People offer toasts for good luck and eat particular foods, such as herring and a rice and bean dish called Hoppin' John, to ensure good fortune for the year.

A superstitious ritual in many families is saving the wishbone (breast bone) from a roast chicken or turkey, drying it, and then letting two children wish on the v-shaped bone. Each child holds one tip, and both make a wish while simultaneously pulling at the bone. Once the bone breaks, the child holding the largest piece of bone supposedly realizes his or her wish.

See also: CHICKEN SOUP; CHINESE NEW YEAR; DRINKING TOASTS; LUNAR NEW YEAR; MEDICINAL FOODS; NEW YEAR'S DAY; NEW YEAR'S EVE.

Reference: Gay. *Keep the Buttered Side Up.* 1995.

SUSHI AND SUSHI BARS

Sushi is not only a food but a traditional Japanese way of eating, which in the 1980s and 1990s has become popular in parts of North America. This trend is apparent with the proliferation of sushi bars, particularly in coastal areas of the West and East. Sushi begins with cooked rice seasoned with rice wine vinegar, sugar, and

Japanese sushi chefs in southern California display small trays of sushi, California rolls, and sashimi, which is served with pickled ginger, and wasabi, a horseradish powder mixed with water to make a green paste.

salt to which a great variety of ingredients can be added. The most common sushi rolls are made with quickly toasted seaweed sheets spread with the seasoned rice and topped with a piece of sliced raw or broiled fish, eel, or squid; smoked oysters or clams; lox; or an egg or a vegetable filling. This concoction is then rolled, sliced, and served with the traditional *wasabi* (a horseradish powder mixed with water to make a thin paste or sauce), tamari or soy sauce, and pickled ginger.

See also: SASHIMI.

SWEDISH MEATBALLS

Small meatballs made with ground beef, veal, and pork are a staple wherever a Swedish smorgasbord or other buffet-style dinner is served. They also may be part of a holiday meal such as Christmas dinner prepared according to Swedish tradition. The meatballs are also very popular items on hors d'oeuvre tables.

See also: APPETIZERS; BUFFET; CHRISTMAS EVE/DAY DINNER; SMORGASBORD.

SWEETBREADS

Sweetbreads are the thymus glands of a variety of animals, but veal and lamb are most often used in the preparation of dishes made with sweetbreads. In Mexico, sweetbreads are called *mollejos,* and because they are in the class of meats known as offal—organ meats—many people consider them taboo foods. Sweetbreads, however, have been a popular dish along the Atlantic Coast of North America since colonial times when fried sweetbreads and sweetbread and oyster pie were common.

Fine dining establishments throughout North America today prepare and serve sweetbreads, keeping alive a centuries-old tradition. In fact, sweetbreads are considered a delicacy in many countries, particularly France where master chefs have concocted numerous classic recipes for *ris de veau* (calf sweetbreads), which frequently are on the menu in North American French-style restaurants. Sweetbreads also may be served at elegant parties, and traditionally are prepared and served at Kentucky Derby celebrations.

References: Root. *Food.* 1980; Simon and Howe. *Dictionary of Gastronomy.* 1970. *Southern Heritage* editors. *The Southern Heritage Celebrations Cookbook.* 1984.

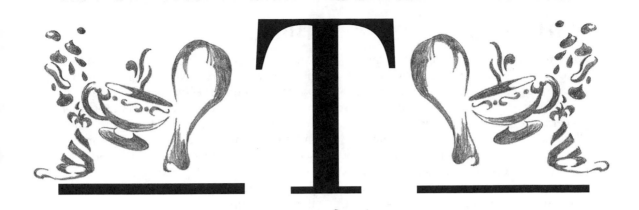

TABLE MANNERS

In every part of the world, sitting down to eat a meal with other people is dictated by numerous customs and rituals. "Table manners are as old as human society, the reason being that no human society can exist without them," wrote Margaret Visser in the opening of her book *The Rituals of Dinner.* Visser and others who have explored food rituals point out that in order to survive, people the world over have had to find and maintain a food supply, establishing rules for procuring, preparing, sharing, and eating meals. Those rules differ with various societies but always form an eating etiquette that people follow when they share a meal.

The rituals for a formal dinner are certainly more elaborate than those for an informal or relaxed meal when rules generally are broken or do not seem to apply. These rituals (because they are repeated over and over and are predictable) help us "interlock with each other" and are a way of expressing a "kind of solidarity," according to Visser. In fact, if people do not follow the rules for eating at a formal meal, they risk being criticized, ridiculed, or ostracized.

Formal meals usually begin with people taking their seats at a table, either designated with place cards or assigned by a host or hostess. A place setting is arranged with a certain number of plates, eating utensils, glassware, a cup and saucer, and a napkin. The meal itself is served in courses, perhaps beginning with an appetizer or soup, progressing through to the main course and then dessert.

Each formal dinner has its own variations, but in U.S. culture, people are expected to behave "properly," eating with the "right" utensils for the corresponding courses, never slurping soup or drinks, never talking and chewing at the same time, using a napkin appropriately, and on and on. Authorities in social etiquette advise on proper manners at mealtime as well as on acceptable behavior for other occasions, filling the pages of hundreds of books, magazines, and columns in major newspapers. In 1993, a dinnerware company surveyed 1,000 people to determine how they identified and ranked poor table etiquette. At the top of the list were talking with one's mouth full and making smacking or other noises while eating. Other kinds of taboo behavior included eating before others are seated and taking food for oneself before offering it to others.

See also: DINNER PARTY; EATING UTENSILS; FINGER BOWL; TABLECLOTHS.

Reference: Visser. The *Rituals of Dinner.* 1991.

TABLECLOTHS

Although it is customary in many cafes, coffee shops, restaurants, and homes to place a cloth on a table before serving a meal, for informal eating most people use placemats or leave a table or counter bare. Placemats are used even when some formal meals are served, but custom usually dictates that formal dinners and banquets be served on a table covered with a white cloth, which has long been associated with wealth and nobility in Europe and with upper-class dining in North America. White cloth napkins also must be placed at each setting when following this ritualistic pattern for preparing a table.

See also: BANQUET; DINNER PARTY; TABLE MANNERS.

Reference: Visser. The *Rituals of Dinner.* 1991.

TACO BARS AND RESTAURANTS

The taco, a corn or flour tortilla generally fried in oil and filled with some kind of meat, cheese, vegetables, and spicy sauce, is a traditional food of Mexico. As the popularity of Mexican cuisine has exploded across the United States, taco restaurants and other such retail outlets that specialize in this food have been opened in many communities well north of the border. Sometimes the best tacos can be found at favorite taco bars, accessible only through walk-up windows where orders are placed and the food is delivered. Behind the scenes, men and women are usually working in cramped quarters to maintain the supply of the product. Quite often, families will open and run these tiny restaurants together, serving the public food that comes from recipes proven over generations within the *familia.* Taco Bell and Taco Time are two of the fastfood versions of these traditional taco bars. Although the food served at these drive-through factories is certainly adequate and sometimes quite good, it is a far cry from the tastes available at such places as Pepe's in Silver Strand Beach or Rose's in Santa Barbara, California.

TAHINLI

An Armenian yeast bread, *tahinli* is traditionally made and served at annual church bazaars and other festive occasions that bring people of Armenian descent together. Before baking, portions of dough are rolled out and spread with a mixture of sesame seed paste (called *tahina or tahina)* and sugar. Then in a two-person operation, the dough is rolled up like a jelly roll, stretched to make it thinner, curled snaillike, allowed to rise, and finally flattened slightly, brushed with an egg mixture, topped with sesame seeds, and baked.

References: Ayto. *A Gourmet's Guide.* 1993; Nathan. *An American Folklife Cookbook.* 1984.

TAILGATE PARTY

What is a college or professional football game without a tailgate party? To tailgating enthusiasts, there is only one answer to this question: the two activities go together. Tailgate parties also take place at other sporting events, such as baseball and soccer games, or just on the spur of the moment at scenic outdoor sites.

As the name suggests, the tailgate of a station wagon, truck, van, or the trunk of a car is the "table" for foods that are served, or the party table might be inside a motor home driven to the event just for that purpose. No particular foods are required to tailgate, and those who plan such parties include their favorite picnic specialties, such as hamburgers, hot dogs, kabobs, and steaks that can be grilled, pasta or potato salad, chips, and beverages. Enjoying food and beverages in a festive atmosphere is what tailgating is all about. Many tailgaters circulate among other enthusiasts. To increase the fun, they bring along musical instruments and good luck charms to boost their favorite team once the game begins.

TAMALES

The tamale is one of Mexico's oldest dishes and one that appears at all of the major Mexican fiestas. From pre-Hispanic days, indigenous peoples have used corn in many ways, and one of the most popular uses has been in the tamale. Dried corn was ground into masa and then flavored with sesame or avocado oil. After the Spanish brought pigs to the continent, lard was used to lighten the mixture. To this masa was added any sort of fillings such as shrimp, fresh corn, coconut, chicken, pork, or beef. The mixture was wrapped in a corn husk, tied off, and finally steam cooked.

In some households in Mexico and in parts of the United States with large Mexican communities, tamales are still prepared in a labor-intensive manner. Since great quantities of this favorite food are eaten at fiesta time, a tamale maker in each household must rise very early to start the process. In many cases, a grandmother or elderly aunt who has "a way with the masa" plus another younger family member assume the responsibility of cooking for an extended family, and when the tamales are ready, relatives stop by to pick up their house's allotment.

In general, though, the production of tamales has moved from the home to a favorite restaurant or other commercial outlet. Ybarras in Brownsville, Texas, has a reputation in that region as one of the finest tamale makers in the world. Their busiest time is the Christmas season when virtually every Mexican family will eat tamales as part of the holiday celebration. The usual time of feasting is midnight, Christmas Eve. On that day Ybarras sells about 1,000 dozen tamales.

TAPAS

Beginning in the 1980s and early 1990s, tapas launched a new eating trend in some American cities. A Spanish term that may have been coined about a century ago, *tapas* refers to a first course in Spain and to appetizers in North America. Apparently,

the Spanish custom of serving tapas began when bartenders put a slice of ham or sausage on top of the glasses of their customers' drinks (usually sherry), creating a kind of top or cover, hence tapas, which literally means "to cover."

Across the United States, Spanish restaurants serve little plates of tapas, and these hors d'oeuvres have become favorites with those who have taken up the habit of grazing or noshing for an evening meal. While tapas are certainly a Spanish dish, they have become so popular that restaurant-goers are finding dozens of hot and cold versions of these tempting tidbits. *Tapas* now is almost a generic term, encompassing a range of appetizer-sized foods, mixing and matching Asian, Mexican, Mediterranean, and Caribbean dishes. Nevertheless, tapas in the Spanish style include such morsels as small portions of mussels in a vinaigrette sauce, puff pastries filled with meat, shrimp in garlic sauce, roasted eggplant, fresh sardines, fried calamari, red beans with snails, stuffed squid, and even mini samplings of main courses. Whether tapas are "authentic" Spanish dishes or a generic blend, they allow people to sample—put together a meal from a number of different foods—and yet eat what appears to be a light meal, although with all the many dishes, the final result can be as much food (or more) as in a regular full-course meal.

See also: APPETIZERS; GRAZING; SARDINES.

TASTE OF . . . FESTIVALS

Taste of Chicago, Taste of Denver, Taste of Orange County, Taste of Wisconsin—festivals celebrating the foods of a city, county, or state—are traditional throughout the United States during the summer and early fall seasons. Many of these festivals are annual three-day to weeklong events featuring musical entertainment, games, craft shows, and other activities along with food booths offering a whole gamut of foodstuffs from the simple to the esoteric. Taste of Orange County in southern California, for example, is a yearly event that features foods from local or nearby eating establishments: a Knotts Berry Farm booth serves its famous boysenberry pie and chicken and dumplings. Mexican-style food such as chili rellenos, quesadillas, chimichangas, burritos, and tacos are part of the menu at other stands. Still others serve traditional Lebanese dishes such as stuffed grape leaves and *shawarma*, barbecued lamb on pita bread. Chinese and Thai foods as well as treats from India (such red-hot tidbits as savory tandoori chicken and samosa—spicy pastry triangles) are served at other street booths.

Some annual taste festivals are known by other names, such as the Annual Media Food Festival and Arts Fair that has been held each September since 1981 in Philadelphia. The event mixes flavors, music, and art in the city's historic downtown shopping district. It always includes a variety of foods to sample: Russian, Ukrainian, Polish, French, German, Italian, French, Asian, and traditional American. **See also:** AMERICAN FOLKLIFE FESTIVAL; AMISH FOOD FESTIVALS; ATLANTIC ANTIC; DANISH DAYS; DYNGUS DAY; ETHNIC FOOD TRADITIONS; FEAST OF SAN GENNARO; FIESTA FILIPINIANA; NATIVE AMERICAN FEASTS; NINTH AVENUE FOOD FESTIVAL; PORTUGUESE HOLY SPIRIT FESTIVAL; SOUTHERN FOOD FESTIVALS; UKRANIAN FESTIVALS.

TASTE PREFERENCES, GENDER-RELATED

Studies and surveys by food marketing experts and psychologists show that there are differences in the taste preferences of American men and women, and these differences appear to be more closely related to social customs than to biological factors. For example, psychologists have found that many men believe they should be "hearty eaters"; therefore, they expect large portions and may insist on meat and potatoes and refuse a lighter fare such as a chicken or fish dinner. Some studies have found that men are much more likely than women to be "primal" about meat, consuming at least 8 percent more beef, pork,

venison, and hearty soups than women do. Some men also believe that it is "effeminate" to order fruits for dessert when eating out and instead will insist on large cuts of cake or pie. Women appear to gravitate to "light" foods not so much because of low caloric content but because these foods are considered "ladylike." Just as gender roles for men and women are changing and becoming less rigid, tastes are also changing, and researchers have found that differences between male and female tastes in food and beverages have become less pronounced, particularly among the more educated in the population.

TEMPURA

Tempura is a style of cooking brought to North America by the Japanese. A light pancakelike batter is used to coat raw vegetables and small pieces of meat, chicken, or fish that are cooked in hot oil. The light, golden-brown food is piled onto a plate or placed in a basket for serving at a table, where diners dip the tempura into an accompanying soy-based sauce. This style of eating has proven to be popular as more and more people have been frequenting Japanese restaurants and sushi bars. In fact, tempura, sushi, and sake have become part of a new way of eating for many westerners.

TEQUILA

Tequila, a traditional alcoholic drink of Mexico, is made from the fermented pulp and double distilled sap of the Blue Agave, one of more than 300 species of the agave plant, which is also called the mescal or century plant. (This plant was erroneously named the century plant because it was believed that it would only bloom after 100 years, but the plant usually only survives until it is about 30 or 40 years old.)

Agave also is used to make an alcoholic drink known to Native Americans and Mexicans as maguey, mexca, or mescal and to make pulque—Mexico's national drink. Mescal and pulque are heavier in flavor than tequila, but are basically the same drink made from the distilled sap taken from roots, leaves, and stalks of the agave.

A common ritual associated with drinking mescal or tequila is swallowing the worm at the bottom of the bottle. The white maguey (or agave) worm, which bores into the agave plant, is actually the larva of a specific butterfly *(Aegiale hesperiaris)* and commercial distillers place one in each bottle of mescal. In the United States, mescal or tequila drinkers make a show of eating or gulping the worm. In Mexican tradition, the person who finishes the last of the mescal in a bottle gets the worm, and swallowing it is supposed to bring good luck!

See also: MARGARITA.

References: Mariani. *The Dictionary of American Food and Drink.* 1993, 1994; Sokolov. *Insects, Worms, and Other Tidbits.* 1989; Trager. *Foodbook.* 1970.

THANKSGIVING DAY DINNER

Thanksgiving celebrations, which are usually associated with a harvest, have taken place in almost every part of the world. In the United States, Thanksgiving Day has been celebrated since 1621 when the Plymouth colonists offered prayerful thanks for a successful harvest. A national Thanksgiving Day holiday was proclaimed by President George Washington in 1789, and in 1863 President Abraham Lincoln established the last Thursday in November as the date for the annual Thanksgiving holiday. In Canada, a day of thanksgiving has been celebrated since 1879, and after World War I it was combined with Armistice Day. Since 1957, the second Monday in October has been celebrated as the Canadian Thanksgiving Day.

Feasting is a part of most Thanksgiving celebrations, and in the United States an estimated 45 million turkeys are prepared annually for the Thanksgiving Day holiday. About 94 percent of Americans prepare and serve turkey at home, and most people stick to a traditional menu for the main meal: turkey with cranberry sauce, mashed white potatoes with giblet gravy, candied sweet potatoes topped with marshmallows, a cooked green vegetable dish, relishes, and pumpkin pie with whipped cream for dessert. Yet, there are also many variations on the way the traditional turkey is prepared. In Italian tradition, for example, the turkey may be flavored with garlic, rosemary, and pancetta and basted with wine and served with gnocchi—dumplings made from mashed potatoes, eggs, and Parmesan cheese that are shaped like macaroni shells and served with a brown gravy or tomato-based sauce. A Puerto Rican–style turkey may be stuffed with *picadillo,* a mixture of ground beef, raisins, olives, and *sofrito,* a cooked tomato sauce with peppers and onions. Cuban-style turkey is marinated overnight in lime or sour orange juice (from a green-orange fruit that tastes like lime) and seasoned with garlic, cumin, oregano, salt, and pepper. A Cajun-style dressing may be made with jalapeño corn bread. One fastfood chain even suggests stuffing birds with prepared hamburgers—minus the pickles and other condiments! Some families cook pheasant or duck along with their turkey. Others prepare a red meat or ham.

In some households, families do not prepare a meal but instead order a "packaged" Thanksgiving dinner from a gourmet grocery store, supermarket, or hotel caterer. In Seattle, for example, the Westin Hotel prepared 250 Thanksgiving turkeys for its 1994 "Reserve-a-Bird" take-out program, which included all the side dishes associated with the traditional feast.

Whether prepared in a hotel or in another type restaurant, a typical Thanksgiving package for six people usually includes a 13- to 14-pound whole roasted turkey with giblet gravy, cranberry-orange walnut relish, sage dressing, sweet potatoes, vegetable side dishes, dinner rolls, perhaps a gelatin mold or tossed green salad, a loaf of sweet bread, and a choice of pumpkin, apple, or mincemeat pie. A bottle of wine also may be included.

The Thanksgiving holiday is also a time when religious and civic groups, social service organizations, and businesses feed the homeless and needy. The traditional dinner is served in shelters, missions, cafes, schools, and other public places. Thousands of turkeys and other foods for a Thanksgiving meal are given away to needy families.

THANKSGIVING EVE

On the Wednesday before Thanksgiving, a drinking ritual takes place in many major U.S. cities and suburbs. Each year thousands of workers leave their jobs early and college students arrive home to celebrate the arrival of a four-day holiday weekend. Many go to nightclubs and taverns to celebrate and toast the night before Thanksgiving, a ritual that in recent years has started to rival the customary toasting and drinking on St. Patrick's Day. Some taverns and restaurants serve special dishes to attract patrons. The ritual also has brought major problems in some communities—alcoholic-related traffic accidents, serious injuries, and deaths.

TOFU

This protein food is certainly not consumed as routinely in North America as it is in Japan, China, and other Asian countries (where it is an essential part of the diet for more than 1 billion people), but it is a popular food for many American vegetarians and others who simply like its versatility. Often called the "meat of the fields," tofu is made from soybeans that are washed, soaked, cooked, and pureed in a blender. The puree is strained to produce soy milk, which is coagulated with magnesium chloride, calcium chloride, Epsom salts, lemon juice, or vinegar, although the latter two coagulants are not used in traditionally made tofu.

The curds that are formed during the coagulation process are usually pressed into a block and stored in cold water. The resultant soy bean "cheese" can be transformed into hundreds of dishes. In fact, the authors of *The Book of Tofu* wax poetic about its endless possibilities: "Pierced

with a skewer, it sizzles and broils above a bed of live coals; placed in a bubbling, earthenware pot over an open fire, it snuggles down next to the mushrooms and makes friends; deep-fried in crackling oil, it emerges crisp and handsome in robes of golden brown; frozen all night in the snow under vast mountain skies, it emerges glistening with frost and utterly changed."

In Canada, the United States, and Mexico, tofu shops and soy dairies supply most of the tofu that consumers purchase for use in dishes prepared at home, ranging from tofu and brown rice casseroles to tofu cream pie. A great many Americans also eat traditional tofu dishes made and served at Japanese, Chinese, and other Asian restaurants.

Reference: Shurtleff and Aoyagi. *The Book of Tofu*. 1979.

TOMATO CELEBRATIONS

Boston has held an annual tomato festival since the mid-1980s, celebrating and promoting Massachusetts' second-largest crop. One of the main events of the August festival is a competition to find the state's best tomato. Judges search for a firm but tender tomato that is flavorful, which means it has to be ripened on the vine.

Although the tomato is botanically a fruit, it is used like a vegetable and was officially declared such by the U.S. Supreme Court in an 1893 decision settling a tariff dispute. Today, tomatoes are the main ingredient in numerous sauces, soups, stews, salads, and condiments, and cooks regularly find new ways to use tomatoes.

Prior to the mid-1800s, the tomato was not widely available as a commercial product in North America. Many people in the United States considered the tomato too acidic to eat, and some clung to a centuries-old European belief that the tomato was poisonous. Initially when tomatoes were used, they were cooked a long time to remove the "poison." In fact, according to food historian Raymond Sokolov, a New Jersey man was declared a hero in 1820 because he ate a tomato in public, hence encouraging more widespread acceptance of the vegetable. The tomato is not only accepted today but is one of the most popular vegetables in the American diet. It is also the number one plant grown in backyard gardens and is part of numerous traditional dishes served in North America.

References: Margen et al. *The Wellness Encyclopedia of Food and Nutrition.* 1992; Sokolov. *Why We Eat What We Eat.* 1991.

TRAIL MIX

Developed as a high-energy resource for hikers and campers who have limited space for carrying food, trail mix has now found its way into children's lunch boxes and onto coffee tables. The recipes for trail mix vary according to taste, but typically ingredients include sunflower seeds (raw or toasted), raisins, roasted soy beans, date pieces, almonds, and other nuts. The point is to include readily digestible energy sources that include plenty of protein and complex sugars. Parents have tried to make trail mix and granola-based snacks more available to their children in an attempt to wean them from the more sugary treats generally consumed by children as snacks.

See also: CAMP/TRAIL FOOD.

TRUCK STOP FOOD

There is a tradition in America that holds: whenever you see a great many trucks parked at a roadside restaurant, the food at that place must be good. It may be useful to debunk this myth with the important observation that more often than not, the only place truckers will stop is where they have room to park. Nevertheless, in the glory years of over-the-road hauling, favorite cafes became regular stops on the route because of the hospitality of the staff, and undoubtedly there were (and are) some good cooks "slinging hash" at truck stops.

Often open for 24 hours a day, 365 days each year, the truck stop cafe still tries to serve the kinds of foods that appeal to its customer base. Because of the mandatory time restrictions on truck drivers, break times or sleeping periods are often arranged around what truckers have determined are the best places to eat, information that is shared by CB radio within the trucking community. Some truck stops have a separate dining area for truckers with booths equipped with telephone jacks so that truckers can make business and personal calls.

Besides corned beef hash (with an egg on top if you like), other country-flavored, comfort fare common on these menus includes: biscuits and gravy, grits, American fries, french fries, huevos rancheros, steak and eggs, chicken-fried steak, Salisbury steak, patty melts, hamburgers, fried chicken, meat loaf, bacon-lettuce-and-tomato (BLT) sandwiches, egg salad sandwiches, tuna sandwiches, and chef's specials for the holidays. Many truckers pick up fastfood—anything that can be purchased quickly and taken into the truck to eat while driving. This cuts down on wasted time and is usually an inexpensive way to appease hunger.

See also: CORNED BEEF HASH; GRITS; HAMBURGERS; HUEVOS RANCHEROS; MEAT LOAF; SANDWICHES.

TURTLE SOUP

Residents and visitors to Louisiana's bayou country and other regions along the Gulf of Mexico may routinely eat turtle soup, and a turtle or terrapin soup is commonly served in fine restaurants along Atlantic coastal regions of the United States. Maryland, for example, is known for its terrapin soup. In an English tradition that established turtle soup as a delicacy about the the mid-1700s, many Canadians also enjoy turtle soup or turtle meat.

This food is no longer as popular as it once was in American colonial times and later periods, when the terrapin, or diamondback turtle as it was known, proliferated along the salt marshes of the Atlantic Coast. Turtle fat and other parts of the turtle were not only used in soup, but they also were the basis for stews, and the meat

was frequently barbecued. The high
demand for terrapin and other turtles
greatly diminished the populations. In
some years, 90,000 pounds of terrapin were
taken from the Chesapeake Bay area alone,
according to food historian James Trager.
By the early 1900s, the terrapin as well as
other species were almost extinct, so con-
servationists encouraged turtle farming—
raising turtles specifically for commercial
use. Although turtles are not widely marketed in North America, they are available
in the coastal regions where they are raised.

See also: SOUP SUPPERS.

References: Fussell. *I Hear America Cooking.*
1986; Trager. *Foodbook.* 1970.

UKRAINIAN FESTIVALS

Many of the early settlers in the Canadian provinces of Manitoba and Saskatchewan came from the Ukraine in the late 1800s and early 1900s. They cleared and farmed the land in this wheat-growing area, which was similar to the homeland where Ukrainians for generations had been making bread and developing the process into an art form. As would be expected, a Ukrainian festival includes bread making as well as preparing and serving other traditional foods. One of the breads served is *paska*, which is the traditional Ukrainian Easter bread. Another is a large wedding bread called *korway* or *korovai*, which is decorated with dough ornaments and greenery. At one time, the wedding bread had to be prepared by seven happily married young women who, according to custom, each brought flour, water, eggs, and butter from different sources in order to assure good fortune for the wedding couple. While that tradition has faded, others have not. Making *varenyky*, a pasta that is also called *pyrohy* (pierogi), is a must. These pasta pillows may be filled with mashed potatoes and cheese, ground meat, mushrooms, or sauerkraut and served with sautéed onions and sausage, or they may be filled with some type of fruit and garnished with sour cream. However they are made, they are avidly consumed in *varenyky*-eating contests. In addition, those who attend a Ukrainian festival will likely taste such traditional foods as stuffed cabbage or perhaps a sauerkraut and sparerib soup.

See also: EASTER.

References: Borghese. *Food from Harvest Festivals and Folk Fairs.* 1977; Clayton. *Cooking across America.* 1993.

VALENTINE'S DAY

Saint Valentine's Day, or simply Valentine's Day, was named for a Christian martyr who was beheaded, according to some historical accounts. Historians have not determined which saint out of at least half a dozen Valentines inspired the feast day celebrated on 14 February, and there is no certainty about how or why the day became associated with exchanging tokens of love and affection. There is little doubt, however, that Valentine's Day has been celebrated for centuries with the tradition of sending "sweets to a sweet." Candy is one of the most popular gifts on this holiday.

The early pilgrims brought with them to North America the European tradition of sending their betrothed confections, and the custom spread as the American colonists began to make homemade candy with messages of love scratched on the surface. By the early 1900s, candy makers were preparing hard candies shaped like hearts and imprinted with words of love. Today, in the United States, Valentine's candy sales total about $655 million annually, and almost two-thirds of all adults give everything from fancy, heart-shaped boxes of chocolates to bags of lollipops as tokens of affection. Not only lovers exchange boxes of candy; schoolchildren also like to give candy as gifts. Cherry-flavored lollipops shaped like hearts; red, white, and pink jelly beans; red-hot hearts; cinnamon jelly hearts; and so-called conversation hearts with short messages on them such as "Be mine" are popular with children.

Along with sharing sweet gifts, adult couples often celebrate Valentine's Day by dining out. In the restaurant business, this day rivals Mother's Day as the busiest day of the year. Some businesses promote going beyond the traditional "couples day" to a more inclusive Valentine's Day celebration, as is the case at the Pinehill Bed and Breakfast in Oregon, Illinois, where the proprietor Sharon Burdick sets aside the whole month of February to celebrate all kinds of loving relationships. Each year, through the entire month of February, Burdick hosts Chocolate Teas, offering a chocolate buffet of treats ranging from chocolate cheesecake to homemade fudge, hot cocoa, and a selection of herbal teas. There is even a checkerboard set up with Hershey's chocolate kisses. Overnight guests are inundated with chocolate treats, from champagne glasses filled with chocolate in their rooms to breakfast treats such as banana and chocolate chip muffins.

See also: CHOCOLATE CANDY; LOLLIPOPS.
References: *Academic American Encyclopedia.* 1994; Carroll. "A Fantasy for Lovers." 1993; *Southern Heritage* editors. *The Southern Heritage Celebrations Cookbook.* 1984.

VEGETARIAN EATING

While not always based on tradition or ritualistic practices, vegetarians follow dietary practices that have a long history. Usually they maintain a diet devoid of animal products, although there are many degrees of commitment to this practice. Some people who call themselves vegetarians consume dairy products and eggs and fit the category of lacto-ovo vegetarians. Others go so far as to shun any products that are of animal origin, including honey and leather. These are the vegans.

About 7 percent of the U.S. population consider themselves vegetarians, according to a Gallup survey conducted for the National Restaurant Association in 1994. The reasons for choosing a vegetarian life-style are many and varied. Typically, religion played a major role in setting the dietary guidelines of some followers. The Seventh-Day Adventists are one group in Western civilization that condemns the consumption of flesh foods. Others may avoid eating animals out of a moral or ethical creed that is more personal and humanist in origin: animals are fellow living creatures occupying space on this earth with a right to thrive equal to that of humans. The Gallup survey, however, showed that concern for animals prompted only 15 percent of U.S. vegetarians to turn to a vegetarian diet. Health, in fact, is a major reason people become vegetarians. Many have decided that meat is a poison to the digestive tract since the human body was not designed to eliminate decaying animals rapidly enough to prevent the creation of degenerative diseases such as cancer, arthritis, and heart disease.

To meet the needs of those on vegetarian diets, an increasing number of food markets and restaurants have been established since the 1960s and 1970s. The types of entrees and other dishes served include vegetarian patties, eggplant lasagna, pasta primavera made with vegetables and topped with a dairy-free sauce, vegetable tofu curry, bean burritos, and lentil loaf. The variety of dishes seemingly is endless, since the foods served depend on the imagination of the vegetarian cook.

Many vegetarian dishes stem from India, and Indian restaurants in North America serve such entrees as spicy chole (chick peas) and *pakoras,* fritters consisting of a mixture of spinach, potato, and onion in a chick pea batter. Lentil and rice dishes, curried vegetables, chutneys, and yogurt are other traditional vegetarian foods served at Indian restaurants.

See also: BEAN DISHES; DELI FOODS; DIWALI; EATING TRENDS; FOOD TABOOS; GAZPACHO; HEALTH/NATURAL FOOD RESTAURANTS; PITA BREAD; TOFU.

VENDING MACHINES

One of the recent trends in American eating customs is buying and consuming food from vending machines. Consumers are spending approximately $28 billion annually for vended foods and beverages, and in response to consumer demands, vending machine companies using new technology have been able to increase the types of food offered from their machines (located in manufacturing companies, shopping centers, airports, rail and bus stations, motels and hotels, and many other public places). Rather than just get an item from a "snack machine," as it was once called, consumers can now get much more from a mechanical vendor. Coffee, cappuccino, sparkling mineral water, vegetarian burgers, gourmet pizzas, fresh fruit, salads, yogurt, and bagels with cream cheese are just a few of the items that vending machines offer today. Not only are single items available, but full meals—everything from frozen, low-fat meals to fastfood-style combination meals—may also be purchased in this fashion. In partnerships with equipment manufacturers and national food processors, companies such as Canteen Corporation—the world's leading provider of vending services—offer popular brand-name entrees, and new vending machines come complete with scanner microwaves that "read" the bar code on the box for appropriate cooking times and temperatures. With more than 4 million machines located throughout the United States (and that number growing annually), vending machine foods will no doubt be part of the North American eating style for decades ahead.

See also: FASTFOOD; MICROWAVE COOKING; SNACK FOODS.

VICHYSSOISE

Because of its name, this cold leek and potato soup is often thought to be of French origin, but it actually was invented by a French chef working at the Ritz-Carlton hotel in New York City. The chef, Louis Diat, named the soup after a spa near his home in France. It is made by blending leaks and potatoes with cream and herbs. The smooth liquid must be chilled in the refrigerator for at least one hour before serving.

Although vichyssoise is not common fare among most Americans, it is often on the menu at fine restaurants and is sometimes served at elegant parties. Still, the soup is a surprise to many who taste vichyssoise for the first time. Expecting their soup to be hot, they are likely to complain to the chef, but once reassured about the temperature of the soup, most diners do enjoy the refreshing taste.

See also: POTATOES; SOUP SUPPERS.

VIDALIA ONION FESTIVAL

Vidalia onions are grown in the town of Vidalia, Georgia, and they are the state's oficial vegetable. Apparently, the soil in the Vidalia area is the only type that produces these onions; attempts to grow them elsewhere have resulted in a bitter-tasting variety. Consequently, onions from Vidalia are legally the only kind that can carry that name, a fact that has been celebrated since 1984 with the Vidalia Onion Festival. Each May this festival draws thousands of visitors, who, of course, taste the many dishes made with Vidalia onions that are offered at food booths.

References: Hill. *Festivals U.S.A.* 1988; Thompson and Carlson. *Holidays, Festivals, and Celebrations of the World Dictionary.* 1994.

WASSAIL AND WASSAIL BOWL

Wassail, a warm fruit cider (usually apple), was a customary drink at feasts in early England, and it is a traditional part of present-day madrigal dinners held during the Christmas season in North America. The term *wassail* is most likely a contraction of the Old English *woes haeil,* meaning "be healthy." A wassail bowl, often laced with brandy, ale, or sherry, also is featured at numerous Christmas, New Year's, and Epiphany celebrations. The drink is used to toast a holiday, a practice based on a custom that was common throughout England—going to the orchard at harvesttime with a jug of cider to toast the bounty of the fruit trees and to sprinkle some of the trees with cider for luck. In early December, a three-day Wassail Celebration in Woodstock, New York, includes not only the traditional wassail bowl but also a fancy ball and horse-and-carriage parade.

See also: DRINKING TOASTS; HOT TODDY; MADRIGAL DINNER.

Reference: Schulz. *Celebrating America.* 1994.

WATERMELON FESTIVALS

Slurping and spitting would hardly be acceptable at a dinner party, but the behavior is expected—and thoroughly enjoyed—at traditional seed-spitting contests that are part of watermelon festivals held during July and August in many small towns across the United States. President Bill Clinton's hometown of Hope, Arkansas, is known as the Watermelon Capital and hosts one of the most famous watermelon festivals in the nation. Thousands of tourists, many of which participated long before Hope's native son became president, attend the event each August.

In Hope and towns such as Pageland, South Carolina, where an annual watermelon festival has been held for about five decades, a seed-spitting contest is a festival highlight. Participants get large wedges of juicy watermelon, preferably with as many seeds as possible; chomp and slurp off a hunk of the fruit; then begin to spit the seeds as fast and as accurately as they can. The seeds have to land in a bucket placed a determined distance from the contestant. It takes skill. A contestant has to maneuver the tongue, lips, and teeth just right in order to make the seeds hit the mark.

As with other food festivals, there is an eating contest to determine who can devour the most watermelon, and a lot of the featured fruit is served to townspeople and visitors.

In some parts of the United States, it is traditional for some individuals to make watermelon rind preserves at festival time, although not necessarily during the festivities themselves. The watermelon rind is first cubed, soaked in lime water, drained, rinsed, soaked in plain water, and boiled to assure crispness. Then the rind is boiled in a syrup made of lemon slices, water, sugar, and perhaps some gingerroot. Sometimes these preserves become part of the ingredients used to make fruitcakes later in the year.

Making a watermelon fruit basket is also a customary activity during watermelon harvest time. The watermelon is cut and carved to resemble a basket and the inside scooped out so that it can be filled with watermelon, honeydew, and cantaloupe balls as well as whole berries or cubes of other fruits in season. A watermelon basket is also a common buffet table item at other summer events.

WEDDING CAKE

See WEDDING FOODS.

WEDDING FOODS

For thousands of years, people have presented and consumed sacred foods and beverages to highlight, and in some cases to actualize, the wedding ceremony. Depending on the cultural background of participants, wedding ceremonies today also may require eating and drinking rituals that stem from the past. At traditional Jewish weddings, for example, dairy products and meats would not be served at the same time because of Jewish dietary laws, but modern North American weddings vary widely in terms of the actual ceremony and the reception where food and beverage items are served to guests.

At some receptions, guests may nibble on mints and nuts washed down with a fruit punch, a common occurrence in earlier decades, or they may be treated to several tables of buffet foods with one featuring hors d'oeuvres, another fruits and vegetables, another salads, and still another with fish, poultry, beef, and ham. Formal wedding sit-down dinners, whether catered, prepared, and served in a private home or in a restaurant, are common as well.

The ritual of preparing and eating a cake is one of the most important parts of a wedding. It is a rite that most likely stems from the Roman practice of creating a special cake *(confarreatio)* that was crumbled over the bride's head to wish her great bounty—in material goods and especially numbers of children—during the marriage.

Different cultures have made and consumed different types of cake. It was once common for the Iroquois bride to bake a cake made of cornmeal to be given to her new husband during the ceremony. A traditional wedding cake among the Pennsylvania Dutch called *schwenkfelder* is flavored with saffron, an expensive spice that German immigrants brought with them to the United States.

Commercial bakers prepare the majority of wedding cakes in North America today, and baking and decorating these cakes is a centuries-old European art. Traditionally, the cakes have been decorated with sugary flowers cascading down multiple tiers. Some present-day bakers use real flowers and ribbons. Almost everyone who marries in North America today will eat a piece of wedding cake as an adjunct to the festivities. In accordance with custom, superstition, and ritual, seldom does the bride or groom taste the cake until the appropriate time.

Cutting the cake is also an integral part of the wedding reception, which usually follows the ceremony. At the designated time, the top tier of a multilayered cake is removed and saved for storage in a freezer, preserving it for the first anniversary celebration, which marks the end of the honeymoon. Modern tradition calls for capturing the first cut of the cake in a photograph or video, with the hands of the newly married couple together on the ceremonial cake knife. It is also a tradition for the new bride and groom to feed each other the first bite of cake. It is, perhaps, a good indicator of

Bride and groom, Elizabeth Taylor and Conrad Hilton, Jr., cut a slice from their five-tiered wedding cake in 1950, performing a centuries-old tradition.

the prospects for the marriage as the guests have an opportunity to observe whether or not the cake is delicately placed on the tongue or unceremoniously shoved into the mouth and/or nostrils.

WELSH RAREBIT

In the early days of America, this dish was referred to as Welsh Rabbit perhaps in humor or as a way to glamorize a simple meal (rather like "Cape Cod turkey" being used as a droll designation for codfish). Welsh Rarebit, however, is a traditional Welsh snack or light meal consisting of a rich cheese sauce, usually served over toast. The sauce is made with a sharp Cheddar cheese that is grated and cooked slowly with butter, Worcestershire sauce, dry mustard, flour, salt and pepper, and a small portion of beer. Some recipes also call for an egg yolk and perhaps a dash of hot sauce. Welsh or not, people who enjoy this light course usually serve it for brunch or a quick supper.

WHISKEY DRINKING

Fermented drinks have been produced since long before recorded history, and it is no surprise that, since colonial times, North Americans have indulged in alcoholic beverages made from fermented fruits, vegetables, and grains (ranging from apples, berries, and grapes to potatoes, turnips, corn, barley, and rye).

When settlers moved to the Kentucky and Tennessee frontier, they used much of the corn and rye they grew to make whiskey, but this was a fairly crude forerunner of the first bourbon whiskey that was developed in Kentucky during the late 1700s or early 1800s. Several Kentuckians have been given credit for the feat, but some historians declare that the Reverend Elijah Craig developed the bourbon whiskey formula that involved mashing chopped kernels of corn and mixing them with limestone water and rye meal, heating and cooling the mash, adding barley malt

and then allowing the mixture to ferment (the basic method that has survived to this day, although modern distillers now use high-tech, sanitary equipment rather than a backyard still to produce their bourbon).

Today, bourbon is considered to be the all-American whiskey and is quite distinct from another popular drink, Scotch whisky (spelled without the "e") distilled from barley. Scotch lovers are likely to drink their whisky straight, although some mix the liquor with water, while bourbon and water over ice is a traditional way to serve bourbon whiskey. Bourbon is the main ingredient in a popular Kentucky drink— the mint julep.

See also: MINT JULEP; MOONSHINE WHISKEY.
References: Carson. *The Social History of Bourbon*. 1963; Simon and Howe. *Dictionary of Gastronomy*. 1970.

WHITE LIGHTNING

See MOONSHINE WHISKEY.

WILD EDIBLES

While meticulous gardeners and lawn-care folks may abhor dandelions and consider them pesky weeds, they are among the most common wild plants that are routinely gathered, prepared, and served as food every spring. Dandelion flowers may be dipped in a flour and egg batter and then fried, while the leaves are often used in salad or cooked like spinach or other greens. Wild watercress, leaks, onions, chives, various mint leaves, and even violets are a few of the other wild plants that are edible.

Those who know how to gather wild edibles caution that people should never harvest and eat wild plants unless they learn which ones are safe, for some are poisonous and deadly. The wild carrot is one plant that looks like the regular garden variety but in the wild it is poisonous hemlock. Some plants are edible at certain times and poisonous at others. Pokeweed is an example of such a plant. The young

shoots that appear in early spring are edible, and people have been gathering and eating these plants for countless seasons, but after the shoots turn red, they are poisonous, and the mature stalks, seeds, and roots of pokeweed are also dangerous.
See also: MUSHROOM HARVESTS AND FESTIVALS; POKEWEED SALAD.

WILD RICING

Harvesting wild rice is an ancient practice passed down over many generations among the Chippewa of Minnesota. At the end of every summer, Chippewa men in times past poled canoes through the rice beds (which are really beds of wild grasses that grow along the shorelines of lakes and streams), while the women used sticks to knock the ripe rice into the canoes. Wild rice is still harvested "by hand" each year, and this is the only legal method for harvesting wild rice that grows naturally in Minnesota. Various commercial growers, however, plant, harvest, and process so-called wild rice with machines.

In recent years, "outsiders"—tourists—have been able to try their hand at wild ricing on the White Earth Reservation, 200 miles northwest of Minneapolis. This ritual harvest is strenuous work and most uninitiated "rice knockers" find that flailing the rice sticks and whacking the grass to make the grains fall into the canoe takes a lot of skill and stamina.

To celebrate the wild rice crop, a staple food for those living on the reservations, a wild rice festival is held annually in mid-September in Nayatahwaush, a small town near the White Earth Reservation.

WINE BARS

Long popular in Europe, wine bars became an "in thing" in the United States during the 1980s. Because restaurants are always looking for new ways to raise the check total, they began installing wine dispensers and special bars that served a variety of fine wines by the glass. This has enabled customers to sample several wines or to have a glass or two of one better wine rather than buying a whole bottle (a logical choice if there are not enough guests in a party to justify such a purchase).

Wine, especially reds, will oxidize and become unpalatable after being opened for more than a few hours. Wine bars rectify this by installing nitrogen displacement dispensers that are capable of holding from one to dozens of different wines. Through a system of surgical tubing, rubber corks, and valves, the wine is pushed out of the bottle and through a spigot under the force of pressurized nitrogen gas. The gas takes the place of any oxygen, and, since it is inert, the wine can remain fresh for weeks if need be.

Some stand-alone wine bars have opened throughout the United States as alternative establishments to smoke-filled, full-service liquor bars. As wine drinking has increased at the expense of hard liquor, these businesses have proven successful.
See also: WINE FESTIVALS; WINE TASTING.

WINE COOLER

Wine with club soda and a shot of 7-Up poured over ice was the original wine "cooler," which was thought to have originated in California during the early 1980s. This drink—also called a wine spritzer—has remained popular, especially on hot days, in bars throughout the United States for many years. Today, when anyone orders a spritzer or a cooler in a tavern, the bartender is likely to point to an array of bottles and ask, "What flavor?" because commercial bottlers have tapped into the demand for sweet, fruity, carbonated alcoholic drinks, which seems to stem from the habit most people develop as youngsters: drinking sweet, syrupy, carbonated soda pop. During the 1990s, there has been a vast increase in sales of such drinks as "peach cooler" and "strawberry mist."

WINE FESTIVALS

With at least 1,700 different wineries in North America producing white, red, blush, sparkling, and dessert wines, it is not surprising that wine events, among them wine festivals, competitions, and tastings, take place each month somewhere on the continent. Almost all states in the United States and provinces in Canada, especially Ontario and British Columbia, produce some type of grape used for wine making. Although Mexico makes some commercial wines, its grapes are used primarily for making brandy.

By far, most wine festivals are held in California where the vast majority of U.S. vineyards are located. New York State, however, is the home of the oldest wineries in the United States, and numerous wineries there and in such eastern states as New Jersey, Connecticut, and Pennsylvania regularly host wine events. Wherever they are held, wine celebrations include tastings and often tours of wineries or seminars about wine. Some wine events are held during the last week in February, which is American Wine Appreciation Week, established by the U.S. Congress to recognize the wine industry and its role in the U.S. economy as well as the traditional use of wine in family, religious, and other cultural ceremonies. Annual international wine festivals are held in various parts of North America throughout the year, and many wine festivals include fund-raising events to benefit the arts, public radio, colleges, and the like.
See also: WINE TASTING.
Reference: Gayot. *Guide to the Best Wineries of North America.* 1993.

WINE TASTING

In grape-growing states such as New York, Michigan, California, and Oregon and in Canadian provinces where there are numerous vineyards and wineries, wine tasting is a traditional summer activity that often includes a picnic lunch or a meal at a restaurant, cafe, or deli on the winery premises or nearby. In Sonoma County, California, for example, there are at least 130 wineries, half of which have picnic facilities. Some wineries feature cook-outs, serving barbecued ribs and chicken each summer weekend through Labor Day. Others offer special luncheons or sunset dinners. Frequently, events such as classic car shows and concerts are staged as additional activities for visitors to the wine country.

Many wineries in North America offer tours not only of their facilities but also of surrounding gardens, which make popular wedding sites. Wineries with adjoining restaurants may serve food and wine that represent the origin of the owners. German, Italian, and French wine festivals are common. In grape-growing regions, wine tasting is also a traditional activity at state fairs where wineries enter their current releases in competitions.

A wine-tasting party is a common way for a civic group or institution to raise funds, whether or not the event is in wine-making regions. Often a wine expert provides information about the featured wines. Such a party may include tasting a "vertical"—several vintages of the same wine—or wines from different regions.

Y

YAMBOREE

"It's a great festive show, where each one should go," according to a march song always played at the East Texas Yamboree in Gilmer. What is a yamboree? A celebration of the sweet potato or yam—a yellow or orange sugary vegetable that is baked and usually served dripping with butter. Foods at the annual yamboree include many baked goods made from sweet potatoes, especially sweet potato pie and sweet potato pone, a dish of grated sweet potatoes, sugar, spices, eggs, flour, and milk. Yam biscuits are popular, too, as is homemade yam ice cream. The sweet potato is also honored in such diverse communities as Benton, Kentucky; Ocilla, Georgia; and Darlington, South Carolina.
References: Hill. *Festivals U.S.A.* 1988; Linck and Roach. *Eats.* 1989.

YOGURT BARS

Frozen yogurt is a relatively new product in North America, developed to take advantage of the movement toward healthier food consumption. As an alternative to ice cream, frozen yogurt generally does have lower fat content, but it is still relatively high in sugar content. Nevertheless, many consumers say they feel "less guilty" eating yogurt than eating ice cream, thus the food has become very popular. Almost every mall has a frozen yogurt outlet. Some are set up as self-serve bars where the customer moves down a line, dispensing the frozen product into a cup, and sprinkling any or all of a wide array of nuts, jimmies, sparkles, and other "goodies" on top of their frozen confection. At the end of the line, an employee weighs the dish to determine the price. Many people enjoy the self-service aspect of the frozen yogurt bar, knowing that here, at least, they can really get it "their way." Sales of this sweet treat have increased by 2,900 percent since 1951 and have continued to triple each year.
Reference: Chalmers. *The Great Food Almanac.* 1994.

YOM KIPPUR

Known also as the Day of Atonement or the Day of Judgment, Yom Kippur is the holiest and most solemn day in the Jewish calendar and is marked by a 24-hour fast; not even water is taken. It is the last of the ten High Holy Days or Days of Penitence that begin with the New Year—Rosh Hashanah—usually in September or October. Beginning at sundown on Yom Kippur Eve, a service of repentance is held, and

Jews acknowledge transgressions and make atonement for such sins as pride, greed, vanity, and lust.

Originally, a sacrificial offering of animals was made in the Temple. Later, a goat, which symbolically carried the sins of the Jewish people, was driven into the desert (this goat became the basis for the term *scapegoat*, meaning an individual or group who bears blame for others). The animal sacrifices were abandoned in the early 1900s, but a chicken or other fowl is frequently killed before the Day of Atonement as an offering, and the bird's meat is eaten later to break the fast.

See also: FASTING.

under a roast (mutton or beef) on a trivet to absorb the juices of the meat. It has been made in Great Britain since the mid-1700s, and the practice of serving it with Sunday dinner came with British colonists migrating to North America. The most common method for making Yorkshire pudding today is pouring meat drippings into a baking pan; adding a batter of flour, eggs, milk, and additional meat juices; and baking it until golden brown.

References: Ayto. *A Gourmet's Guide.* 1993; Mariani. *The Dictionary of American Food and Drink.* 1993, 1994; Simon and Howe. *Dictionary of Gastronomy.* 1970.

YORKSHIRE PUDDING

A traditional British dish, Yorkshire pudding is a batter pudding originally baked

ZAKUSKI

At a formal Polish dinner, the *zakuska* or *zakuski* is a traditional introductory course of hors d'oeuvres presented as pleasingly as possible to whet the appetite. The practice probably stems from the days of the Russian tzars when the *zakuski* consisted of numerous dishes and bowls of food and bottles of vodka on a table. In Polish tradition, the *zakuski* may be served buffet-style or it may be arranged on platters and passed to diners at the table. Typically, it includes fish and seafoods such as anchovy fillets and smoked oysters, clams, mussels, salmon, or whitefish; cold meats and poultry; assorted cheeses; pickled mushrooms and onions; and breads such as pumpernickel and rye.

See also: APPETIZERS.

References: Davis. *The Potato Book*. 1973; Simon and Howe. *Dictionary of Gastronomy*. 1970.

ZUCCHINI BREAD

Small loaves of sweet zucchini bread wrapped in foil or plastic wrap are popular gifts during the Christmas holiday, and these breads often are sold at fund-raising bazaars and bake sales. This bread is also an essential part of an annual ritual in Harrisville, New Hampshire, where an International Zucchini Festival is held every summer. Not only is the familiar zucchini bread sold and consumed, but a great variety of other zucchini-based dishes also are eaten. The vegetable is fried, pickled, used as a base for spicy gazpacho, marinaded with pasta, cooked to make a jam or jelly, served in casseroles, and even used as a topping for granola or blended in ice cream. In most other parts of North America, however, grating zucchini to bake in bread is probably the most traditional use of this food, particularly if it is part of a holiday ritual.

APPENDIX

Eating and Drinking Traditions, Customs, and Rituals by Category

Eating and Drinking Places
Airport Dining/Drinking
Bed and Breakfast
Biker "Hangouts"
Bistro Dining
Bookstore Cafe or Deli
Brew Pubs
Cafes
Cafeteria Dining
Catering-Truck Foods
Coffee Houses
Convenience Store Foods
Cookie Bars/Shops
Cruise Ship Dining
Dining by Rail
Espresso Bars
Executive Dining
Firehouse Food
Food Courts
Food Fairs
Grocery Store and
    Supermarket Meals
Health/Natural Food
    Restaurants
Lemonade Stand
Meals-On-Wheels
Oyster Bars
Salad Bars
Soup Kitchen
Street Food
Taco Bars and Restaurants
Truck Stop Food
Vending Machines
Wine Bars
Yogurt Bars

Ethnic and National Foods,
Beverages, and Events
Agutuk
American Folklife Festival
Amish Food Festivals
Antipasto
Apple Pandowdy
Atlantic Antic
Bagels
Basque Boarding-House
    Dining

Bastille Day
Beltane Cakes
Challah
Chiles
Chinese Buffet
Chitterlings
Cioppino
Curry
Danish Days
Eintopf
Enchiladas
Feast of San Gennaro
Fiesta Filipiniana
Gazpacho
German Potato Salad
Glogg
Goulash
Greek Food Festivals
Green Corn Festivals
Gumbo
Huevos Rancheros
Irish Coffee
Jambalaya
Juneteenth
Kolaches
Kwanzaa
Las Posadas
Luau
Lunar New Year
Lutefisk
Margarita
Matzoh
Menudo
Mexican Fiestas
Mole
Moon Cakes
Native American Feasts
Navajo Fry Bread
Ninth Avenue Food Festival
Oktoberfest
Pasty
Persian New Year
Pesto
Pierogies
Piñata
Pita Bread
Pitcha

Poi
Polenta
Poor Soup
Portuguese Holy Spirit
    Festival
Posole
Potlatch
Purim Feast
Ramadan
Rivels
Saganaki
Saguaro Cactus Syrup
Saint Joseph's Day Feast
Saint Lucia Day
Saint Patrick's Day
Sake
Salsa
Sashimi
Sauerkraut
Scrapple
Seder
Shaker Foods
Shavout
Shish Kebab
Shoofly Pie
Shortbread
Smorgasbord
Sopaipillas
Soul Food
Spring Rolls
Stuffed Grape Leaves
Succot
Sunflower Festival
Sushi and Sushi Bars
Swedish Meatballs
Taco Bars and Restaurants
Tamales
Tapas
Taste of . . . Festivals
Tempura
Tequila
Tofu
Ukrainian Festivals
Wassail and Wassail Bowl
Welsh Rarebit
Yorkshire Pudding
Zakuski

267

Life-Cycle Events and Foods
Baby Food
Bachelor Party
Bar Mitzvah/Bat Mitzvah
Birthday Cake
Children's Table
Christening Party
Funeral Food
High School Class Reunion
High School
   Graduation Party
Prom Night
Rehearsal Dinner
Spring Break
Showers, Bridal and Baby
Wedding Foods

Holiday Eating and Drinking
All Kings Day
All Souls Day
Bastille Day
Chanukah
Chinese New Year
Christmas Bazaar
Christmas Candy
Christmas Cookies
Christmas Eve/Day Dinner
Cinco de Mayo
Diwali
Dyngus Day
Eggnog
Fruitcake
Gingerbread Cookies/
   Houses
Halloween
Independence Day
   Celebrations
Labor Day
Madrigal Dinner
Mardi Gras
Memorial Day
Mother's Day
New Year's Day
New Year's Eve

Obon
Thanksgiving Day Dinner
Thanksgiving Eve
Valentine's Day

Religious Ceremonies and Foods
Easter
Epiphany Feast
Eucharist
Las Posadas
Lent
Portuguese Holy
   Spirit Festival
Purim Feast
Ramadan
Rosh Hoshanah
Seder
Shrove Tuesday
Succot
Yom Kippur

Special Occasions (note: most food promotion and harvest festivals could be considered special occasions, but the entries below represent events that are not scheduled for any set date each year)
Art Show Opening
Bake Sale
Banquet
Barn-Raising
Buffet
BYOB Party
Candlelight Dinner
Carnival and Fair Food
Catered Events
Cheese Tasting
Chuck-Wagon Supper
Church Dinners/Suppers
Cocktail Party
Dining by Rail
Dining on Delivery
Dinner Party

Eating Out
Family Reunion
Fondue Party
Hog Roast
Ice Cream Social
Kaffeeklatsch
Keg Party
Open House
Progressive Dinner
Wine Tasting

Sports Events and Foods
Baseball Park
   Eating and Drinking
Camp/Trail Food
Shore Lunch
Sports Bars
Sports Drinks
Stadium and Arena Eating
   and Drinking
Superbowl Supper
Tailgate Party
Trail Mix

Time-of-Day Foods, Drinks, and Rituals
After-Dinner Drinks
After-Dinner Mints
Afternoon Tea
After-Theater Dining
Aperitif
Bedtime Snack
Breakfast
Breakfast Sandwiches
Continental Breakfast
Family Dinner
Happy Hour
Ladies' Luncheon
Lunch
Nightcap
Sunday Brunch
Sunday Dinner

BIBLIOGRAPHY

Academic American Encyclopedia (online version). Danbury, CT: Grolier, 1994.

Adler, David. *The Life and Cuisine of Elvis Presley.* New York: Crown Publishing, 1993.

Aidells, Bruce, and Denis Kelly. *Real Beer and Good Eats: The Rebirth of America's Beer and Food Traditions.* New York: Alfred A. Knopf, 1992.

Airola, Paavo. *Are You Confused?* Phoenix, AZ: Health Plus Publishers, 1971.

Algren, Nelson. *America Eats.* Iowa City: University of Iowa Press, 1992. (A collection of writings compiled during the 1930s and published posthumously).

American Heritage editors. *The American Heritage Cookbook and Illustrated History of American Eating and Drinking.* New York: Simon & Schuster, 1964.

Andoh, Elizabeth. *An American Taste of Japan.* New York: William Morrow, 1985.

Angers, W. Thomas. *Cajun Cuisine: Authentic Cajun Recipes from Louisiana's Bayou Country.* Lafayette, LA: Beau Bayou Publishing, 1985.

Arnett, Alison. "Beef Eaters." *Chicago Tribune,* 21 January 1993, p. 1.

Ayto, John. *A Gourmet's Guide: Food and Drink from A to Z.* Oxford, England: Oxford University Press, 1993.

Baldridge, Letitia. *The New Manners for the '90s.* New York: Rawson Associates, 1990.

Barbour, Celia. "Hot Chocolate." *Martha Stewart Living,* February 1996, p. 83.

Bernardino, Minnie. "Squid: Appreciative Fans Say Tasty Mollusk Is an Inexpensive Delicacy Offering High-Protein, Low-Fat Meat as Well as an Interesting Texture." *Los Angeles Times,* 14 May 1987, p. B-1.

Bernbaum, Rose Levy. *Rose's Melting Pot: A Cooking Tour of American Ethnic Celebrations.* New York: William Morrow, 1993.

Betz, Bob, ed. *Tastes of Liberty: A Celebration of Our Great Ethnic Cooking.* Woodinville, WA: Chateau Ste. Michelle, 1985.

Biro, Charlotte. *Flavors of Hungary.* San Francisco: 101 Productions, 1973.

Blofeld, John. *The Chinese Art of Tea.* Boston: Shambhala Publications, 1985.

Borden, Leslie Michlin. "Matzoh and More." *St. Petersburg Times,* 24 March 1994, Section D, p. 1.

Borghese, Anita. *Food from Harvest Festivals and Folk Fairs.* New York: Thomas Y. Crowell, 1977.

Boyle, Robert H. "The Joy of Cooking Insects." *Audubon,* September/October 1992, pp. 100–103.

Boyton, Sandra. *Chocolate: The Consuming Passion.* New York: Workman, 1982.

Bragdon, Allen D., ed. *Joy through the World.* New York: Allen D. Bragdon Publishers, 1985.

Brallier, Jess M. *The Hot Dog Cookbook.* Old Saybrook, CT: The Globe Pequot Press, 1993.

Brown, Dale, ed. *American Cooking.* New York: Time-Life Books, 1968.

Brownson, JeanMarie. "Oaxaca's History Is Linked to Its Luscious Chocolate." *Chicago Tribune,* 17 February 1994, Food Guide section, p. 6.

Bunnelle, Hasse. *Food for Knapsackers.* San Francisco, CA: Sierra Club, 1973.

Burroughs, Stanley. *Healing for the Age of Enlightenment.* Kailua, HI: Stanley Burroughs, 1976.

Cahill, Robert Ellis. *Olde New England's Sugar and Spice and Everything.* Salem, MA: Old Saltbox Publishing House, 1991.

Camp, Charles. *American Foodways.* Little Rock, AR: August House Publishers, 1989.

Campagna, Darryl. "Shuffle Off to Bison." *Albany Times Union,* 11 January 1996, p. C-1.

Campbell-Platt, Geoffrey. *Fermented Foods of the World.* Cambridge, England: Butterworths, 1987.

Carroll, S. R. "A Fantasy for Lovers—Of Chocolate, That Is," *Chicago Tribune,* 7 February 1993, Tempo section, p. 5.

Carson, Gerald. *The Social History of Bourbon.* Lexington: University Press of Kentucky, 1963.

Chalmers, Irene. *The Great Food Almanac.* San Francisco, Collins Publishers, 1994.

Chalmers, Irene, with Milton Glaser and friends. *Great American Food Almanac.* New York: Harper & Row, 1986.

Child, Julia. *The Way To Cook.* New York: Alfred A. Knopf, 1989.

Choate, Judith. *The Great American Pie Book.* New York: Simon & Schuster, 1992.

Clark, Libby, ed. (for the National Council of Negro Women). *The Black Family Reunion Cookbook*. New York: Simon & Schuster, 1993.

Clark, Marian. *The Route 66 Cookbook*. Tulsa, OK: Council Oak Books, 1993.

Clayton, Bernard. *Cooking across America*. New York: Simon & Schuster, 1993.

Coffin, Tristram Potter, and Hennig Cohen, eds. *Folklore from the Working Folk of America*. Garden City, NY: Anchor/Doubleday, 1973.

Cohen, Hennig, and Tristram Potter Coffin. *America Celebrates! A Patchwork of Weird and Wonderful Holiday Lore*. Detroit: Visible Ink Press/Gale Research, 1991a.

———. *The Folklore of American Holidays*. Detroit: Gale Research, 1991b.

Cook, John. *Diet and Your Religion*. Santa Barbara, CA: Woodbridge Press, 1976.

Coutelle, Dee. *The Perfect Croissant*. Chicago: Contemporary Books, 1983.

Coyle, L. Patrick, Jr. *The World Encyclopedia of Food*. New York: Facts on File, 1982.

Craig, Betty. *Don't Slurp Your Soup: A Basic Guide to Business Etiquette*. New Brighton, MN: Brighton Publications, 1991.

Cunningham, Scott. *The Magic in Food*. St. Paul, MN: Llewellyn Publications, 1990.

Dailey, Pat. "Best Quality Ingredients Give Fruitcake a Shelf Life That You Can't Laugh Off." *Chicago Tribune*, 18 November 1990, Food section, p. 10.

Davids, Kenneth. *Coffee: A Guide to Buying, Brewing, and Enjoying*. San Ramon, CA: 101 Productions, 1987.

Davis, Myrna. *The Potato Book*. New York: William Morrow, 1973.

Denton, Patti. "Ostrich: Expecting To Fly." *Indianapolis Star*, 3 November 1993, p. D1.

DeWitt, Dave, and Nancy Gerlach. *The Whole Chile Pepper Book*. Boston: Little, Brown, 1990.

DeWitt, Dave, and Arthur J. Pais. *A World of Curries*. Boston: Little, Brown, 1994.

Dickson, Paul. *The Great American Ice Cream Book*. New York: Galahad Books, 1972.

Digby, Joan, and John Digby, eds. *Inspired by Drink: An Anthology*. New York: William Morrow, 1988.

Dolamore, Anne. *The Essential Olive Oil Companion*. Topsfield, MA: Salem House Publishers, 1989.

Dornfield, Cindy. "Oyster Feed Not for the Faint-Hearted." *Idaho Falls Post Register*, 9 September 1993, p. 81.

Dosier, Susan. "BBQ Deep in the Heart of Texas." *Southern Living*, 1 August 1993, p. 52.

Dufty, William. *Sugar Blues*. New York: Warner Books, 1975.

Egerton, John. *Southern Food: At Home, on the Road, in History*. Chapel Hill: University of North Carolina Press, 1993.

Elkort, Martin. *The Secret Life of Food*. Los Angeles: Jeremy P. Tarcher, 1991.

Epstein, Benjamin. "It's All Big Game: Dining on Lion, Peacocks, Gators." *Los Angeles Times*, 17 November 1994, p. 36.

Evans, Elizabeth. "The Bagel Boom!" *Orange City Register*, 26 January 1996, p. F7.

Fantasia, Ruth. "Time Line of Food Products and Lifestyle Changes from More Than a Century." *The Virginia Pilot*, 13 March 1995.

Farb, Peter, and George Armelagos. *Consuming Passions: The Anthropology of Eating*. Boston: Houghton Mifflin, 1980.

Farr, Sidney Saylor. *More Than Moonshine: Appalachian Recipes and Recollections*. Pittsburgh, PA: University of Pittsburgh Press, 1983.

Farrell, Kenneth T. *Spices, Condiments and Seasonings*. New York: Van Nostrand Reinhold, 1990.

Fehr, Stephen C. "The Mall in the Airport." *Washington Post*, 14 March 1994, p. A1.

Feirstein, Bruce, and Lee Lorenz. *Real Men Don't Eat Quiche*. New York: Pocket Books, 1982.

Fiddes, Nick. *Meat: A Natural Symbol*. New York: Routledge, 1991.

Finklestein, Joanne. *Dining Out: A Sociology of Modern Manners*. Washington Square: New York University Press, 1989.

Funk, Charles Earle. *2,107 Curious Word Origins, Sayings, and Expressions*. New York: Galahad Books, 1993.

Fussell, Betty. *I Hear America Cooking*. New York: Viking Penguin, 1986.

———. *The Story of Corn*. New York: Alfred A. Knopf, 1992.

Garcia, Juan, and Melanie Grizzel. "A Year's Worth of Leftovers." *Dallas Morning Star*, 27 December 1995, p. F-1.

Gay, Kathlyn. *Keep the Buttered Side Up*. New York: Walker, 1995.

Gayot, André (for the American Automobile Association). *Guide to the Best Wineries of North America*. Los Angeles: Gault Millau, 1993.

Geffen, Alice M., and Carole Berglie. *Food Festival*. New York: Pantheon Books, 1994.

Gerlach, Nancy, and Jeffrey Gerlach. *Foods of the Maya: A Taste of the Yucatan*. Freedom, CA: Crossing Press, 1994.

Goldstein, Joyce Esersky. *The Mediterranean Kitchen*. New York: William Morrow, 1989.

Gordon, Jeff. "Morning Briefing upon Further Review." *St. Louis Post-Dispatch*, 7 May 1995, p. 2-F.

Grant, Bruce. *Concise Encyclopedia of the American Indian*. New York: Crown Publishers, 1989 (first published by Dutton, 1958).

Grimes, William. *Straight Up or on the Rocks: A Cultural History of American Drink*. New York: Simon & Schuster, 1993.

Groff, Betty. *Betty Groff's Pennsylvania Dutch Cookbook*. New York: Macmillan, 1990.

Gutierrez, C. Paige. *Cajun Foodways*. Jackson: University Press of Mississippi, 1992.

Hanes, Phyllis. "India's Chefs Expand Repertoire." *Christian Science Monitor*, 1 November, 1989.

Harris, Marvin. *Good To Eat: Riddles of Food and Culture*. New York: Simon & Schuster, 1985.

Henderson, Jim. "The Tabasco of Louisiana." *Bon Appetit*, March 1994, pp. 38 and 40.

Hendrickson, Robert. "Since 1928 It's Been Boom and Bust with Bubble Gum." *Smithsonian*, July 1990, pp. 75–83.

Herbst, Sharon Tyler. *Food Lover's Companion*. Hauppauge, NY: Barron's Educational Series, 1990.

———. *The Food Lover's Dictionary*. New York: Hearst Books, 1994.

Hill, Kathleen Thompson. *Festivals U.S.A.* New York: John Wiley & Sons, 1988.

Holt, Geraldene. *A Cup of Tea: An Afternoon Anthology of Fine China and Tea Traditions*. New York: Simon & Schuster, 1991.

Holt, Tamara. *Bean Power*. New York: Dell Publishing, 1993.

Hooker, Richard J. "Food and Drink in America: A History. New York: Bobbs Merrill Company, 1981.

Hostetler, John A. *Amish Society*. Baltimore, MD: Johns Hopkins Press, 1968.

Hutchison, Ruth. *Pennsylvania Dutch Cook Book*. New York: Harper & Brothers, 1948.

Ickis, Marguerite. *The Book of Festivals and Holidays the World Over*. New York: Dodd, Mead, 1970.

Jamison, Cheryl Alters, and Bill Jamison. *Texas Home Cooking*. Boston: Harvard Common Press, 1993.

———. *Smoke and Spice*. Boston: Harvard Common Press, 1994.

Jones, Evan. *American Food: The Gastronomic Story*. Woodstock, NY: Overlook Press, 1990.

Kant, Joanita. *The Hutterite Community Cookbook*. Intercourse, PA: Good Books, 1990.

Karnow, Stanley. "Year In, Year Out, Those Eateries Keep Eggrolling Along." *Smithsonian*, January 1994, pp. 86–94.

Kaufman, Peter, and T. K. Woods. *The Great American Meatloaf Contest Cookbook*. New York: Hearst Books, 1994.

Kirlin, Katherine S., and Thomas M. Kirlin. *Smithsonian Folklife Cookbook*. Washington, DC: Smithsonian Institution, 1991.

Knab, Sophie Hodorowicz. *Polish Customs, Traditions, and Folkore*. New York: Hippocrene Books, 1993.

Kump, Peter. "Practical Cook." *Chicago Tribune*, 14 July 1994, Section 7, p. 4.

Lagasse, Emeril. *Emeril's New New Orleans Cooking*. New York: William Morrow, 1993.

Lang, Jennifer Harvey. *Larousse Gastronomique: The New American Edition of the World's Greatest Culinary Encyclopedia*. New York: Crown Publishers, 1990.

Langlois, Stephen, with Margaret Guthrie. *Prairie: Cuisine from the Heartland*. Chicago: Contemporary Books, 1990.

Lee, Edwige. "Give Winter Dishes a Taste of Tropical Climes with Coconut." *The Houston Chronicle*, 27 December 1995, Food section, p. 2.

Levenstein, Harvey. *Paradox of Plenty: A Social History of Eating in Modern America*. Oxford: Oxford University Press, 1993.

Linck, Ernestine Sewell, and Joyce Gibson Roach. *Eats: A Folk History of Texas Foods*. Fort Worth: Texas Christian University Press, 1989.

Lipske, Mike. "A New Gold Rush Packs the Woods in Central Oregon." *Smithsonian*, January 1994, pp. 35–44.

Livingston, A. D., and Helen Livingston. *Edible Plants and Animals*. New York: Facts on File, 1993.

Lundy, Ronni. *The Festive Table*. New York: North Point Press, 1995.

MacClancy, Jeremy. *Consuming Culture: Why You Eat What You Eat*. New York: Henry Holt, 1992.

McClester, Cedric. *Kwanzaa*. New York: Gumbs & Thomas Publishers, 1993.

MacDonald, Margaret Read, ed. *The Folklore of World Holidays*. Detroit: Gale Research, 1992.

McGee, Harold. *On Food and Cooking: The Science and Lore of the Kitchen*. New York: Collier Books/Macmillan, 1984.

Mackle, Elliott. "Hot Stuff: A Chili Round-Up." *Atlanta Journal and Constitution*, 5 October 1991, Leisure section, p. 20.

Mahany, Barbara. "Pablum Rebellion." *Chicago Tribune*, 20 May 1994, Tempo section, p. 1.

Malpezzi, Frances M., and William M. Clements. *Italian-American Folkore*. Little Rock, AR: August House Publishers, 1992.

Marcin, Marietta Marshall. *The Complete Book of Herbal Teas*. New York: Congdon and Weed, 1983.

Margen, Sheldon, and editors of the University of California at Berkeley "Wellness Letter." *The Wellness Encyclopedia of Food and Nutrition*. New York: Rebus, 1992.

Mariani, John F. *The Dictionary of American Food and Drink,* New York: Ticknor and Fields, 1993; Hearst Books, 1994.

Miller, Mark Eric, ed. *Amish Cooking.* Scottdale, PA: Herald Press, 1980.

Miller, Jeannette L., and Elisabeth Schafer. *Lunches To Go!—Brown Bagging It.* Carbondale, IL: Pearl Publications, 1991.

Minifie, Bernard W. *Chocolate, Cocoa, and Confectionery.* Westport, CT: AVI Publishing, 1980.

Mintz, Sidney W. *Sweetness and Power: The Place of Sugar in Modern History.* New York: Penguin Books, 1985, 1987.

Morris, Stephen. *The Great Beer Trek* (revised edition). New York: Stephen Greene Press/Pelham Books, 1990.

Mothershead, Alice Bonzi. *Dining Customs around the World.* Garrett Park, MD: Garrett Park Press, 1982.

Naj, Amal. *Peppers.* New York: Alfred A. Knopf, 1992.

Nash, Helen. *Kosher Cuisine.* New York: Random House, 1984.

Nathan, Joan. *An American Folklife Cookbook.* New York: Schocken Books, 1984.

Neal, Bill, and David Perry. *Good Old Grits Cookbook.* New York: Workman, 1991.

Neufeldt, Victoria, ed. *Webster's New World Dictionary of American English.* New York: Prentice Hall, 1994.

Neustadt, Kathy. *Clambake: A History and Celebration of an American Tradition.* Amherst: University of Massachusetts Press, 1992.

Newall, Venetia. *An Egg at Easter: A Folklore Study.* London, Boston: Routledge & Kegan Paul, 1971, 1984.

Norman, Barbara. *Tales of the Table: A History of Western Cuisine.* Englewood Cliffs, NJ: Prentice Hall, 1972.

Ojakangas, Beatrice A. *Pot Pies.* New York: Clarkson/Potter, 1993.

O'Neill, Molly. *New York Cookbook.* New York: Workman, 1992.

Ortiz, Yvonne. *A Taste of Puerto Rico.* New York: Penguin Books, 1994.

Parrinder, Geoffrey, ed. *World Religions: From Ancient History to the Present.* New York: Facts on File, 1983.

Paston-Williams, Sara. *The Art of Dining: A History of Cooking and Eating.* London: National Trust Enterprises, 1993.

Pavlik, Pamela. "Even without the Memories, You'll Enjoy These Ukrainian Dishes." *Phildelphia Inquirer,* 14 April 1993, p. F2.

Poister, John J. *The New American Bartender's Guide.* New York: Penguin Books, 1989.

Pool, Michael. "Flavored Coffee Has the Taste of Success." *St. Petersburg Times,* 17 March 1994, p. B3.

Prudhomme, Paul. *Chef Paul Prudhomme's Louisiana Kitchen.* New York: William Morrow, 1984.

Purgavia, Dermot. "Calling All Meat-Eaters." *Associated Newspapers, Mail on Sunday,* 24 November 1995, pp. 15–16.

Pyles, Stephan. *The New Texas Cuisine.* New York: Doubleday, 1993.

Quintana, Patricia, with Carol Haralson. *Mexico's Feasts of Life.* Tulsa, OK: Council Oaks Books, 1989.

Raichlen, Steven. *Miami Spice.* New York: Workman, 1993.

Rand McNally editors. *The Official Baseball Atlas, 1994 Edition.* Chicago: Rand McNally, 1994.

Rhoades, Robert E. "Corn, the Golden Grain," *National Geographic,* June 1993, pp. 92117.

Rice, Bernard. "Pioneers' Ketchups Avoided Tomatoes," *South Bend Tribune,* 11 December 1994, p. E8.

Rice, William. "What's Cooking on Campus?" *Chicago Tribune,* 24 February 1994, Food Guide section, p. 1.

Robbins, Jim. "Care for a Little Hellish Relish? Or Try a Hotsickle." *Smithsonian,* January 1992, pp. 42–51.

Robertson, Patrick. *The Book of Firsts.* London: Rainbird Reference Books, 1975.

Rolnick, Harry. *The Complete Book of Coffee.* Hong Kong: Melitta, 1982.

Root, Waverley. *Food.* New York: Simon & Schuster, 1980.

Root, Waverly, and Richard de Rochemont. *Eating in America: A History.* New York: Ecco Press, 1981.

Rothrock, Millicent. "Wing Ding of a Price Surge." *Greensboro News and Record,* 24 May 1995, p. D1.

Rozin, Elisabeth. *Blue Corn and Chocolate.* New York: Alfred A. Knopf, 1992.

Schivelbusch, Wolfgang, and David Jacobson (trans.). *Tastes of Paradise: A Social History of Spices, Stimulants, and Intoxicants.* New York: Pantheon Books, 1992.

Schulz, Phillip Stephen. *Celebrating America.* New York: Simon & Schuster, 1994.

Schwartz, Arthur. *Soup Suppers.* New York: HarperCollins, 1994.

Schwartz, John. "The Great Food Migration," *Newsweek,* Special Issue, Fall-Winter 1991, pp. 58–62.

Senaur, Ben, Elaine Asp, and Jean Kinsey. "Food Trends and the Changing Cuisines." St. Paul, MN: Eagen Press, 1991.

Shapiro, Laura. "No Time To Make Dessert?"

Newsweek, 9 May 1994, p. 63.

Shemanski, Frances. *A Guide to Fairs and Festivals in the United States.* Westport, CT: Greenwood Press, 1984.

Sherman, Josepha. *A Sampler of Jewish American Folklore.* Little Rock, AR: August House Publishers, 1992.

Shosteck, Joan. *A Lexicon of Jewish Cooking.* Chicago: Contemporary Books, 1979.

Shurtleff, William, and Akiko Aoyagi. *The Book of Tofu: Food for Mankind.* New York: Ballantine Books, 1979.

Simmons, Marie. *365 Ways To Cook Pasta.* New York: HarperCollins, 1992.

Simon, Andre L., and Robin Howe. *Dictionary of Gastronomy.* New York: McGraw-Hill, 1970.

Simonds, Nina. *China's Food: A Journey through China's Culinary Landscape.* New York: HarperCollins, 1990.

Simoons, Frederick J. *Eat Not This Flesh: Food Avoidances in the Old World.* Madison: University of Wisconsin Press, 1967.

Smith, Jeff. *The Frugal Gourmet Cooks American.* New York: William Morrow, 1987.

———. *The Frugal Gourmet Cooks Three Ancient Cuisines.* New York: William Morrow. 1989.

———. *The Frugal Gourmet on Our Immigrant Ancestors.* New York: William Morrow, 1990.

Sokolov, Raymond. "Insects, Worms, and Other Tidbits." *Natural History,* September 1989, pp. 84–88.

———. *Why We Eat What We Eat.* New York: Summit Books, 1991.

Solomon, Jay. *Lean Bean Cuisine.* Rocklin, CA: Prima Publishing, 1995.

Southern Heritage editors. *The Southern Heritage Celebrations Cookbook.* Birmingham, AL: Oxmoor House, 1984.

"Spamming the Globe." *Newsweek,* 29 August 1994, p. 8.

Staten, Vince. *Can You Trust a Tomato in January?* New York: Simon & Schuster, 1993.

Stehlin, Dori. "A Little 'Lite' Reading." *FDA Consumer Special Report,* May 1993.

Stein, Stephen J. *The Shaker Experience in America.* New Haven and London: Yale University Press, 1992.

Steinberg, Sally Levitt. *The Donut Book.* New York: Alfred A. Knopf, 1987.

Stern, Jane, and Michael Stern. *GoodFood.* New York: Alfred A. Knopf, 1983.

———. *Real American Food.* New York: Alfred A. Knopf, 1986.

———. *A Taste of America.* New York and Kansas City: Andrews and McMeel, 1988.

Stewart, Martha. *Entertaining.* New York: Clarkson N. Potter, 1982.

Suffes, Susan, ed. *Mr. Boston's Official Bartender's and Party Guide.* New York: Warner Books, 1994 (first pub. 1935).

Sunset magazine editors. "Join the Portuguese for a Festa." *Sunset,* May 1989, pp. 20–22.

Tannahill, Reay. *Food in History.* New York: Stein and Day, 1973.

Tarantino, Jim. *Sorbets!* Freedom, CA: Crossing Press, 1988.

Taylor, Joe Gray. *Eating, Drinking, and Visiting in the South: An Informal History.* Baton Rouge: Louisiana State University Press, 1982.

Thompson, Sue Ellen, and Barbara W. Carlson, eds. *Holidays, Festivals, and Celebrations of the World Dictionary.* Detroit: Omnigraphics, 1994.

Tossaint-Samat, Maguelonne. *History of Food.* Cambridge, MA: Blackwell Publishing, 1992.

Tourneau, Isabelle. *Cooksource.* New York and London: Doubleday, 1990.

Trager, James. *Foodbook.* New York: Grossman, 1970.

———. *The Food Chronology.* New York: Henry Holt, 1995.

Vanberg, Bent. *Of Norwegian Ways.* New York: Harper & Row, 1970.

Visser, Margaret. *Much Depends on Dinner.* New York: Grove Press, 1986.

———. "Family Goals, Values and Rituals Eroded by Changes in the Way We Eat." Los Angeles Times. 5 April 1990, Food section, p.43.

———. *The Rituals of Dinner.* New York: Grove Weidenfeld, 1991.

Wason, Betty. *A Salute to Cheese.* New York: Hawthorn Books, 1966.

Weatherford, Jack. *Indian Givers.* New York: Fawcett Columbine, 1989.

Weiner, Hal, and Marilyn Weiner. *World of Cooking.* New York: Macmillan, 1983.

West, John O. *Mexican-American Folkore.* Little Rock, AR: August House, 1988.

Williams, Susan. *Savory Suppers and Fashionable Feasts.* New York: Pantheon Books/Random House, 1985.

Wolf, Christopher. "A Taste of Tomorrow's Foods," *The Futurist,* May/June 1994, pp. 16–20.

Wolfert, Paula. *Mediterranean Cooking.* New York: HarperPerennial, 1994.

Woods, Sylvia, and Christopher Styler. *Sylvia's Soul Food.* New York: William Morrow, 1992.

Wyman, Carolyn. *I'm a SPAM Fan: America's Best-Loved Foods.* Stamford, CT: Longmeadow Press, 1993.

Young, Gordon. "Chocolate: Food of the Gods," *National Geographic,* November 1984, pp. 664–686.

ILLUSTRATION CREDITS

6 Chacma Incorporated. Courtesy Nabisco, Inc., East Hanover, New Jersey.
10 Courtesy California Artichoke Advisory Board.
14 UPI/Bettmann.
16 Charles Krupa, AP/Wide World Photos.
19 Peter Menzel. Stock, Boston.
21 AP/Wide World Photos.
26 Art Abeier, *New York Daily Mirror*. UPI/Bettmann.
28 Arthur Leipzig. UPI/Bettmann.
34 Paul Vathis, AP/Wide World Photos.
35 Courtesy Princess Cruises, Los Angeles, California.
38 Marty Lederhandler, AP/Wide World Photos.
42 Courtesy Bordon, Inc., Columbus, Ohio.
43 Photofest.
45 Courtesy The Catfish Institute, Belzoni, Mississippi.
49 Mark Elias, AP/Wide World Photos.
51 Courtesy Cheyenne Frontier Days, Cheyenne, Wyoming.
69 Courtesy Nabisco, Inc., East Hanover, New Jersey.
72 UPI/Bettmann.
74 Courtesy Ocean Spray Cranberries, Lakeville-Middleboro, Massachusetts.
75 John McGurk II from *You Can Too* by Jeanette McGurk. Baton Rouge, Louisiana: Cajun Pantry, 1987.
79 Courtesy Princess Cruises, Los Angeles, California.
82 Courtesy Solvang (California) Conference & Visitors Bureau.
83 AP/Wide World Photos.
85 Courtesy Princess Cruises, Los Angeles, California.
86 Courtesy Napa Valley Wine Train.
89 Courtesy Door County Chamber of Commerce, Sturgeon Bay, Wisconsin.
97 Bob Galbraith, AP/Wide World Photos.
104 Photofest.
112 Elise Amendola, AP/Wide World Photos.
120 Courtesy Gilroy Garlic Festival Association, Gilroy, California.
123 UPI/Bettmann.
131 Courtesy National Live Stock and Meat Board, Chicago.
133 Courtesy Celestial Seasonings, Boulder, Colorado.
134 UPI/Bettmann.
139 AP/Wide World Photos.
151 Mike Okoniewski, AP/Wide World Photos.
153 UPI/Bettmann.
154 UPI/Bettmann.
158 Courtesy Yosemite Concession Services Corp.
163 Frank Mastro. Bettmann Archive
165 Courtesy National Live Stock and Meat Board, Chicago.
168 AP/Wide World Photos.
178 Alex Quesada, AP/Wide World Photos.
182 Courtesy Fredericksburg (Texas) Convention and Visitors Bureau.
185 Courtesy Westin Hotel, Galleria Dallas, Dallas, Texas.
188 Photofest.
193 UPI/Bettmann.
202 UPI/Bettmann Newsphotos.
218 UPI/Bettmann.
220 AP/Wide World Photos.
224 UPI/Bettmann.
227 UPI/Bettmann.
229 Joe Marquette, AP/Wide World Photos.
231 Courtesy Hormel Foods Corporation, Austin, Minnesota.
232 Douglas C. Pizac, AP/Wide World Photos.
235 Courtesy California Strawberry Commission.
237 Mark Lennihan, AP/Wide World Photos.
241 Ellis Herwig. Stock, Boston.
259 UPI/Bettmann.

INDEX